Duncan Petersen's

CHARMING SMALL HOTEL GUIDES

BRITAIN
& IRELAND

Duncan Petersen's

CHARMING SMALL HOTEL GUIDES

BRITAIN
& IRELAND

Consultant editor Fiona Duncan

Hotel critic, *The Sunday Telegraph*

Duncan Petersen

18th edition

Conceived, designed and produced by
Duncan Petersen Publishing Ltd,
Studio 6, 82 Silverthorne Road, Battersea, SW3 8HE

Editorial director Andrew Duncan
Consultant editor Fiona Duncan
Editor Ella Carr
Contributing editors Jonathan and Joan Noble, Belinda and Hamish
Alexander, David Perkins, Ella Carr
New edition editor Ella Carr
Cover design Nicky Collings
Maps Map Creation Ltd
Photo credits see below for individual details

A CIP catalogue record for this book is available
from the British Library

ISBN 978-0-9956803-4-0

DTP by Duncan Petersen Publishing Ltd
Printed in Bulgaria by Pulsio

Grays Court credit (page 331): Dominic Wright
Red Lion Freehouse credit (page 101): Nick Cunard
Ballyvolane credit (page 383): bathroom shot by James Fennell and exterior
shot by Kostar photography
Covent Garden Hotel (page 121): Simon Brown
Cover photos: The Horn of Plenty (front left), The Quay House (front, top
right), Inis Meáin (front, bottom right), Howard's House (back), Corsewall
Lighthouse (spine)
Title page: The Pier, Harwich

Contents

Introduction

From the consultant editor, Fiona Duncan

Welcome to the 18th edition of Charming Small Hotel Guides Britain & Ireland – a guide with a long history. It was first published in 1988 by my husband Andrew Duncan, his co-director Mel Petersen and with Chris Gill as the editor. I took over as editor in the mid 1990s and looked after several editions until 2006 when I began writing my hotel column in *The Sunday Telegraph*. Since then it has been looked after by Duncan Petersen with myself as consultant editor, giving advice on new entries and which to drop.

The guide's focus on smaller places, usually with four to 12 bedrooms, is especially close to my heart – and to my view on hotel keeping – which is that small is, mostly, beautiful because large places find it hard to create a place with that elusive quality of character and charm, where the guest feels like a person, not just a customer.

I have not been able to visit every single entry in the guide, though most are known to me in some way. Though all the entries are faithful to our idea of a charming small hotel, I do like some better than others; and I have had to trust that the detailed work of updating facts has been done well. Those aside, I believe that the guide is as unique and as valuable as it was when first published in 1988. I hope you agree.

Happy travels.

This new edition reflects all the recent changes in our sector of the hotel industry:

• It's larger than ever before – with nearly 60 new hotels.

• There have been a substantial amount of closures since the last edition.

• There are many more 'boutique' inns than in previous editions, with rooms to a high standard and often very good food.

In all other respects, the guide remains true to the values and qualities that make it unique (see below), and which have won it so many devoted readers. It has sold hundreds of thousands of copies in the U.K., U.S.A. and in five European languages.

Why are we unique?

This is the only independent (no hotel pays for an entry) UK-originated accomodation guide that:

• concentrates on places that have real charm and character;

• is highly selective and fussy about size. Most hotels have fewer than 20 bedrooms; if there are more, the hotel must have the feel of a much smaller place. Time and again we find that a genuinely warm welcome is *much* more likely to be found in a small hotel;

• gives proper emphasis to description – doesn't use irritating symbols;

• is produced by a small company with like-minded reporters.

Above all, the text doesn't read as if it's an advert, paid for by the hotel, which is the case with most other guides. Our reviews are honest: objective, distanced and they mention negatives *and* positives.

Glengorm Castle, Tobermory

So what exactly do we look for?
Our selection criteria

• A peaceful, attractive setting. Obviously, if the entry is in an urban area, we make allowances.

• A building that is handsome, interesting, historic or characterful.

• Adequate space, but on a human scale. We don't go for places that rely too much on grandeur.

• Good taste and imagination in the interior decoration. We reject standardized, chain hotel fixtures, fittings and decorations.

• Bedrooms that look like real bedrooms, not hotel rooms, individually decorated.

• Furnishings and other facilities that are comfortable and well maintained. We like to see interesting antique furniture that is there to be used, not simply revered.

• Proprietors and staff who are dedicated and thoughtful, offering a personal welcome, but who aren't intrusive or overly effusive.

• Interesting food.

• A sympathetic atmosphere; an absence of loud people showing off their money; or the 'corporate feel'.

No fear or favour

To us, taking a payment for appearing in a guide seems to defeat the object of producing a guide. If money has changed hands, you can't write the whole truth about a hotel, and the selection cannot be nearly so interesting. This seems to us to be proved at least in part by the fact that pay guides are so keen to present the illusion of independence: most only admit taking payment in small print inside.

Not many people realize that on the shelves of British bookshops there are many more hotel guides that accept payments for entries than there are independent guides. This guide is one of the few that do not accept any money for an entry.

A fatter guide, but just as selective

In order to accommodate extra entries with a whole or half page description and colour photograph, we've had to print more pages. But we have maintained our integrity by keeping the selection to around 500 entries. Since our last edition, the number of places to stay that deserve to be in the guide has increased – many new revamped inns and restaurants-with-rooms have opened and have been included. But the guide is all about places that are more than just a bed for the night. Every time we consider a new hotel, we ask ourselves whether it has that extra special something, regardless of category and facilities, that makes it worth seeking out.

Types of accommodation in this guide

Despite its title, the guide does not confine itself to places called hotels or places that behave like hotels. On the contrary, we actively look for places that offer a home from home (see page 8). We include small and medium-sized hotels; pubs; inns; restaurants-with-rooms; guest-houses and bed-and-breakfasts. Some places, usually private homes which take guests, operate on house-party lines, where you are introduced to the other guests, and take meals at a communal table. If you don't like making small talk to strangers, or are part of a romantic twosome that wants to keep itself to itself, this type of establishment may not be for you. On the other hand, if you are interested in meeting people, perhaps as a foreign visitor wanting to get to know the locals, then you'll find it rewarding.

Home from home

Perhaps the most beguiling characteristic of the best places to stay in this guide is the feeling they give of being in a private home – but without the everyday cares and chores of running one. To get this formula right requires a special sort of professionalism: the proprietor has to strike the balance between being relaxed and giving attentive service. Those who experience this 'feel' often turn their backs on all other forms of accommodation – however luxurious.

Our pet dislikes

Small hotels are not automatically wonderful hotels; and the very individuality of small, owner-run hotels, makes them prone to peculiarities that the mass-produced hotel experience avoids. For the benefit of those who run the small hotels of Britain – and those contemplating the plunge – we repeat once more our list of pet hates:

Price too high Prices tend to be higher, like for like, than in France and Italy. This is not always the fault of hotels, but it is disappointing.

Not entirely child-friendly Again, compared with mainland European hotels, children are much more often seen as a nuisance by hoteliers.

Poor English at reception The surge in recent years of foreign workers, prepared to work for low wages, means guests sometimes have to adapt to a non-fluent English speaker. Especially irritating if you arrive tired after a long journey.

'Contemporary-formulaic' decoration Too many hotels think they can appeal simply by putting 'modern' paint on the walls. The more we see of this, the more of a cliche it becomes.

The hushed dining room Owners have a duty to create an atmosphere in which conversation can flow.

The ordinary breakfast Even hotels that go to great lengths to prepare special dinners are capable of serving prefabricated orange juice, sliced bread and tea made with tea bags at breakfast.

The schoolteacher mentality If you run a hotel, you should be flexible and accommodating enough to deal with the whims of travellers.

The inexperienced waiter Or waitress. Running a small operation does not excuse the imposition on the paying public of completely untrained (and sometimes ill-suited) staff who can spoil the most beautifully cooked food.

The lumpy old bed Beds have improved much in recent years. There's no excuse for a creaking frame or an old mattress.

The erratic boiler It doesn't often happen, but tepid baths are unforgiveable. Even the cheapest places should regard this as a basic.

Check the price first

In this guide we have adopted the system of price bands, rather than giving actual prices as we did in previous editions. This is because prices were often subject to change after we went to press. The price bands refer to the approximate price of a standard double room (high season rates) with breakfast for two people. Prices for Ireland are quoted in Euros. They are as follows:

£	under £80	€	under 90 euros
££	£80 – £150	€€	90 – 170 euros
£££	£150 – £200	€€€	170 – 230 euros
££££	more than £200	€€€€	more than 230 euros

Always check what is included in the price (for example service, breakfast, afternoon tea) when booking.

Introduction

How to find an entry

In this guide, the entries are arranged in geographical groups. First, the whole of Britain and Ireland are divided into five major groups, starting with Southern England and working northwards to Scotland; Ireland comes last. Within these major groups, the entries are grouped into smaller regional sub-sections such as the South-West, Wales, the Midlands and the Highlands and Islands – for a full list, see page 5. Within each sub-section, entries are listed alphabetically by nearest town or village; if several occur in or near one town, entries are arranged in alpha order by name of hotel.

To find a hotel in a particular area, use the maps following this introduction to locate the appropriate pages.

To locate a specific hotel, whose name you know, or a hotel in a place you know, use the indexes at the back, which list entries both by names and by nearest place name. The name of the county follows the town name in the heading for each entry.

The five main sections of the book (Southern England, Central England, The North, Scotland and Ireland) are introduced by area introductions.

Using the guide

We use three different hotel entry formats in order to give you perspective on the character and quality of the places to stay. Although all are worthy of the guide, some are better than others. The **whole page** entries are the cream of our selection – mainstream charming small hotels that tick all or most of our boxes. **Half pages** shouldn't be overlooked or under-rated. They are also true charming small hotels, some of them good, some excellent. Usually, but no means always, because of their larger size, they don't conform as closely to our criteria as the whole page hotels. They are grouped at the end of each regional section, after the whole page entries. **Section opener** entries are useful back-up entries with small photos and brief descriptions. They are found on the five area introduction pages – see above. Again, don't overlook these: they are great places that have attracted our attention but not quite as faithful to our criteria as whole and half page entries.

So within each region you need to look in three different places to get the whole range of recommendations, and the entire contents are also easily accessible by using the maps on pages 15-25 and the indexes on pages 415-429.

Introduction

HOW TO READ AN ENTRY

Postal address and other key information.

Places of interest within reach of the hotel.

This sets the hotel in its geographical context and should not be taken as precise instructions as to how to get there; always ask the hotel for directions.

Rooms described as having a bath usually also have a shower; rooms described as having a shower only have a shower.

This information is only an indication for wheelchair users and the infirm. Always check on suitability with the hotel.

Essential booking information.

THE SOUTH-WEST   SOUTHERN ENGLAND

Milton Abbot, Devon

Milton Abbot, Tavistock, Devon
PL19 0PQ

Tel (01822) 870000
Fax (01822) 870578
e-mail mail@hotelendsleigh.com
website www.hotelendsleigh.com

Nearby Tavistock market, Tamar Valley, Plymouth historic dockyards, Exeter cathedral
Location 15 minutes from Tavistock down mile long drive in own extensive grounds; ample car parking
Food breakfast, lunch and dinner
Price ££££
Rooms 18; all have bath and shower; all have phone, TV, DVD player, internet access
Facilities dining room, sitting room, garden, terrace, library, helipad, use of local country club (swimming, gym, spa) **Credit Cards** AE, MC, V
Children accepted
Disabled good access, 1 ground floor suite with private garden
Pets accepted, dog beds provided
Closed never
Proprietors Olga Polizzi

Hotel Endsleigh
Country house hotel

Endsleigh, on the edge of Dartmoor, and sister hotel of Olga Polizzi's Tresanton in Cornwall (page 72), was one of the most talked about new British hotels when it opened eight years ago. Our reporter found it 'effortlessly elegant and – crucially – unpretentious, unlike many of its try-hard, oh-so-hip rivals.'

It's down a mile-long private drive in 'one of the loveliest locations I've seen in 20 years of writing about hotels'. The sixth Duke of Bedford built the 16-bedroom fishing and shooting lodge as a retreat, in the cottage *orné* style. The gardens are by Humphry Repton.

Olga Polizzi has decorated it in her cool, inimitable style, but the spirit of the old house remains intact – old pull-down maps of Devon in the hall, the family crests in the dining room, the floor made of sheeps' knuckles on the veranda. Bedrooms are lovely: stylish and unfussy, with original baths and basins and a welcome lack of puzzling technology. You'll get a TV and DVD player, but you are more likely to spend time pouring over the absorbing collection of books in the library. Apart from that, there's little to do, other than to fish, walk or picnic in the grounds, a fantasy of dells and grottoes. The food is good, but not quite as good as at its sister hotel, though prices are similar.

59

Introduction

City, town or village, and region, in which the hotel is located.

Name of hotel.

Type of establishment.

Description – never vetted by the hotel.

Breakfast is normally included in the price of the room. Other meals, such as afternoon tea, may also be available. 'Room service' refers to food and drink, either snacks or full meals, which can be served in the room

Always let the hotel know in advance if you want to bring a pet. Even where pets are accepted, certain restrictions may apply, and a small charge may be levied.

Children
Where children are welcome, there are often special facilities, such as cots, high chairs, baby listening and high teas. Always check whether children are accepted in the dining room.

We list the following credit cards:
AE American Express
DC Diners Club
MC Mastercard
V   Visa
Most hotels accept many other credit cards.

Reporting to the guide

Please write and tell us about your experiences of small hotels, guest houses and inns, whether good or bad, whether listed in this edition or not. As well as hotels in Britain & Ireland, we are interested in hotels in Austria, France, Italy, Spain, Germany and Switzerland.

Readers whose reports prove particularly helpful may be invited to join our Travellers' Panel. Members give us notice of their own travel plans; we suggest hotels that they might inspect, and help with the cost of accommodation.

The address to write to us is:

Editor, *Charming Small Hotel Guides*
Studio 6, 82 Silverthorne Road, Battersea, SW8 3HE.

Checklist

Please use a separate sheet of paper for each report; include your name, address and telephone number on each report.

Your reports will be received with particular pleasure if they are typed, and if they are organized under the following headings:

Name of establishment
Town or village it is in, or nearest
Full address, including postcode
Telephone number
Time and duration of visit
The building and setting
The public rooms
The bedrooms and bathrooms
Physical comfort (chairs, beds, heat, light, hot water)
Standards of maintenance and housekeeping
Atmosphere, welcome and service
Food
Value for money

We assume that in writing you have no objections to your views being published unpaid, either verbatim or in an edited version. Names of major outside contributors are acknowledged, at the editor's discretion, in the guide.

Hotel location maps

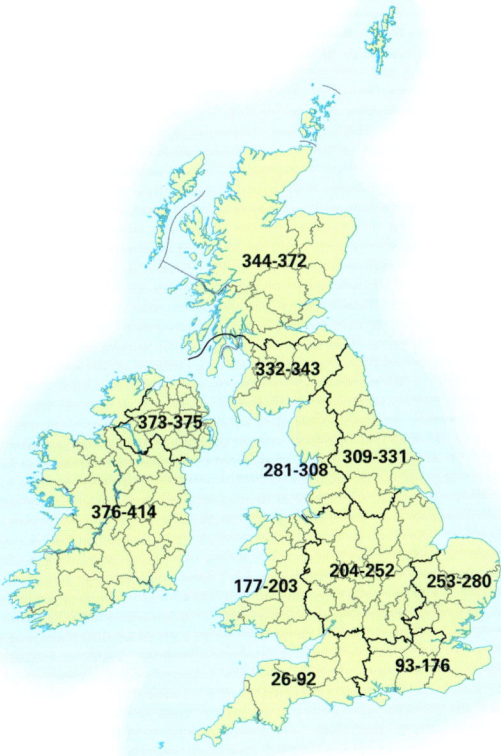

344-372

332-343

373-375

281-308

309-331

376-414

204-252

177-203

253-280

26-92

93-176

Carmel Head • Amlwch
Holyhead • • Benllech
Rhosneigr • Llangefni

Bontnewydd 179
Dolydd 203
Nant Gwynant 194

Pwllheli 197

Aberdaron •
Ganllwyd 187
Penmaenpool 196
Tal-y-llyn 199

Cardigan
Eglwysfach 185
Bay
Aberystwyth

Aberaeron 178
Tregaron •

Cardigan • Lampeter •
Strumble Head Newport •
St. David's • Brechfa 180
Haverfordwest • Carmarthen
Narberth 194
Pontarddulais
Pembroke • Llanelli
Penally 195 *Carmarthen* SWANSEA
Bay
Reynoldston 177

B r i s t o l

St. George's Channel

Barnstaple •

Hartland Pt.
Hartland •
Great Torrington

Bude 39 Holsworthy 53
A3072
Virginstow 92
Lewdown 54 Chagford 26
Lifton 55, 90 Milton Abbot 59
Tresco 81 Rock 66
St Mary's 70 Padstow 62, 63 St Minver 73 Gulworthy 51
Hugh Town Mawgan Porth 26
Newquay 91 PLYMOUTH
St. Austell 68
Fowey 49
St. Ives Redruth Bigbury-on-Sea 34
Zennor 86 Truro Mevagissey 91
Carbis Bay 40 Rosevine 67
Penzance 64, 65 St.Hilary 69 St.Mawes 71, 72
Mousehole 60 Falmouth 47
Land's End Coverack 42
Black Head
Lizard Pt.

16

LIVERPOOL
Llandudno 191
Rhyl
Birkenhead
SHEFFIELD
Wilmslow
Chester
Macclesfield
Chesterfield
Baslow 245
Denbigh 184
Ashford-in-the Water 205
Rowsley 236
Sutton-in-Ashfield
Capel Garmon 182
Crewe
Biggin-by-Hartington 245
Belper 207
WREXHAM
Newcastle-under-Lyme
Ashbourne 204
Llandrillo 190
DERBY
NOTTINGHAM
Rhydycroesau 235
M6
Llanarmon Dyffryn-Ceiriog 188
LEICESTER
Shrewsbury 251, 177
Cannock
Ironbridge 248
Tamworth
Llanbrynmair 189
Bishops Castle 208
Norton 230
Cound 177
Llangurig
Worfield 244
BIRMINGHAM
Bridgnorth
Knighton
Milebrook 203
Kidderminster
COVENTRY
Rhayader
Leintwardine 249
Rugby
Penybont
Titley 240
Redditch
Leamington Spa 249
Leominster
Worcester
Llyn Brianne
Builth Wells 181
Hereford 225
Malvern Wells 229
Llyswen 202
247
Three Cocks 200
Little Malvern 228
Winchcombe 241
246-247
209
213
Brecon
Llanthony 192
Corse Lawn 216
246
248
Crickhowell 177, 183
250
Felin Fach 186
250 221
231
Abergavenny 201
Skenfrith 198
Painswick 233
210
211, 212
Shipton-under-Wychwood 251
Ebbw Vale
Clearwell 214
206
217 238 231,232
Aberdare
219 [see page 18]
Pontypool
Crudwell 44
Faringdon 218
Pontypridd
Tetbury 239
SWINDON
Port Talbot
NEWPORT
Shefford
Yattendon 176
BRIDGEND
CARDIFF
Nettleton 61
Woodlands 147
Newbury
BRISTOL 88
Whitley 26
Kintbury 167
Channel
BATH 29-31, 87
Baughurst 94
Bradford-on-Avon 35, 36, 87
East Chisenbury 101
Allerford 27
Mells 58
Frome 90
Burnham-on-Sea
Stockbridge 151, 152
Exford 89
Wedmore 92
Longleat 26
Teffont Evias 78
Winchester 155, 174
Williton 26
Street
Winsford 84
Lower Swell 26
57 38
77
Romsey 140
Beercrocombe 33
83
88
79 80
Southampton 150
Hinton St George 52
85 Sherborne
76 89
Cranborne 43
Cullompton
41
Wickham 175
East Chelborough 46
Brockenhurst 97
Bucklers Hard 98
Gittisham 50
Beaminster 32
Lower
Lymington 170
Gurnard 166
Exmouth
Branscombe 37 Dorchester 26
Bockhampton 56
Wareham 82
BOURNEMOUTH
East End 102
Babbacombe 28
Weymouth
Swanage
Studland 75
Yarmouth 156
Ventnor 153, 173
Dittisham 45
Bill of Portland
Seaview 172
Strete 74
Prawle Point
English
Channel

Bruton 38
Buckhorn Weston 88
Chettle 41
Fonthill Gifford 48
Fontmell Magna 89
Lovington 57
Sturminster Newton 76
Swallowcliffe 77
Tisbury 79
Tollard Royal 80
Wincanton 83
Yeovil 85

Channel Islands:
Alderney 157
Guernsey 158-160, 176
Herm 161
Jersey 162-164

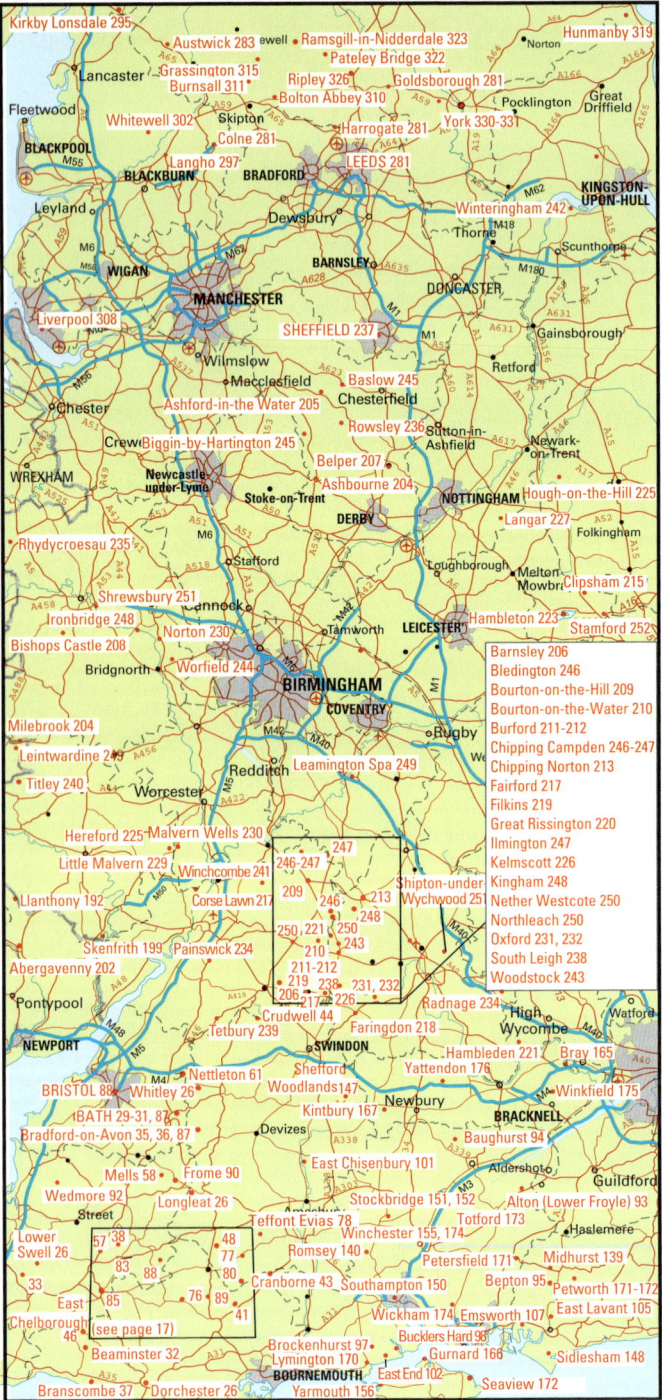

Kirkby Lonsdale 295
Austwick 283 ewell Ramsgill-in-Nidderdale 323 Hunmanby 319
Pateley Bridge 322 Norton
Lancaster Grassington 315 Goldsborough 281 Great Driffield
Burnsall 311 Ripley 326 Pocklington
Fleetwood Whitewell 302 Bolton Abbey 310 York 330-331
Skipton
BLACKPOOL Colne 281 Harrogate 281
M55 Langho 297
BLACKBURN BRADFORD LEEDS 281 KINGSTON-UPON-HULL
Leyland Dewsbury Winteringham 242
M6 Thorne Scunthorpe
WIGAN BARNSLEY M18
M62 DONCASTER M180
MANCHESTER A628
Liverpool 308 M1 Gainsborough
SHEFFIELD 237 A631
Wilmslow Retford
Chester Macclesfield Baslow 245
Ashford-in-the-Water 205 Chesterfield Newark-on-Trent
Crewe Biggin-by-Hartington 245 Rowsley 236 Sutton-in-Ashfield
WREXHAM Newcastle-under-Lyme Belper 207 Hough-on-the-Hill 225
Stoke-on-Trent Ashbourne 204 NOTTINGHAM
Rhydycroesau 235 DERBY Langar 227 Folkingham
Stafford Clipsham 215
Shrewsbury 251 M6 Loughborough Melton Mowbray
Ironbridge 248 Cannock LEICESTER Hambleton 223 Stamford 252
Bishops Castle 208 Norton 230 Tamworth
Bridgnorth Worfield 244 BIRMINGHAM
Milebrook 204 COVENTRY M1
M42 M40 Rugby
Leintwardine 243 A456
Titley 240 Redditch Leamington Spa 249
Worcester
Hereford 225 Malvern Wells 230 247
Little Malvern 229 Winchcombe 241 246-247
Llanthony 192 Corse Lawn 217 209 246 213 Shipton-under-Wychwood 251
250 221 250
Skenfrith 199 Painswick 234 210 248
Abergavenny 202 211-212 243
219 238 231, 232
Pontypool 206 217 226
Crudwell 44 Radnage 234 High Wycombe Watford
NEWPORT Tetbury 239 Faringdon 218 Hambleden 221 Bray 165
SWINDON
Nettleton 61 Shefford Yattendon 176 Winkfield 175
BRISTOL 88 Whitley 26 Woodlands 147
BATH 29-31, 87 Kintbury 167 Newbury BRACKNELL
Bradford-on-Avon 35, 36, 87 Devizes Baughurst 94
A338 Aldershot
Mells 58 Frome 90 East Chisenbury 101 Guildford
Wedmore 92 Longleat 26 M3 Alton (Lower Froyle) 93
Street Stockbridge 151, 152 Totford 173
Teffont Evias 78 Winchester 155, 174 Haslemere
Lower Swell 26 57 38 48 Romsey 140 Petersfield 171 Midhurst 139
33 83 88 77 80 Cranborne 43 Southampton 150 Bepton 95 Petworth 171-172
East 85 76 89 41 Wickham 174 Emsworth 107 East Lavant 105
Chelborough (see page 17) Brockenhurst 97 Bucklers Hard 98 Sidlesham 148
46 Beaminster 32 Lymington 170 Gurnard 166
Branscombe 37 Dorchester 26 Yarmouth 156 BOURNEMOUTH East End 102 Seaview 172

Barnsley 206
Bledington 246
Bourton-on-the-Hill 209
Bourton-on-the-Water 210
Burford 211-212
Chipping Campden 246-247
Chipping Norton 213
Fairford 217
Filkins 219
Great Rissington 220
Ilmington 247
Kelmscott 226
Kingham 248
Nether Westcote 250
Northleach 250
Oxford 231, 232
South Leigh 238
Woodstock 243

Hornsea

Withernsea

North

Sea

Grimsby

Louth

Mablethorpe

Horncastle
A158
A158
Coningsby

A52

Skegness

Brancaster 254
Holkham 263
Morston 270
Cley-next-
the-Sea 257

Boston
Hunstanton
Cromer

Donington
Burnham Market 255
Thorpe Market 275
Fakenham

Snettisham 272

Spalding
A17
King's Lynn 265, 266
A10
Wroxham

A47
A47
Coltishall 277

Wisbech
A1122
Swaffham 274
Norwich 271, 278
A149

Great
Yarmouth

March
Fritton 260

Mundford
Lowestoft

Chatteris
Brandon

Ely
Thetford
Diss
A140

Huntingdon 264
A14
Walberswick 276
Southwold 279-280

Burwell
Bury St Edmunds 256
Saxmundham 177

Cambridge
Newmarket

Long Melford 268
Bildeston 253
Woodbridge 280
Orford 279
Clayton

Royston
Lavenham 267, 277, 278

Great Waldingfield 261
Stoke by Nayland 273

M11
Dedham 258, 259
Harwich 262

Stevenage
Braintree
Mistley 269

Stansted

Clacton-on-Sea

Chelmsford

Maldon

Chigwell

Rayleigh

M25
SOUTHEND-ON-SEA

LONDON 26, 111-137, 168-170
Thames Estuary

Sheerness
Herne
Bay
Margate 138

Dartford
Faversham 166
Sandwich 146

M25
Maidstone
M2
Canterbury

Banstead
M26
M26

Reigate

East
Grinstead 103
Egerton 106
Dover

Sissinghurst 149
Ashford
Folkestone

Cuckfield 100
West Hoathly 154

Fletching 108
Rye 142-144, 26
Littlestone 110

Rushlake Green 141
Camber 99

East Hoathly 104
Hastings 109

Herstmonceux 167
St Leonards-
on-Sea 145

Brighton 96,165
Eastbourne

Strait of Dover

19

Strontian 366
Kinlochleven
Killiecrankie 355
Tobermory 367
Pitlochry 359
Lochaline
Aberfeldy
Ballinluig
Salen
Port Appin 360
Loch Lyon
Craignure
Connel 369
Isle of Eriska 352
Oban
Tyndrum
Perth
Isle of Mull 354
Mull
Dalmally
Fionnphort
Seil
Balquhidder 345
Comrie 369
Auchterarder
Luing
Inveraray
Cairndow
Callander
Scarba
Strachur 370
Dunblane
Kinross
Colonsay
Kilmartin
Luss
Loch Lomond
Stirling
Dunfermline
Ardlussa
M80
Bo'ness
Jura
Knapdale
Kirkintilloch
Cumbernauld
Craighouse
Greenock
M8
Bridgend
Kilberry 337
Largs
Johnstone
GLASGOW 332, 335
Islay
Clachan
Hamilton
Carluke
Ardbeg
Lochranza
Strathaven
Arran
Brodick
Kilmarnock
Galston
Machrihanish
Lamlash
Ayr
Muirkirk
Abington
Campbeltown
Cumnock
Rathlin Island
Sanda Island
Turnberry
Sanquhar 341
Girvan
SOUTH AYRSHIRE
Moniaive
Beattock
Thornhill
Closeburn 333
Bennane Head
St. John's Town of Dalry
Lochmaben
Ballantrae
Barrhill
Loch Ken
Dumfries
Kirkcolm 338
Cairnryan
Creetown
Dalbeattie
Stranraer
Wigtown
Portpatrick 340
Kirkcudbright
Aspatria
Drummore
Whithorn
Maryport
Mull of Galloway
Burrow Head
Wasdale Head 301
Ramsey
Peel
Laxey
Isle of Man
Port Erin
Douglas
Castletown
Irish Sea
Carmel Head
Amlwch
Holyhead
Llandudno 191
Conwy
Bangor
Denbigh 184
Bontnewydd 179
Dolydd 202
Capel Garmon 182
Nant Gwynant 193
Coed
Corwen

North

Sea

Montrose
Alyth
Forfar
Lunan Bay
Arbroath
Carnoustie
DUNDEE
St. Andrews Bay
Cupar 334
Fife Ness
Leven
Isle of May
Kirkcaldy
Firth of Forth
Gullane 342
EDINBURGH 342
Grantshouse
Penicuik
Ayton
Berwick-upon-Tweed
Lauder
Greenlaw
Galashiels
Kelso 332
Cornhill-on-Tweed 313
Melrose 339
Heiton by Kelso 336
Wooler
Hawick
Jedburgh 343
Alnwick
Amble
Kielder Water
Otterburn
Langholm
Longtown
Haltwhistle
Whitley Bay
Gretna
Brampton 288
NEWCASTLE UPON TYNE
GATESHEAD
SUNDERLAND
Consett
Alston
Durham 314
Stanhope
Crook
Hartlepool
Tees
Romaldkirk 327
Redcar
284
282
290
299-300
Kirkby Stephen 294
Whashton 281
MIDDLESBROUGH
Brough
285
281
292
Kelleth 281
Millgate 321
Stokesley
Whitby
Robin Hood's Bay
307
303-305
Barngate 307
Reeth 324
Richmond 325
293
286-287
289
298
291
Hawes 317
Arkengarthdale 306
Northallerton
Lastingham 320
Aysgarth 306, 309
West Witton 281
Hawnby 318
Scarborough
Kirkby Lonsdale 295
Byland 312
Harome 316
Kettlewell
Hunmanby 319
Austwick 283
Ramsgill-in-Nidderdale 323
Sheriff Hutton 328
LANCASTER 296
Grassington 315
Pateley Bridge 322
Bridlington
Ripley 326
Goldsborough 281
Burnsall 311
Bolton Abbey 310
York 330, 331
Fleetwood
Whitewell 302
Skipton
South Dalton 329
BLACKPOOL M55
Colne 281
Harrogate 281
Beverley
Langho 297
BRADFORD
LEEDS 281
Howden
BLACKBURN
KINGSTON-UPON-HULL
Leyland
Huddersfield
Winteringham 242
Ormskirk
M6
Scunthorpe
Brigg
WIGAN
BARNSLEY
Doncaster
Market Rasen
MANCHESTER
Liverpool 308
SHEFFIELD
Gainsborough
Knutsford
Wilmslow
Worksop
Chester
Macclesfield
Baslow 245
Chesterfield
Mansfield
Ashford-in-the-Water 205
Crewe
Biggin-by-Hartington 245
Rowsley 236
Hough-on-the-Hill 225
Newcastle-under-Lyme
Hucknall
Ashbourne 204

Askham 282
Bassenthwaite Lake 284
Borrowdale 285
Bowness-on-Windermere 286-287
Clifton 290
Crosthwaite 291
Great Langdale 307
Hawkshead 293
Sawrey 298
Seatoller 281
Ullswater 299-300
Windermere 286-287

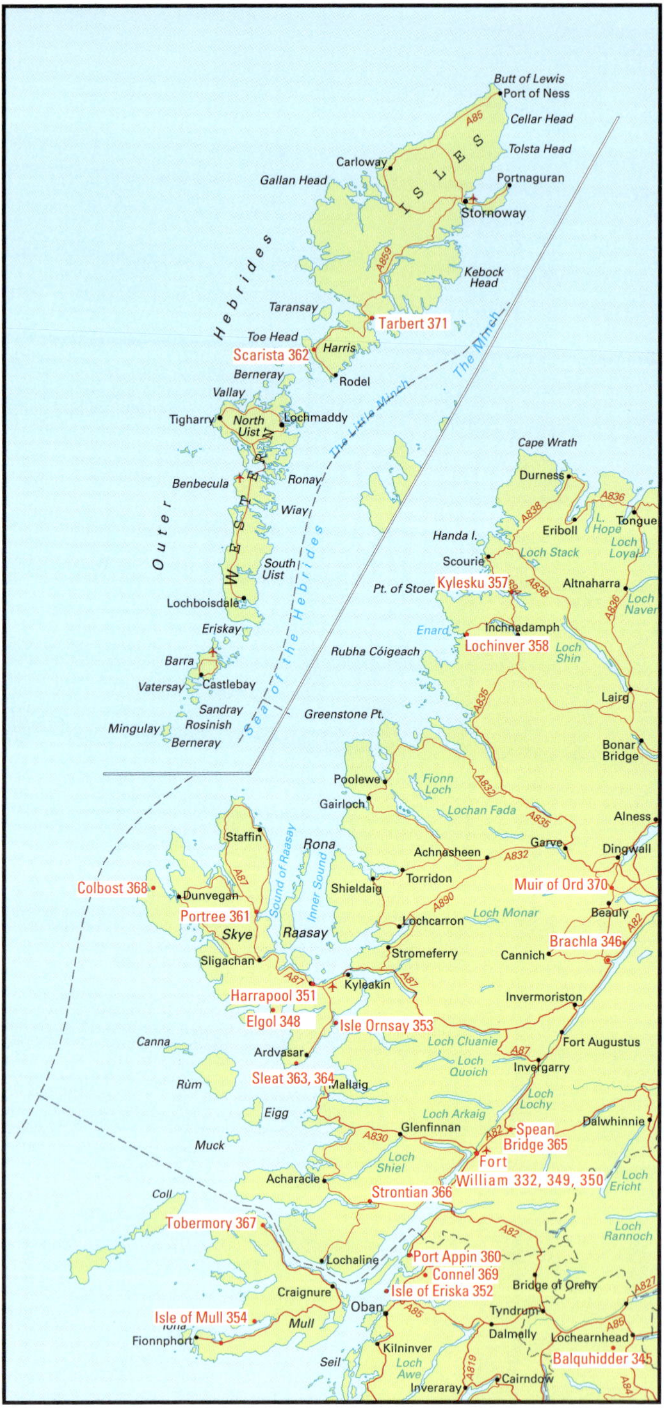

Butt of Lewis
Port of Ness
Cellar Head
Tolsta Head
Carloway
Gallan Head
ISLES
Portnaguran
Stornoway
A85
A859
Kebock Head
Hebrides
Taransay
Tarbert 371
Toe Head
Scarista 362
Harris
Berneray
Rodel
Vallay
Tigharry
North Uist
Lochmaddy
The Minch
The Little Minch
Cape Wrath
Durness
Benbecula
Ronay
WESTERN
Wiay
Outer
Eriboll
Tongue
L. Hope
Loch Loyal
A836
A838
Handa I.
Loch Stack
Scourie
South Uist
Sea of the Hebrides
Pt. of Stoer
Kylesku 357
Altnaharra
Lochboisdale
Loch Naver
Eriskay
Enard
Inchnadamph
Lochinver 358
Loch Shin
Rubha Cóigeach
Barra
Vatersay
Castlebay
Sandray
Rosinish
Mingulay
Berneray
Greenstone Pt.
A835
Lairg
Bonar Bridge
Poolewe
Fionn Loch
Gairloch
A832
Lochan Fada
Alness
Staffin
Rona
Garve
Dingwall
Achnasheen
Sound of Raasay
Inner Sound
Torridon
Colbost 368
Dunvegan
Shieldaig
Muir of Ord 370
A87
A890
Portree 361
Loch Monar
Beauly
Skye
Raasay
Lochcarron
A82
Brachla 346
Sligachan
Stromeferry
Cannich
Kyleakin
Harrapool 351
Invermoriston
Elgol 348
Isle Ornsay 353
Canna
Loch Cluanie
Fort Augustus
Ardvasar
Loch Quoich
Invergarry
Sleat 363, 364
Mallaig
Rùm
Loch Lochy
Eigg
Loch Arkaig
Dalwhinnie
Glenfinnan
Spean Bridge 365
Muck
A830
Loch Shiel
Fort William 332, 349, 350
Acharacle
Loch Ericht
Coll
Strontian 366
Loch Rannoch
Tobermory 367
Port Appin 360
Lochaline
Connel 369
Craignure
Isle of Eriska 352
Bridge of Orchy
A827
Isle of Mull 354
Oban
Tyndrum
Iona
Mull
Fionnphort
Dalmally
Lochearnhead
Kilninver
Balquhidder 345
Seil
Loch Awe
A819
Cairndow
Inveraray
A84

ORKNEY ISLANDS

Papa Westray
North Ronaldsay
Westray
Sanday
Sanday Sound
Rousay
Eday
Stronsay
Brough Head
Shapinsay
Mainland
Finstown
Kirkwall
Stromness
Mull Head
St. Mary's
Rora Head
Hoy
Burray
South Ronaldsay
Burwick

Pentland Firth

SHETLAND ISLANDS

Haroldswick
Unst
Gutcher
Fetlar
Isbister
Mid Yell
Hillswick
Yell
Ulsta
Toft
Sullom
Whalsay
Mainland
Walls 372
Lerwick
Scalloway
Bressay
Sumburgh
Sumburgh Head

Strathy
Scrabster
Thurso 371
John o' Groats
Melvich
Dounreay
Loch
Sinclair's Bay
A897
A9
Loch More
Kinbrace
Latheron
Lybster
A9
Helmsdale
A839
Golspie
Dornoch 332, 347
Tarbat Ness
A838
Tain
Dornoch Firth

Burghead
Lossiemouth
Cromarty
Urquhart 372
Cullen
Fraserburgh
Elgin
Fochabers
Forres
Aberchirder
Mintlaw
Auldearn 344
Rothes
Keith
Turriff
Peterhead
Charlestown of Aberlour
Dufftown
Huntly
Grantown-on-Spey
Oldmeldrum
Ellon
Carrbridge
Rhynie
Inverurie
A96
Aviemore
Tomintoul
Alford
Kintore
Dyce
ABERDEEN
Girdle Ness
Kingussie 356
Ballater
Banchory
Peterculter
Newtonmore
Crathie
Aboyne 368
Braemar
Stonehaven
Laurencekirk
Inverbervie
Milton Ness
Killiecrankie 355
Brechin
Montrose
Pitlochry 359
Kirriemuir
Scurdie Ness
Loch Tummel
Lunan Bay
Kenmore
Blairgowrie
Meigle
Forfar
Arbroath
DUNDEE
Perth
Newport-on Tay
St. Andrews Bay
Comrie 369
Auchterarder
Newburgh
Cupar 334
Fife Ness

North Sea

Atlantic

Ocean

Aran Island

Gweebarra Bay

Rossan Pt.   Ardara 377

Killybegs

Dunkineely 391

Donegal Bay

Benwee Hd.   Downpatrick Head   Inishmurray

Erris Hd.

Belmullet   Killala Bay   Sligo Bay   Sligo

Inishkea   Bangor Erris   Dromore West   Ballysadare

Blacksod Bay   Crossmolina   N59   Ballina   S L I G O

Ballycroy   L.Conn   Tobercurry

Achill Island   Mulranny 373   M A Y O   Riverstown 407   L. Gara

Newport   Swinford   Boyle

Clare   Castlebar   Ballaghaderreen

Clew Bay   Westport   Ballymote 379   Castlerea

Inishturk   Ballyhaunis   N60

Inishbofin   L. Mask   Claremorris

Inishark   L. Carra   N17

Leenane 397

Clifden 384-385, 410   Tuam

Slyne Head   CONNEMARA   Recess 406   N84

Cashel Bay 382   G A L W A Y

Ballinasloe

Inishmore   Galway Bay

Aran   Inis Meáin 395   Loughrea

Islands

Inisheer   Ballyvaughan 380   Gort   Portumna

Lisdoonvarna   N67   Lough Derg

Hags Head   398, 399   mon   N18

Liscannor Bay   Milltown Malbay

C L A R E

Ennis   Newmarket-on-Fergus 404   Nenagh 403

Kilkee   Kilrush   Shannon

Loop Head   Foynes   Limerick

Mouth of The Shannon   Ballybunion

Kerry Head   Listowel   Rathkeale

Brandon Head   Tralee Bay   L I M E R I C K   Tipperary

Castlegregory 373   Tralee   Abbeyfeale   Rath Luirc   Kilmallock

Dingle 387   Castleisland   Ballingarry 409

Slea Head   K E R R Y   Mitchelstown

Dingle Bay   Killorglin   Fermoy

Caragh Lake   L. Leane   Killarney   Mallow 404

381   Aghadoe 376   Castlelyons 383

Valencia I.   Cahirciveen   C O R K   Cloyne 411

Bray Head   Kenmare 412   Macroom   Midleton

Bolus Head   Cobh

Glengarriff   Innishannon 411   Cork Harbour

Ballylickey 410   Bandon   Kinsale

Dursey Head   Bantry Bay   Shanagarry 413

Clonakilty

Goleen 392, 393   Skibbereen   Galley Head

Mizen Head

24

Tory Island
Fanad Head
Rathlin Island
Fair Head
Sanda Island
Carndonagh
Moville
Portrush
Ballycastle
Buncrana
Bushmills 375
Tory Sound
Lough Foyle
Limavady
Ballymoney
Rathmullan 413
Gweedore
Letterkenny
Londonderry
Garron Pt.
N56
Glenties
Ballybofey
Strabane
Kilrea
Ballymena
Larne
DONEGAL
Magherafelt
A6
M2
Omagh
Cookstown
Antrim
Carrickfergus
Bangor
NORTHERN
Donaghadee
A5
Ballyshannon
IRELAND
Newtownards
Bundoran
A32
A4
Lough Neagh
ARDS
L. Melvin
Lower L. Erne
Irvinestown
Magheralin 374
Strangford Lough
FERMANAGH
Manorhamilton
Enniskillen
Blackwater
A3
Dromore
N16
Monaghan
A28
Downpatrick 375
Ardglass
Upper L. Erne
Clones 386
Newry
Newcastle
L. Key
Drumshanbo
MONAGHAN
Belturbet
Warrenpoint
Kilkeel
LEITRIM
Cavan
A1
Carrick-on-Shannon
Carrickmacross
Dundalk
Ballagan Pt.
CAVAN
LOUTH
Dundalk Bay
N4
Virginia
N52
Clogher Head
Longford
L. Sheelin
N3
Ceanannus Mor (Kells)
Drogheda
Drogheda Bay
Roscommon
N55
Slane 408
Balbriggan
Lough Ree
Multyfarnham 402
Mullingar
Navan
Trim
Boyne
DUBLIN
Grand Canal
WEST MEATH
MEATH
Swords
Athlone
N6
Moate
Kinnegad
M1
Tullamore
Grand Canal
N4
Lucan
M50
Dublin 373, 389, 390
Dun Laoghaire
OFFALY
Droichead Nua
M7
Naas
M11
Bray
Portarlington
Birr
Mountmellick
Monasterevin
M9
Poulaphouca Res.
Roscree
Mountrath
N7
Portlaoise
Athy
N9
Rathnew 405
LAOIS
Abbeyleix
Mountrath 401
Carlow
WICKLOW
Wicklow
Rathdrum
Templemore
Tullow
N11
Mizen Head
Thurles
CARLOW
Arklow
TIPPERARY
Kilkenny 414
Kilgraney 412
Gorey 394
KILKENNY
Thomastown
N80
Cahore Point
Cahir
N24
Carrick-on-Suir
Inistioge 396
Enniscorthy
Clonmel
New Ross
WEXFORD
Ballymacarbry 378
Drinagh 388
Wexford
WATE
Woodstown 414
Waterford
Rosslare
Tramore
Rosslare Harbour
Dungarvan
N25
Helvick Head
Waterford Harbour
Hook Head
Saltee Islands
Carnsore Point
St. George's Channel
Youghal
Ardmore 409
Youg Bay

Area introduction

This first section covers the most important summer tourist counties of Britain: Devon and Cornwall, with their spectacular coastlines and wonderful patchwork countryside, their sunken lanes and timeless villages. Add to them Somerset and Wiltshire, Dorset and south-west Hampshire, and you have what is loosely known as the West Country – what used to be, more or less, the early medieval Kingdom of Wessex. The rest of the section consists of densely populated south-east England – East and West Sussex, Kent, Berkshire and Greater London. Here, as elsewhere, you can scarcely go a mile without discovering somewhere worth seeing: a picturesque village, a Georgian town or a spectacular view. Charming small hotels are thick on the ground. We draw the border dividing southern England from Central England roughly along the M4, or a line linking London in the east with Bristol in the west.

Below are some useful back-up places to try if our main selections are fully booked:

Gidleigh Park
Country house hotel, Chagford
Tel 01647 432367
www.gidleigh.co.uk
Luxury, fine dining.

The Casterbridge
Town guesthouse, Dorchester
Tel 01305 264043
www.casterbridgehotel.co.uk
Relaxed guesthouse offering bed-and-breakfast service.

The Bath Arms
Village hotel, Longleat
Tel 01985 844308
www.batharms.co.uk
Quirky country hotel on The Longleat Estate.

Langford Fivehead
Restaurant-with-rooms, Lower Swell
Tel 01460 282020
www.langfordfivehead.co.uk
'Farm to plate' fine dining.

The Scarlet
Coastal hotel, Mawgan Porth
Tel 01637 861800
www.scarlethotel.co.uk
Eco-friendly, grown-ups only hotel for relaxation.

The Pear Tree Inn
Restaurant-with-rooms, Whitley   Tel 01225 704966
www.peartreewhitley.co.uk
Marco Pierre White's chic steakhouse in the Cotswolds.

The White House
Town house hotel, Williton
Tel 01984 632306
www.whitehousewilliton.co.uk
Family-run guesthouse, comfortable Somerset base.

B&B Belgravia
City bed-and-breakfast, London Tel 020 72598570
www.bb-belgravia.com
Upmarket, stylish bed-and-breakfast accommodation.

Chiltern Firehouse
Town house hotel, London
Tel 020 7073 7676
www.chilternfirehouse.com
Luxury hotel with a Michelin starred chef.

The Mermaid Inn
Town inn, Rye
Tel 01797 223065
www.mermaidinn.com
Charming inn in pretty Rye, dating back to 1420.

Hotel du Vin
Town mansion hotel, Tunbridge Wells
Tel 084474 89266
www.hotelduvin.com
Elegant hotel in spa town.

Longueville Manor
Country house hotel, St Saviour Tel 01534 725501
www.longuevillemanor.com
Traditional Relais & Chateaux hotel, high standards.

Allerford, Somerset

Allerford, Minehead, Somerset
TA24 8HW

Tel 01643 863276
e-mail info@crosslanehouse.com
website www.crosslanehouse.com

Nearby Exmoor National Park,
Coleridge Way, West Somerset
Rural Life Museum
Location just off the A39 in the vil-
lage of Allerford
Food breakfast, lunch, dinner, picnic
baskets on request
Price ££-£££
Rooms 3; 2 double with bathroom
and 1 suite with bathroom
Facilities dining room, sitting room,
terrace,
Credit cards MC, V
Children not under 16
Disabled access to ground floor only
Pets dogs welcome, not in public
rooms
Closed Jan
Proprietors Max and Andrew

Cross Lane House
Village hotel

Cross Lane House has stood on the same corner of Allerford village for more than 500 years – but you'd be for-given for not realizing this. Recent owners Max and Andrew have carefully renovated the late medieval building, turning it into a striking up-to-date hotel. Set back from the road by a charmingly haphazard stonewall and a trim, winding footpath, the exterior shows Max's and Andrew's atten-tion to detail.

Wherever possible they have retained the house's original features – we especial-ly like the dining room where the massive stone lintel over the fireplace and original timber panelling are good examples of their old-and-new style.

Upstairs the four generously sized bed-rooms are decorated in country house style – each room has the kind of thought that we look for. The neutral tones are complemented with floral splashes, adding colour to an otherwise pastel palette.

The location – in Exmoor National Park – gives you access to some of the most beautiful walking routes in south-west England. It is also close to the Coleridge Way: a 36-mile (58 km) footpath noted as one of the UK's best autumnal walks.

Babbacombe, Devon

Oddicombe Beach Hill,
Babbacombe, South Devon TQ1
3LX

Tel 01803 327110
e-mail enquiries@caryarms.co.uk
website www.caryarms.co.uk

Nearby Babbacombe Bay, Torquay.
Location turn onto Babbacombe
Downs Road, continue along the
Downs with the sea on your left then
turn left onto Beach Road.
Food breakfast, lunch, dinner
Price ££££ **Rooms** 10 sea-facing
rooms and suites at inn; 3 restored
fisherman's cottages: all rooms have
phone, TV, hairdryer, tea/coffee
facilities. 8 deluxe beach huts/suites;
each with terrace, sitting room, wet
bar, fire, bathroom **Facilities** residents' sitting room with fire, Yon-Ka
Spa, conservatory, bar, dining room,
wi-fi **Credit cards** MC, V
Children welcome over 12
Disabled 1 ground-floor room **Pets**
dogs in 2 bedrooms and the cottages
Closed never
Proprietor Lana de Savary

Cary Arms & Spa
Beach inn

Special places need a special effort to
reach them. Set beneath the cliffs on
the beach at Babbacombe, the Cary Arms'
location is spectacular, but its approach, via
an alarmingly steep single-track road, is
not for the faint hearted. Queen Victoria
was equally enchanted 150 years ago, rowing ashore with Prince Albert from the
Royal Yacht on several occasions.

The present hotel was built in the late
1880s: a solid, reassuring building with a
stone walled, slate floored bar at its core.
Here, superior gastropub dishes are
served. Try the local Devon beef or Lyme
Bay lobster.

There are ten bedrooms and three self-
catering cottages, all delightful, with retro
red leather bed-heads, pretty wardrobes,
sticks of rock on snow white pillows and
walls adorned by old posters advertising
the delights of Devon and colourful photographs (recalling de Savary's passion) of
racing yachts. Recent additions are the
eight deluxe beach huts lining the water's
edge. Each hut sleeps two, and quirkily
combines vintage seaside style with
bespoke contemporary art. There is also a
new spa offering luxury Thalgo treatments.

Chic and secluded doesn't come cheap,
but it's worth it. Their standard double
rooms are £245 – this price includes
breakfast. The manageress, Jen, is superb.

1 Upper Oldfield Park,
Bath, Avon BA2 3JX

Tel (01225) 426336
e-mail info@dorianhouse.co.uk
website www.dorianhouse.co.uk

Nearby Bath centre.
Location from Bath, take A367
signposted Shepton Mallet, after 1
minute's drive, take first road on the
right; with car parking
Food breakfast
Price ££
Rooms 13 doubles; all with bath or
shower, all rooms have TV, phone,
hairdryer, wi-fi
Facilities sitting room, dining room,
honesty bar; garden
Credit cards MC, V
Children accepted by arrangement
Disabled access difficult
Pets not accepted
Closed 24th and 25th Dec
Proprietors Tim and Ros Forester

Dorian House
Bed-and-breakfast

Although Bath has a large number of hotels, Dorian House stands out as a place of elegance and charm. Tim Hugh has made the most of this Victorian building built in 1880 of Bath stone, standing on a hill overlooking the city centre – bedrooms have splendid views towards Royal Crescent.

With high ceilings and large windows (including some impressive bay windows), rooms are drenched in light and, with tan, beige and cream tones, have a feeling of airiness. The house retains all of its original features and many rooms have fireplaces and fine antiques. The elegant decoration combines Asian antiques with contemporary pieces and works of art.

The high-quality breakfast is taken in a tastefully decorated Orangery in the Japanese-inspired garden, also with views of the city. The sitting room (with honesty bar) is equally refined. You can't have dinner here, but there are plenty of good restaurants in Bath and Tim provides a book of menus collected from the better restaurants in town.

Since our last edition Dorian House has changed hands, though we hear standards have remained high. Reports welcome.

Hunstrete House, Hunstrete,
Pensford, Bath, BS39 4NS

Tel 01761 490490
e-mail info@thepignearbath.com
website https://www.thepighotel.
com/near-bath

Nearby Hamburger Hill (Bristol
Outdoor Pursuits, 0.5m), Bath (6m)
with Roman Baths, Royal Crescent,
Thermae Bath Spa, Fashion
Museum
Location down a rural road in
unspoilt countryside, car park
Food breakfast, lunch, dinner
Price ££-££££
Rooms 29; doubles and 2 suites;
twin bedding, cots and extra beds
available in some rooms. All have
shower or bath, TV, tea-making
facilities; some have larder, drinks,
Nespresso machine **Facilities**
grounds, kitchen garden, treatment
room, lounge, library, restaurant
Credit cards V, MC, AE **Children**
welcome **Disabled** has an accessible
room suitable for a wheelchair **Pets**
not accepted **Closed** never
Manager Sarah Holden

The Pig - near Bath
Country house hotel

This Grade II-listed house, dating back to
1820, stands in the Chew valley, imposing and dignified, surrounded by its own
deer park. It became the third of the Pig
hotels, a venture conceived by Robin
Hutson and David Elton that's now grown
into a fully formed family of five hotels.

The style is rural shabby-chic and it
works beautifully: stripped wooden floors,
painted timber-panelled walls and velvet
curtains create a grand but informal atmosphere. Robin's wife Judy is responsible for
the interior design: mismatched rugs and
fabrics create a feeling of relaxed glamour,
while every object has been chosen with
taste and panache. The bedrooms are consistent with the style: comfortable and laid
back. They include 'larders' stocked with
snacks and large bathrooms. As well as the
rooms in the country house, there are four
delightful garden rooms and two 'hideaway
rooms' in the kitchen garden, with wood-
burning stoves and freestanding baths.

The large kitchen garden provides much
of the produce used in the kitchen, freshly
picked on the day. The flavoursome dishes,
with local game such as wild rabbit and
duck, are uncomplicated and satisfying. It's
hard to find fault here: an all-round good
address, where you will feel relaxed and
spoiled. (See other Pig hotels on pages 50,
75, 97 and 150).

Russell Street, Bath, Somerset BA1
2QF

Tel (01225) 447928
Fax (01225) 446065
e-mail reservations@thequeensber-
ry.co.uk **website** www.thequeensber-
ry.co.uk

Nearby Assembly Rooms; Museum
of Costume; The Circus.
Location in middle of city, close to
main shopping area; paved gardens
behind; daytime car parking restrict-
ed – but valet parking available
Food breakfast, lunch, dinner
Price £££
Rooms 29, 1 with shower, rest with
bath; all rooms have phone, TV,
hairdryer, CD player
Facilities sitting room, bar, restau-
rant; courtyard
Credit cards AE, MC, V
Children welcome
Disabled accessible, lift/elevator
Pets guide dogs only
Closed never
Proprietors Laurence and Helen
Beere

The Queensberry
Town house hotel

This Bath hotel is slightly large for our
purposes, but cannot be allowed to
escape the net. Laurence and Helen Beere
bought this discreet, quiet and beautifully
decorated haven right in the centre of
Bath in 2003. It has the advantage of a lift
to all levels, which cuts down on confusion
in the maze of stairwells, corridors and different levels resulting from the linking of
three buildings. Despite the small-scale
appearance of the hotel, the majority of
the bedrooms are surprisingly spacious,
and are kitted out to the highest standards
of comfort and elegance. Double beds
generally mean king-size here, almost
guaranteed to give you a good night's
sleep, and are made up with lovely cotton
sheets. Rooms on the first floor are
largest, with armchairs and breakfast
tables; bathrooms are lavish, with quality
toiletries and proper towels.

The rooms have a contemporary feel,
while still making use of the original features and antiques.

Downstairs, the principal sitting room is
beautifully furnished in muted colours. The
award-winning basement restaurant, the
Olive Tree, attracts non-residents.

Beaminster, Dorset DT8 3AY

Tel (01308) 862200
Fax (01308) 863700
e-mail enquiries@bridge-house.co.uk
website www.bridge-house.co.uk

Nearby Mapperton Gardens; Forde Abbey; Abbotsbury Swannery & Sub-Tropical Gardens.
Location on A3066 in centre of town; ample car parking
Food breakfast; lunch; dinner
Price £££
Rooms 13; 7 double, 3 twin, 1 single, 2 family, all with bath or shower; all rooms have phone, TV, wi-fi
Facilities sitting room, bar, restaurant, 2 conservatories; outdoor dining area, walled garden
Credit cards AE, MC, V
Children accepted
Disabled 4 bedrooms with easy access **Pets** dogs accepted in selected rooms **Closed** never
Proprietors Mark and Joanna Donovan

Bridge House Hotel
Country hotel

Dating from the 13th century, Bridge-House is reputedly a former clergy house and the oldest building in Beaminster. Whatever its antecedents, it is certainly a venerable and charming building and has been run as a hotel by Mark and Joanna Donovan for the last thirteen years. Mark, a former television producer, and Joanna, a former retail buyer, took on the hotel as a major change of lifestyle. Their aim has been to create a stylish country town retreat by 'updating where necessary, without destroying the building's unique charm'.

The sitting room and bar areas have medieval character; local artists' paintings hang on the walls. Lunch and dinner are served in the Georgian panelled dining room or the conservatory. In summer, guests can also eat outside under a large 'Gazova', which looks out on to the walled gardens. The restaurant has an excellent reputation, with a seasonal menu reflecting an area blessed with quality local produce: fish, meat and cheese all come from nearby. Bread, biscuits and ice-cream are all made in the Bridge House kitchens; even the marmalade that accompanies the satisfying breakfasts is made on the premises.

Bedrooms, with mahogany beds and Frette Italian linen, are all different, as would be expected in a building so full of nooks and crannies – including a priest hole.

Beercrocombe, Somerset

Hatch Beauchamp, Taunton,
Somerset TA3 6AF

Tel 01823 481883
email frogstreet@hotmail.com
website www.frogstreet.co.uk

Nearby Barrington Court; Vale of
Taunton.
Location on SW side of village, 10
miles (16 km) SE of Taunton; in gardens, with ample car-parking
Food breakfast, dinner (for parties of
6 or more)
Price £
Rooms 4; 1 family suite, 2 doubles,
1 super king with private sitting
room and entrace; all rooms have
bath/shower, hairdryer, tea-making
facilities, Sky TV, free wi-fi.
Facilities sitting room, dining room;
terrace, garden
Credit cards all major
Children accepted by arrangement
Disabled not suitable
Pets not accepted
Closed 6 weeks in the winter period
Proprietors Louise and David

Frog Street Farmhouse
Farm guesthouse

This longhouse dates back to the 15th
century and can be found at the end of
a lane in deepest Somerset. The house has
considerable character and warmth, with
Jacobean panelling and a handsome oak-
beamed inglenook in the sitting room.
Guests walk through the front door straight
in to the highly polished dining room where
breakfast is served. When possible Louise
and David use their own produce: eggs
come from their own hens, tomatoes from
the organic garden, with homemade bread
and preserves.

Bedrooms look out on to farmland, cider
apple orchards and the pretty garden. They
are all spacious and comfortable, with white
duvets, and a mix of antique furniture. Since
the last edition, the Orchard suite has been
expanded into two bedrooms to incorpo-
rate families; The Snug has a private sitting
room and entrance. The bathrooms in all
rooms have been renovated and are airy,
with freestanding roll-top baths or showers.
The atmosphere is friendly, restful and
unpretentious.

Bigbury-on-Sea, Devon

Folly Hill, Bigbury-on-Sea, Devon
TQ7 4AR

Tel (01548) 810240
e-mail info@thehenleyhotel.co.uk
website www.thehenleyhotel.co.uk

Nearby Burgh Island, Avon Estuary.
Location 20 minutes from A38
beyond Bigbury-on-Sea towards sea;
ample car parking
Food breakfast, dinner (give 3 days
notice)
Price ££-£££
Rooms 5; all double and 3 can be
twin, all have bath/shower; all have
phone, TV, radio
Facilities conservatory/dining room;
garden, private cliff path and steps to
beach, beach
Credit cards AE, MC, V
Children over 12 only
Disabled not suitable
Pets dogs welcome (£5 per day)
Closed Nov to Mar
Proprietors Martin Scarterfield and
Petra Lampe

The Henley
Coastal hotel

Recommended to us by an astute reader, The Henley was described to us as 'the sort of place that I always hope to discover on holiday, and alas, rarely do.' Originally built as a holiday cottage during Edwardian times, the hotel has a beach-house feel and spectacular views that stretch from the Avon Estuary around to Burgh Island. And if simply looking at the sea isn't enough, you can climb down the private cliff path to a stretch of pristine beach.

Although owner Martyn Scarterfield was a PE and Art teacher in a previous life, he comes from a family hotel in Sidmouth and has been in the trade for many years. Co-owner Petra Lampe brings both charm and a sense of warmth and elegance to the hotel. Together, they create a relaxing atmosphere that is, above all, unpretentious.

Bedrooms are simple, yet comfortable and spacious. The dining room has Lloyd Loom furniture and overlooks the sea. Martyn does the cooking and it can be described as 'real home cooked food' – excellent quality without any artificial presentation. The dining menu is limited but often includes fresh, locally caught fish (three days notice required).

A winning combination of great food, beautiful views and friendly owners.

Bradford-on-Avon, Wiltshire

4 Masons Lane, Bradford-on-Avon,
Wiltshire BA15 1QN

Tel (01225) 866842
Fax (01225) 866648
e-mail
csh@bradfordoldwindmill.co.uk
website
www.bradfordoldwindmill.co.uk

Nearby Bath; Kennet and Avon
Canal; Longleat.
Location just N of town centre;
with cottage garden and parking for
3 small cars
Food breakfast, dinner (Mon, Wed,
Thur, Sat only)
Price ££
Rooms 3; 2 double, 1 family suite,
all with bath; all rooms have TV
Facilities sitting room, dining room;
terrace **Credit cards** MC, V
Children welcome over 6
Disabled access difficult
Pets not accepted
Closed Nov to Mar
Proprietors Peter and Priscilla
Roberts

Bradford Old Windmill
Town guesthouse

Peter and Priscilla Roberts' extraordinary home, an old windmill, continues
to provide guests with a unique experience. Built in 1807, the windmill functioned
for only 20 years but left a memorable
building in its stead. It boasts a 4-storey
Cotswold stone tower, conical roof, point-
ed Gothic windows and restored sail galley.

The rooms, some with curved walls and
oddly-angled corners, offer excellent views
over old Bradford and beyond. The Fantail
Suite includes a minstrel gallery and Great
Spur is round with a circular bed. Each
room contains curiosities and guidebooks
from the Roberts' extensive travels.
Bathrooms have been updated.

Breakfast is served at the communal
table or occasionally, weather permitting,
on the pretty terrace that also overlooks
old Bradford.

The breakfast menu is extensive and
includes free-range bacon. Ingredients are
90 per cent organic. Priscilla will prepare a
home-made soup tray at short notice for
those who do not wish to go out to eat.
This is a very different kind of guesthouse,
and one with great character. See also our
other windmill, Cley Mill (page 257).

Bradford-on-Avon, Wiltshire

Newtown, Bradford-on-Avon,
Wiltshire BA15 1NQ

Tel (01225) 862230
e-mail priorysteps@clara.co.uk
website www.priorysteps.co.uk

Nearby Barton Tithe Barn; Bath.
Location off A363 on N side of
town; in 0.5 acre garden, with car
parking
Food breakfast, dinner (to order)
Price ££
Rooms 5 double and twin, all with
bath; 1 self-catering apartment in the
Coach House; all rooms have TV
Facilities sitting room, dining room;
terrace, garden
Credit cards MC, V
Children accepted
Disabled access difficult
Pets not accepted
Closed occasionally
Proprietors Carey and Diana
Chapman

Priory Steps
Town guesthouse

High above the lovely little wool town of
Bradford-on-Avon, Carey and Diana
Chapman's converted row of weavers' cottages
look out over the predominantly Georgian
houses interspersed with a smattering of Saxon
and medieval buildings. Although only a three
minute walk from the centre, Priory Steps is
not easy to find. It is so discreetly signposted
that it looks like a private home – which it is
for the Chapmans and their (now grown-up)
children. As a result, the pictures and pieces
that decorate the house have family connections and the atmosphere is informal and easy-
going, especially in the book-lined sitting room.

Each of the bedrooms has a theme –
Indian, Chinese and so on. In spite of the cottage architecture, there is nothing cramped
about them: they are light and airy, with wonderful views. Beautifully decorated, each is
furnished mainly with antiques. This is a well-
maintained place with a continuing refurbishment programme.

Diana is a keen cook and dinner is served
either at a communal table in the elegant dining room or, on fine days, out on the terrace
of the garden looking down over the town.
Dinners are three courses, with no choice,
but special requirements are happily met,
given notice. You will be made to feel like a
house guest in a particularly well-run home.

Branscombe, Devon

Branscombe, Devon
EX12 3DJ

Tel (01297) 680300
e-mail reception@masonsarms.co.uk
website www.masonsarms.co.uk

Nearby South Devon coastal path;
Sidmouth.
Location in village 8 miles (11 km) S
of Honiton, off A3052 between
Sidmouth and Seaton; with ample
car parking
Food breakfast (for residents), lunch,
dinner
Price ££-£££
Rooms 27; 7 in the main inn; 15
cottage rooms; 6 above car park; all
rooms have phone, TV, hairdryer
Facilities bar, restaurant; garden
Credit cards MC, V
Children welcome
Disabled some facilities but access a
little difficult
Pets accepted **Closed** never
Proprietors St Austell Brewery
Company Ltd
Managers Simon and Alison Ede

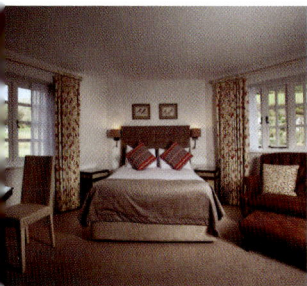

Masons Arms
Seaside village inn

Branscombe is a picturesque little
Devon village, at the end of a winding
lane, surrounded by steep, wooded hillsides
and overlooking the sea. The National Trust
owns most of the land around, and the
South Devon Coastal Path passes through
it. In other words, this village is a hive of
activity, inspiring visits from walkers in winter and beachcomers in summer, many of
whom pitch up at the Masons Arms.
Welcoming, yes; popular, certainly. It's what
a village pub should be, although its success
has led to expansion: what was a simple
inn, converted from four cottages, now has
a restaurant and a bar serving food, a large
function room, plus 27 rooms spread out
between the main inn, cottage rooms and
above the car park.

For the past seven years St Austell
Brewery Company Ltd have been making
improvements while preserving the character of the place. They have refurbished
the cottage rooms and restaurant, and
most rooms now have their own bath.

The bedrooms have a cottagey feel, with
pretty fabrics, beamed ceilings and sloping
floors. The recently upgraded cottage
rooms are modern and stylish. Bathrooms
were refurbished in early 2017. The food is
several notches above pub fare, with the
restaurant and bar offering the same menu.

28 High St, Bruton, Somerset BA10 0AE

Tel 01749 814070
e-mail bedrooms@atthechapel.co.uk
/restaurant@atthechapel.co.uk
website atthechapel.co.uk

Nearby Bath
Location central Bruton
Food breakfast, lunch, dinner
Price ££
Rooms 8 double, all with wi-fi, iPod docking station, TV, safe, tea/coffee facilities
Facilities sitting room, dining room, bar, brasserie, gun lockers
Credit cards AE, MC, V
Children welcome
Disabled access to the restaurant
Pets not accepted
Closed Christmas Day
Proprietors Catherine Butler & Ahmed Sidki

At the Chapel
Town guesthouse

This handsome 19thC congregational chapel has been brilliantly transformed. Catherine Butler, the inspired owner, along with her partner Ahmed, spent eight years restoring it, and rapidly established it as an indispensable meeting place ("it's the town piazza" a regular tells us) – a hub for the community, just as it was when it was first built.

You wake in a bedroom dominated by floor-to-ceiling stained-glass and stone-framed windows: what an estate agent would call the the wow factor. Freshly-baked croissants are delivered from the in-house bakery to your room at seven each morning. The smell wafts temptingly through the door (handmade by Ahmed, like all the doors, much of the furniture and the stone bread oven in the bakery).

Things just happen here. Sergei Polunin and other Royal Ballet stars have danced here; the night we stayed, there was a showing of local boy Julian Temple's film *London: The Modern Babylon* downstairs in the 'club room' ... and on it goes. "People just suggest things," says Catherine. "The building has the right chemistry; I believe it always did."

Bude, Devon

Summerleaze Crescent, Bude,
Devon EX23 8HJ

Tel 01288 389800 **Fax** 01288
389820 **e-mail** enquiries@thbeachat-
bude.co.uk
website www.thebeachatbude.co.uk

Nearby Bude heritage centre and
museum, the National Coastal Path,
surfing and seawater swimming pool
available on the beach, Boscastle village, the ruins of King Arthur's
Castle in Tintagel **Location** Bude,
some car-parking available
Food breakfast, lunch, dinner
Price ££-££££
Rooms 17; all with flat-screen TV,
Blu-Ray player, direct-dial telephone, hairdryer, fridge, safe, hospitality tray. **Facilities** restaurant, bar,
terrace, club room, wi-fi **Credit
cards** AE, MC
 Children accepted, extra bed £30
per night, £50 per night for 5-16
year olds.
Disabled there is a lift to all floors,
and 1 ground-floor room
Closed select dates over Christmas
Manager Will and Susie Daniel

The Beach
Coastal hotel

The Beach can claim to be one of the
hottest places on the north Cornwall
coast. The old Victorian building has kept
its character, with rooms of different shapes
and sizes, but a modern feel has been
added by thoughtful, contemporary redecoration.

Guests especially enjoy the bedrooms,
describing them as comfortable and homely.
All the rooms are decorated in cool colours
– in the New England seaside style – with
fashionable design features and accessories,
particularly in the bathrooms. It is the combination of the views over Summerleaze
Beach and the stylish decoration that make
them so appealing – most have views that
also extend over the spectacular Cornish
scenery surrounding Bude, including the
Downs at Efford and the Bude canal.

Since our last edition they've opened a
restaurant, presided over by head chef Joe
Simmons who previously worked at the
Michelin-starred Priory Hotel in Bath, with a
menu championing seafood and local produce. Their bar – popular with locals – has
views across Summerleaze beach, and is
especially lively during weekends and
evenings. If you prefer to eat out, the interesting town of Bude has a medley of local
restaurants. This is definitely a place for more
than one night's stay.

Carbis Bay, Cornwall

Boskerris Road, Carbis Bay, St Ives,
Cornwall, TN26 2NQ

Tel (01736) 795295
e-mail
reservations@boskerrishotel.co.uk
website www.boskerrishotel.co.uk

Nearby St Ives 2.9m; Porthminster
beach; Eden Project 40m; Lands
End, Minnack Theatre 18m
Location above Carbis Bay beach,
on the edge of St Ives
Food breakfast, afternoon tea &
sandwiches, light dinner **Price** £££-
££££ **Rooms** 15; (ocean view) 3
super-king; 4 king; 1 twin; (not
ocean view) 3 king, 1 twin. All have
hairdryer, phone, TV radio,
coffee/tea **Facilities** guest sitting
room, bar, outside decked terrace;
treatment room, small dining room,
breakfast room **Credit cards** all
major accepted **Children** 10+ are
allowed **Disabled** Classic Deluxe
room is on ground floor, with a
walk-in rain shower **Pets** not accepted **Closed** early Nov-mid March
Proprietor Jonathan and Marianna
Basset

Boskerris
Coastal hotel

The relaxed vibe of Cornwall combined
with a touch of St Tropez glamour
characterizes this small, family-run hotel,
nestled on the Cornish coast. Its decoration is bright and breezy, Mediterranean-
coast style. It looked a little drab when we
visited in November, but one could easily
imagine its magic in summer, when light
pours in from the floor-length windows
and guests can enjoy a drink on the elegant decked terrace, with panoramic views
from St Ives bay towards Newlyn
(Godevry Lighthouse, which inspired
Woolf's modernist novel, can be spied in
the distance). After a day in St Ives (a convenient three-minute train journey away)
the turquoise sitting room, filled with
twinkling music and aromatic smells from
their luxury spa, is the perfect bolt-hole.
The bar is well-stocked, and George can
whip up cocktails (try the negroni).

The bedrooms (most with sea views)
vary in size and comfort, and reflect the
Mediterranean theme, with white walls
offset by colourful headboards, though we
felt some of the Classics could do with a
bit of a decorative lift.

Their Bits and Bites menu is short,
unfussy, but sophisticated nonetheless. The
breakfasts are first rate, with a daily buffet
spread and cooked menu including French
toast with fried bananas, bacon and syrup.

Chettle, near Blandford Forum,
Dorset, DT11 8DB

Tel (01258) 830096
Fax (01258) 830051
e-mail
enquiry@castlemanhotel.co.uk
website www.castlemanhotel.co.uk

Nearby Kingston Lacy House;
Cranborne Chase; Salisbury.
Location in village, signposted off
A354, 6 miles (9 km) NE of
Blandford; ample car parking
Food breakfast, Sunday lunch,
dinner **Price** ££
Rooms 8 doubles, all with bath; all
rooms have phone, TV, hairdryer
Facilities dining room, 2 sitting
rooms, bar; garden
Credit cards MC, V
Children welcome
Disabled access difficult
Pets not accepted in house; 2 stables
available for guests' horses and dogs
Closed Feb
Proprietor Barbara Garnsworthy

Castleman

Country house hotel

Chettle is one of those rare estate villages that has hardly changed in the 150
years it has been in the benign ownership of
one family, who live in the fine Queen Anne
manor house. The late Teddy Bourke, one of
the family, took on the decrepit ex-dower
house ('locals all thought it was haunted') in
1996, along with his partner Barbara
Garnsworthy (who continues to run it
today). Together they transformed it into a
charmingly eccentric and very reasonably
priced hotel and restaurant. Part of the
building dates back 400 years, but it was
much altered in Victorian times when it was
tricked out with a galleried hall; a richly
carved oak Jacobean fireplace was also
installed in one of the reception rooms (the
other is Regency style) with bookcases to
match. Upstairs, the elegant proportions of
the rooms have been left intact, and bedrooms are just right: comfortable and in good
taste, but without room service or unneces-
sary frills so as to keep prices sensible; several of the bathrooms have Victorian roll-top
baths. The 'large' rooms are enormous, one
with a huge bay window overlooking the
fields, whilst the smaller ones are still spacious. The Castleman's restaurant – a long,
rather plain room at the rear – serves straightforward traditional and modern British dishes, and the bill is not indigestible. 'Superb
value', say regular guests.

Coverack, Cornwall

Coverack, Nr Helston, Cornwall,
TR12 6TF

Tel 01326 280464
e-mail reception@thebayhotel.co.uk
website www.thebayhotel.co.uk

Nearby Lizard Peninsula, the Eden
project, Trebah gardens, Iron-Age
fort, open-air theatre, St Michael's
Mount, Falmouth, Helston,
Penzance, Truro, St Ives
Location M5 Motorway: junction
31 onto A30 into Cornwall, then
onto Broads.
Food breakfast, lunch, dinner
Price £££-££££ **Rooms** 13 double
and twin; hairdryers, tea and coffee
making facilities **Facilities** restaurant, terrace, wi-fi, flatscreen televisions, private parking **Credit cards**
MC, V **Children** not under 8
Disabled some ground floor rooms
Pets small and medium dogs welcome but not in public rooms; £8
valeting charge per dog per day; pet
food arrangeable. **Closed** Dec-Feb
Proprietors House family

The Bay Hotel
Seaside hotel

Peace and quiet. One visitor remarked
that during her whole time here, she saw
"no more than fifty people on the entire
beach." Nestling in the fishing village of
Coverack, the hotel is a second's walk from
miles of unspoilt coastline.

Inside, proprietors the House family have
gone to great lengths to create a peaceful
and calming atmosphere. Rooms are decorated in mellow, coastal tones, which perfectly complement the sea views most visitors will have. Some are smallish, but all are
well furnished with more than enough storage space. You can really switch off here:
none of the rooms have a phone, and the
area itself has no mobile reception. There is,
however, free wi-fi.

The hotel has a terrace and a superbly
decorated conservatory restaurant, which
looks out across the sea. Guests should
expect to sit down to top food – chef and
proprietor Ric House has a reputation for
creating excellent dishes. Ingredients are all
local, and, of course, all fish is freshly caught.
Service is excellent in the restaurant, as it is
throughout the rest of the hotel. The House
family have more than 30 years of experience within the hotel business, and the welcoming atmosphere crops up continually in
guests' comments.

As we went to press they were due to reopen after repair work following flooding.

Cranborne, Dorset

Cranborne, Wimborne, BH21 5PZ

Tel 01725 551 133
e-mail enquiries@10castlestreet.com
website www.10castlestreet.com

Nearby Cranborne gardens and local walks (500m), Wimborne (11km), Salisbury (27km), Poole beach (27km), Sandbanks beach
Location Cranborne village; ample parking
Food breakfast, lunch, dinner, snacks, afternoon tea, room service
Price £££-££££
Rooms 9; 2 luxury doubles, 5 lovely doubles, 1 snug double, 1 double with separate bathroom; all have TV, wi-fi, tea and coffee making facilities, bath products, robes
Facilities 2 sitting rooms, restaurant with separate dining room for small groups, garden room, large grounds
Credit cards V, MC, DC, AE
Children welcome **Disabled** not suitable **Pets** well behaved dogs allowed in some rooms (£10); welcome in bar **Closed** Christmas day
Proprietors Gretchen and Alex Boon

10 Castle Street
Country house hotel

Don't be fooled by the humble name: 10 Castle Street is a grand and sumptuous 18th century Queen Anne house. Former family home of the Countess of Litchfield before Alex and Gretchen Boon took up the lease and transformed it into a restaurant/bar and private members club.

The concept is novel and we think it has potential. On the ground floor the restaurant, drawing room, terrace and bar are open to all; while the first floor with a billiard room, kids' playroom and sitting room is reserved for members. Members have access to discounted room rates, special events, and full use of the spa. Hotel guests become 'passing members' for the time of their stay. This arrangement, and the jovial atmosphere fostered by Alex and Gretchen, makes you feel like your staying in an old friend's house rather than a hotel.

The nine bedrooms are furnished with attractive sofas and an eclectic mix of art. The marble-clad bathrooms are lovely, as are the views on to the phenomenal garden. Enjoy dinner at the restaurant decorated with art from Messum's gallery in London, in the intimate Blue Room or in the Tasting Room, where you can watch your dishes being prepared: each is unique. Head Chef Alex Fullock prepares sophisticated dishes with meat reared on the grounds and hand-picked herbs and vegetables.

Crudwell, Wiltshire

Crudwell, Malmesbury
Wiltshire SN16 9EP

Tel (01666) 577194
e-mail info@therectoryhotel.co.uk
website www.therectoryhotel.com

Nearby Cotswolds
Location village of Crudwell on the
edge of the Cotswolds with car park-
ing **Food** breakfast, lunch, dinner
Price ££-£££
Rooms 15 doubles, most with bath
and shower, radio, TV, skincare
products
Facilities bar/sitting room,
Victorian walled garden, croquet,
outer heated swimming pool
Credit cards AE, MC, V
Children welcome
Disabled not suitable
Pets dogs accepted (charges apply)
Closed never
Proprietors Alex Payne and Khalil
Toukan

The Rectory
Village hotel

A real find: this hotel is as soothing as it
is professional. Assured, and stylishly
simple, devoid of gimmicks, it's unaffected
but excellent. Recently refurbished and
reopened in 2017 by its new owners, The
Rectory stands on the edge of the
Cotswolds in the village of Crudwell. The
entrance hall is homely as well as contemporary.

The reception area opens on to a wide,
light, flagstoned corridor, with interesting
antique maps adorning the walls. Opening
off it are a lovely panelled dining room, and
contemporary Glass House where breakfast can be taken. This leads in to a sophisticated bar serving up cocktails, draft beer
and all-day canapes. Guests can head to the
elegant and warmly decorated Drawing
Room for after dinner drinks, and sometimes a projected film.

The dining room offers a seasonal
menu, or if you prefer to eat out, try The
Potting Shed Pub (their sister property) in
Crudwell village, which produces great pub
fare with some interesting twists.

The 15 bedrooms could have been furnished and decorated just for this guide.
They are all different, attractive without
being fancy, sensibly priced homes from
home in which it's a pleasure to spend time.

Dittisham, Devon

Old Coombe Manor Farm,
Dittisham, near Dartmouth, Devon
Q6 OJA

Tel (01803) 722398
Fax (01803) 722401
e-mail info@fingals.co.uk
website www.fingals.co.uk

Nearby Dartmouth Castle.
Location 7 miles (6 km) N of
Dartmouth, 1 mile (1.5 km) from vil-
lage; with garden and car parking
Food breakfast, dinner
Price ££-££££
Rooms 3 double - 1 interconnected
to en-suite single; 5 self-catering for
2-6 people, all with bath or shower;
all rooms have phone, some have TV
Facilities dining room, bar, sauna,
snooker, swimming pool, croquet,
tennis, table-tennis; rowing boat.
Credit cards AE, MC, V
Children accepted
Disabled access difficult
Pets accepted in bedrooms
Closed after New Year to before
Easter **Proprietor** Richard Johnston

Fingals
Manor house bed-and-breakfast

Fingals is different, and those who love it will really love it – which sums up why we remain enthusiastic about this manor farmhouse in a secluded valley close to the River Dart. The 17thC house, with Queen Anne front additions, has plenty of charm. Inside, new and old furniture, pine and oak blend stylishly.

Fingals has always come closer to a 'country house party' type of guesthouse than a hotel. In 2014 the number of rooms were reduced to three doubles, alongside five self-catering properties for families, or for those who want extra space and privacy while still being able to use the hotel's facilities. It is also suited to large family gatherings – the owners frequently host parties that sleep up to 30 across all generations.

Fingals is an exceptionally relaxed place – you pour your own drinks, eat breakfast until 10 in the morning – and those who insist on everything being just so are likely to be disappointed. The three-course dinners are offered two nights a week depending on how many people are staying. They are chosen from a short menu, are modern in style, competent in execution, and ample in quantity.

A laid-back place with a laid-back yet thoroughly professional proprietor.

East Chelborough, Dorset

East Chelborough, near Dorchester, Dorset DT2 0QA

Tel 01935 83362
e-mail relax@woodencabbage.co.uk
website www.woodencabbage.co.uk

Nearby Lyme Regis, Charmouth, Lulworth Cove, Abbotsbury and Cerne Abbas, Bridport, Beaminster.
Location 12 miles north of Bridport and Dorchester, 10 miles south-west of Sherborne
Food breakfast
Price ££
Rooms 3; 2 double rooms and 1 twin all with en-suite; all rooms have flat screen TV, wi-fi, hairdryers and tea trays
Facilities garden room with cosy sitting room area, TV and wi-fi, hall, garden and terraces, gazebo, tea/coffee facilities; private parking (under cover if necessary) **Credit cards** via Sagepay (2% fee) **Children** normally over 4 years **Disabled** no access
Pets not accepted in the house
Closed during winter months please enquire
Proprietors Susie and Martyn Lee

Wooden Cabbage
Country house bed-and-breakfast

'Wooden cabbage' is the local jargon for the many small oak trees that grow around here and this house named after them is superbly sited on a gently sloping hill with satisfyingly long views over gentle unspoilt Dorset countryside. It's a former keeper's cottage that has been enlarged to quite gracious proportions – there's an airy feeling of space in the main rooms and it's furnishings are elegant – owners Martyn and Susie Lee's family heirlooms are everywhere, some of them fine pieces, but with homely touches such as family photos.

Bedrooms are like the rooms you would find in a cared-for family home – stylish without being over the top. Service is exceptionally good for an operation such as this – professional but relaxed. Our series editor Fiona Duncan says that if Oscars were awarded for guesthouses, Martyn and Susie would get one.

The flavourful breakfast includes Susie's home-made granola, garden fruits and local ingredients; tea is served upon arrival in the thatched gazebo overlooking the valley views.

Prices are very fair. Martyn's vegetable garden will make amateur kitchen gardeners want to go home and give up: it's not only functional but a key feature of the garden at one end of the house.

22 Melvill Road, Falmouth,
Cornwall, TR11, 4AR

Tel 01326 314466
e-mail info@highcliffefalmouth.com
website
www.highcliffefalmouth.com

Nearby 3 beaches in walking distance; Maritime Museum (1km); Pendennis Castle; several gardens 5 min by car; Heligan 1hr, Eden Project 1hr, St Ives 1hr, Penwith **Location** 1 min walk from sea front, 6 min walk from main town **Food** breakfast; picnic baskets delivered to rooms on request **Price** £-£££ **Rooms** 8; 3 super-king double (1 can be twin); 3 king-size double; 2 single; all ensuite; all with iPod/iPhone docking station, digital flat TVs with DVD, hairdryer, wi-fi, robes, Molton Brown troiletries **Facilities** sitting room, free parking, wi-fi **Credit cards** all except AE **Children** only 8+ allowed **Disabled** 1 ground floor suite, but no special facilities **Pets** not allowed **Closed** Dec to mid-Jan **Proprietors** Simon and Vanessa Clark

Highcliffe B&B
Contemporary bed-and-breakfast

The 'contemporary' in the title is no misnomer. Nearing its ten year anniversary, Highcliffe constantly regenerates to keep up with its trendy Falmouth clientèle. Every December they shut for upkeep, and every second year Vanessa redecorates almost every room. The general effect is Scandi-chic: white painted walls and floorboards offset by flashes of colour and bespoke lighting. One bedroom we saw, with *Toile du Jouy* wallpaper and a handmade pleated headboard, was about to be upholstered with navy velvet and matching curtains; guests should feel like they're the first to use them. All are kitted with Molton Brown toiletries, Egyptian cotton bedding and monsoon showers. You'd be hard-pushed to find the same luxury at this price in the area.

The breakfast is as versatile as the interiors, with guests encouraged to cherry pick from the menu. Choices can be adapted to any dietary requirement without fuss, as can their daily specials. The homemade granola even has its own Facebook page, set up by an admiring guest.

For all its trendiness, Highcliffe is a family-run bed-and-breakfast that offers a highly personal experience. Vanessa and Simon go the extra mile to adapt to their guests needs, and advise them on the best of Cornwall.

Fonthill Gifford, Wiltshire

Fonthill Gifford, Tisbury, Wiltshire,
SP3 6PX

Tel 01747 870385
e-mail info@beckfordarms.com
website www.beckfordarms.com

Nearby Fonthill Estate; Tisbury sta-
tion (5 minute drive); Rushmore
Golf Club
Location just off the Fonthill Estate,
near Tisbury
Food breakfast, lunch, dinner
Price ££
Rooms 10; 8 rooms above the pub
and 2 private lodges a short walk
away; all with own bath or shower,
TV with DVD player and internet
radio
Facilities traditional pub bar, large
garden; terrace
Credit cards DC, MC, V
Children welcome except in the
lodges
Disabled only to downstairs rooms
Pets welcome (except in the lodges)
Closed on Christmas day
Proprietors Dan Brod and Charlie
Luxton

The Beckford Arms
Country pub

Although a night-time fire threatened
to destroy the Beckford Arms a few
years ago, new owners Charlie Luxton and
Dan Brod have taken this event in their stride
and used it to create something exceptional.

Our series editor Fiona Duncan notes
that it's a bit of a hybrid – traditional country pub, restaurant and charming place to
stay all in one. You can either eat at the bar,
where mulled wine and cider are warmed
over an open fire during winter, the elegant private dining room, the laid back
conservatory, or even the sitting room if
you like. The food can't be faulted.

After dinner, you can retire to one of
their ten small but well-appointed bedrooms, where a range of comforts await
you: Siberian goose-down duvets, vintage
Welsh blankets and woolly hot-water bottles. We particularly enjoyed the quirky
drawings by local artist Zebedee Helm.

Outside, the garden rambles towards a
professional *boules* court. There are ham-
mocks, a games area for entertaining children, even a dog bath. On the Fonthill
Estate, opposite The Beckford, there are
two beautiful private lodges. Arrive to a
fully-stocked fridge and cook yourself breakfast in the morning, or saunter over to The
Beckford for their famous eggs benedict. On
summer weekends they have a BBQ, and a
woodfired oven serves pizzas.

Fowey, Cornwall

28 Fore Street, Fowey, Cornwall
PL23 1AQ

Tel (01726) 833302
Fax (01726) 833668
e-mail info@theoldquayhouse.com
website www.theoldquayhouse.com

Nearby The Eden Project; The
Lost Gardens of Heligan;
Lanhydrock; coastal walks
Location on main street; no hotel
car park but in summer low-cost
permits available for car park 800
yards away
Food breakfast, lunch, dinner
Price £££
Rooms 11 double, all with shower,
some with bath; all have phone, TV,
video player, wi-fi
Facilities restaurant, sitting areas,
bar, riverfront terrace
Credit Cards AE, DC, MC, V
Children not under 12
Disabled not suitable
Pets guide dogs only
Closed never
Proprietors Fair Tree Capitol
Manager Martin Nicholas

Old Quay House
Seaside hotel

Location, location, location. This is a
long, thin building jutting out over the
wonderful Fowey River in the heart of
charming Fowey, loved by yachties and the
rest, and it is rightly geared around the
endless amusement you'll get from the
comings and goings on the river, not to
mention the prettiness of it all.

You can eat or just sit with a drink on
the terrace right over the water watching
it all go by, or, when cold, move just inside
to a sitting area. Most of the bedrooms
have the view, the best being corner
rooms and the (£340) top-floor suite. The
interior design is cool, uncluttered, contemporary, to attract a core market of
30s-50s: grey paint, pine floors, perspex
tables. The long, thin, downstairs combined
bar, restaurant and sitting area has recently
been redecorated. Food was fairly priced
at around £30 for three courses when we
visited; the list of wines by the glass has
been extended since then.

They aim for a personal welcome and
with 11 bedrooms, and the current competent, friendly management, that's a reasonable claim. However, with so many non-
residents coming in to eat, it's not especially strong on the private, unique character
we appreciate. It's a 'hotel and restaurant'
formula, one that can work well, but in different hands might be merely formulaic.

Gittisham, Devon

Gittisham, Honiton, EX14 3AD

Tel 01404 540 400
website www.thepighotel.com/at-combe/
e-mail info@thepigatcombe.com

Nearby Honiton (1.5m), Allhallows Museum of Lace and Antiquities (2m), Honiton Golf Club (4.5m), South Devon coast (8m), Seaton Wetlands (10m), Exeter (16m)
Location down rural road in unspoilt countryside, car park
Food breakfast, lunch, dinner
Price ££-££££
Rooms 27; king/superking, 1 family room with bunk beds; twin, cots and extra beds available. All have shower or bath; some have larder, drinks, Nespresso machine
Facilities large grounds, kitchen garden, treatment rooms, restaurant, garden folly, sitting room
Credit cards MC, V, AE
Children accepted
Disabled 1 adapted room
Pets not allowed **Closed** never
Proprietors Fiona Moores

The Pig - at Combe
Country hotel

The latest arrival in The Pig litter is a dreamy Grade I-listed Elizabethan manor surrounded by undulating Devon countryside and grazing horses. Previously the traditional Combe House Hotel, already loved by this guide, it's now also sexy, says our series editor Fiona Duncan.

Step directly into the wood-panelled, glamorous bar (formerly the reception hall), with shelves of colourful glasses stacked against the windows and a blazing fire. In the dining room, a tall bricked-up window has been revealed, bringing in light and beautiful views. The old garden folly has been transformed into an atmospheric bar and outdoors dining space serving woodfired pizza; the potting sheds are now treatment rooms. The restored kitchen gardens and Victorian greenhouses provide fresh herbs and ingredients for the restaurant's "25-mile" menu.

Judy's design talent is evident in the bedrooms: they are traditional and stylish, with quirky touches (such as pantries hidden inside antique cupboards), and they are conceived for practicality and comfort. One occupies a converted row of stables stalls; many have charming vintage furniture and freestanding baths. The hotel's location just off the A30 makes it easy to reach — although going back to routine after a stay here might not be as easy.

Gulworthy, Devon

Gulworthy, Tavistock,
Devon PL19 8JD

Tel (01822) 832528
website www.thehornofplenty.co.uk
 e-mail
enquiries@thehornofplenty.com
Nearby Cotehele House, Dartmoor,
Plymouth, The Garden House,
Buckland Abbey
Location 3 miles (5 km) W of
Tavistock on A390; with ample car
parking
Food breakfast, lunch, dinner
Price ££-£££
Rooms 16; 4 in main house, 6 in
new original Coach House, 6 in new
Coach House; all can be double or
twin; all have bath/shower; all rooms
have phone, TV, DVD, minibar,
hairdryer, tea/coffee facilities
Facilities sitting room, bar, restau-
rant; terrace, garden
Credit cards MC, V
Children accepted
Disabled 2 suitable bedrooms
Pets not allowed in the main house
Closed never
Proprietors Julie Leivers and
Damien Pease

The Horn of Plenty
Country hotel

The Horn of Plenty has been in guide from the very start. Its stock has continued to rise since a change of ownership in 2010, which involved a major reinvestment. All the rooms are a high standard, including one imaginatively done in mauve: this goes for those in the main house and those in the coach house (the Garden Rooms), overlooking the charming walled garden.

Built in 1830 by the Marquess of Tavistock, the secluded house is approached down a short drive and has a splendid location overlooking the Tamar Valley, a view shared by the bedrooms, some of which have small terraces.

The Horn of Plenty is no longer primarily a restaurant. However, under head chef Scott Paton the menus are constantly changing in accordance with seasonal produce. Your food is served in front of picture windows in the two-part dining room.

It's not especially cheap (although prices have gone down with the new owners), but we reckon you get what you pay for here – a view backed up by a guest we overheard expressing his satisfaction. Competent, friendly manager.

Hinton St George, Somerset

High Street, Hinton St George
Somerset, TA17 8SE

Tel (01460) 73149
e-mail steveandmichelle@lord-
poulettarms.com
website www.lordpoulettarms.com

Nearby local cider makers;
Montacute House, Sherborne
Castle, Forde Abbey;
Jurassic coast, Blackdown Hills.
Location in village street, plenty of
free car parking; own small private
car park.
Food breakfast (for residents), lunch,
dinner
Price ££ **Rooms** 4; 2 with bath in
the room, two with separate private
bathroom across corridor; all rooms
except one have WC, radio, leaf tea
and coffee making **Facilities** bar,
garden, boule area **Credit cards** all
except Amex **Disabled** not suitable
Children one room can be converted to family room **Closed** Christmas
Day, Boxing Day and 1st Jan
Proprietors Steve Hill and Michelle
Paynton

The Lord Poulett Arms
Country inn

We reacted with pleasure to this country inn from the moment we were through the door. First, the arresting birdcage pattern wallpaper in the passage. Then the pleasant atmosphere in the bar – actually divided into three areas. A cheery local was installed in his favourite spot. Two mothers with babies were meeting for a tomato juice. Steve and Michelle, the proprietors, who took over in 2002 with no previous experience of the business, say they wanted to create a country get-away for visitors and a meeting place for locals – and they have. Tables and chairs are a mellow jumble of different antique country types. Food was the best we can remember in a pub. Upstairs, the bedroom corridor was decorated with a bold, striped wallpaper reminding us of a French inn, as did the four simple and homely bed-rooms; these were charming, pretty but not over-feminine, again relying on unusual wallpapers rather than contemporary sludge-colours. Prices are fair.

At the back are two gardens for eating out in fine weather, one a herb garden, the other grassy, with an old *pelota* or fives wall at the end.

A pub that's got it just right, thanks to the owners' natural taste and emphasis on quality and things that matter.

Holsworthy, Devon

Clawton, Holsworthy,
Devon EX22 6PS

Tel (01409) 271219
e-mail courtbarnhotel@talk21.com
website www.courtbarnhotel.co.uk

Nearby Bude; Boscastle; Tintagel;
Hartland Abbey; Dartmoor.
Location on A388 from Launceston
to Holsworthy, at Clawton; ample
car parking
Food breakfast, dinner
Price ££
Rooms 6; 3 double, 1 twin, 2 single,
all with bath; all rooms have phone,
TV, hairdryer, books, wi-fi
Facilities restaurant, breakfast
room, 2 sitting rooms, bar, garden,
croquet
Credit cards AE, DC, MC, V
Children accepted
Disabled restricted access and facili-
ties for people with mobility needs
Pets no pets allowed; Guide Dogs
only
Closed late Dec to early Jan
Proprietors Robert Wood

Court Barn
Country house hotel

Court Barn lacks any trace of stuffiness or pretentiousness, and it has an abundance of easy-going warmth. It is a four-square house, dating from the 16th century but partly rebuilt in 1853, where antiques, souvenirs, books and games jostle with sometimes unusual furnishings in a carefree medley of patterns. The result is reassuring: this home-like environment spells comfort far beyond the meretricious harmony of hotels colour-matched by designers. And its owners, Susan and Robert Wood, spare no effort to make you feel at home and welcome.

Downstairs, there is a sitting room with open log fire and views over the garden, a breakfast room which looks out on to the croquet lawn, and an elegant restaurant which is candle-lit in the evenings. The food, on our most recent visit, was satisfying, accompanied by an extensive wine list.

Beautifully kept park-like grounds surround the house; croquet hoops offer plenty to do outside. Beyond are gently rolling hills; and Court Barn is perfectly placed for exploring Devon and Cornwall.

Lewdown, near Okehampton,
Devon EX20 4PN

Tel (01566) 783222
e-mail info@lewtrenchard.co.uk
website www.lewtrenchard.co.uk

Nearby Dartmoor; Tintagel; Exeter;
Boscastle.
Location from old A30 at Lewdown,
take road signposted Lewtrenchard;
in 11-acre grounds with ample car
parking
Food breakfast, lunch, dinner, after-
noon tea
Price £££–££££
Rooms 14; all double and 8 can be
twin, all have bath/shower; all rooms
have phone, TV, hairdryer
Facilities drawing room, library bar
lounge, restaurant, breakfast room,
ballroom; garden, croquet
Credit cards AE, MC, V
Children accepted
Disabled ramp, 1 room with dis-
abled facilities, disabled loo, chairlift
Pets accepted
Closed never
Proprietors Murray family

Lewtrenchard Manor
Manor house hotel

Driving east down the narrow road
from Lewdown, on the edge of
Dartmoor, nothing quite prepares you for
the first sight of Lewtrenchard Manor, a
magnificent 16thC stone manor house,
with some Victorian additions, approached
by an avenue of beech trees and set in
stunningly beautiful grounds which lead
down to a lake studded with swans.

The interior is equally impressive. The
massive reception rooms are rich in ornate
ceilings, oak panelling, carvings and large
open fireplaces. Despite its size, however,
the hotel has the warm, hospitable atmosphere of a much humbler building, engen-
dered in great part by its hostess, Sue
Murray. The drawing room invites you to
curl up with a good book.

On the first floor, a splendid long gallery,
full of family paintings and portraits, leads
to the spacious bedrooms, all of which
have extensive views through leaded windows and over the Devon countryside.

A former owner of Lewtrenchard was
the Reverend Sabine Baring Gould (who
wrote, amongst others, the hymn *Onward,
Christian Soldiers*). Mercifully, he largely
resisted the Victorian habit of embellishing
an already beautiful building. The Murray
family took over in 2012.

Lifton, Devon

Lifton, Devon, PL16 0AA

Tel (01566) 784666
e-mail
reservations@arundellarms.com
website www.arundellarms.com

Nearby Dartmoor; Tintagel;
Boscastle; Port Isaac; Exeter.
Location 3 miles (5 km) E of
Launceston, just off A30 in Lifton;
with ample car parking
Food breakfast, lunch, dinner
Price £££
Rooms 27; all double; fisherman's
cottage (sleeps 4); all with bath; all
rooms have phone, TV, hairdrier,
fax/modem points **Facilities** 2
restaurants, 2 bars, games room, dry-
ing room; garden, salmon and trout
fishing, fishing lake, fly fishing les-
sons, organised shooting parties
Credit cards AE, DC, MC, V
Children accepted
Disabled access possible
Pets dogs accepted
Closed never
Proprietor Adam Fox-Edwards

The Arundell Arms
Fishing inn

A 200-year-old coaching inn, on a site
that dates back to Saxon times, which
is famous – indeed an institution – for fishing and for food. Traditional country pursuits are taken seriously here: the Arundell
Arms has been one of England's premier
fishing hotels for more than half a century.
Anglers have 20 miles of private fishing and
a 90-feet-deep lake at their disposal (con-
taining some very large, wily trout). When
autumn comes, the fisherman go, shooting
parties arrive with spaniels and labradors,
and talk at the bar is of high birds and driv-
en snipe. Lifton is surrounded by some of
the loveliest countryside in England.
Fishing arrangements are flexible – don't
be shy of visiting if you're a beginner.

Then there's the food. Head Chef Steven
Pidgeon has the accolade of being a
Master Chef of Great Britain – one of only
80. His food is meticulously prepared and
beautifully presented, complemented by
good wines and attentive, friendly service.

From the sitting room you can see the
garden and the 250-year-old former cock-
pit, now a tackle room. There are two
rather grand interconnecting dining rooms
and a friendly bar. Bedrooms are homely,
pretty and fresh. Home-made chocolates
are placed in the sitting room for guests
after dinner and there are vases of fresh
flowers. A unique place.

Lower Bockhampton, Dorchester

Lower Bockhampton, Dorchester,
DT2 8PZ

Tel 01305 262 382
e-mail
enquiries@yalburycottage.com
website www.yalburycottage.com

Nearby Thomas Hardy's birthplace
(Upper Bockhampton), 1 mile;
Dorchester, 5 miles
Location 3km east of Dorchester,
on a single track road. 5 minutes'
drive from the A35. **Food** breakfast;
Farmers' Market lunch on Sundays;
dinner for guests 7 days a week; non-
guests Tues - Sat **Price** £-££
Rooms 8 double; 1 can be adapted
to take 4 people, 2 can be twin/dou-
ble; all have tea/coffee facilities,
complimentary water, hairdryer, toiletries, TV, wi-fi
Facilities breakfast room, restaurant, lounge, bar **Credit cards** MC,
V **Children** welcome, though no
under 10s in restaurant after 8pm
Disabled not suitable **Pets** allowed
in some rooms (£7.50)
Closed 4 weeks from Dec 23rd
Proprietors Ariane Jones

Yalbury Cottage
Country hotel

If you love 19thC English literature, then
this could be for you. This pretty 17thC
thatched cottage is an ideal base for
exploring Thomas Hardy's Wessex. He was
born a mile away in Higher Bockhampton
and set all his fiction in this area, widely
known as Thomas Hardy's Wessex.

With eight bedrooms, this is a personal
and characterful place to stay. Rooms are
tastefully decorated using creams, whites
and lilacs. There is also a sitting room for
guests' use. Pre-dinner drinks are at seven
o'clock. The cosy and highly rated restaurant accommodates just 26 people and
serves earthy food in hearty portions. On
Sundays, a special lunch is prepared using
local ingredients purchased from the local
Farmer's Market earlier in the day.

If the Thomas Hardy trail is not for you,
there is still plenty to do. Dorchester is
just two miles away, with its Roman
remains and architecture, shops and museums. From there, it's another 15-minute
drive to the famous Jurassic Coast (including Chesil Beach), and the popular seaside
town of Weymouth.

Lovington, Somerset

Lovington, Castle Cary, Somerset
BA7 7PT

Tel 01963 240600
e-mail
jjools@pilgrimsrestaurant.co.uk
website
www.pilgrimsrestaurant.co.uk

Nearby Glastonbury, Wells, Bath &
West Showground, Wincanton
Races, Fleet Air Arm Museum,
Bath, Jurassic Coast
Location in Lovington on B3153, 3
miles west of Castle Cary and 1 mile
east of A37 Fosse Way at Lydford-
on-Fosse **Food** breakfast, lunch,
dinner, Sunday lunch (last Sunday of
the month) **Price** £-££ **Rooms** 5; 4
double and 1 twin, all en suite; double rooms have bath and wet-room
showers, twin has wet-room shower;
all have TV, hairdryer, wi-fi, tea/cof-
fee **Facilities** bar, restaurant, wi-fi
Credit cards MC, V **Children**
accepted over 14 **Disabled** access
possible **Pets** not accepted in bedrooms **Closed** rarely **Proprietors**
Sally & Jools Mitchison

The Pilgrims Restaurant
Restaurant-with-rooms

We especially like places that evolve
over time under the same hands-on
owner managers. Julian (Jools) and Sally
bought the place in 1997 as a dead-beat
village pub. Into the nothing-special building they inserted a rather good restaurant
and set about persuading not just the pub-
supporting locals but people further afield
that it was worth driving some way for the
rather special food. People came, and the
restaurant prospered – but the place was
still an awkward hybrid – a restaurant in a
pub building with no accommodation. Then
on the back of the restaurant's success,
they added five rooms. So then they had a
restaurant-with-rooms, and suddenly their
operation was fully in its skin.

The ground-level bedrooms (step
straight in from outside) are in a clean,
modern style. Basics are right: quality beds,
good linen. Details such as wind-up torch-
es in bedside drawers get good feedback.
You're on a B road with lightish traffic at
times, not audible in bedrooms, which are
steps away from the restaurant entrance.

The food is again the product of spade-
work and inspiration. Jools worked hard at
finding top, local ingredients and maintaining relationships with the suppliers. He
tries to let the ingredients speak for themselves–"not to do too much to them".

Mells, Somerset BA11 3PN

Tel 01373 812254
e-mail info@talbotinn.com
website www.talbotinn.com

Nearby Longleat Estate; Shepton
Mallet; Wells; Farrington Golf
Course.
Location the estate village of Mells
Food breakfast, lunch, dinner
Price ££-£££
Rooms 8; all with king- or emperor-
sized beds, own bath or shower,
Smart TVs, internet radio and wi-fi
Facilities pub bar, coach house grill
room, garden, cobbled courtyard, in-
room massage
Credit cards DC, MC, V
Children accepted, 1 family room
Disabled no special access
Pets not accepted
Closed never
Proprietors Dan Brod, Charlie
Luxton and Matthew Greenlees

The Talbot Inn
Country inn

Our series editor Fiona Duncan visited
this off-the-beaten track inn recently
and rated it highly. Owners Charlie and
Dan, proprietors of the Beckford Arms
(see page 48) bought the lease from the
present Earl of Asquith and Oxford and
reopened in 2013. Their new venture is up
there with the Beckford Arms because they
know how to combine style, value for
money and character.

The Talbot gets a head start with the
charm of its location, the pretty Somerset
village of Mells, and this is reinforced as
you approach through the unevenly sur-
faced, cobbled courtyard. Inside there is a
choice of cosy dining areas, a sitting room
across the courtyard in a barn dating from
the 1500s, and the Grill Room housed in
the old coach house. The speciality here is
meat and fish cooked over an open fire.
When it's busy at weekends the atmosphere is bustling and jolly.

There are eight stylish but unpretentious bedrooms which are very fairly priced.
We especially like spacious no 6: relax in a
deep freestanding bath, have a rain shower
or chill out in the sitting room with two
sofas. Witness the sawn logs stacked in the
fireplace, the woolly hot water bottle covers and pegs with hangars doing the work
of wardrobes.

Milton Abbot, Devon

Milton Abbot, Tavistock, Devon
PL19 0PQ

Tel (01822) 870000
Fax (01822) 870578
e-mail mail@hotelendsleigh.com
website www.hotelendsleigh.com

Nearby Tavistock market, Tamar Valley, Plymouth historic dockyards, Exeter cathedral
Location 15 minutes from Tavistock down mile long drive in own extensive grounds; ample car parking
Food breakfast, lunch and dinner
Price ££££
Rooms 18; all have bath and shower; all have phone, TV, DVD player, internet access
Facilities dining room, sitting room, garden, terrace, library, helipad, use of local country club (swimming, gym, spa) **Credit Cards** AE, MC, V
Children accepted
Disabled good access, 1 ground floor suite with private garden
Pets accepted, dog beds provided
Closed never
Proprietors Olga Polizzi

Hotel Endsleigh
Country house hotel

Endsleigh, on the edge of Dartmoor, and sister hotel of Olga Polizzi's Tresanton in Cornwall (page 72), was one of the most talked about new British hotels when it opened eight years ago. Our reporter found it 'effortlessly elegant and – crucially – unpretentious, unlike many of its try-hard, oh-so-hip rivals.'

It's down a mile-long private drive in 'one of the loveliest locations I've seen in 20 years of writing about hotels.' The sixth Duke of Bedford built the 16-bedroom fishing and shooting lodge as a retreat, in the cottage *orné* style. The gardens are by Humphry Repton.

Olga Polizzi has decorated it in her cool, inimitable style, but the spirit of the old house remains intact – old pull-down maps of Devon in the hall, the family crests in the dining room, the floor made of sheeps' knuckles on the veranda. Bedrooms are lovely: stylish and unfussy, with original baths and basins and a welcome lack of puzzling technology. You'll get a TV and DVD player, but you are more likely to spend time pouring over the absorbing collection of books in the library. Apart from that, there's little to do, other than to fish, walk or picnic in the grounds, a fantasy of dells and grottoes. The food is good, but not quite as good as at its sister hotel, though prices are similar.

Mousehole, Cornwall

The Parade, Mousehole, Penzance,
Cornwall TR19 6PR

Tel 01736 731222
e-mail bookings@oldcoastguardho-
tel.co.uk
website
www.oldcoastguardhotel.co.uk

Nearby by the sea; 1 hour away
from Newquay
Location situated above the harbour
wall of Mousehole; St Clement's Isle
in front
Food breakfast buffet, lunch, dinner
Price ££-£££
Rooms 15 double and twin; all
rooms have bathroom with either
shower or bath, Roberts Radio,
books, tea and coffee facilities, most
have sea views and some have a balcony. **Facilities** sub-tropical garden,
seating area, dining room, bar, private access to beach **Credit cards**
DC, MC, V **Children** welcome
Disabled not suitable **Pets** welcome
Closed Christmas day and 1 week a
year, usually in January
Proprietors Edmund and Charles
Inkin

The Old Coastguard
Seaside hotel

Not everyone likes the style of the Inkins' hotels, writes our series edi-
tor, Fiona Duncan, but if you agree with the *Charming Small Hotel Guide* attitude that a jar of fresh flowers and a stylish old radio are as good as a large flat screen TV in the bedroom, then you'll get the point of The Old Coastguard.

It was a boring Victorian seaside hotel until its recent makeover, but the Inkins have avoided formulaic designer dodges to bring it up to date. They have spent money instead on the basics – the beds are soundly comfortable, there are thick tow-els, and properly served, not over-ambi-tious food.

The downstairs sitting area is the hotel's ace card: full of sunlight. You relax on deep armchairs and sofas looking out over the harbour and sea through a wall of big win-dows that capitalise on a view that will keep you stationary for hours.

The 14 bedrooms are gradually being made over to Charlie Inkin's taste for tongue-and-groove panelling behind the beds, mustard yellow paint and striped curtains in greens and blues. We like bed-rooms 1, 2 and 3 the best (even with fixed toiletry dispensers), and 5 with its bath facing the sea. See the Inkins' other hotels: Gurnard's Head and The Felin Fach Griffin Inn on pages 86 and 186.

Nettleton Shrub, Nettleton, near
Chippenham, Wiltshire SN14 7NJ

Tel (01249) 782286
Fax (01249) 783066
e-mail caroncooper@fossefarm-house.com
website www.fossefarmhouse.com

Nearby Castle Combe; Cotswolds.
Location in countryside off B4039,
6 miles (9.5 km) NW of
Chippenham, in 1.5 acres of garden
with car parking
Food breakfast, lunch, dinner
Price £££
Rooms 9; sleeps max. 24 guests; 1
double and 1 twin/family room in
The Stables; 2 double and 1 sofa bed
in Garden House; 1 double and 1
sofa-bed in Dovecote.
Facilities sitting room, dining room,
tea room; terrace, garden
Credit cards MC, V **Children**
accepted **Disabled** The Garden
House only **Pets** dogs allowed in
main building and Stables at
£15/night **Closed** never **Proprietor**
Caron Cooper

Fosse Farmhouse
Country bed-and-breakfast

Former cookery presenter Caron Cooper presides over a small corner of France in the Wiltshire countryside. She has decorated Fosse Farmhouse with style, bringing together English vintage and French brocante. Antiques, including many French pieces, fill the house and the adjoining cottages.

Since our last visit Caron has added two more self-catering cottages, The Dovecote and The Garden House – making three along with the converted Stables. All follow the style of the main building and can be hired individually or as a group.

Some more recent renovations mean the bedrooms in the main house feel homely and Caron has added some charming detail to each, with the bathrooms being finished to a high standard.

While Fosse Farmhouse claims it is only a bed-and-breakfast, two and three course dinners are available if booked in advance. Caron's food blends French with English influences. You might get rack of lamb with a mint and port wine sauce or chicken basquaise; dessert might be sticky toffee pudding or crème brûlée.

16/18 High Street, Padstow,
Cornwall, PL28 8BB

Tel 01841 550 950
e-mail
stay@padstowtownhouse.co.uk
website https://www.paul-
ainsworth.co.uk/padstow-town-
house/

Nearby Paul Ainsworth at no.6,
Camel Estuary, Rock, Polzeath
Location Padstow's High Street (a
quiet residential street in Old Town)
Food breakfast, Paul Ainsworth at
Number 6 down the road, for dining
Price ££££
Rooms 6 suites; all come with TV,
wi-fi, mini bar, Car Rosa products
Facilities parking, 'honesty larder',
electric car on hand
Credit cards all major
Children only 16+ allowed
Disabled not suitable
Pets not allowed
Closed 24 -26 Dec; restaurant
closed in Jan (dates vary yearly)
Proprietors Paul Ainsworth

Padstow Townhouse
Town guesthouse

We're usually wary of chefs-turned-hoteliers: bedrooms rarely live up to the food. Paul Ainsworth has bucked this trend by a mile with his five-bedroom guesthouse, set up to compliment his Michelin-starred restaurant. When you dig a little deeper this isn't surprising: he and his sister Michelle, with whom he runs it, grew up in a B&B. The attention to detail is noticeable from the moment you walk in the door – literally: the welcome mat is changed three times daily to read 'Morning/Afternoon/Evening'. Their 'honesty pantry' brims with delicious treats guests can pile into wicker baskets and take to their rooms. Michelle is kindness itself, bringing beef and seaweed pasties on arrival, and a flask of hot chocolate after dinner.

The rooms (named after ingredients in Paul's Fairground dessert) have been decorated by Paul's wife, Emma (it's a proper family affair) with the designer Eve Cullen-Cornes. They are simultaneously decadent and cocooning: ours (Honeycomb) had a bold black and gold scheme, and wrought-iron bed made by local craftsmen. They're well-equipped with Smart TVs (Apple ones for films) and voluminous baths and showers. Breakfast is as expected from a top chef, served in Rojano's – which guests are transported to in the hotel's electric car. Ainsworth style, you want for nothing.

Riverside, Padstow,
Cornwall PL28 8BY

Tel (01841) 532700
e-mail reservations@rickstein.com
website www.rickstein.com

Nearby surfing beaches; Trevose
Head **Location** in village centre, 4
miles (6 km) NW off A39 between
Wadebridge and St Columb; various
car parks in Padstow; parking included for some rooms.
Food breakfast (included), lunch,
dinner **Price** £££
Rooms 35 doubles, (some can be
twins) in 3 different buildings, most
with bath, some with shower; all
rooms have phone, TV, hairdryer;
some have minibar **Facilities**
Seafood Restaurant: bar, conservatory, terrace; St Petroc's: Ruby's Bar
next door, garden **Credit cards** MC,
V **Children** welcome in St Petroc's
Hotel and the Café, over 3 in The
Seafood Restaurant **Disabled** access
possible (except at Rick Stein's Cafe)
Pets dogs accepted in selected
rooms **Closed** Christmas; restaurants closed on 1st May **Proprietors**
Rick and Jill Stein

The Seafood Restaurant & St Petroc's Hotel
Restaurant-with-rooms

Rick Stein's Padstow empire has grown exponentially in recent years to include seven different places to stay, at varying prices, as well as seven places to eat/drink: his flagship Seafood Restaurant, the Bistro in St Petroc's Hotel, Rick Stein's Cafe, Stein's Fish & Chips, The Cornish Arms, The Seafood Bar and Ruby's Bar. If you are intent on eating at the quayside Seafood Restaurant (superb seafood, straight from the fishing boats, served in a lively dining room) then the bed-rooms above make the best choice for a night's stay. They are spacious and under-stated; a couple of them offer superb estu-ary views. What the place lacks in public rooms, it makes up for in laid-back atmos-phere and its prime position on the quay. St Edmund's House, behind the restaurant, has six new pricey suites. Less expensive, but no less tasteful, are the rooms in St Petroc's Hotel just up the hill, a little removed from the bustle of the quayside. This is an attrac-tive white-painted building with views across the older parts of town and the estu-ary. The place exudes a friendly ambience, not least in the Bistro, where a short, very reasonably priced menu serving seafood and meat. There are three attractive rooms above the Café in Middle Street, and self-catering properties just outside of Padstow in Trevone.

20 Chapel Street, Penzance,
Cornwall TR18 4AW

Tel 01736 365 664
e-mail
penzance@artistresidence.co.uk
website www.artistresidencecorn-wall.co.uk

Nearby St Michael's Mount, Lands
End, St Ives, Minack Theatre &
Porthcurno Beach, Tate St Ives,
Eden Project (48 miles) Newquay
Airport (41 miles)
Location historic Chapel Street in
Penzance's old quarter
Food breakfast, lunch, dinner
Rooms 21; 20 in main hotel, and 3-
bed cottage; all have wi-fi, hairdryer,
TV **Facilities** restaurant, beer gar-
den, bar/sitting room
Credit cards AE, DC, MC , V
Children welcome
Disabled no special facilities
Pets accepted in 2 ground floor
rooms, enquire before
Closed Jan
Proprietors Charlotte and Justin
Salisbury

Artist Residence Cornwall **Town hotel**

It was no surprise when a new Artist Residence popped up on Cornwall's cre-ative west coast, choosing ramshackle Penzance over picture-perfect St Ives. Loyalists to the brand won't be disap-pointed by the hotel's artful rusticity and olde worlde charm, complete with wood-burning stoves, stacks of logs, distressed leather armchairs, and candle lanterns peppering its cosy interior. They'll also find something new in its laid back Cornish atmosphere – the staff are young, local and extremely friendly.

The original 'arty' rooms were decorat-ed by British painters (Jo Peel's mural of historic Chapel Street, and Mat McIvor's pop-art confection are the two most pop-ular). The bedrooms in the newer wing are done up in AR's 'house' style. Our loft suite, The Look Out, had the feel of a Parisian garret: slanted walls with exposed beams, a freestanding copper bath, and its own balcony terrace, with views across Penzance. Bedrooms come with an irre-sistible minibar, stocked with pork scratch-ings, chocolate-covered honeycomb and Cornish ale, while the informal Cornish Barn restaurant downstairs serves hearty smokehouse classics such as ribs and beer-can chicken (though the vegetarian dishes could do with a bit of a lift). In summer, they fire up a barbecue in the beer garden.

Penzance, Cornwall

Chapel House, Chapel Street,
Penzance, Cornwall TR18 4AW

Tel 07810020617 / 01736362024
e-mail hello@chapelhousepz.co.uk
website chapelhousepz.co.uk

Nearby St Michael's Mount, Lands
End, St Ives, Minack Theatre &
Porthcurno Beach, Tate St Ives,
Eden Project (48 miles) Newquay
Airport (41 miles)
Location historic Chapel Street, in
the old quarter of Penzance
Food breakfast, dinner 3 times
weekly (by arrangement), Sunday
brunch, cake available at all times
Rooms 6 double; all have en suite,
waterfall showers, sea views, iPad
dock with local info & room service
Facilities sitting room, kitchen, gar-
den, terrace, boot room
Credit cards all major
Children welcome
Disabled no special facilities
Pets well behaved dogs allowed
Closed never
Proprietor Susan Stuart

Chapel House
Town bed-and-breakfast

Former accountant Susan Stuart has transformed this elegant Georgian townhouse with great aplomb, marrying original features and antique pieces with the clean lines of Cornish modernism. Her personal service goes well beyond the remit of a 'bed-and-breakfast'. In the kitchen-basement she whips up exquisite breakfasts for her guests every morning, along with three mid-week meals (by arrangement). There's a perennial supply of home-made cake and tea, as well as stacks of wellies, wax jackets and winter-warmers for ill-equipped townies. In summer, guests breakfast in the garden, or have a g+t on the terrace – staying here is like being in a house party: relaxed and unregimented.

The six bedrooms (all with sea views) each have unique individual features: bespoke oak bed frames (the four-poster in Room 3 is particularly striking), two Hepworth-esque oval bathtubs, a wood burning stove – and a glass roof/window in Room 6, with panoramic views across Penzance (the more modern loft rooms build up into the rafters). Each is kitted with an iPad – the fount of Susan's local knowledge and a conduit to room service through her FaceTime. Encouraged by a number of accolades, Susan also recently bought the house next door, where she has plans for several more bedrooms.

Rock, Wadebridge, Cornwall
PL27 6LA

Tel (01208) 863394
e-mail info@enodoc-hotel.co.uk
website www.enodoc-hotel.co.uk

Nearby Polzeath 2 miles; Padstow
(by ferry).
Location overlooking the Camel
Estuary, bordering St Enodoc golf
course in Rock, 2 miles off B3314
from Wadebridge; car park
Food breakfast, lunch, dinner
Price £££
Rooms 20; 16 double, all with
bath/shower, 4 suites; all rooms have
phone, TV, radio, hairdryer, fan
Facilities sitting room, library, din-
ing room, bar, billiard room, sauna;
outdoor heated swimming pool
Credit cards AE, DC, MC, V
Children welcome
Disabled adapted WC on ground
floor **Pets** not accepted
Closed Jan to mid Feb
Manager Kate Simms

St Enodoc
Seaside hotel

Well-heeled British families have flocked to Rock for their bucket-and-spade holidays for generations, but styl-ish hotels were thin on the ground here-abouts – until, that is, the emergence in 1998 of the old-established St Enodoc Hotel from a change of ownership and total makeover.

The imposing building is typical of the area: no beauty, but solid and purposeful, with pebbledash walls and slate roof.

Weathered delabole slate floors, quirky fabrics and 20thC Cornish paintings make up their decorative scheme, combined with clean lines and easy-going comfort. Bedrooms, with bright colours and original artwork on the wall, feel like bedrooms rather than hotel rooms, with marvellous views across the Camel Estuary.

The restaurant is run by James Nathan, who has worked in the kitchen of luminar-ies such as Rick Stein and Jamie Oliver, since winning Masterchef in 2008. He focusses on buying the freshest market fish. The restaurant has panoramic views, with a wide terrace for outdoor eating.

Rosevine, South Cornwall

Rosevine, near Portscatho,
South Cornwall, TR2 5EW

Tel (01872) 580644
e-mail info@driftwoodhotel.co.uk
website www.driftwoodhotel.co.uk

Nearby Eden Project, Tate Gallery,
the gardens of Heligan, Glendurgan
and Trebah.
Location in countryside just off
A3078, S of Truro; ample parking
for cars and boats
Food breakfast, dinner
Price ££££
Rooms 14 double and 1 twin, 3 with
bath, 1 with shower; rest with bath
and shower, cabin with double and
twin; all rooms have phone, TV,
hairdryer **Facilities** sitting room,
drawing room, TV room, dining
room, bar; garden, beach
Credit cards AE, MC, V
Children welcome
Disabled access difficult
Pets not accepted
Closed mid Dec to beginning of Feb
Proprietors Paul and Fiona
Robinson

Driftwood Hotel
Coastal hotel

'Situated on seven glorious acres of Cornwall's finest heritage coastline,' says the brochure – and Driftwood does indeed provide all you could want on a sea-side break. It's a clapboarded converted family house that has been refurbished and renovated into a stylish yet comfortable haven by interior designer Fiona and husband Paul. All fourteen bedrooms, including the cabin overlooking the beach, have a clean, fresh style that helps maximise the space, as do the cosy sitting and drawing rooms.

Those who love seafood will be happiest here, but the rest of the food is good too. The menu is concentrated on well prepared dishes with fresh local ingredients. The Michelin-starred restaurant has spectacular views of the rugged Cornish coastline. For children there is a TV room with computer games and video library. If you fancy getting out and about there are numerous small pubs and restaurants nearby St Mawes; or hampers can be made up for lazing on the beach.

All around Driftwood there are varied activities that suit different tastes. Great walks and gardens such as Trelissick, the Eden Project, within a short drive; for art lovers, the Tate Gallery at St Ives; or for the energetic, watersports, riding, tennis and golf.

St Austell, Cornwall

Boscundle, St Austell, Cornwall
PL25 3RL

Tel (01726) 813557
e-mail stay@boscundlemanor.co.uk
website www.boscundlemanor.co.uk

Nearby Eden Project, Heligan
Gardens, Lanhydrock House
Location 2.5 miles (4 km) E of St
Austell, close to A390; in 5 acre
woodland gardens; ample car parking
Food breakfast, dinner
Price £££ **Rooms** 13; 4 standard
doubles, 1 excecutive suite, 3 in-
house suites, 1 garden suite, 3 superior, 1 single; all rooms have phone,
TV, safe, fridge
Facilities sitting room, bar, restaurant; heated indoor pool; hot tub;
spa treatment room; garden, croquet, woodland walks, civil wedding
licence **Credit cards** MC, V
Children welcome **Disabled** access
difficult **Pets** dogs in selected rooms
Closed never **Proprietors** David
and Sharon Parker

Boscundle Manor
Country house hotel

When David and Sharon Parker
bought this charming wisteria-
draped property sixteen years ago, the
hotel (which had already been a mainstay
in the guide for many years) was beginning
to become a bit tired and frayed around
the edges. They turned it around with a
full-scale refurbishment, introducing new
furniture and oriental mahogany throughout. They continue to redecorate the bedrooms, with new wallpapers and licks of
paint – though we felt the bold patterns
and colour schemes looked a touch dated.

The grounds include five acres of terraced gardens and woodland, with several
pleasant walks through the woods. There
are ponds and old tin mine remains.

Sharon herself has now taken the helm
of the kitchen, serving flavourful, hearty
dishes such as *confit de canade* with beans
and sausage cassoulet. As before, they use
Cornish products whenever available. The
butter on the table comes from hand-
milked, West Country cows and is hand-
packed at the local dairy.

St Hilary, Cornwall

St Hilary, Penzance, Cornwall
TR20 9BZ

Tel (01736) 740262
e-mail info@ennys.co.uk
website www.ennys.co.uk

Nearby Lands End; Penzance;
Lizard peninsula; St Michael's
Mount; St Ives.
Location in gardens with car parking; from B3280 from Marazion turn
left into Trewhella Lane, between St
Hilary and Relubbus
Food cottages are self-catering with
welcome tea, luxury suites come with
welcome breakfast hamper **Price** ££
Rooms 3 cottages and 2 luxury
suites. All double with TV, sitting
room, kitchen/kitchenette, all with
shower/bath **Facilities** heated swim-
ming pool. grass tennis court (May-
Sept); conservatory with sofas, books
and local information; laundry room,
free parking **Credit cards** MC, V
Children babies and 12+ welcome
Disabled access difficult
Pets not accepted **Closed** Nov 1 to
Mar 1 **Proprietor** Kristofer and
Raphaela Allerfeldt

Ennys
Self-catering cottages

Ennys is a beautiful, creeper-clad 17thC
Cornish manor house situated at the
end of a long tree-lined drive in little St
Hilary, a few miles from Penzance. The sheltered gardens include a swimming pool and
a grass tennis court. The fields stretch
down to the River Hayle, along which you
can walk and picnic.

Since our last edition, Ennys has acquired
new owners and a new format – no longer
offering bed-and-breakfast in the main
house, but instead renting out three cottages and two luxury suites, all self-catering. This isn't to say the experience isn't
spoiling. Raphaela and Kristopher are both
perfect hosts, full of enthusiasm and local
knowledge.

The two family suites are in an adjacent
converted stone barn, near the three cottages. Each is its own microcosm, with
kitchen facilities, sitting rooms and televisions – perfect for families or couples
seeking seclusion and intimacy. The real
draw is the impressive facilities on the
Georgian estate: a grass tennis court and
heated swimming pool spread across lus-
cious grounds. Guests in the luxury suites
are welcomed with a complimentary hamper, and there's a wealth of restaurants
nearby. A peaceful oasis from which to
explor Cornwall.

St Mary's, Isles of Scilly

St Mary's, Isles of Scilly,
TR21 0TA

Tel (01720) 422317/423342
Fax (01720) 422343
e-mail info@star-castle.co.uk
website www.star-castle.co.uk

Nearby other Scilly islands including Tresco; bird watching; swimming with seals
Location in own grounds
Food breakfast, lunch, dinner
Price ££-£££
Rooms 38 (8 in castle, 30 Guard House rooms); 4 singles with shower; 34 double or twin with bath and shower; all rooms have phone, TV
Facilities sitting room, bar, 2 restaurants, tennis, indoor swimming pool
Credit Cards AE, MC, V
Children accepted
Disabled difficult, but some ground level rooms
Pets accepted
Closed 3 days before Christmas, 4 weeks after New Year
Proprietor James Francis

Star Castle Hotel
Island hotel

There's only a handful of upmarket hotels in the Scillies, some of which strive to appeal to the mainland's chic set. They tend to lack heart, but this one decidedly does not. The welcome begins at the airport, or ferry, where James – who has now taken over the hotel from his father, Robert – or the hotel's driver comes to meet guests.

Castles often make dismal hotels, but this one, inside its walls in the shape of an eight-pointed star, has something of the charm and intimacy of a Cotswold cottage. As well as the cosy bar, first floor sitting room and ground floor, stone-walled dining room, there are eight charming bedrooms in the castle itself. In 2017 the rooms were redecorated with new licks of paint, curtains and some new bathrooms fitted.

Each morning at breakfast, James enquires from his guests what they feel like doing, arranging boat trips and providing packed lunches and maps for walkers. Many regulars simply say they are "going with Tim", a hugely popular local boatman who takes guests on trips to the off-islands.

The spacious bedrooms in the annexe have also been overhauled. An exotic garden is growing up between the two wings to detract from their somewhat Butlinesque appearance. We could not fault the food, and there's an interesting personal wine list. This is not a chic hotel, but a very good one.

St Mawes, Cornwall

Harbourside, St Mawes, Cornwall, TR2 5AN

Tel (01326) 270270
e-mail info@idlerocks.com
website www.idlerocks.com

Nearby St. Mawes, Trelissick, Glendurgan, Heligan and Trebah gardens; Truro; Eden Project; National Maritime Museum.
Location follow signs for the castle which will bring you down to the harbour side, allocated spaces in St Mawes Public Car Park
Food breakfast, lunch, dinner; afternoon tea, children's high tea at 5.30pm **Price** ££££
Rooms 19; 4 in separate annexe, all ensuite, with underfloor heating, some family rooms
Facilities bar, lounge, terrace, children's room, baby listening
Credit cards all major
Children welcome **Disabled** annexe has some disabled access **Pets** 2 dog-friendly room in the annexe
Closed 2 weeks in Jan
Proprietors Karen & David Richards

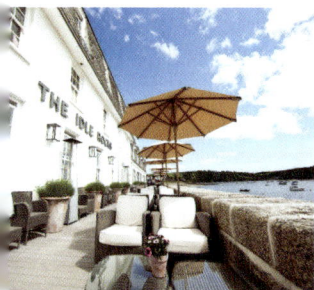

Idle Rocks
Seaside hotel

No surf here on the beautiful Roseland Peninsula, but there's 'harbour jumping' from St Mawes' harbour wall instead – a long-established St Mawes pastime at high tide. "We bet our friends to do it, and give the money to charity," says David Richards, owner of The Idle Rocks.

This is one of those seaside hotels so close to the water you can hear the waves from your bedroom window: magical. With 20 nigh-on faultless (though not large) bedrooms, kids' playroom, elegant dining room and stone-walled terrace where chilled music plays. As this guide goes to press the hotel enters its fifth year, having grown into the Richards' vision and attracting an increasingly sophisticated clientèle. Everything is fresh, new and of the highest quality, predominantly white but liberally splashed with vibrant pattern and colour.

The food has also been edging toward Michelin standard. The menu is correctly pitched to reflect the ambience and location. focussing on fresh Cornish produce, locally sourced – served in a relaxed setting. Their Sunday lunch comes especially recommended.

St Mawes, Cornwall

St Mawes, Cornwall
TR2 5DR

Tel (01326) 270055
Fax (01326) 270053
e-mail info@tresanton.com
website www.tresanton.com

Nearby Trelissick, Glendurgan,
Heligan and Trebah gardens; Truro;
Eden Project; National Maritime
Museum.
Location in town, just below castle,
14 miles (22 km) S of Truro; car
parking
Food breakfast, lunch, dinner; room
service **Price** ££££
Rooms 30; 26 double and twin, 4
suites, all with bath; all rooms have
phone, TV and DVD player,
hairdryer, free wi-fi
Facilities sitting room, dining room,
bar, cinema, terraces; 8-metre yacht,
beach club **Credit cards** AE, MC, V
Children welcome
Disabled not suitable
Pets accepted in 4 rooms **Closed** 2
weeks in Jan
Proprietor Olga Polizzi

Tresanton
Seaside town hotel

It's easy to drive past the hotel, as it has no obvious entrance, particularly for cars. Look closer and you will see a discreet sign and some steps next to a pair of white-painted garages. Stop, and within seconds someone will appear to welcome you, take your luggage and park your car. This is not any old seaside hotel.

Tresanton was opened in the summer of 1998 by Olga Polizzi, daughter of Lord Forte, and it is now well established as the West Country hotel for chic townies who prefer not to forego sophistication at the seaside. Yet St Mawes is a happy-go-lucky holiday village, full in summer of chirpy families, bucket and spade in hand, and the two must rub along together. A whitewashed former sailing club and a cluster of cottages on the sea front make up the hotel, which was well known back in the 1960s, but had long lost its glamour before Olga Polizzi came across it. She set about redesigning it in minimalist, elegant style, using restful, muted tones of oatmeal and flax, accentuated by blues, greens, browns or yellows. Bedrooms are a study in understated luxury and have stunning sea views. The warm and comfortable sitting room and bar are more traditional, and there's a new Mediterranean beach club. The food is also gaining many plaudits. Tresanton can claim to be one of the most sought-after hotels in the South West.

St Minver, Cornwall

Trewornan Bridge, St Minver,
Wadebridge, Cornwall. PL27 6EX

Tel (0) 1208 812359
e-mail
enquiries@trewornanmanor.co.uk
website www.trewornanmanor.co.uk

Nearby Rock, Polzeath,
Wadebridge, Padstow
Location set in 25 acres of land. Off
the B3314. Ample parking.
Food breakfast
Price ££-££££
Rooms 5 double; all with emperor
size beds, large en suites, TVs, hos-
pitality tray with homemade buis-
cuits, bathrobes, wi-fi
Facilities sitting room with honesty
bar, breakfast room, 8 acres mature
garden **Credit cards** all major
Children not allowed
Disabled not suitable
Pets not allowed
Closed never
Proprietor Paul and Lesley
Stapleton

Trewornan
Country bed-and-breakfast

Paul and Lesley have perfected the
romantic 'getaway', marrying the
romance of their 13thC Grade II-listed
manor house with supreme comfort and
stylishness. Perched in 8 acres of well-tended garden (and 25 acres of farmland)
Trewornan has the feeling of intimate seclusion, whilst being a ten-minute drive from
the north coast heavyweights of Rock, Port
Isaac and Padstow. The decoration is plush,
without obliterating original features:
crushed velvet furnishings sit alongside
arched portals and a flagstone hall. The five
guest bedrooms are superb, with Emperor
beds, upholstered headboards and views
across the garden (our room, Porthilly, was
especially luxuriant, with a huge bathroom).

At breakfast guests are greeted by a regal
spread, including cooked dishes whipped up
by Paul's mother. Paul is the perfect host:
quietly efficient without being overbearing,
and always on hand for insider advice. Small
touches combine to make guests feel special, from jars of sweets in bedrooms to the
well-stocked honesty bar in the sumptuous
living room.

The couple have plans to convert a study
into a second living room, and add two bedrooms to the outbuilding – further cultivat-
ing a sense of privacy and relaxation (which
drives their no child, no pet policy). A very
special new addition to this guide.

Strete, Devon

Totnes Road, Strete, Dartmouth,
Devon TQ6 0RU

Tel 01803 770364 **Fax** 01803
771182
e-mail info@stretebarton.co.uk
website www.stretebarton.co.uk

Nearby Slapton Ley, Slapton Beach,
South West Coast Path, Blackpool
Sands, Greenway (NT), Coleton
Fishacre (NT), Salcombe,
Dartmouth, boating, golf **Location**
access from A38 and A384, see website for full details
Food breakfast; 2 restaurants serving
lunch and dinner within a minute's
walk **Price** ££-£££ **Rooms** 5 double
and 1 cottage suite, with flat-screen
television and DVD/CD player, wi-
fi, fresh flowers, hairdryer, magazine
selection **Facilities** drawing room,
dining room, garden, massage treatments available **Children** 8 years
and over **Disabled** no access **Pets**
welcome in the Cottage Suite only –
additional £7/pet/night **Closed**
rarely **Proprietor/Manager** Stuart
Litster & Kevin Hooper

Strete Barton House
Country bed-and-breakfast

Nestling in the peaceful coastal village of Strete, this smart B&B within reach of award-winning beaches and the Slapton Ley Nature Reserve will appeal to nature lovers with a taste for luxury.

The refurbished 16thC manor house has five smart bedrooms in a variety of eye-catching styles, with sea views, king-sized sleigh beds and flat-screen TVs. There's additional accommodation in the Cottage Suite, with its log-burning stove and inglenook fireplace. On arrival, the wel-coming hosts will offer you a hot drink and a slice of home-made cake.

Strete is in the hilly area of south Devon known as the South Hams, with great walking and cycling, to give an extra dimension to the coastal scenery. If the weather's poor, book a massage appoint-ment with the qualified therapist.

They make a serious effort with the buffet breakfast here, served in a pleasant room overlooking the large gardens. There's no lunch or dinner, but the hosts can recommend local restaurants.

According to one recent visitor, "hosts Stuart and Kevin deserve the highest of praise", while another termed Strete Barton "one of the most beautifully appointed guesthouses we have ever stayed in".

Studland, Dorset

Manor House, Manor Road,
Studland, Swange, BH19 3AU

Tel 01929 450288
e-mail info@thepigonthebeach.com
website https://www.thepighotel.
com/on-the-beach/

Nearby Studland to Swanage trail,
Studland Sea School, Studland
Beach and Nature Reserve, Studland
Stables, Shell Bay, Durlston Country
Park, Corfe Castle, Bournemouth
Beach. **Location** just outside the village of Studland; car parking **Food**
breakfast, lunch, dinner **Price** ££-
££££ **Rooms** 27; a combination of
king, super-king and twin bedrooms;
2 shepherd huts and 2 dovecotes;
twin bedding, cots and extra beds
available in some rooms. All have
shower or bath; some have larder,
drinks, Nespresso machine **Facilities**
restaurant, bar, sitting room, spa,
terrace, garden **Credit cards** V, AE,
MC **Children** welcome **Disabled**
has an accessible room suitable for a
wheelchair **Pets** guide dogs only
Closed never
Hotel Director Lora Strizic

The Pig - on the beach
Coastal hotel

A quirky fantasy with gargoyles and an overlapping stone roof, this manor house might remind of you of the witch's gingerbread house in Hansel and Gretel, says our series editor Fiona Duncan. With its yellow exterior and terrific position overlooking Studland Bay, you are likely to fall for its enchantment from the moment you see it. Taken over in 2014 by Robin Hutson and David Elton of the Pig hotels, it is relaxing outside and cosy inside.

Once the holiday home of a historic landed family, it retains an eccentric atmosphere, with antiques, curios, chandaliers and vintage finds. It's been extended to include a new wing, and 23 spacious rooms have been refurbished – while preserving period features and reclaimed floorboards. In one bedroom you will find Portuguese carved woodwork, while in another a four-poster bed. The bedrooms are exceedingly well-stocked, with excellent bathrooms. There is also a terrace with dramatic views over Old Harry Rocks, to be enjoyed in summer.

As in all The Pig hotels, the restaurant is decorated with herbs and edible flowers, a reminder that the kitchen garden provides plenty of the fresh ingredients picked and used daily. The focus is on fresh fish, which, like breakfast, is superb. See other Pig hotels on pages 30, 50, 97 and 150.

Sturminster Newton, Dorset

Hazelbury Bryan Road, Sturminster Newton, Dorset DT10 2AF

Tel (01258) 472507
Fax (01258) 473370
e-mail book@plumbermanor.co.uk
website www.plumbermanor.co.uk

Nearby Thomas Hardy country; Shaftesbury; Sherborne.
Location 2 miles (3 km) SW of Sturminster Newton; private car parking
Food breakfast, Sun lunch, dinner
Price ££-£££
Rooms 16; 14 double, all with bath, 2 small doubles with bath; all rooms have phone, TV, tea/coffee facilities with shortbread, hairdryer
Facilities dining room, sitting room, bar; garden, croquet, tennis court
Credit cards AE, DC, MC, V
Children welcome
Disabled 2 courtyard rooms with wheelchair access and handrails, dining room and hotel facilities are wheelchair accessible **Pets** accepted by arrangement, £10 **Closed** Feb
Proprietor Richard Prideaux-Brune

Plumber Manor
Manor house hotel

This is a handsome Jacobean manor house, 'modernized' in the early 20th century, that has been in the Prideaux-Brune family for well over 300 years. Since 1973, brothers Richard and Brian have been running it as an elegant but relaxed restaurant with comfortable bedrooms. Richard Prideaux-Brune is much in evidence front-of-house, as is his brother Tim. Together with Brian, who is responsible for the highly-regarded food, they draw in restaurant customers from far and wide – expect plenty of bustle on Friday and Saturday evenings, and non-residents in the dining room.

The brothers make charming hosts, and have created a very relaxed and welcoming atmosphere. Old family portraits hang in the house; labradors lounge in the bar; the decoration is homely and comfortable rather than smart. The large bar area might detract from the feeling of a family home, but it helps the Prideaux-Brunes' operation in a practical way (shooting parties are a feature in winter).

Bedrooms are divided between those in the main house (which lead off a gallery hung with portraits) and those in a converted stone barn and courtyard building which overlook the extensive gardens and stream. They are all spacious and comfortable.

Swallowcliffe, Wiltshire

Swallowcliffe Salisbury. Wiltshire
SP3 5PA

Tel 01747 870211
e-mail hello@royaloakswallow-
cliffe.com **website** www.royaloak-
swallowcliffe.com

Nearby walking routes, Cranborne
Chase, Shaftesbury hill top market
town (8m), Wilton House, Salisbury
Cathedral (13m), Stonehenge, Bath
(32m), Studland Beach (40m)
Location Swallowcliffe, car park
available **Food** breakfast, lunch, dinner, tea, snacks, informal room service **Price** ££ **Rooms** 6; 3 doubles, 2
doubles or twins, 1 double with sofa
bed. 2 rooms can be connected. All
have hairdryer, radio alarms, tea and
coffee making facilities, wi-fi
Facilities garden, dining room, oak
room, lounge area, pub **Credit
cards** V, MC **Children** welcome;
cots, z-beds and games available
Disabled 2 rooms are accessible
through lift (1 king room and 1 twin
room) **Pets** 1 room suitable, £10 fee
Closed Christmas Day **Proprietor**
Mark Treasure, chef-patron

Royal Oak Inn
Village inn

In 2015 this traditional village inn rose like
a phoenix from the ashes thanks to the
efforts of three residents who campaigned
to give Swallowcliffe back its pub, after
seven years of neglect had put its future in
serious doubt. Extensive renovations and a
spot-on refurbishment has had a hugely
beneficial effect on the 19thC building.

The traditional thatched-roof exterior
belies a modern, stylish interior. The bar and
restaurant areas on the ground floor combine low ceilings and an open hearth fireplace with Matthew Burt's custom-made
furniture and contemporary landscape
paintings. There is an oak and glass garden
extension, which impresses with its light-
ness and simplicity. Upstairs, six individually
designed bedrooms are extremely peaceful
thanks to the pub's location in a quiet village street, with its back to the valley. They
are comfortable, with huge beds and luxurious duvets and toiletries. Two rooms also
have freestanding baths.

Chef-patron Mark Treasure's imaginative
take on pub grub, with a focus on local produce, has been popular among residents
and visitors. You might find slow roast pork
belly, smoked haddock and homemade
baked beans among the choices, but the
menu changes often. For breakfast, expect
freshly baked bread, seasonal fruit and
scrambled eggs.

Teffont Evias, Wiltshire

Teffont Evias, Salisbury,
Wiltshire SP3 5RJ

Tel (01722) 716392
Fax (01722) 716820
e-mail enq@howardshousehotel.com
website
www.howardshousehotel.co.uk

Nearby Salisbury Cathedral; Wilton
House; Stonehenge; Old Sarum,
Longleat.
Location in village, off B3089 (sign-
posted from Teffont Magna), 10
miles (16 km) W of Salisbury; car
parking
Food breakfast, lunch, dinner
Price ££-£££
Rooms 9; 7 double (including twin),
1 four-poster, 1 superior, all with
bath and shower; all rooms have
phone, TV, hairdryer
Facilities dining room, sitting room;
terrace, garden, croquet
Credit cards AE, MC, V
Children welcome
Disabled Coach House is suitable
Pets accepted
Closed 23rd-27th Dec
Proprietor Simon Greenwood

Howard's House
Country house hotel & restaurant

Teffont Evias, in the Nadder Valley, has
been owned by the same family, father to
son, since 1692. It is picturesque and has
great charm without being twee. In the
grounds stands Howard's House, opposite a
marvellously knotty topiary hedge, and
embellished by a Swiss gabled roof in the
early 19th century – its then owner had fall-
en for all things Swiss on the Grand Tour. It
is surrounded by two acres of pretty garden.

Its *raison d`être* is the food, created by
chef Nick Wentworth. Dishes might
include seared scallops with *sauce vierge*
and crab mayonnaise, rack of lamb with
onion puree and tomato and olive salsa,
followed by summer berry jelly and elder-
flower ice cream. The smallish dining room
is a soft cream and off-balanced by some
striking artwork, as is the decoration in the
cosy sitting room. The bedrooms: pastel-
coloured walls, floral fabrics, oak furnishings. The four-poster room is the prettiest;
rooms 1 and 2 have garden views.

Breakfast here is well above average:
excellent coffee, warm croissants and
toast wrapped in a white napkin, and the
mouthwatering orange juice. You might
choose a boiled egg, or something more
sophisticated such as poached egg tartlet
with Hollandaise sauce.

The newly restored Coach House is an
ideal facility for private events.

West Hatch, Tisbury, Wiltshire SP3 6PA

Tel (01747) 870 444
e-mail info@pythousekitchengarden.co.uk
website www.pythousekitchengarden.co.uk

Nearby Tisbury, Salisbury, Old Wardour Castle, Stone Henge
Location on a small country lane betwen villages of Tisbury and Semley
Food breakfast, lunch, dinner, fire cooking, Sunday roast **Price** ££
Rooms glamping village; 6 bell-tents, with comfy beds, fresh linen, kitchenette, breakfast/cocktail bar, WCs, hot showers
Facilities restaurant, terrace, walled garden, bar, glamping. Can be rented out for private parties and weddings. **Credit cards** all major
Children welcome
Disabled no special facilities
Closed Glamping season is Mar-Oct; restaurant open all year round
Proprietor Sophia and Piers Milburn

Pythouse Kitchen Garden **Glamping**

An unconventional new entry, not much known outside its neighbourhood. The charm is in the way the huge conservatory dining room – a masterpiece of shabby-chic interior decoration – interfaces with the huge 18thC walled garden. Out of sight behind a hedge at the bottom are the six comfortable, heated bell tents, set up for 'glamping': comfortable beds, fresh linen, a large covered dining area, breakfast bar, kitchenette, smart WCs and hot showers, open from March to October.

The tenting comes into its own in summer, of course, when in fine weather the terrace will be your sitting room. If you want to be indoors, hang out in the homely coffee shop area with its nicely displayed homemade cakes and biscuits.

The four seasonal menus offer simple, traditional British kitchen garden food, cooked inside on the stove or outside over a beechwood fire pit. They vary a little each day depending on what the gardener brings in – one of the most popular items is the Garden Board, reflecting just that. The fire pit is a major feature, with meat and fish expertly and deliciously cooked or smoked. The whole set-up artfully satisfies city dwellers' nostalgia for the good life and its homegrown trappings – every area of paint deliberately left peeling, every painted (or unpainted) chair – contributes something.

Tollard Royal, Wiltshire SP5 5PS

Tel 01725 516207
e-mail info@kingjohninn.co.uk
website www.kingjohninn.co.uk

Nearby Thomas Hardy country;
Shaftesbury; Salisbury, Rushmore
Golf Club, Todber Manor Fisheries,
Cranborne Chase.
Location village of Tollard Royal on
Wiltshire/Dorset border
Food breakfast, lunch, dinner
Price ££££-££££
Rooms 8; 5 in the inn, 3 in the
coach house opposite (with self-
catering facilities); all doubles and all
have bath/shower, all have TV, tele-
phone, wi-fi **Facilities** pub, restau-
rant, terraced garden and outdoor
kitchen **Credit cards** DC, MC, V
Children welcome at lunch, can stay
from 2 years **Disabled** one room in
coach house with disabled facilities
Pets dogs allowed by prior arrange-
ment (£15)
Closed Christmas Day and New
Year's Eve
Proprietors Alex and Gretchen
Boon

King John Inn
Village inn

At weekends the King John is jammed
with urban couples, though locals
come here too – it has a strong feel of village pub turned weekend hang-out. The
charming new 'outdoor kitchen', with a
cosmopolitan seafood bar under a
Victorian-style pavilion, is popular in the
summer. In the evening, don't be surprised
to find a lively throng on the terrace outside, keeping warm from the wood-burning braziers.

Up the steep, hessian-carpeted stairs
are the five bedrooms (there are also
three in a converted coach house). They
are decorated with an eye for the past as
well as the present, and have a choice of
fabrics that makes them refreshingly different from others of their ilk. Ours had a bay
window dressed in a beautiful woven fabric and a great feeling of space. The bathroom was a little dark, but had both free-
standing bath and shower.

Downstairs, the simple wooden tables
quickly fill up and the noise levels can
climb. We thought the pork and mustard
pies 'good pub fare', and the snails, crab on
toast and fish from Poole Harbour better
than expected. The home-made bread and
fudge are great.

Tresco, Isles of Scilly

Tresco Estate, Isles of Scilly, TR24 0QQ

Tel (01720) 422849
e-mail contactus@tresco.co.uk
website www.tresco.co.uk

Nearby Tresco's sub-tropical Abbey Garden; boat trips to other Scilly Isles; ferry to Bryher.
Location Tresco island.
Food breakfast, lunch, dinner
Price very variable, see website
Rooms 16; 7 self-catering, 9 self-catering with hotel services (eg daily clean), for 2-10 people. See website for details of individual cottages
Facilities restaurants and pubs (eg New Inn in New Grimsby), swimming pool, gym, spa, bike hire, golf buggies **Credit cards** DC, MC, V
Children welcome
Disabled no special access (golf buggies available for people with reduced mobility)
Pets not accepted
Closed Dec-Feb (although self-catering cottages run all year)
Proprietor Tresco Estate

Sea Garden Cottages
Self-catering cottages

The whole of Tresco is in effect a multi-faceted holiday destination, unique in Britain. The Island Hotel has disappeared, to leave a mix of timeshare and rental accommodation dotted all over the island. The Sea Garden Cottages – built from sympathetic wood and stone – comprise seven self-catering cottages and nine cottages that have certain hotel facilities as part of the package.

Our cottage suite was faultless: comfortable, well-equipped kitchen and garden, seaside-fresh decoration. It also had some interesting modern art, much of it from the collection of Tresco's proprietors, Robert and Lucy Dorrien-Smith.

There's an indoor pool and tennis court by the cottages. Guests can also eat in the stylish restaurant at the Flying Boat Club at New Grimsby or in the new restaurant, The Ruin. This shares the same electrifying sea views as the rooms, and does tasty food – although we preferred the surf'n'turf at The New Inn at New Grimsby, its menu was tantalising and made choosing difficult.

Accommodation on Tresco is expensive. However, it's a no-car, protected environment and under blue skies the archipelago dances in the sunlight. If you want the full hotel experience think about Hell Bay Hotel (http://www.hellbay.co.uk/), on Bryher, also owned by the Dorrien-Smiths.

Wareham, Dorset

Church Green, Wareham,
Dorset BH20 4ND

Tel (01929) 551666
Fax (01929) 554519
e-mail reservations@theprioryho-tel.co.uk **website** www.theprioryho-tel.co.uk

Nearby Poole Harbour; Swanage; Lulworth Cove.
Location in town near market square; in 4.5 acre gardens with ample car parking
Food breakfast, lunch, dinner
Price ££££
Rooms 17; 13 double, 5 suites, all have bath/shower; all rooms have phone, TV, hairdryer, minibar
Facilities drawing room, bar, restaurant; terrace, garden, croquet, pontoon, organised goldf outings **Credit cards** DC, MC, V
Children accepted over 8 in restaurant, over 14 in hotel **Disabled** facilities available in restaurant, access difficult in hotel **Pets** guide dogs only **Closed** never **Proprietors** Turner family

The Priory
Country town hotel

Hidden behind the church, this 16thC Priory is the perfect retreat for anyone who appreciates a sense of history, as well as peace, comfort and good food. It has been run for the last fourty-one years by the Turner family, and is currently under the guiding hand of Jeremy, who is ensuring that everything, from the excellent antiques to the pretty fabrics in the bedrooms, has been done with taste and in keeping.

The bedrooms are all that should be expected from a 16thC priory: beams, sloping ceilings and floors, as well as being supremely comfortable and well-equipped with books (no *Reader's Digest* here) and attractive toiletries in the bathrooms. To keep up with the demand for rooms the boathouse has been converted to provide four extra bedrooms, or rather suites, equipped with luxury baths and French windows opening on to the River Frome. Indeed, it's possible to arrive by boat to The Priory: moorings are available and, after a quick walk through the stunning gardens (from which Mrs Turner gathers flowers for the arrangements) you can relax with a pre-dinner drink on the terrace. The food is richly sastisfying, with a mainland European flavour emanating from the menu.

Wincanton, Somerset BA9 8BS

Tel 01963 824466
Fax 01963 32681
e-mail
enquiries@holbrookhouse.co.uk
website www.holbrookhouse.co.uk

Nearby Wincanton Race Course;
many National Trust attractions;
Bath; Longleat Safari Park
Location 1 mile from Wincanton,
Somerset; from M3 south, exit at
junction 8 onto the A303, then take
the A371 sign-posted to Wincanton
and Castle Cary.
Food breakfast, lunch, dinner
Price £–££
Rooms 21; all double, 14 can be
twin, 4 suites, all with bath; all
rooms have phone, hairdryer
Facilities Health Club, Spa, 4 sitting
rooms, cafe **Credit Cards** all accepted **Children** welcome **Disabled** 1
room with disabled facilities **Pets**
accepted **Closed** never
Proprietors John & Patricia
McGinley

Holbrook House
Country house hotel

John and Pat McGinley bought Holbrook House in 1998 on a whim. Passing by, they popped in for a cup of tea and found it was for sale. The current manager, Darren (the McGinleys' son) was a successful DJ before he took over – as we arrived we listened to a cool compilation of background music, mixed by Darren himself.

The place seems to defy time, what with Darren's music – he hopes, too, that per-formers at Glastonbury might stay here. The McGinleys completely redecorated when they took over, but you wouldn't know it, so quietly old-fashioned are the furnishings. We particularly liked the feel of the main hall.

In the 20 acres of grounds that surround the house there is a grass tennis court – a rarity these days – plus an enormous old cedar tree and a steep drop to a deep gully that eventually reaches the River Cale.

Value for money is exceptional. As we went to press, two people could pay as little as £100 on a weekday: for this they get for a huge room, beautiful grounds, use of the hotel's spa and pool and tennis court (rack-ets provided) and breakfast and dinner. In summer, many weekends are given over to weddings.

Winsford, Exmoor National Park,
Somerset TA24 7JE

Tel 01643 851455
e-mail
enquiries@royaloakexmoor.co.uk
website www.royaloakexmoor.co.uk

Nearby Exmoor Pony Centre;
Dunster Castle; Tarr Steps;
Caracatus Stone; Stone Age Burial
Site **Location** in centre of village on
B road, 1.5miles from junction with
A396, ample parking in hotel car
park and on street
Food breakfast, lunch, dinner
Price ££
Rooms 12; 6 doubles under the
thatch (5 with four poster beds), 2
twins, 2 doubles in annexe; all rooms
have bath/shower, telephone, TV,
hairdryers, tea/coffee making facilities **Facilities** residents lounge, dining room, bar, wi-fi, garden
Credit Cards all major **Children**
welcome **Disabled** access possible to
annexe rooms **Pets** accepted in bar
and some of the bedrooms **Closed**
1st-8th Feb **Proprietors** Mark &
Sally Bradley

The Royal Oak
Village inn

This Exmoor institution has been improving steadily since the Henrys took over
in 2011, followed by the Bradleys a few
years later. Locals popping in for a drink feel
relaxed because their custom is valued and
they have their own bar area. Hotel guests
have a peaceful refuge at the far end of the
building – a large sitting room replete with
Victorian-style deep-buttoned chairs and
sofas. Along with the rest of the public areas
and bedrooms, it's conservatively rather
than imaginatively decorated – 30 and 40-
somethings won't like it as much as their
parents – but it's appropriate to Exmoor.

There's room in the dining area for the
shooting parties not to swamp the regular
guests. Several menus, including a family one,
and a long wine list, offer the wide choice
needed to satisfy these different groups. We
liked the chunky, brown-stained tongue-and-
groove panelling throughout the ground
floor – quite smart and pleasing because it
pulls it all together in an unpretentious way.
Ceilings are low, beams are everywhere and
because of the thatch overhang, the ground
floor is darkish. We also liked the spacious
bedrooms, with conventional repro and
antique furnishings and adequate, plain
white bathrooms. No 4, at £140, is especially roomy. No 3, the smallest, is roomy by
comparison with what other similar places
offer for £120.

Barwick, near Yeovil, Somerset
BA22 9TD

Tel (01935) 423902
Fax (01935) 420908
e-mail info@littlebarwick.co.uk
website
www.littlebarwickhouse.co.uk

Nearby Brympton d'Evercy;
Montacute House; Sculpture by the
Lakes, Sherborne.
Location 2 miles (3 km) S of Yeovil
off A37; car parking
Food breakfast, lunch, dinner
Price ££
Rooms 7 double and twin, all with
bath or shower; all rooms have TV,
hairdryer, phone, iPod dock, radio,
wi-fi
Facilities sitting room, dining room,
bar/private dining room; garden
Credit cards MC, V
Children welcome over 5
Disabled access difficult
Pets accepted
Closed 2 weeks Jan
Proprietors Emma and Tim Ford

Little Barwick House
Restaurant-with-rooms

Emma and Tim Ford have built up a reputation for fine food at this restaurant with rooms in Somerset. Tim is one of Britain's finest chefs: he trained at Sharrow Bay and spent time in several top hotels refining his art. Previously he was head chef at Summer Lodge in Evershot, but he and his wife Emma, who was front-of-house there, have now been running Little Barwick for 18 years.

Locally-sourced meat, game and fish provide the cornerstone of Tim's cooking (our inspector enjoyed pink roasted rump of Dorset lamb with aubergine caviar and black olive sauce), while the lunch menu is a simpler variation of the dinner menu. The wine list is extensive, including many wines by the glass or half bottle.

Little Barwick has featured in these pages for years, recommended for its friendly informality, and this has remained the case through changes of ownership. The Fords have completed a programme of redecoration that has freshened up both the interior and exterior of this lovely listed Georgian dower house. The dining room is decorated with a pretty Farrow and Ball stripe wallpaper. Bedrooms remain cheerful with fresh flowers, real coffee in cafetières and homemade shortbreads.

Treen, Zennor, Cornwall
TR26 3DE

Tel (01736) 796928
e-mail
enquiries@gurnardshead.co.uk
website www.gurnardshead.co.uk

Nearby Tate Galley at St Ives; South
West Coast Path; Trengwainton
Location on the B3306 between St
Ives and Land's End; ample car
parking
Food breakfast, lunch, dinner
Price £££
Rooms 7; 4 double, 3 twin, some
with a bath and all with shower; all
with phone, Roberts Radio and
hairdryer.
Facilities bar, dining room; garden
Credit cards MC, V
Children welcome
Disabled no special facilities
Pets dogs welcome
Closed Christmas day and 1 week in
early Dec
Proprietors Charles and Edmund
Inkin; they also own The Old
Coastguard (page 60) and Felin Fach
Griffin (page 186) in Wales

The Gurnard's Head
Seaside inn

An early 17thC coaching inn near
Zennor, standing like a beacon on the
windswept coastal road that runs between
St Ives and Land's End. Brothers Charles
and Edmund Inkin's motto is 'the simple
things in life done well' and they reckon on
applying this to all aspects of The Gunard's
Head, as also to their other establishments.

The stunning location and views of the
Atlantic make this inn popular with walkers, tourists and city dwellers looking for
tranquility, although the sounds and smells
from the neighbouring farm may not be for
urban-outdoor types. The bedrooms are
simple and tastefully decorated, with hand-
made beds and good linen. Each room is
lined with old books and local pictures and
maps – you might be staying with friends.

With the Atlantic 500 metres away,
locally caught fish is a highlight of the seasonal menu. The lunch menus suit most
guests, from the hungry walker to those
who want to settle in for a fixed-price
menu with a carafe of wine. In the evening,
the menu is short and delicious, changing
daily according to what suppliers bring
through the back door. Drink from a choice of
well-chosen and affordable wines or local
real ales and cider. Too good to be true?
Our reporter, food writer Mark Taylor's,
reply: 'Except for the quibble about the
farmyard smells, it really is that good.'

Bath

Apsley House
Town hotel

Once upon a time this was a grand house with huge grounds leading down to the River Avon. The grounds were sold off long ago to make way for the houses which now surround Apsley House, leaving enough garden to ensure privacy for the occupants.

There is a large, comfortable drawing room, with a grand piano for guests' use, as well as a licensed bar.

Owners Claire and Nicholas Potts have updated the bedrooms and bathrooms, and generally set about making the place "a lot cleaner". Since the last edition the Potts have opened up three further bedrooms in the hotel, complete with four-poster beds.

Claire does some of the cooking and is rightly proud of her breakfasts.

Newbridge Hill,
Bath, BA1 3PT

Tel (01225) 336966
e-mail info@apsley-house.co.uk
website www.apsley-house.co.uk
Food breakfast
Price ££
Closed 25th-26th Dec
Proprietors Claire and Nicholas Potts

Bradford-on-Avon, Wiltshire

The Swan Inn
Town inn

In 2007 this 600-year-old Bradford-on-Avon institution got a new lease of life – a complete makeover. However, the listed building was hard to renovate, and the result lacks finesse. This shouldn't stop you staying here, if you want what it offers: a mixture of small town hotel, pub and informal restaurant. Locals and residents enjoy the bar and the (good) food; prices are fair. This includes hearty pub classics as well as a traditional Thai menu. It's a serious alternative to lodging in Bath, where hotel prices are now higher than in London.

The interior design relies a bit too much on predictable 'contemporary' colours, carpets and curtains, but the current owners are constantly working to keep the interiors fresh and welcoming. Rooms 8 and 12 in particular are spacious and good value.

1 Church Street, Bradford-on-Avon,
Wiltshire, BA15 1LN

Tel (01225) 868686
e-mail stay@theswanbradford.co.uk
website www.theswanbradford.co.uk
Food breakfast, lunch, dinner
Price £££ **Closed** never
Proprietors James

Bristol

Hotel du Vin
Town house hotel

Since our last edition, the Hotel du Vin chain has been taken over by Frasers Hospitality, a large group. However, this is probably still the most interesting and stylish place to stay in Bristol.

Converted from a collection of derelict 18thC sugar warehouses, the hotel's gracious Queen Anne frontage belies the wizardry behind. Open brickwork, painted girders and sweeping stairs with a curving steel bannister combine industrial elements with contemporary style to great effect.

The huge bedrooms contain custom-made beds, alongside equally huge bathrooms with showers and free-standing baths. The aptly-named Sugar Bar has whitewashed walls, wood flooring and rugs that contribute to the unhurried, plantation house feel.

The Sugar House,
Narrow Lewins Mead,
Bristol, Avon BS1 2NU

Tel 0117 9255577
email
website www.hotelduvin.com
Food breakfast, lunch, dinner
Price £££
Closed never
Proprietors Frasers Hospitality

Buckhorn Weston, Dorset

The Stapleton Arms
Village inn

In deepest Dorset lies this new-wave village inn, the type you might describe as 'urban-chic with a country twist'. With pillared portico and elegant proportions, it looks more like a gentleman's residence than a long-established hostelry. Step inside, and the scene is contemporary: open-plan, leather sofas and chunky tables.

The bedrooms are great, especially for the price: airy and well-proportioned. We had a lovely bathroom, with large, free-standing tub and generous toiletries.

Dinner, contrary to reports, was a little disappointing: we called more than once for missing cutlery and water. However, when the place is humming, as it often is, it makes a great stop-off en route to the West Country.

Church Hill, Buckhorn Weston,
Gillingham, Dorset SP8 5HS

Tel 01963 370396
e-mail relax@thestapletonarms.com
website www.thestapletonarms.com
Food breakfast, lunch, dinner
Price ££
Closed on Christmas day only open
2 hours for drinks
Proprietor Steve Philpot

Exford, Somerset

The Crown Hotel
Country inn

A reliable, unpretentious, friendly Exmoor base, run by Lancastrian Sarah Whittaker. The bar and restaurant food is above-average (for the price). Furnishings are traditional, not imaginative or modern – but then a contemporary designer hotel would seem unnatural on Exmoor. There's enough room to accommodate locals, hotel guests and shooting parties at the same time – they don't always mix. The eating areas in the bar are pleasantly informal. All the basics are right, including properly warm bedrooms and bathrooms, and fair prices.

Exford, Somerset TA24 7PP

Tel 01643 831554
Fax 01643 831665
e-mail
info@crownhotelexmoor.co.uk **website** www.crownhotelexmoor.co.uk
Food breakfast, lunch, dinner
Price ££-££££ **Closed** never
Proprietors Sarah Whittaker

Fontmell Magna, Dorset

The Fontmell
Village inn

'It's a traditional country inn deeply rooted in the local community,' says new owner John Crompton. A formerly run-down village inn that's been done up in contemporary country style (Farrow & Ball, mismatched antique dining chairs). It's more boutique hotel than rural drinking spot, but while we reclined in front of a wood-burning stove before dinner, six gents dropped in to prop up the bar and exchange the day's news.

The stair carpet is grubby, but the rooms are all different – imaginative with comfortable beds. There are glitches – thin walls, nowhere for shower gel, missing soap. But the dining room is attractive; the food 'enjoyable, not outstanding', and we liked that the village stream ran between the bar area and the dining room extension.

Fontmell Magna, Shaftesbury, Dorset SP7 0PA

Tel 01747 811441
e-mail info@thefontmell.com
website www.thefontmell.com
Food breakfast, lunch, dinner
Price £-££
Closed never
Proprietor Simon Crumplin & John Crompton

Frome, Somerset

Babington House
Country house hotel

Babington was the idea of Nick Jones, owner of the trendy Soho Club in London, and bought as a country retreat for club members. In practice anyone can stay here, although it might be better if you were young, or at least young at heart. Having said that, everyone is made to feel welcome, in a laid-back yet professional, atmosphere. It's a contemporary hotel set in an elegant country house that offers metropolitan and unpretentious luxury. Bedrooms are wonderful, with huge bottles of complimentary lotions in the bathrooms. You can have any number of beauty treatments in the Cowshed, where there is also an indoor pool and a gym. Small children are kept occupied in the well-equipped crêche.

Babington, near Frome,
Somerset BA11 3RW

Tel (01373) 812266
e-mail
reception@babingtonhouse.co.uk
website www.babingtonhouse.co.uk
Food breakfast, lunch, dinner, room
service **Price** ££££
Closed never
Proprietors Nick Jones

Lifton, Devon

Tor Cottage
Country bed-and-breakfast

Tor Cottage is described as a hideaway on the edge of Dartmoor and it is true that if you make the trip to this remote hotel, you will find a pleasant hotel full of little touches that give Tor Cottage an edge over other similar hotels: for example, a jug of sparkling wine awaits your arrival, as do champagne truffles, fresh fruit and flowers in your bedroom and the bonus of access to a heated outdoor swimming pool for those guests interested in taking a late-night dip under the brilliantly clear skies of Dartmoor.

Maureen prides herself on good service and genuinely enjoys pampering her visitors. As a result, Tor Cottage has picked up a large amount of awards and guests claim to leave suitably rejuvenated.

Chillaton, nr Lifton, Devon PL16
0JE

Tel 01822 860248
Fax 01822 860126
e-mail info@torcottage.co.uk
website www.torcottage.co.uk
Food breakfast
Price £££
Closed mid-Dec to mid-Jan
Proprietors Maureen Rowlatt

Mevagissey, Cornwall

Trevalsa Court
Seaside hotel

This is a cliff-top hotel with spectacular views, courteous staff, a simple but refreshingly different style – and an interesting history. It was built in the 1930s as a private, cliff-top home with breathtaking sea views and a Daphne du Maurier character: oak-panelled walls and stone-framed mullion windows.

The bedrooms and bathrooms vary in size, and though decorated mostly neutrally, the bigger ones have eclectic wallpaper, art and solid wooden furniture.

Trevalsa isn't isolated: houses have grown up around it. We don't rate this as ideal for a beach holiday, but it's a great base for the local sights. The coastal path is literally at the bottom of the garden, reached by a vertiginous metal stairway.

School-Hill, Mevagissey, South Cornwall PL26 6TH

Tel (01726) 842468
e-mail stay@trevalsa-hotel.co.uk
website www.trevalsa-hotel.co.uk
Food breakfast, lunch, dinner
Price ££
Closed Dec-Jan
Proprietors John and Sue Gladwin

Newquay, Cornwall

The Headland Cottages
Self-catering cottages

Talk about a Victorian pile. The Headland Hotel's outward appearance is so frightening it was the setting for the 1990 film adaptation of Roald Dahl's *The Witches*.

The 39 one- to three-bedroom self-catering cottages make an attractive alternative to staying at the hotel – indeed any hotel – with all the benefits of hotel facilities close by. They are built in Cornish village style with rough stone and granite walls. Ours was airy and freshly painted in seaside colours, and had an excellent kitchen and gas log fire too.

You can mix self-catering with meals in the hotel. The Headland also has a fully equipped new spa, to which cottage guests have full access. The cottages, food and spa are worth seeking out.

Fistral Beach, Newquay, Cornwall TR7 1EW

Tel 01637 872211 **e-mail** reception@headlandhotel.co.uk
website www.headlandhotel.co.uk/accommodation/cottages **Food** breakfast, lunch, dinner **Price** £££-££££
Closed never **Proprietors** Mr and Mrs Armstrong

Virginstow, Devon

Coombeshead Estate, Virginstow,
Devon EX21 5EA

Tel 01409 211236
e-mail info@percys.co.uk
website www.percys.co.uk
Food breakfast, dinner
Price £££
Closed never
Proprietors Tony and Tina
Bricknell-Webb

Percy's Country Hotel
Country hotel and restaurant

Percy's Country Hotel was originally bought as a retirement home by the Bricknell-Webbs, who ran a restaurant in London called Percy's. The bedrooms, in an adjacent converted barn, are spacious and (after recent refurbishment) smart in an understated way: the showers are power showers, the beds are king-size, and the real coffee comes in cafetieres. Two rooms, with stripped wood floors, flowers and a wood-burning stove make up the intimate and calming restaurant – residents only. Tina cooks in the modern English style, with almost all ingredients, such as salad, eggs and venison, coming from the estate. Fish features strongly, and it is very good. The wine list is equally good, and almost all wines are available by the glass.

Wedmore, Somerset

Cheddar Road, Wedmore, Somerset
BS28 4EQ

Tel 01934 710337 **e-mail**
info@theswanwedmore.com **website**
www.theswanwedmore.com **Food**
breakfast, lunch, dinner, afternoon
tea, snacks, Sunday lunch **Price** ££
Closed Christmas Day drinks only
Proprietor Stay Original Co.

The Swan
Country inn

Another dead-beat country pub restored and converted eight years ago into a comfortable up-to-date haven. Owner Rob Greacen has kept faith with the place's inherited country pub ambience by going for wooden floors, log burners and a choice of real ales. The food, served all day, is hearty country fare – chef Tom Blake was at Hugh Fearnley-Whittingstall's River Cottage. Rare-breed pork is a speciality.

The bedrooms are striking: quality beds and linen, some charming furniture and interesting auction room finds here and there.

Alton (Lower Froyle), Hampshire

Lower Froyle, Alton, Hampshire
GU34 4NA

Tel 01420 23161
e-mail info@anchorinnatlower-
froyle.co.uk
website www.anchorinnatlower-
froyle.co.uk

Nearby Hampshire.
Location 1.8 miles from Bentley,
just off the A31
Food breakfast, lunch, dinner
Price £££
Rooms 5; all with shower
Facilities 2 bar areas, dining room,
private dining rooms, courtyard
Credit cards AE, DC, MC, V
Children welcome
Disabled access to the dining rooms,
not to the bedrooms
Pets dogs allowed in the bedrooms
and bar area
Closed never
Proprietors Kiran Shukla

The Anchor Inn
Country Inn

As a pleasant place to stay, it works well. You
might even ask yourself, why spend
more in a hotel when you can stay just as
comfortably here? Our room felt spacious,
with French doors on to a balcony rising
to a high apex, and room for a sofa and
table. All the extras of a fully-fledged hotel
are in place: a choice of teas and coffees;
Bush radio; antique-style sleigh bed;
Egyptian cotton linen. The decoration is
fashionable yet full of character, with oriental carpets on sisal, pale sage walls covered in pictures and shelves of books.

A number of classic English touches
help achieve the pleasant effect of staying
in a country house rather than a hotel: fabrics in tweed patterns, eccentric *objets
d'art,* pewter goblets and mochaware can
be found in the bedrooms and dining
room – which is illumined by particularly
cosy lighting.

The night we stayed we were chilly in
the wood-panelled dining room, but that
was probably a one off. We got used to the
low beams in the bar and kept our heads,
but it's good sport watching new arrivals
lose theirs. The food is properly English
and enjoyable. Breakfast is excellent, and
the staff friendly.

Baughurst, Hampshire

Baughurst Road, Baughurst,
Hampshire RG26 5LP

Tel 0118 9820110
e-mail
hello@thewellingtonarms.com **website** www.thewellingtonarms.com

Nearby Highclere Castle, The
Vyne, Silchester Roman Wall,
Bishopswood Golf Course, Sandford
Springs Golf Club
Location on Baughurst Road, lead-
ing south from Baughurst
Food breakfast, lunch, dinner
Price £££-££££
Rooms 4 doubles; all with shower,
heated floors, wi-fi, TV and mini bar
Facilities bar, restaurant, large gar-
den **Credit cards** DC, MC, V
Children welcome, no special facili-
ties **Disabled** wheelchair access pos-
sible **Pets** dogs welcome
Closed Sunday evenings
Proprietor Jason King and Simon
Page

The Wellington Arms
Pub restaurant-with-rooms

Our series editor, Fiona Duncan, writes:
'The Wellington Arms is a dining pub
with four rooms so immaculate that even in
plutocratic north Hampshire, it stands out
like a supermodel in a street market – oak
furniture, Hungarian goose down bedding
and slate flagstones with underfloor heating
are just some of the features that set it
apart. Partners Simon and Aussie born
Jason have owned, run and gently expanded
this pretty former shooting lodge of the
Duke of Wellington for twelve years and it
looks and feels special.

'Just an hour's drive from central London
yet set in peaceful countryside, it ticks all
the boxes for urbanites seeking rural idyll;
immaculate, fulsome flower- and vegetable
gardens, which the owners and kitchen staff
tend themselves; orchards; they even keep
rescue hens – not to mention the beehives,
flock of Jacob sheep and Tamworth pigs.
They have tea cosies knitted by Simon's
mum from their own sheep, and fabric hens
dangling from the room keys. 'Jason's cooking takes pub dining to its highest level:
home made, locally sourced and tasty, with
a state of the art cheese soufflé. After lunch,
take the footpath from the door of the
Wellington Arms, which leads through
woods and fields, or perhaps head for
Watership Down, site of Richard Adam's
famous book of the same name'.

Bepton, West Sussux

Bepton, Nr Midhurst,
West Sussex GU29 0JB

Tel 01730-819020/819000
Fax (01730) 819099
e-mail reservations@parkhouseho-
tel.com **website** www.parkhouseho-
tel.com

Nearby Petworth; Goodwood;
Cowdray Park Polo Club;
Chichester. **Location** on the B2226
in the village of Bepton; ample car-
parking **Food** breakfast, lunch, dinner; room service **Price** ££-£££
Rooms 21 double: 12 in main house,
6 in South Downs Cottage, 2 in Polo
Cottage and 1 in Bay Tree Cottage.
All have tea, coffee, wi-fi, TV, radio,
bathrobes, hairdryer, room service
Facilities dining, drawing room,
conservatory, bar; gardens, outdoor
swimming pool, two grass tennis
courts, croquet lawn, bowls green,
golf, spa **Credit cards** MC, V
Children welcome **Disabled** adapted ground-floor bedroom, South
Down Cottage has lift, spa has lift
Pets by arrangement **Closed** never
Proprietor Seamus O'Brien

Park House
Country hotel

Park House has been in the O'Brien family for more than 50 years, and has
always retained the atmosphere of a private
country house thanks first to the careful
attention of Ioné O'Brien, and now to
Seamus. A 16thC farmhouse with Victorian
additions with its cream-painted roughcast
walls, at first it looks rather suburban.

Inside, however, the elegant public rooms
strike a very different note. The honesty
bar, festooned with mementoes and photographs of polo players (Cowdray Park is
close at hand) is admirably well-stocked,
while the drawing room, particularly
appealing at night, gleams with polished parquet floor, velvet-backed alcoves filled with
books and china, yellow walls, and table
lamps which cast a golden glow.

Bedrooms are traditional. The Polo is
perhaps the best cottage, adjacent to the
main house with entrance to a private garden. The dinner menu has been expanded
(it used to be quite limited) and features
traditional English food. Dinner might
include lamb rump with aubergine and puy
lentils, followed by pistachio, chocolate and
rasberry soufflé.

The extensive facilities include the likes
of grass tennis courts and golf, as well as the
Park House Spa – a luxurious area with an
indoor pool, gym and fitness suite, saunas,
steam rooms and a jacuzzi.

Brighton

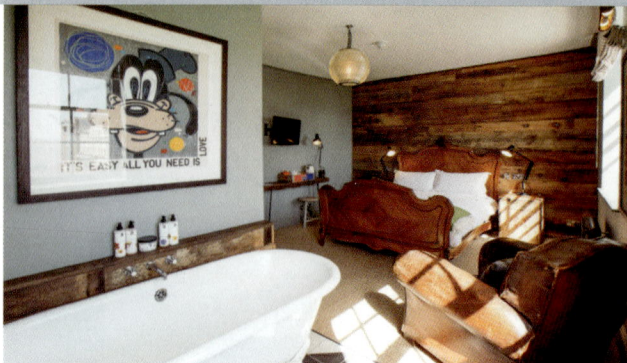

33 Regency Square, Brighton, BN1 2GG

Tel 01273 324 302
e-mail
brighton@artistresidence.co.uk
website www.artistresidence-brighton.co.uk

Nearby beach, Brighton Pier, The Royal Pavilion, The Lanes, Brighton Dome, Brighton Wheel, Komedia, train station. **Location** in historic Regency Square **Food** breakfast, snacks, lunch, dinner, tapas **Price** £-££££ **Rooms** 24; 17 double; 5 twin or triple, one suite, one bunk house room (for groups of up to four sharing, 4 built in single bunk beds); all rooms have wi fi, TV with freeview, hairdryer, tea and coffee making facilities. **Facilities** Ping pong, cocktail bar, breakfast room/art gallery, sitting room, meeting room, event space **Credit cards** AE, DC, MC, V **Children** welcome **Disabled** no special access **Pets** not allowed **Closed** never
Proprietor Charlotte and Justin Salisbury

Artist Residence, Brighton **Town hotel**

When 20-year-old Justin Salisbury quit university to help his injured mother run her ailing guesthouse, he made a call to arms to local artists on gumtree: to decorate in return for free board. Thus Artist Residence – now four branches strong – was born. Their flagship in Brighton has also expanded over the years, acquiring the house next door and a new restaurant. The nine original 'Arty' rooms are supplemented by 14 rooms, done up in their 'House' style – a mixture of rustic shabby-chic and faux-industrial. We stayed in the art-themed No. 4, muraled with a fantasy cityscape, and hung with photographs by an artist called Bonnie & Clyde. The fairly basic bathrooms and bedrooms in these rooms are elevated by the wacky and creative surroundings – perfect for its trendy Brighton setting. Their restaurant, The Set, is run by head chef Danny Kenny. Diners are given the option of four set tasting menus, and can then watch the dishes being prepared in the open kitchen. They also have the Set Cafe for informal dining with music, and the Cocktail Shack.

The hotel's original concept may whiff of gimmick but our series editor, Fiona Duncan, calls this is the real deal. It may be 'funky' but it certainly isn't naff. On top of this, the staff are charming.

Beaulieu Road, Brockenhurst,
Hampshire SO42 7QL

Tel 01590 622354
e-mail
info@thepighotel.com
website www.pighotel.com

Nearby Beaulieu National Motor
Museum, Bucklers Hard;
Lymington; New Forest wildlife
centres. **Location** in own extensive
grounds, in the heart of the New
Forest, close to Brockenhurst; ample
private car-parking **Food** breakfast,
lunch, dinner **Price** ££–£££ **Rooms**
26; 16 in main house, 10 in stable
yard; all with monsoon showers.
Most have larder cabinet, television,
DVD player. Family rooms have a
log burner or a freestanding bath.
Facilities restaurant, lounge, bar, spa
treatments, vegetable garden, guided
walks, cycling, tennis courts, pigsty
with pigs **Credit cards** AE, DC,
MC, V **Children** welcome **Disabled**
no special access **Pets** not allowed
Closed never
Proprietor Robin Hutson
Manger Jorge Gertrudes

The Pig
Country house hotel

In its earlier incarnations, we thought of
this place as a benchmark for the sort of
establishment we didn't want in the guide
– it was one of hundreds of nothing-special country house hotels. But now that
Robin Hutson, creator of the Hotel du Vin
chain and one of Britain's most inspired
hoteliers, has practised his magic on the
place, the result is hard to ignore.

Robin's wife Judy did the interior. It's
quite a contrast to the controlled, Georgian
exterior: a set piece of shabby-chic with
touches of anarchy. The conservatory-din-
ing room is the big draw: an imaginative,
light-filled space with a wonderful tiled
floor, pots of herbs on wooden boxes lining the outside windows and on every
table. Over the corridor in the drawing
room shabby-chic reasserts itself emphatically. The floor boards are distressed, and
'damaged' plasterwork on the walls
reveals areas of brickwork beneath – only
it's not damaged, it's *trompe l'oeil*. The bedrooms are truly comfortable.

Don't leave without a stroll through the
walled kitchen garden, where they grow
some of what's eaten in the dining room.

See also The Pig - near Bath, The Pig - at
Combe, The Pig - on the Beach and The Pig
- in the Wall (pages 30, 50, 75 and 150)
Their website: www.thepighotel.com

Bucklers Hard, Hampshire

Bucklers Hard, Beaulieu,
Hampshire SO42 7XB

Tel (01590) 616253
Fax (01590) 616297
e-mail enquiries@themaster-
builders.co.uk **website** www.themas-
terbuilders.co.uk

Nearby New Forest; Beaulieu;
Lymington.
Location overlooking Beaulieu river
at Bucklers Hard, 2 miles (3 km) SE
of Beaulieu, 9 miles (14 km) SE of
Lyndhurst; ample car parking
Food breakfast, lunch, dinner
Price £££ **Rooms** 26 double, 18 can
be twin; all rooms have phone, TV,
hairdryer, wi-fi, tea/coffee facilities,
complimentary Godminster vodka
Facilities sitting room, Riverview
restaurant, yachtsman's bar; terrace,
garden, pontoon available
Credit cards MC, V **Children** wel-
come **Disabled** access difficult
Pets 7 dog-friendly rooms
Closed never
Proprietors Hillbrooke Hotels

The Master Builder's
Riverside hotel

The location of this hotel really is special,
and historic, at the bottom end of a row
of 18thC shipwrights' cottages, looking
down on to the Beaulieu River. It contains a
bar that's popular with visiting yachtsmen,
and nearby is a maritime museum.

When Hillbrook Hotels took over some
years ago they carried out a well-needed
overhaul. The bedrooms in the main building
have a quirky character, combined with luxury. The 18thC house was lumbered some
years back with an unsympathetic modern
annexe, the Henry Adams Wing. Since our
last edition this has been refurbished, offering Posh Classic Rooms decorated with a
coastal feel. While these were always comfortable and attractive, they now have more
character.

The reception area is sophisticated, and
the newly refurbished Riverview restaurant
is designed to reflect a forest, and stream-
lined to creative intimate dining settings for
couples and parties. Expect 'modern British'
dishes. There is a large outdoor eating area,
again with great views of the Beaulieu River,
which comes into its own in summer when
the barbecue operates.

Hillbrooke Hotels specialise in hotels and
inns on country estates. In this edition of the
guide we also feature their places to stay in
Stamford (page 252).

Camber, East Sussex

New Lydd Road, Camber, Rye, East Sussex TN31 7RB

Tel 01797 225 057
e-mail
reservations@thegallivant.co.uk
website www.thegallivant.com

Nearby Camber Sands, Romney Salt Marshes, Dungeness, Rye.
Location 90 minutes from central London, 5 minutes from Rye, car park opposite **Food** breakfast, lunch, dinner **Price** £££–££££
Rooms 20 doubles; 4 Luxury Garden Rooms, 3 Baby Hampton Rooms, 2 Deck Rooms and 1 Snug Cain. All rooms have wi-fi, telephone, DVD player, flat-screen television, hairdryer, tea and coffee and Bramley toiletries
Facilities 2 function rooms, Beach Hut spa treatment room, coastal garden and shingle courtyard
Credit cards MC, V **Children** welcome **Disabled** access possible and all rooms are ground floor **Pets** dogs welcome **Closed** sometimes for a week in Jan
Manager Harry Cragoe

The Gallivant Hotel
Beach hotel

The Gallivant started in the Sixties as the Blue Dolphin Motel, when no doubt it saw its fair share of gallivants and their girls. It's still identifiable on the outside as being inspired by the California coast motel, but it's also buzzy, inexpensive and in a great location: Camber Sands is over the road, and Rye is five minutes by car.

The sunny restaurant, with bleached wood bar, simple tables and chairs, has a Scandi/New England feel, and the food is spot on – with ingredients sourced within 15 miles of the hotel. On a predominantly piscatorial menu, we enjoyed a pungent fish soup and salt-marsh lamb, with a creamy buttermilk panna cotta. The wine list has a lovely array of local sparkling varieties from which to choose.

When we visited, the bedrooms were motel rooms given a makeover – compact, with beach shack-style furniture, taupe walls and curtains – and in need of a bit of a lift. Since then new owner Harry Cragoe and his wife Sigrid have completely refurbished nine rooms, incorporating quirky retro touches, with an eye to The Hamptons, the expensive residential enclave on Long Island, near New York city. All bedrooms come with King or Super-King Hypnos mattresses, along with plump goose-down bedding.

Ockenden Lane, Cuckfield,
West Sussex RH17 5LD

Tel (01444) 416111
e-mail reservations@ockenden-
manor.co.uk
website www.hshotels.co.uk

Nearby Nyman's; Sissinghurst;
Wakehurst Place; Gatwick;
Brighton.
Location 2 miles (3 km) W of
Haywards Heath close to middle of
village, off A272; in 9-acre grounds,
with ample car parking
Food breakfast, lunch, afternoon tea,
dinner
Price £££
Rooms 28; 26 double, 2 single, all
with bath; all rooms have phone, TV,
hairdryer
Facilities sitting room, bar, dining
room; terrace, garden, spa
Credit cards AE, DC, MC, V
Children welcome
Disabled access possible in a couple
of rooms (enquire before); ramp
available to restaurant **Pets** not
accepted **Closed** never **Proprietors**
Miranda Carminger

Ockenden Manor
Manor house hotel

Anne Goodman made many changes
for the better here after taking over
this attractive 16th/17thC manor house.
Now her daughter Miranda owns the
hotel, and continues to keep up her high
standards.

Bedrooms are spacious and individual
(and crammed with giveaways); a superb
master suite with sombre panelling relies
on reds and greens to give a feeling of
brightness. Several of the bathrooms are
notably spacious, and they are well-equipped.
The main sitting room, though lavishly furnished, has a personal feel. Staff are friendly and obliging. (A notice in the hotel
states that whatever a hotel's character
and charm, it is only as good as its staff.)

Dinner, which is served in the new dining room with sweeping views towards the
Souths Down National Park, is another
highlight. Food is based on local produce,
with vegetables and herbs from the garden.

Although Ockenden Manor is popular
with business people, it is a human, comfortable hotel. 'Hidden away behind trees
and a high wall; quiet; good value', says our
reporter.

East Chisenbury, Wiltshire

East Chisenbury, Pewsey, Wiltshire
SN9 6AQ

Tel 01980 671124
e-mail troutbeck@redlionfree-
house.com

Nearby Area of Natural
Outstanding Beauty; Salisbury
Cathederal & Magna Carta;
Stonehenge; Longleat House &
Gardens; Safari Park; Avebury;
White Horse Trail. **Location** East
Chisenbury village
Food breakfast, lunch, dinner**Price**
£££ **Rooms** 5 doubles, 1 can also be
twin, all rooms have riverside views
& private decking, wi-fi, TV, tea &
coffee, outdoor weather kit, organic
handmade toiletries
Facilities dining room, pub, bar;
garden, private fishing
Credit cards MC, V **Children** wel-
come in pub **Disabled** 1 room with
wheelchair access **Pets** dogs wel-
come in pub and The Manser Room
Closed one week in Jan
Proprietors Brittany & Guy
Manning

Red Lion Freehouse
Village inn

The Red Lion is a quintessential English
village pub – *à la mode* – with a
Michelin star and five glamourous bedrooms. The delightful chef/patron, Guy
Manning, runs the pub with his equally
charming and hard-working wife and general manager, Brittany.

There's everything you could wish for in a
thatched pub: a log burner, beams, blackboards and assorted wooden tables and
chairs. However, we missed comfy sofas –
their absence made it feel static.

The food was superb for an inn, but perhaps
quite expensive compared with other similar establishments. But the care that Guy
and his close-knit team put into what is
essentially home cooking is of the highest order.
The rich and gamey menu features dishes
like herb roasted partridge served with
potato *mille'feuille,* parsnips, prunes and
roasting juice – Guy doesn't hold back on
flavour.

The five bedrooms are in a converted
bungalow, Troutbeck, along the lane. They
are a bit glitzy: silvery furniture and fake fur
throws, but the standard is high, and they
are an exhilarating contrast to the inn.
Thoughtful extras include well-stocked
minibar; a list of items you may have forgotten,
which Brittany can then provide for you; and
especially the views of the Hampshire
Avon, running through the garden.

East End, Hampshire

Lymington Road, Hampshire SO41
5SY

Tel 01590 626223
website www.eastendarms.co.uk

Nearby Exbury Gardens, Cowes,
New Forest, Buckler's Hard, Motor
Museum, Beaulieu.
Location on Lymington Road, half
way between Beaulieu and
Lymington, close to Solent shore
Food breakfast, lunch, dinner (not
Sunday night)
Price ££
Rooms 5 double/twin, all have
bath/shower, all with TV, wi-fi, gun
safe, tea/coffee facilities
Facilities bar, restaurant, terrace
Credit cards DC, MC, V
Children accepted
Disabled only to ground floor
Pets dogs in bar but not restaurant
or bedrooms
Closed 3-6 o'clock Monday to
Friday
Proprietor John Illsley

East End Arms
Country inn

An honest, affordable base on the
southern edge of the New Forest in a
backwater between Beaulieu and Lymington.
It's part of the renaissance since 2005 in
New Forest places to stay, joining the
quite recently refurbished Master
Builder's (page 98) and The Pig (page 97).

When owner John Illsley (the former
bass guitarist of Dire Straits) bought the
pub in the mid 1990s he got a letter from
the regulars: 'Hands off our bar' – they
wouldn't even let him repair the hole in
the ceiling. Most new owners of old pubs
would have turned the whole of the lower
floor into a gastropub eating area, but
Illsley had the sense to keep the old public bar intact. If you want posh food turn
left after the front door; if you want a
plain, bare floored room, with coal in the
grate and murmuring locals, real ale and a chatty bar maid, turn right.

Upstairs, John's wife Steph has created
five truly charming bedrooms: crisp
sheets, king-sized beds, OKA furniture,
Mulberry fabrics, walls decorated with
John's paintings. The result is a country
pub that is an up to date, comfortable
place to stay yet retains its integrity and
sense of identity. The food is mostly reliable, sometimes imaginative, above average for the price.

East Grinstead, West Sussex

Vowels Lane, near East Grinstead,
West Sussex RH19 4LJ

Tel (01342) 810567
e-mail info@gravetyemanor.co.uk
website www.gravetyemanor.co.uk

Nearby Wakehurst; Nyman's
Gardens; Glyndebourne
Location 4.5 miles (7 km) SW of
East Grinstead by B2110 at
Gravetye; in 35 acre grounds with
ample car parking
Food breakfast (for residents), lunch,
dinner, room service **Price** ££££
Rooms 17; 16 double, 1 single, all
with bath; all rooms have phone, TV,
hairdryer, bluetooth speaker on
request, wi-fi; 8 rooms have air con-
ditioning
Facilities 2 sitting rooms, bar, din-
ing room; terrace, garden, croquet
Credit cards AE, MC, V **Children**
welcome over 7 **Disabled** ramp
access but no adapted rooms
Pets not accepted (1 mile from ken-
nel) **Closed** never
Proprietors Jeremy and Elizabeth
Hosking

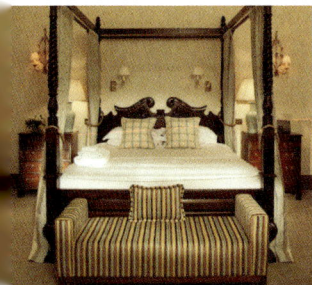

Gravetye Manor Hotel & Restaurant **Country hotel**

The country house hotel, now so much a part of the tourist scene in Britain, scarcely existed when Peter Herbert opened the doors of this serene Elizabethan house over 50 years ago. Under new ownership from February 2010, it had a multi-million pound refurbishment, and standards in every department remain unflaggingly high. Service consistently achieves the elusive aim of attentiveness without intrusion, while the food can still claim to be among the best in the county. A recent visitor, who had known the hotel for 30 years, remained as impressed as ever: 'A sleek operation that doesn't compromise.' However, another commented on 'lots of wealthy-looking people in sunglasses and strange-looking jogging suits'.

The pioneering gardener William Robinson lived in the house for half a century until his death in 1935. Great care is taken to maintain the various gardens he created; Robinson was also responsible for many features of the house as it is seen today – the mellow oak panelling and grand fireplaces in the calm, gracious sitting rooms, for example. Bedrooms – all immaculate – vary in size from the adequate to the enormous, and prices range accordingly.

East Hoathly, Sussex BN8 6EL

Tel (01825) 840216
Fax (01825) 840738
email stay@oldwhyly.co.uk
website www.oldwhyly.co.uk

Nearby Glyndebourne, Charleston Farm House, East Sussex National Golf Course, Batemans.
Location just off A22 S of Uckfield on road to Halland, ample car parking
Food breakfast, dinner
Price ££
Rooms 4 double with bath, 1 with shower
Facilities sitting room, dining room; terrace, garden, croquet, hard top tennis court, heated swimming pool, lake, walking paths
Credit cards not accepted
Children welcome
Disabled access difficult
Pets by arrangement
Closed never
Proprietor Sarah Burgoyne

Old Whyly
Country house guesthouse

Driving up to Old Whyly in the springtime is magical; owner Sarah Burgoyne has planted 4,000 tulip bulbs and at the right season, the lawn is ablaze with colour. Set in 40-acre grounds, with a duck-dotted lake, well-maintained gardens and walks that take in the nearby 600-acre stud farm, this Grade II listed 18thC manor has an enviable setting

Once you cross the well-gravelled drive and climb the front steps, you will be welcomed in Sarah's (and her dog, Noodle's) antique-filled home. The impressive family painting collection lines the walls, including a full-length portrait of Sarah herself. The sitting room has a roaring fire with inviting furniture – perfect for admiring the china collection or just reading a book. Bedrooms are spacious and comfortable. However, one of the best reasons to stay at Old Whyly is the food. Sarah, a passionate cook who trained in Paris, prepares excellent dishes and, although many of her customers tend to eat at Glyndebourne, Sarah is more than happy to provide dinner.

Breakfast includes honey from Sarah's bees kept in the orchard and eggs from the hens that wander about on the lawn.

East Lavant, West Sussex

Pook Lane, East Lavant, West
Sussex PO18 0AX

Tel 01243 527434
e-mail
info@royaloakeastlavant.co.uk
website
www.royaloakeastlavant.co.uk

Nearby Chichester, Littlehampton.
Location turn off A3 at Milford
Junction onto the A286 via
Haslemere and Midhurst. On enter-
ing Lavant take the left turn sign-
posted East Lavant. Royal Oak is just
past hump-back bridge
Food breakfast, lunch, dinner
Price ££-£££
Rooms 6 doubles, all have
bath/shower. 2 additional self-cater-
ing cottages
Facilities bar, restaurant, terrace,
garden **Credit cards** AE, MC, V
Children welcome
Disabled not suitable
Pets allowed in bar area, restaurant
and a couple of the rooms
Closed never
Proprietor Cirrus Inns

The Royal Oak
Country inn

The Royal Oak is in beautiful
Goodwood country just two miles
from Chichester. With a widespread reputation for its food – the restaurant serves
a combination of French, Mediterranean
and New English cuisine with wines to
match – the Inn is always busy at night, and
a stay in one of six well-appointed rooms
makes for an encapsulating short break.

Each room is lavishly furnished and with
all mod-cons, including flat-screen TV and
a DVD player. The exposed beams and
brick work offer a pleasant old-and-new
style we particularly liked.

Rooms in the Sussex Barn and Deluxe
Flint Cottage however, just a few short
steps from your dinner table, are univer-
sally acclaimed. A touch small, perhaps, but
greatly prepared and provided for and
with every angle and idea covered (including cots for children and complimentary
morning papers for those with a little
more time on their hands). Staff are always
on hand and obliging and the buffet breakfast is top-notch.

The Street, Egerton, Kent, TN27 9DJ

Tel 01233 756 599
e-mail digin@thebarrowhouse.co.uk
website thebarrowhouse.co.uk

Nearby Leeds Castle (7.3 m),
Biddenden Vineyards (9.8 m), The
Granary Spa (5.9 m) and Woodside
spa (6.9 m). Chart Hills Golf Club
(7.4 m)
Location halfway between
Maidstone and Ashford in the idyllic
village of Egerton
Food breakfast, lunch, dinner & bar
menu, Pizza menu available from
spring-autumn
Price ££ **Rooms** 3; 2 large doubles,
1 double/twin; 2 have shower/bath, 1
has shower only; all rooms come
with coffee/tea, TV, wi-fi
Facilities bar, live music
Credit cards V, D, VD, M
Children welcome
Disabled not suitable
Pets no access (dogs allowed in bar)
Closed never
Proprietors Dane & Sarah
Allchorne

The Barrow House
Village inn

This pub has much in common with its
sister-pub The Milk House (page 149).
Its white weatherboard exterior has all the
traditional features you'd expect from an
inn dating back to 1576, when it was built
using timbers from sailing ships (the name
refers to an ancient barrow in a nearby
field). Inside it's been given a contemporary
makeover, with Farrow & Ball paintwork in
chalky blues and creams. These are artfully
combined with more rustic features, such
as stone floors, antler chandeliers and two
open fires in the cosy bar area — which still
bears the signatures of American and
Canadian airmen who frequented The
George when they were stationed nearby
during the Second World War.

There are three comfortable and attractive bedrooms upstairs (our only quibble
was with the somewhat cramped bathrooms). They're ideal bolt-holes from
which to explore Egerton: that rare breed
of village that still exudes a thriving sense
community spirit. It's dominated by the
13thC ragstone church at its centre, with a
network of small lanes leading out of the
village, offering stunning views of the Weald
of Kent and Ashford Valley.

The menu goes well beyond traditional
pub grub, with diverse options for 'Tear &
Share', 'Grazing', 'Small Plates' as well as
sides and mains.

Emsworth, Hampshire

47 South Street, Emsworth,
Hampshire PO10 7EG

Tel 01243 375592
Fax 01243 372257
email info@36onthequay.co.uk
website www.36onthequay.co.uk

Nearby Hayling Island, Portsmouth,
Chichester, South Downs National
Park, Portsmouth ferries 10 minutes
Location Emsworth is on A259
between Havant and Chichester
Food breakfast, lunch, dinner
Price £££-££££
Rooms 7; 5 doubles with bath/show-
er; rooms have TV, phone, tea/coffee
facilities, iPod docking station, wi-fi
Facilities restaurant, bar
Credit cards DC, MC, V
Children accepted
Disabled access to restaurant only
Pets dogs accepted in the cottages
Closed 2 weeks in Jan, one week in
May and 1 week in Oct/Nov
Proprietors Raymon and Karen
Farthing

36 on the Quay
Village restaurant-with-rooms

Chef Ramon Farthing got his Michelin
star in 1997, but Restaurant 36 on the
Quay only became a place to stay recently. He and wife Karen (front of house)
developed the accommodation cautiously ,
achieving five doubles plus two cottages
over several years.

In fact the operation feels like a wise
balance of form with content. The food,
served in an appropriately smart (but not
flashy or unrelaxing) dining room overlooking Emsworth Quay and Bay, is consistently delicious and imaginative. Ramon's
training was French classical, he migrated
to modern British and has now added a
Scandinavian influence – fresh, clean
flavours, ingredients that speak out. One
pudding, peanut parfait, could be unique.

The reasonably priced, comfortable
rooms have quirky corners (the house is
listed). Saffron is an apartment with kitchenette, useful for a family; Nutmeg has a
great harbour view; Vanilla, the top room,
has a lovely bay window seat, again with
the harbour view. Neutral, off whites and
variations on vanilla predominate.

There's nothing like this in the area –
the waterfront location is charming and
endlessly interesting. It would make a great
weekend break, or a spoiling stopover
before an early ferry from Portsmouth.

Fletching, East Sussex

Fletching, near Uckfield,
East Sussex TN22 3SS

Tel (01825) 722890
Fax (01825) 722810
e-mail info@thegriffininn.co.uk
website www.thegriffininn.co.uk

Nearby Sheffield Park;
Glyndebourne; Ashdown Forest.
Location in village 1 mile (1.5 km)
E of A275; with car parking
Food breakfast, lunch, dinner
Price ££
Rooms 12 double and 1 twin, 6 with
bath, 7 with shower; all have wi-fi,
TV with DVD and radio, hairdryer
Facilities bars, restaurant, bar bil-
liards; terrace, patio, garden
Credit cards AE, DC, MC, V
Children welcome
Disabled 2 rooms on ground floor
Pets accepted in bar, but not in bed-
rooms or restaurant
Closed Christmas Day
Manager Samantha Barlow

The Griffin Inn
Village inn

On our latest visit to the Griffin Inn, the
pub was packed, the dining room was
almost full and the kitchen was bustling.
Successful? Evidently. But still welcoming and
cosy? Definitely.

This 16thC village inn has been owned by
the Pullan family for 35 years and it maintains its winning combination of good food
(it can claim to be Britain's first gastro-pub)
and pretty bedrooms with beams, low ceilings and four-poster beds. Everything is a bit
uneven, quaint, on a small scale – but
endearing rather than cramped. Beds are
inviting and bathrooms are in an attractive
Victorian style, with funky porthole mirrors.
That said, some of the rooms were looking
a little tired on our last visit; but we imagine
that re-investment is on the way.

The pub has more beams, panelling, open
fires and hunting prints, while the old public
bar has been turned into the 'Club Bar', with
a sofa and a woodburner. Good food is
always at hand either in the pub or in the
restaurant, which uses fresh seasonal ingredients and local organic vegetables. Both
menus change daily. The wine list has over
100 wines, many of which are priced at
under £25 per bottle. You can take your
drink out to the garden overlooking
Sheffield Park and enjoy live jazz at the
weekends. In summer, there's a full-scale
BBQ serving Modern European dishes.

1 Hill Street, Hastings, East Sussex
TN34 3HU

Tel 01424 430014
email res@swanhousehastings.co.uk
website
www.swanhousehastings.co.uk

Nearby town centre, 1066 country,
Rye, Camber Sands
Location in town centre, just behind
East Parade which runs along
seafront
Food breakfast
Price ££-£££
Rooms 4 doubles with TV, DVD
Facilities sitting room, telephone,
wi-fi, outdoor patio
Credit cards AE, MC, V
Children accepted
Disabled 1 ground-floor bedroom
Pets not accepted
Closed Christmas
Proprietors Brendan McDonagh
and Lionel Copley

Swan House
Town house guesthouse

In its building dating from the 14th century,
Swan House, Hastings, could hardly lack
old world charm. Aged timbers surface
everywhere, while each of the four bedrooms has its own antique theme. The
Garden Room uses dark wood and heavy
curtains; the Renaissance Room is lighter,
with lace curtains and hand-painted walls,
while the Artisan Room is full of light and
bright dashes of colour. Homely charm
threads the whole interior. They are proud
of breakfast here, using local produce in a
choice of traditional cooked dishes. They
even produce their own toiletry range for
guests.

Swan House is in the middle of Hastings,
so parking can be a problem, but owners
Brendan and Lionel provide permits for
the municipal car parks nearby. Some
reporters mention noise from adjoining
rooms and passages, a natural hazard in
buildings this old, but for most visitors this
would be a quibble: this place offers a nice
combination of charm and careful management.

Littlestone, Kent

Coast Road, Littlestone,
New Romney, Kent TN28 8QY

Tel (01797) 364747
Fax (01797) 367156
email enquiries@romneybayhouse-hotel.co.uk **website** www.romney-bayhousehotel.co.uk

Nearby Rye; Dungeness Lighthouse; Sandwich.
Location in New Romney, take Station Road to sea front, turn left, and follow hotel signs for 1 mile; car parking
Food breakfast, weekday sandwich lunch, weekend light lunch, dinner
Price ££-£££
Rooms 10 double and twin, all with bath or shower; all rooms have TV, hairdryer
Facilities sitting room, dining room, look-out room, tea room; terrace, garden, croquet, boules, beach adjacent to golf course
Credit cards AE, MC, V
Children accepted over 14
Disabled access difficult
Pets not accepted **Closed** Christmas
Proprietors Clinton and Lisa Lovell

Romney Bay House
Seaside hotel

The approach through sprawling Littlestone is unpromising, particularly in the dark when you don't know where you're heading. But this dignified 1920s house, built by Clough Williams Ellis for American columnist Hedda Hopper, has a superb position between the sea and Romney Marsh. Clinton and Lisa Lovell took over Romney Bay House in 2003, and have kept the style of the interior much the same, while upgrading the bathrooms. The interiors are reminiscent of a small hotel in Provence, with plenty of French furniture and fabrics. This is a thoroughly relaxed place: the cosy bar; the warm, fire-lit sitting room packed with groups of comfortable, inviting chairs; breakfasts in the pretty conservatory; drinks or cream teas on the terrace in fine weather. Dinner is a non-choice four-course menu, planned around the resident diners each evening and made with local produce.

An upstairs 'look-out' room has the feel of a beach house, with piles of towels for swimming, wicker chairs and sea shells. Bedrooms have creamy cottons, fresh white bedlinen, bright checks, and antiques; those on the first floor have full length windows, allowing uninterrupted views out to sea.

66 Turnmill Street, London, EC1M 5RR

Tel 0207 7014 0240
e-mail enquiries@blueprintlivinga-partments.com
website www.blueprintlivingapart-ments.com/66-turnmill-street

Nearby 1 min from Farringdon Rail Station. St Pancreas Rail Station, Hatton Garden (jewelry quarter) St Paul's Cathedral, Smithfield and the Barbican. Parking nearby. **Location** Clerkenwell **Food** self-catered apartments; restaurants near by **Price** ££££ **Rooms** 14 apartments with bedroom, bathroom, living room and kitchen; all with air-condi-tioning, iPod dock, direct dial phone, safe, television, kitchen uten-sils) **Facilities** wi-fi, air-condition-ing, maid service, CCTV, luggage storage, lift **Credit cards** AE, MC, V **Children** welcome- cots and high chairs available on request **Disabled** lift to all floors **Pets** not allowed **Closed** never **Proprietor** Blueprint Living Apartments

66 Turnmill Street
Self-catering apartments

The entrance to 66 Turnmill Street is down an insignificant side street close to Farringdon Station, but once inside the atmosphere is stylish and sophisticated. We think these apartments will suit a wide range of tastes and needs, and they offer a winning combination of homely comfort with professional style.

When we visited soon after opening, most of the apartments were already booked. Each is similar in size and style: only colour scheme and layout differed a little in each. Heavy wooden panelling, grey fabrics and solid, comfortable furniture are key elements. A bit of colour is added in the kitchen units and the quirky cushions on the sofa, but overall the effect is muted and calm. Apartments on the higher floors are the best: they have more light and views of the historical buildings surrounding Turnmill Street. Bathrooms are white, bright and modern.

52 Cambridge Street, Pimlico,
London, SW1V 4QQ

Tel 0203 019 8610
email london@artistresidence.co.uk
website www.artistresidencelon-
don.co.uk

Nearby Victoria station, Sloane
Square, Belgravia, Tate Britain,
Houses of Parliament, Big Ben,
London Eye, Saatchi Gallery,
Oxford St
Location a quiet road in Pimlico, 5
mins from Victoria Train Station
Food breakfast, lunch, dinner,
snacks **Price** £££-££££
Rooms 10; 7 double, 1 double/twin,
2 suites; all have wi-fi, TV, radio, air
conditioning, mini fridge, tea and
coffee making facilities, safe, show-
er; largest rooms have baths
Facilities restaurant, cocktail bar,
sitting room, private dining room
Credit cards AE, DC, MC, V
Children accepted
Disabled no special facilities
Pets not accepted **Closed** never
Proprietors Justin and Charlotte
Salisbury

Artist Residence
London **City hotel**

This Georgian townhouse, once a run-
down pub, is a welcome addition to
our London section, and the newest hotel
in the Art Residences' mini-chain. Like its
siblings it has been characterfully converted into a stylish but relaxing place. Rooms
and suites are split across three floors and
vary in size, but make the most of their
Georgian dimensions: even the smallest
rooms have been thoughtfully designed.
The modern-rustic style, with exposed
brick, distressed leather and wooden
floorboards, is low key, but only in comparison to its more extrovert sister hotels
and we like the bathrooms, with their
retro tiles and modern fittings.

Their popular bistro-style restaurant,
The Cambridge Street Kitchen, is run by
head chef Radek Nitkowski and serves
seasonal British produce. After dinner,
relax in a comfy chair in front of an open
fire in the Club Room. Adjoining is a room
with a ping-pong table that can also be
used for meetings or private dining.

In the basement is the trendy cocktail
lounge where 'mixologists' serve drinks
infused with celery and foamed with egg-
whites. It's snug, dimly lit and decorated
with iconographic prints and modern-
retro furniture. Very well located for a
London hotel: on a quiet street five minutes walk from Victoria station.

499 Old York Road, Wandsworth
SW18 1TF

Tel 020 8870 2537
email alma@youngs.co.uk
website www.almawandsworth,com

Nearby Wandsworth Common,
Wimbledon Common, Battersea
Park, Kew Gardens
Location Waterloo 15 minutes by
train, on-street parking available
Food breakfast, lunch, dinner
Price ££-£££
Rooms 23; 13 doubles, 3
double/twin, 6 twin; all have
bath/shower, with TV, phone,
tea/coffee facilities, hairdryer, iron-
ing board
Facilities bar, restaurant, wi-fi, lug-
gage storage
Credit cards AE, MC, V
Children accepted
Disabled 2 easy access rooms
Pets not accepted
Closed never
Proprietors Young's

The Alma
City restaurant-with-rooms

Built in 1866 and named to commemo-
rate the Crimean Battle of Alma in
1854, shiny green tiles and a domed roof
mark this place out as an example of the
London pub boom of the 19th century.

Now it has a new lease of life. Young's
the brewer landlord have turned four
pokey ground-floor rooms into one
impressive one, with a circular bar in the
centre. A fine white plasterwork frieze was
revealed during conversion, as were the
solid mahogany staircase, woodwork and
fin de siècle mosaics.

Despite claiming to be 'a friendly, local
pub' on its website, The Alma is more than
that now, with a restaurant as well, adjacent to the bar. You'll find all sorts: chaps in
pinstripes propping up the bar, blokes in
overalls arguing on the pavement after
watching the football on a screen. Food is
served in the dining room by busy waitresses from a kitchen open to view and a
country-style pine table that doubles as a
work station. Bar and dining spaces inter-
act well; in either room everyone is happy.

The 23 bedrooms are well equipped,
with armchairs, desks and the latest technology. The decoration is lively, and some
have floor to ceiling windows. A laidback
option for those who don't want the
prices or chic formality of central London.

50 Great Cumberland Place, Marble
Arch, London W1H 7FD

Tel 0207 724 4700
e-mail info@thearchlondon.com
website www.thearchlondon.com
Nearby Hyde Park, Oxford Street,
the City
Location north-east corner of Hyde
Park, short walk from Marble Arch
tube
Food breakfast, lunch, dinner in
Hunter 486 restaurant, 24 hour
room service
Price ££££
Rooms 82; all have bath/shower,
with TV, wi-fi, internet radio, DVD
player, iPod docking station,
Nespresso machine
Facilities restaurant, bar, Le Salon
de Champagne, 3 conference rooms
Credit Cards all major
Children welcome
Disabled ramp, disabled rooms on
ground floor
Pets welcome
Closed never
Proprietor Mr Bejerano

The Arch
City hotel

With 82 bedrooms The Arch is signifi-
cantly larger than our usual entry, but
it feels intimate. A two-minute walk from
Marble Arch tube, the lovely Georgian
townhouse is a quiet haven for guests who
want to be in the centre of town. It may be
luxurious, but it's not pompous – one of the
new breed of city hotels for people who
take the latest gadgets in their rooms for
granted and who want to feel relaxed in
their surroundings.

The striking bedrooms are more
designed than homely, but with welcome
extras such as complimentary soft drinks,
Nespresso machines and bedside digital
radios. We liked the common theme in the
rooms and suites of a single wall decorated
with individual, retro wallpaper.

The hotel's cleverest concept is the cocktail lounge that flows into a zinc-topped bar
area and on into a dining space with an
open-to-view kitchen. This is the heart of
the operation, and you can dine and breakfast anywhere you like in these three areas.
Dishes are well-executed. Its Hunter 486
Restaurant & Bar, named after the 1950s
dialling code for Marlybone, presents a 'Best
of British' inspired seasonal menu drawing
on classics like fish & chips. It produces its
own jams, chocolates, breads and speciality
éclairs for afternoon tea – impressive for a
boutique London hotel just off Oxford Street.

12 Folgate Street, Spitafields,
London, E1 6BX

Tel 020 7377 4390
Fax 020 7377 4391
e-mail
reservations@battylangleys.co.uk
website www.battylangleys.com

Nearby Dennis Severs' House,
Christ Church, East End/West End
of London **Location** in heart of
Spitafields, located on site of
Medieval priory St Mary Spital; now
a residential area thronged with bars
and restaurants **Food** breakfast-in-
bed, 24 hr room service
Price ££££
Rooms 29; 28 double, 1 single; 7
with sofa-beds to accomodate chil-
dren or extra adult; 2 suites and 1
deluxe with access to private terrace
Facilities 3 sitting rooms, books,
honesty bar, courtyard garden area
Credit Cards V, MC, AE, Debit
Children welcome
Disabled 1 specially adapted room
for wheelchair access, lift
Pets not allowed **Closed** never
Chief Executive Caroline Conaty

Batty Langley's
City hotel

The third hotel, and period-passion-proj-
ect, of Douglas Blain and Peter McKay
(see Hazlitts, page 124 and The Rookery,
page 134), Batty's was spun out lovingly over
five years, before quietly opening its doors in
2015. Georgian-themed with all the trimmings, everything – from the carved wooden
bedsteads to the housekeeping trolleys – has
been faithfully sourced, or recreated by an
army of local artisans. The result is an explo-
sion of deep-wine hues, sumptuous damasks
and gilded stucco – with characterful portraits and *objets d'art* at every turn.

Not that Batty's takes itself too seriously.
Taking their cue from Georgian wit, visual
riffs abound: mirrors that fold away to reveal
TVs, toilet-cum-thrones – even secret
rooms. The 29 regal bedrooms are named
after historic Spitafield residents, with espe-
cial preference for 'tarts and thieves'.

Batty's may be grand but it's also homely,
and eminently private. Because they eschew
mass-marketing (preferring word-of-mouth)
you'll often have the sitting room to yourself,
along with its well-stocked honesty bar. An
indulgent breakfast in bed is almost manda-
tory, while the charming staff are on-call 24
hours a day for room service. The hotel is
filled with 3,500 antique books that are playfully moved about between rooms – an apt
expression of a hotel bent on storytelling.
A Spitafields institution in the making.

33 Beaufort Gardens, London
SW3 1PP

Tel (020) 7584 5252
Fax (020) 7589 2834
e-mail enquiries@thebeaufort.co.uk
website www.thebeaufort.co.uk

Nearby Harrods; Victoria and
Albert Museum.
Location off Brompton Road, just
W of Harrods; pay and display park-
ing in street
Food breakfast; room service
Price ££££
Rooms 29; 18 double and twin, 7
suites and 4 single, all with bath or
shower; all rooms have phone, TV,
Sky, CD player, air-conditioning,
fax/modem points, hairdryer; wi-fi,
fax/answering machines on request
Facilities sitting room, bar **Credit
cards** AE, DC, MC, V
Children accepted
Disabled access difficult
Pets not accepted
Closed never

The Beaufort
City bed-and-breakfast

Three Harrods doormen in a row gave
our inspector unerring directions for
the hundred-yard walk to The Beaufort,
part of a Victorian terrace overlooking a
quiet Knightsbridge cul-de-sac. This is still
one of the few hotels in the world which
surprises you with what doesn't appear
later on your bill. Feel like a bottle of
water? No charge. Soft drink? Cream tea?
The answer's still no charge.

All the rooms are different, some decorated in muted pastels, others following in
the cheerful footsteps of the public areas.
Each room has a CD player and portable
stereo and, for those who need added pro-
tection from the English weather, there are
also chocolates, shortbread and umbrellas.
And then there are the flowers. Plenty of
them. Many are real, but most are hanging
on the walls as part of the enormous collection of English floral watercolours.
Noted for the friendiness of its staff, the
Beaufort has many faithful regulars.

61-63 Petersham Road, Richmond
Upon Thames, London TW10 6UT

Tel (020) 8940 0902
e-mail info@thebingham.co.uk
website www.thebingham.co.uk

Nearby Thames, Hampton Court
Palace, Royal Botanic Gardens at
Kew, Syon House, Ham House
Location 20 mins from Heathrow
on A307, 8 min walk from
Richmond station
Food breakfast, lunch, afternoon tea,
dinner
Price ££££
Rooms 15 double and twin; air-con-
ditioning, TV, DVD player, radio,
iPod dock, wi-fi, shower
Facilities dining room, 2 conference
rooms, bar
Credit cards AE, DC, MC, V
Children welcome
Disabled lift access to event rooms,
access to restaurant
Pets guide dogs only
Closed never
Proprietor Samantha Trinder

The Bingham
Riverside restaurant-with-rooms

Here's a good example of an 'amateur'
London hotel keeper competing with
the 'professionals' – ie corporate hotel groups
– and being every bit as good if not better.

The Bingham is slick and glamorous, and
could be, almost, part of a hotel group: its
contemporary, interior designed look is
one you often see. It seemed, at first
glance, 'professional' rather than 'amateur'.
But you soon realize that it isn't: because
of the warmth of the staff; the pristine way
the place is kept; and the cohesive atmosphere which makes people feel at home.

In 1984, the Trinders bought the two
Georgian town houses and turned them
into a B&B. In 2001, their daughter
Samantha joined and turned it into what it
is today – a lovely place to dine and stay.

When we visited the rooms were
soothing, spotless and well equipped, with
comfortable beds, if a bit dull. They've since
been refurbished, and we'd be interested
to hear reports. You wake to the river at
the end of the garden, with the towpath
and rowing boats beyond. A balcony runs
the length of the restaurant – this is a subtly opulent room that is successful by anyone's standards.

Chef Andrew Cole's immaculate dishes are
the equal of their surroundings. Professionalism,
mixed with the pride of an independent
'amateur' owner, is at work here.

22 Basil Street, London SW3 1AT

Tel 0207 589 5171 **Fax** 0207 225 0011 **email** reservations@capitalhotel.co.uk **website** www.capitalhotel.co.uk

Nearby Harrods, Harvey Nichols, Sloane Street, Brompton Arcade, Hyde Park, South Kensington Museums **Location** Knightsbridge, close to Harrods and Harvey Nichols **Food** breakfast, lunch, dinner, afternoon tea **Price** ££££ **Rooms** 49; 8 suites and 7 doubles. All rooms have air-conditioning, radio, television, TV, emails and films on demand, hairdryer, mini-bar **Facilities** Outlaw's restaurant, 2 function rooms, wi-fi, laundry/dry cleaning, international newspapers, cot, babysitting, private car-parking, 24 hour room service, The Peak health club and gym **Credit cards** all major **Children** welcome **Disabled** access unavailable **Pets** guide dogs **Closed** never **Proprietor** Warwick Hotels **Manager** Kate Levin

The Capital
City hotel

A firm favourite of our series editor Fiona Duncan, The Capital's outstanding reputation has been long established and remains unfaltering. Opened in 1971, it remains faithful to its original concept, to be a family-run hotel in the busy and popular heart of Knightsbridge. Guests can be near Harrods, Harvey Nichols and Hyde Park and get relief from the bustle back within the hotel's luxurious, comfortable atmosphere.

Staff are notoriously brilliant: Clive, the head concierge, can claim to be London's finest, and always goes beyond expectations. He will even take guests jogging around Hyde Park. Likewise in the cosy bar, César the barman holds cocktail master classes for guests, promising a wonderfully fun evening. Nathan Outlaw runs the Michelin-starred seafood restaurant Outlaw's, and hosts events and masterclasses throughout the year.

In each bedroom the decoration is typically English, with tasteful colour schemes and traditional furniture. Luxury, handmade mattresses and Egyptian cotton sheets add to the comfort.

Bathrooms are marble and beautiful, with the attention to detail of bathrobes and toiletries that we like.

Camberwell Church Street,
London SE5 8TR

Tel (020) 7703 5984
Fax (020) 7385 4110
e-mail info@churchstreethotel.com
website www.churchstreethotel.com

Location in busy high street near
Camberwell Green; parking in nearby residential street with permits
(£5) from reception.
Nearby South London Gallery, Oval
cricket ground, clubs, London Eye
20 minutes by bus, also County Hall
(Saatchi Gallery); leisure centres
Food breakfast, dinner **Price** ££
Rooms 28; 18 double, 9 single, 1
triple; all rooms have own bathroom
except 3 doubles and 5 singles which
have shared bathroom; all rooms
have TV, hairdryer; most have flat-
screen TV, DVD, air-con **Facilities**
breakfast 24-hour room-bar, with
honesty bar; tapas restaurant
Cards AE, MC, V **Disabled** not
suitable **Children** welcome; under
six, free in parents' room **Closed**
never **Proprietors** Jose and Mel
Raido

Church Street Hotel
City hotel

The conventional name and restrained exterior give no hint of what's inside. In reception, a gold painted altar for the desk; colourful ikons on the walls; French tiles on the floor. Swirly patterned carpets lead you upstairs; lurid religious paintings hang in the passages; custom-made brown bedroom doors have iron studs. The signals are a little confusing, but hip-60s-Latin-American with a contemporary twist more or less sums it up. Your bedroom is likely to burst with colour: our reporter's was cobalt blue with a comfortable hand-made wrought-iron bed, painted crucifixes in high alcoves and hand-painted Mexican tiles in the bathroom.

Spanish-Greek brothers José and Mel Raido created this place, wanting to do something refreshing and affordable – and they have. Their success is borne out by the generally youthful, cool crowd from all over the world that you'll meet in the walnut-panelled breakfast room/bar. The Angels and Gypsies restaurant, downstairs, is a delight. It's tapas, done well – fine local ingredients; relaxed and highly-skilled staff. A cocktail bar called 'Communion' has recently opened in the basement.

Located in noisy, multi-ethnic Camberwell, just along from the Green, but Oval tube, with fast access to the centre, is just around the corner. Nothing like this anywhere else in Britain.

2 Warrington Crescent, Little
Venice, London W9 1ER

Tel (020) 7286 1052
e-mail reservations@colonnadeho-
tel.co.uk
website www.colonnadehotel.co.uk

Nearby Little Venice.
Location 1-minute walk from
Warwick Avenue tube, 3 car parking
spaces in garage, £15 per night, must
be pre-booked
Food breakfast, lunch, dinner, 24 hr
room service, brunch, afternoon tea
Price £££
Rooms 43; 35 double, 5 twin, 3 sin-
gle, most with shower, some with
bath; all rooms have TV, stereo,
phone, minibar, safe, hairdryer,
trouser press, iron
Facilities sitting room, restaurant
with terrace, bar
Credit cards AE, DC, MC, V
Children welcome
Disabled not suitable
Pets guide dogs only
Closed never
Manager Dev Nandy

The Colonnade
City hotel

Set in Little Venice, with its canals and bridges, The Colonnade manages to overcome the trappings of a large hotel to provide a private place to stay. The building itself occupies two Victorian town houses that were built in 1865 as private resi-dences. In the late 1800s, it was used as a girls' school and, in the early 1900s, it became a maternity hospital. Alan Turing, creator of the first computer and the man who solved the Enigma code, was born here, and you'll find a suite named after him. When the building later became a hotel, Sigmund Freud stayed here while waiting for his house in Hampstead to be finished. In his suite, a bed sits in a gallery above a sitting room with enormous floor-to-ceiling win-dows. In the JFK Suite, you can sleep in the four-poster bed built for President Kennedy's state visit in 1962. The rest of the bedrooms are done out in three smart colour schemes: black and gold, green and gold or red and gold. In the sitting room, comfy sofas, attractive stripy chairs, an open coal fire and complimentary sherry, port and lollipops offset the strange artificial topiary.

In the lower ground floor, the achingly hip bar and restaurant – recently refurbished with very smart results, and renamed Banu – serves European and Persian fare.

10 Monmouth Street, London
WC2H 9HB

Tel (020) 7806 1000
Fax (020) 7806 1100
e-mail covent@firmdale.com
website www.firmdale.com

Nearby Covent Garden; Royal
Opera House; West End theatres.
Location in fairly quiet street
between Shaftesbury Avenue and St
Martin's Lane; metered parking or
public car park nearby
Food breakfast, lunch, dinner; room
service
Price ££££ **Rooms** 58; 52 double
and twin, 6 suites; 6 single, all with
bath; all rooms have phone, TV,
video, CD player, fax/modem point,
air-conditioning, minibar, hairdryer
Facilities drawing room, restaurant,
bar, library, work-out room, beauty
treatment room, screening room,
meeting rooms **Credit cards** AE,
MC, V **Children** accepted **Disabled**
access possible, lift/elevator
Pets not accepted **Closed** never
Proprietors Tim and Kit Kemp

Covent Garden Hotel
City hotel

The group of seductive London hotels
owned by Tim and Kit Kemp includes
eight sprinkled across London and two in
New York. They began with Dorset Square
and then opened several more similar
town house hotels, before becoming more
expansive here in Covent Garden, but
without losing any of their previous assur-
ance. The latest addition is Ham Yard Hotel
opening in 2014.

Monmouth Street is an attractive and
quiet cobbled street ideally placed for theatre and boutique shopping. The building
was formerly a French hospital, which Tim
and Kit (she is the Design Director responsible for all the decoration) have transformed into a hotel that at once feels glamorous, yet welcoming and not in the least
intimidating. A stunning drawing room and
library stretches across the first floor, with a
well-stocked honesty bar at one end, where
guests can help themselves. On the ground
floor is Brasserie Max bar and restaurant,
serving tasty, simply cooked dishes, or
there's a well-balanced room service menu.

Bedrooms have been individually
designed, although each possesses a matching fabric-covered mannequin, and they all
have superb granite bathrooms. One bedroom has a memorable four-poster bed.
The cosy attic rooms are also delightful.

9 Camp Road, Wimbledon
Common, London SW19 4UN

Tel (020) 8619 1300
e-mail reservations@foxand-
grapeswimbledon.co.uk
website www.foxandgrapeswimble-
don.co.uk

Nearby Wimbledon village, central
London
Location Camp Road, short drive
from Wimbledon train and under-
ground station
Food breakfast, lunch, dinner
Price ££
Rooms 3 doubles, all have
bath/shower, all with TV and
tea/coffee facilities
Facilities restaurant, wi-fi
Credit cards AE, DC, MC, V
Children accepted but no extra beds
for children over 2
Disabled access possible to restau-
rant and pub, but not to rooms
Pets not accepted in bedrooms
Closed never
Proprietor Jolly Fine Pubs

Fox and Grapes
Restaurant-with-rooms

It's not a bad idea, staying in this modest
pub on Wimbledon Common instead of
an expensive central hotel. Kensington is
40 minutes away, yet the feel of the Fox
and Grapes is that of a country inn, especially at weekends, when it is jammed with
muddy dogs and their owners.

Or rather, according to *les frères français*, the
Bosis, who started the place, an English
version of something peculiarly French – a
bouchon – a neighbourhood bar where the
food is hearty, and the owner is key.

Chef Director Paul Merrett oversees a
menu of robust dishes that echo meat-
heavy *bouchon* fare. Quality cuts of steak,
braised ox cheek – eaten at plain deal
tables quickly laid with cutlery when you
are ready to begin.

The building itself is unusual – one huge
room, a beamed village-hall-style extension, with a stylish bar and a kitchen open
to view. The atmosphere is certainly convivial (though noisy when busy).

The bedrooms are quite well decorated
and equipped, but small, with nowhere to
put a sponge bag in our tiny bathroom.
Breakfast is taken in the pub, somewhat
desolate in the early morning and smelling
of beer. Nevertheless, the Fox and Grapes
is *très sympa*, as the French say.

190 Queen's Gate, London
SW7 5EX

Tel (020) 7584 6601
Fax (020) 7589 8127
e-mail reservations@gorehotel.com
website www.gorehotel.com

Nearby Kensington Gardens; Hyde
Park; Royal Albert Hall; Harrods.
Location on Queen's Gate; metered
parking and public car park nearby
Food breakfast, lunch, dinner
Price ££££
Rooms 50; 44 double, 6 single or
twin, all with bath or shower; all
rooms have phone, TV, DVD, mini-
bar, hairdryer, safe, wi-fi, 24 hr
concierge
Facilities library/sitting room, bar,
restaurant
Credit cards AE, MC, V
Children welcome
Disabled access possible, lift/elevator
Pets not accepted
Closed never
Proprietor Starhotels Collezione

The Gore
City hotel

In 1990 the team who opened Hazlitt's (see opposite) bought this Victorian town house (long established as a hotel) set in a wide tree-lined street near Kensington Gardens and Hyde Park, and gave it the Hazlitt treatment: bedrooms furnished with period antiques, walls enlivened with pictures, and they recruited a young and friendly staff, trained to give efficient but informal service. It's since been taken over by Starhotels, but the smart Victorian interiors remain in tact.

It has character by the bucketload; walls whose every square inch is covered with prints and oil paintings; bedrooms furnished with antiques, each with its own style – a gallery in one room, Judy Garland's bed in another. There is also an impressive dossier in each room describing what to do locally – 'put together with verve and a feel for what the guest might really want'. The panelled bar on the ground floor is a popular rendezvous for non-residents as well as guests. Across the hallway is their restaurant, 190 Queen's Gate, headed by Michelin-starred chef Daniel Galmiche. which offers lighthearted French dishes with a British twist. The place is stylish, with rosewood panels and red chairs.

Reports on the new management are welcome.

6 Frith Street, Soho Square, London
W1D 3JA

Tel (020) 7434 1771
Fax (020) 7439 1524
e-mail reservations@hazlitts.co.uk
website www.hazlittshotel.com

Nearby Oxford Street; Piccadilly
Circus; Covent Garden; theatres.
Location in Soho, between Oxford
Street and Shaftesbury Avenue; pub-
lic car parks nearby
Food breakfast; room service
Price ££££
Rooms 30; 24 doubles, 3 suites, 3
singles; all with bath; all rooms have
phone, TV, fax/modem point,
hairdryer, safe, minibars, air-condi-
tioning and wi-fi.
Facilities sitting room, library with
honesty bar, meeting room
Credit cards AE, DC, MC, V
Children welcome
Disabled not suitable
Pets not accepted
Closed never
Proprietors Peter McKay and
Douglas Blaine

Hazlitt's
City hotel

There is no quarter of central London
with more character than Soho; and
there are few places to stay with more
character than Hazlitt's, formed from
three Georgian terraced houses off Soho
Square. The sloping, creaking floorboards
have been retained (it can be an uphill
walk to your bed), and the rooms decorated with suitable antiques, busts and
prints. Restoration work has revealed
original fireplaces and Georgian panelling
that's 300 years old. The bedrooms, named
after some of the people who visited or
stayed in the house where the eponymous
essayist himself lived, are delightfully different from most London hotel rooms, some
with intricately carved wood headboards,
others with delightful four-posters, all with
free-standing bath tubs and Victorian fittings in the bathrooms.

As befits an establishment with such literary connections, Hazlitt's is particularly
popular with visiting authors, who leave
signed copies of their works when they
depart. Sadly, the dresser in the little sitting
room in which they are kept is now locked
to protect the books, which had a habit of
going missing. Continental breakfast is
served in the bedrooms, as well as light
dishes such as pasta and filled baguettes. A
hotel for people who like their comforts
authentic, yet stylish.

162-166 Chiswick High Road,
London
W4 1PR

Tel (020) 8742 1717
Fax (020) 8987 8762
e-mail reservations.highroad@soho-house.com
website www.highroadhouse.co.uk

Nearby Hampton Court Palace, Twickenham, Richmond, Kew Gardens
Location on Chiswick High Rd (A315) with no parking but hotel can feed your meter. Nearest tube Turnham Green
Food breakfast, lunch, dinner, room service **Price** £££
Rooms 14; 13 standard doubles, 1 superior; all have showers, superior has bath; all rooms have phone TV/DVD player, wi-fi, phone, hairdryer **Facilities** dining room, bar, games room, tv plasma room, brasserie **Credit cards** AE, DC, MC, V **Children** accepted **Disabled** 1 adapted room **Pets** not accepted **Closed** never
Proprietor Nick Jones

High Road House
City hotel

You can hope that a hotel owned by Nick Jones (proprietor of Soho House and Babington House) is going to be interesting and this doesn't disappoint. The decoration is city chic but doesn't feel cold: the colours bring the place to life and add an air of cosiness. The bar and dining room are buzzy, with masses of light and are not so cramped that you think that your next door neighbour can hear your thoughts. The food is traditional English with French twists, but nothing too pretentious.

Downstairs in the basement is a fantastic space painted in grey-blue with retro furniture which can be a nightclub; a place for meetings; a place for private sports parties (big plasma screen); a children's activity area or a place for chilling out and playing pool or mini football.

The bedrooms are, as you would expect, very cool (maybe a bit too white) with comfy beds, delicious Cowshed toiletries in the bathrooms and very quiet. All the windows are triple glazed, which is just as well as there is a very busy yet fun, trendy road outside.

This a great hotel for all ages; and it is especially popular with mothers and children – activities for the latter are supervised by minders on Sundays, while parents have some time off.

55 Hanger Lane, London
W5 3HL

Tel (020) 8991 4450
email info@hotel55-london.com
website www.hotel55-london.com

Nearby Heathrow (20 mins), Ealing
Common, Central London (20
mins), North Ealing Tube
Location on A406 Hanger Lane,
parking for 5 cars, ample space
behind hotel in NCP
Food breakfast, lunch, dinner
Price £-£££
Rooms 29 (inc. 3 suites); all double,
all with shower, 5 with bath and
shower; all rooms have phone, TV,
hairdryer, air-con, wi-fi, safe,
tea/coffee facilities
Facilities restaurant, bar lounge,
bar, garden, garden room
Credit cards AE, MC, V
Children welcome (in a few rooms
extra beds are provided)
Disabled 2 suitable rooms
Pets not accepted
Closed never
Proprietor Sanjay Tohani

Hotel 55
City hotel

This young hotel had only been open a
year when we went to press. It's well
placed for Heathrow: the Piccadilly line
(North Ealing) is right behind the hotel,
and takes you in without a change.

Tiberius, the charming and helpful manager, greets you as you step through the
automatic doors. Straight through the
ground floor and you are in the chic bar
area, with walls clad in leather, low seating
and a plasma screen. But the real joy of
this place is the garden room leading on to
a landscaped garden – rare in London. It's
surprisingly quiet, considering the hotel is
on a busy road and the tube is so close.
You can have your continental breakfast in
the garden room, read the papers or have
a light lunch. The restaurant is now oper-
ated by Momo Japanese Restaurant.

The bedrooms and bathrooms are
small, but nicely done, and with some
interesting furniture in the bigger ones.
They too are refreshingly quiet (double
glazing): the ones overlooking the garden
are particularly peaceful. If climbing stairs
is an effort, (there's no lift) then flop on to
the orthopaedic mattress (in every room)
while sipping your environmentally friendly water. Plenty of business people here –
which does affect the atmosphere.

28 Basil Street, London SW3 1AS

Tel (020) 7589 6286
email
reservations@thelevinhotel.co.uk
website www.thelevinhotel.co.uk

Nearby Harrods; The V&A;
Knightsbridge; Hyde Park;
Buckingham Palace.
Location between Sloane Street and
Harrods; public car park opposite and
at Capital Hotel, if available
Food The Knightsbridge Metro
serves breakfast and lunch **Price** ££££
Rooms 12; 8 std/exec doubles, 3
deluxe, 1 suite; all with bath and
shower; all rooms have phone, flat
screen TV, wi-fi, digital radio, mini-
bar, Nespresso machine, safe, air-con
Facilities lounge, The Metro Bar &
Bistro, honesty bar **Credit cards** AE,
DC, MC, V **Children** welcome
Disabled access difficult (steps), but
has 1 ground floor room and lift/ele-
vator **Pets** accepted by arrangement
Closed restaurant only, Sun lunch
and dinner **Proprietor** Warwick
Hotels & Resorts **Manager** Kate
Levin

The Levin
City hotel

This impressively-situated hotel, in the heart of Knightsbridge, opened in late 2007. The Levin has renewed its appeal with a multi-million pound renovation.

The stylishness strikes you as you walk in – everything is 'designer' and top quality – George Smith chairs, hand-blown ice-blue crystal chandeliers by Refer and Star, and a five-storey glass chandelier by renowned lighting designer Sharon Marston. Whether or not the names matter to you, the effect is impressive and everything is immaculate. Bedrooms are beautifully designed, with contrasting colours and textures. Fabric-covered back-lit headboards give the rooms a cosy feel. The non-uniform room shapes of this old building have been imaginatively put to use, with sofas built into large bay windows. Original fireplaces add further character. Bathrooms are a fair size, with Italian marble and under-floor heating: stylish and spotlessly clean.

Attention to detail is superb, with all the technical wizardry you could want and also – uniquely, we believe – a mini-champagne-cocktail-bar in each room, with champagnes, mixers and a book of cocktail recipes.

Despite its design credentials, The Levin has a friendly atmosphere and manages to avoid pretentiousness. It is hard to find fault with the place.

135-137 Ebury Street, London,
SW1W 9QU

Tel 020 7730 8191
e-mail info@limetreehotel.co.uk
website www.limetreehotel.co.uk

Nearby Victoria Station,
Buckingham Palace, Westminster
Abbey, Houses of Parliament,
Natural History Museum, Harrods,
all within one mile
Location on a residential road in
south Belgravia, surrounded by
restaurants, cafés and boutiques
Food breakfast
Price ££-££££
Rooms 25; 12 doubles, 4 twins, 3
triples, 6 singles; all have bathroom,
wi-fi, widescreen TV, tea/coffee mak-
ing facilities, safe, hairdryer, tele-
phone, toiletries **Facilities** breakfast
room, small sitting room, garden
Credit cards MC, V
Children aged 5 and above
Disabled not suitable
Pets not suitable
Closed never
Proprietor Charlotte and Matthew
Goodsall

Lime Tree Hotel
City hotel

Our series editor Fiona Duncan investi-
gated Lime Tree Hotel on a hunch,
enticed in by its pretty Georgian façade and
overflowing window boxes. What she found
was a hotel with a personal, relaxed atmosphere combined with fantastic value – a
rarity in London.

The secret to Matt and Charlotte's success? Matt puts it down to zero hotel experience, which has helped them avoid the
pitfalls towards becoming an impersonal
engine, joining OTAs and bringing in PRs
who hike up the prices. Instead they've run
it in their own independent style, and as a
result have enjoyed 100 per cent occupan-
cy most of the year.

All bedrooms have luxury beds, draped
with Osborne & Little, or Cole & Son curtains. They can be on the small side and only
three have baths, but all are priced accordingly. Ours, at £220 a night, had a double
and single bed, a widescreen television and
an original Victorian fireplace. Singles start
at £125, making this an excellent option single travellers, who are made to feel welcome by the remarkably friendly staff.

The hotel (which connects two
Georgian houses) has a countrified feel,
with homely touches such as painted furniture and breakfast options being chalked on
a board in the kitchen (these include croissants, yoghurt and cooked dishes).

25 Courtfield Gardens, London
SW5 0PG

Tel (020) 7244 2255
Fax (020) 7244 2256
email kensington.info@nadlerho-tels.com
website www.nadlerhotels.com

Nearby Royal Albert Hall, Hyde Park, Earl's Court, Natural History Museum, V&A Museum, Science Museum, Kensington Palace, London Olympia
Location Courtfield Gardens, walking distance from Earl's Court tube, private parking spaces
Food breakfast
Price ££-£££
Rooms 65; all have bath/shower, with TV, wi-fi, phone, hairdryer, safe, ironing board, mini-kitchen
Facilities lounge reception area
Credit cards AE, MC, V
Children welcome
Disabled lift access, 1 room with disabled access **Pets** only guide dogs accepted **Closed** never
Proprietor Robert Nadler

The Nadler, Kensington
Self-catering hotel

The Nadler is not the sort of place we usually recommend – with 65 standardised rooms, neutrally decorated, at first sight it looks like an upmarket stopover for travelling businessmen. Rooms are neutrally decorated.

But it has some useful features that break the mould. We like the (fairly original) concept of a self-catering hotel. The compact kitchenettes in each room are not ideal for cooking, but they do offer the essentials: a fridge, kettle, microwave, sink with a Brita tap and Nespresso machine. Breakfast can be delivered to your room. Soft carpets warm up otherwise sterile corridors; two rooms have recently been sacrificed to make a reception area furnished with antiquarian books and sofas – a shame there's no separate sitting room for guests. For families, the hotel offers flexibility: there are pull-out beds in bigger doubles and rooms with bunk-beds. Bespoke artworks hang on the walls.

For their size, the rooms are value for money (as we went to press, a standard double was from £169) The friendly staff will provide you with the names of local restaurants and cafes that offer exclusive discounts to guests. Their sister hotel in Soho has been booked up since it opened in June, and there's a branch in Liverpool (all on www.nadlerhotels.com).

Doughty Street, London WC1N 2PL

Tel 020 7014 0240
e-mail enquiries@blueprintlivinga-
partments.com
website www.blueprintlivingapart-
ments.com/no-5-doughty-street

Nearby Great Ormond Street
Hospital, Charles Dickens Museum,
Gray's Inn Fields, West End the-
atres, restaurants and bars
Location literary district of
Bloomsbury, close to the Financial
District
Food self-catering
Price £££-££££
Rooms 11 serviced apartments; all
with fully-equipped kitchen, shower
room, flat screen television, free wi-
fi, direct dial telephone, radio, CD
player and iPod dock **Facilities** wi-
fi, safe deposit box, laundry room,
DVD library, babysitting services
Credit cards AE, MC, V
Children welcome
Disabled no lift **Pets** no
Closed never **Proprietor** Marldon

No. 5 Doughty Street
Self-catering apartments

Tucked away in the heart of London's
literary district, yards from The
Charles Dickens Museum and Gray's Inn
Fields, lies Doughty Street, one of the
most picturesque Georgian streets in
London. These 11 luxury, serviced apartments in a Grade II listed building offer
spacious comfort and value for money.
While other serviced apartments tend to
have stale, corporate decoration, No.5
Doughty street has the tasteful interior
design of a modern boutique hotel, with all
the contemporary trimmings, while
remaining faithful to the period architecture of the building.

A range of studio, one-bedroom and
two-bedroom apartments is on offer. Each
has a fully-equipped kitchen, free wi-fi, flat
screen television, direct dial telephone and
iPod dock. Due to the building's listed status, a lift could not be fitted, but the stairs
up to the fifth floor apartment are well lit
with a large airy skylight. Once inside this
top-floor apartment, admire the great
view down the Georgian street below.
Room service is limited to a linen change
and clean once a week (a tip can be given
to the staff for extra attendance). The location, mid-way between the West End and
The City and wealth of nearby sights and
restaurants, could hardly be better.

16 Sumner Place, London
SW7 3EG

Tel (020) 7589 5232
Fax (020) 7584 8615
e-mail sixteen@firmdale.co.uk
website www.firmdalehotels.com

Nearby South Kensington
museums; Knightsbridge; Kings
Road.
Location off Old Brompton Road;
no private car parking
Food breakfast, lunch, dinner and
Afternoon Tea served in The
Orangery or garden; room service
Price ££££
Rooms 41 double, all with bath/
shower; all rooms have phone, TV,
iPod dock, minibar, hairdrier, safe,
umbrellas, wi-fi
Facilities sitting room, bar,
conservatory; small garden
Credit cards AE, DC, MC, V
Children accepted
Disabled access possible,
lift/elevator **Pets** not accepted
Closed never
Manager Fanny Royol

Number Sixteen
City bed-and-breakfast

Number Sixteen is one of London's
most characterful luxury bed-and-
breakfast establishments. The original
building has spread along its early Victorian
South Kensington terrace, to encompass
four adjoining houses – all extensively
refurbished a few years ago.

Public rooms and bedrooms alike are
brimful of pictures, including a huge eye-
catching abstract in the reception room.
Downstairs there are always big bowls of
fresh flowers – sweet peas or roses perhaps – and the large rear patio garden is
well kept and full of colour. Inside, the decoration is richly traditional and harmonious. A series of small sitting rooms with
Victorian moulded ceilings, polished antiques
and luxurious drapes, lead to an award-
winning conservatory, from where, on
summer days, you can sit and admire the
profusion of flowers outside.

Bedrooms are generously proportioned, comfortable and stylish, largely furnished with period or contemporary
pieces; some have French windows opening on to the garden. Breakfast is served in
your room or in the drawing room, library,
conservatory or garden. The hotel has no
dining room but there are plenty of restaurants on the Old Brompton Road nearby.

37 Pimlico Road, London SW1W
8NE

Tel 020 7881 9844
e-mail
reservations@theorange.co.uk
website www.theorange.co.uk

Nearby Victoria station, Ranelagh
Gardens, Kings Road, Saatchi
Gallery, Tate Britain
Location Pimlico Road, walking dis-
tance from Sloane Square station
and Belgravia, Victoria station short
drive away
Food breakfast, lunch, dinner
Price ££-££££
Rooms 4 doubles, all have
bath/shower, all have air-condition-
ing, wi-fi, iPod docking station, TV
Facilities restaurant, bar
Credit cards all major
Children accepted
Disabled disabled toilets
Pets not accepted
Closed never
Proprietor Cubitt House

The Orange
City pub-with-rooms

This place was once evidently a public house, and the ground-floor bar still acts as a meeting and drinking spot for locals, albeit noisy, well-heeled ones – it stands opposite Daylesford Organics, on Pimlico Road. They love its wooden floors, country furniture and shabby-chic atmosphere and decoration. However, as a pub with rooms there aren't many guest facilities, and as we went to press a standard room was £205 – not dissimilar to rates of fully-fledged hotels, but without the same level of comfort.

Of the four rooms, two are compact, two a decent size. The best is Pimlico, charming with original floorboards, lofty ceiling criss-crossed with rafters and pine panelling. There was a desk, a whitewashed wardrobe and a bedside radio.

There are tables on the first floor and downstairs. The starter of smoked salmon tartare was enjoyable, as was the main course of slow-cooked beef cheeks. Breakfast was beautifully presented, but is not included in the room rate. Despite these reservations, The Orange makes a useful, informal London stopover.

181-183 Cromwell Road, London
SW5 0SF

Tel 020 7244 2000
e-mail enquiries@therockwell.com
website www.therockwell.com

Nearby Kensington High Street,
Earl's Court, South Kensington,
Heathrow (30 minutes on underground) **Location** on Cromwell
Road. Pay parking behind hotel 8.30
am to 6.30 pm and (usually) free
spaces after 6.30. NCP car park in
Holiday Inn – details from reception. **Food** breakfast, lunch, dinner
Price £££ **Rooms** 40; 27 double, 13
single, all with shower only, air conditioning, telephone, voicemail, flat
screen satellite TV, free broadband,
safe, minibar **Facilities** bar, dining
room, garden, reception sitting area,
conference room, laundry service,
24-hour room service **Credit cards**
AE, DC, MC, V **Children** welcome
Disabled no specially adapted rooms
but some rooms on ground floor;
lift/elevator **Pets** not accepted
Closed never **Proprietor** Marldon

The rockwell
City hotel

We must declare an interest: one of the
backers of The rockwell, which
opened back in 2006, is architect Michael
Squire, neighbour and sailing cronie of the
guide's publisher. How to write about it
without bias? Some years ago, Squire and his
partners acquired two large, adjoining houses at the impersonal west end of the
Cromwell Road, opposite the Cromwell
Hospital, and first thought of making them
rooming houses for students. Then, unexpectedly, they got permission for change of
use. Overcoming their worries about the
location, they spent serious money turning
it into a contemporary hotel. The bedrooms, though created out of a variety of
spaces, and very comfortable, seemed at
first a little too much like conventional city
hotel rooms for this guide. But, staying the
night, they grew on us, with their beautiful
oak fittings and large beds with fine sheets.
Most are far from being boxes. Fairly priced,
too. And we found the corridors and connecting parts unusually well lit and congenial. But the essential charm we seek came
home when we had drinks in the attractive
garden followed by dinner in the cosy but
coolly decorated little dining room.
Imaginative, carefully prepared food, relaxed
but friendly service and again, fair prices.
Londoners could do a lot worse than eat
out here (see above left for tips on parking).

Peter's Lane, Cowcross Street,
London EC1M 6DS

Tel (020) 7336 0931
Fax (020) 7336 0932
e-mail reservations@rookery.co.uk
website www.rookeryhotel.com

Nearby The City; St Paul's;
Smithfield; Farringdon tube station.
Location in pedestrian street in
Clerkenwell, near Smithfield and
City; parking in nearby public car
park
Food breakfast, 24 hour room serv-
ice **Price** ££££
Rooms 33; 27 double, 3 single, 3
suite, all with bath; all rooms have
phone, TV, minibar, hairdryer, safe,
wi-fi
Facilities conservatory, honesty bar;
terrace
Credit cards AE, DC, MC, V
Children accepted
Disabled 2 bedrooms on ground
floor **Pets** not accepted
Closed never
Proprietors Peter McKay and
Douglas Blaine

The Rookery
City hotel

Opened by the owners of the imaginative Hazlitt's (see page 124), this
homely little hotel full of old curiosities and
flights of fancy is in a traffic-free alleyway
among the restaurants of fashionable
Clerkenwell. Created from a row of converted listed Georgian cottages, it is packed
with character and 'time-warp' detail: wood
panelling; period shutters; open fires; flagged
floors; even a special creaky sound put into
the treads of the new stairs to make them
seem old. Pretty bedrooms have little half-
shutters, Egyptian cotton sheets, summer
and winter duvets. Minibars and 'worksta-
tions' are discreetly hidden behind antique
doors. Bathrooms are delightful, with
Victorian fittings, exposed copper pipes and
wainscotting. One suite, on two floors, has
a rococo French bed, attendant blackamoor
and an Edwardian bathing machine; an elec-
tronically controlled panel shuts off the
upper floor for business meetings.

A conservatory, with open fire and leather
chairs, serves as a day room, opening on to a
tiny terrace garden. Breakfast, continental, is
on trays: fresh orange juice, coffee and croissants prepared and baked by the hotel's own
pâtissier. We visited recently and enjoyed the
vaguely Dickensian atmosphere as much as
ever. Try nearby Luca restaurant on St John
Street – good Italian food.

9-11 Sydney Street, London,
SW3 6PU

Tel (020) 7376 7711
e-mail
info@sydneyhousechelsea.co.uk
website
www.sydneyhousechelsea.com

Nearby Harrods, Victoria & Albert
Museum, Natural History Museum
Location between Fulham Road and
Kings Road; no parking but two
NCP car parks nearby (corner of
Sydney St & Kings Road, Sloane
Avenue) **Food** breakfast, 24 hour
room service (limited after 10pm)
Price ££££
Rooms 21 double, plus 'room at the
top'; all have shower, 11 have baths.
All have telephone, flat-screen TV,
DVD player, hairdryer, combination
safe and internet access **Facilities**
sitting room, bar, breakfast room
Credit cards AE, DC, MC, V
Children welcome **Disabled** not
suitable **Pets** not accepted **Closed**
never **Proprietor** Andrew
Brownsword

Sydney House Chelsea
City guesthouse

On a handsome residential street,
announced only by a subtle name-
plate, Sydney House could be a private
residence – clearly a draw for its many
regular guests, some of whom stay weekly
while in London on business.

Andrew Brownsword, owner of Gidleigh
Park and The Bath Priory, bought this elegant grade II listed Georgian town house in
2002, totally refurbishing it. Original features are found alongside sophisticated,
modern decoration and furnishings.
Neutral colours dominate the reception/sit-
ting area, where a large palm, modern tapestries and matching cushions in the
suede-covered chairs add splashes of colour.

Bedrooms are smart and fresh, with
clean, light bathrooms. The 'room at the
top', set on the fifth floor, is perhaps surprisingly small, but leads out on to its own
generously-sized private terrace, with
wooden table and chairs and an area
heater – so you can take in the impressive
views over London year-round.

The staff at Sydney House are immaculately presented, professional and courteous but seemed to be feeling the strain of
too many visitors. We wondered whether
the high volume of guests might take its
toll on the interior, or on the service.
Reports welcome.

185 Kennington Lane, Kennington Cross, SE11 4EZ

Tel (020) 7735 1061
e-mail info@thetommyfield.co.uk
website www.thetommyfield.com

Nearby Kennington, Kia Oval, Vauxhall, Elephant & Castle
Location on main road Kennington Lane 5 min walk from Kennington tube
Food breakfast (weekends only), lunch, dinner
Price ££-£££
Rooms 6; all double, all have bath and/or shower, wi-fi, satellite TV, fan, hairdryer, safe, fridge, Nespresso machine
Facilities pub/restaurant, private function room
Credit cards MC, V
Disabled no speical facilities
Pets accepted in pub
Closed never
Proprietors Three Cheers Pubs Co.

The Tommyfield
City pub-with-rooms

We like The Tommyfield because it's different. Part of the Three Cheers Pubs co. south London mini-chain, it's been refashioned as a pub-with-rooms. The ground floor pub has a trendy modern-rustic look: exposed brick, tiled walls and copper light fittings. There's no reception, so the welcome can be hit-or-miss, especially if the place is busy. Once you've checked in, you can come and go as you please as the rooms have a separate entrance. The pub itself draws a young, local crowd in the evenings that enjoy the quiz and comedy nights. The food is unpretentious and good value: pies, burgers, fish and chips, and specials. On our recent visit we ordered grilled lamb chops with cous-cous and were pleasantly surprised.

The six rooms, spread over the two upper floors, continue the shabby-chic style of downstairs: painted white brick walls are offset by colourful furnishings and bold prints. Bathrooms are well-proportioned and well-stocked: ours had a huge walk-in shower, with enough space for two, and a warm slate floor. Beds are huge and comfortable, and though The Tommyfield is on a main road, we weren't disturbed by noise. Unfortunately, breakfast is only served at the weekend, but porridge-pots, fruit and juices are provided in the room.

St Johns Square, 86-88 Clerkenwell
Road, London, EC1M 5RJ

Tel (020) 7324 4444
Fax (020) 7324 4445
e-mail info@thezetter.com
website www.thezetter.com

Nearby Farringdon tube, Barbican,
Old Spitalfields Market, Liverpool
St Station **Location** Location: off
A5201 Clerkenwell road; NCP parking around the corner (residents at
hotel get discount) **Food** breakfast,
lunch, dinner **Price** £££-££££
Rooms 59; all doubles with shower;
all rooms have phone, TV,
CD/DVD players, hairdryers, safe,
air-con, wifi, Penguin paperbacks,
hot-water bottles in knitted tea
cosies, colourful mood lighting;
rooms on 5th floor have tea/coffee
facilities   **Facilities** restaurant, sitting room, terrace with tables, 2
board rooms with private kitchen
Credit cards MC, V **Children**
accepted **Disabled** 2 rooms **Pets** not
accepted **Closed** never
 Proprietors Mark Sainsbury and
Michael Benyan

The Zetter
City hotel

This is one of the new breed of eco-
friendly hotels gaining popularity in
London. Water is pumped from its own
bore hole, supplying the rooms and air-
conditioning. When it gets too hot, the sky-
lights in the glass atrium pop open for ven-
tilation; the room keys control the lights, so
no energy is wasted when you leave.

The bar, restaurant and terrace are all
done out in kitsch, retro style which manages, thankfully, not to be garish. The
restaurant is wonderfully light thanks to
the floor-to-ceiling windows. In early 2017
head chef Ben Boeynaems took the reigns,
with a simple and well-balanced menu that
allows the high-quality ingredients to
shine. In keeping with The Zetter's sustain-
able ethos, the produce is seasonal and
sourced fom local suppliers.

The bedrooms are stacked over 5 storeys,
clustered around the central atrium: quite
a dizzying sight from the ground floor. Each
room is individually designed in a quirky
retro style, with splashes of colour from
bedspreads and rugs. The colours might
not be to everyone's taste: neon pinks,
greens and blues – but they are all of a
fairish size and peaceful, with homey
touches like Penguin paperbacks and hot
water bottles in hand-knitted cosies. The
seven roof-top suites have great views
from their private balconies.

Margate, Kent

31 Hawley Square, Margate, Kent
CT9 1PH

Tel 01843 225166
e-mail
info@thereadingroomsmargate.co.uk
website www.thereadingroomsmar-
gate.co.uk

Nearby Shell Grotto, Powell
Cotton Museum, Turner
Contemporary Art Centre, outdoor
activites
Location Hawley Square in Margate
old town, 5 minutes from beach and
Old Town Quarter
Food breakfast
Price £££
Rooms 3; all double and all have
bath/shower
Facilities room service
Credit cards all major, not AE
Children not accepted
Disabled no lift
Pets not accepted
Closed Christmas and Boxing Day
Proprietors Louise Oldfield and
Liam Nabb

The Reading Rooms
Town bed-and-breakfast

There are two big reasons to make a special visit to has-been Margate: the new Turner Contemporary Art Centre, and this luxury B&B on a Georgian square five minutes from the seafront, with restricted views to the sea from some of the rooms. It's a little unconventional: each of the three large rooms occupies its own floor, and there is no guest sitting room or dining room, so your room, though large, is your world. Breakfast is delivered to the bedroom – and is unusually good. Bathrooms are huge and glitteringly luxurious.

There's no lift – rooms on the top floors mean climbing the staircase, but the hosts will offer to carry your bags. As we went to press, rooms cost from £170 a night (occasionally lower), which might seem high for a place with no facilities except the rooms. But you'll be happy to pay this if you are, for example, a sophisticated metropolitan type who values quality, style and bespoke service, and the privacy that comes with not interacting with other guests. The rooms are beautiful and gracious, one with floor-to-ceiling windows.

Midhurst, West Sussex

Church Hill, Midhurst, West Sussex
GU29 9NX

Tel 01730 812990
mobile 07875 971368
website www.churchhousemid-hurst.com

Nearby South Downs National
Park, Petersfield, Cowdray Park,
Goodwood, Langham Brewery
Location central Midhurst, unlimited free parking on Church Hill
Food breakfast
Price £££
Rooms 5; all doubles, 3 suites
Facilities sitting room, dining room,
conservatory, garden
Credit cards MC, V
Children welcome
Disabled access possible to Dali
suite **Pets** not accepted
Closed Christmas Eve, Christmas
Day, Boxing Day
Proprietors Fina and Jaque Jurado

The Church House
Town bed-amd-breakfast

You think you're about to enter the modest hall of a small town house in a Midhurst side street... in fact you step into a huge, beautifully designed ground floor space stretching into the distance. The scale could be that of a stately home, but the laid-back country house ambience, the antiques to be used, not revered, the use of colour are something else. Fina Jurado, who is Spanish, fashioned her highly original B&B out of four town houses in 2011, having run Gaudis, a well known restaurant here for years. She lives two doors away – guests have the run of it – and is a characterful, naturally friendly hostess.

The bedrooms (some huge, such as the master suite, Silver) combine English country house and European style elements. Comfortable, not staid, each is stylishly individual but homely in its way.

You start asking yourself, why stay in a hotel when this is so much more interesting – a place where you can be yourself. The ground floor, resolving into several sitting areas, plus the garden, is big enough for three or four guest groups to co-exist privately. Dinners are cooked to order; tea is with home-made cakes; help yourself to a drink – singles are free; or buy a bottle.

Romsey, Hampshire

Market Place, Romsey, Hampshire
SO51 8ZJ

Tel 01794 512431
Fax 01794 517 485
e-mail
thewhitehorse@twhromsey.com
website
www.thewhitehorseromsey.co.uk

Nearby Broadlands; Romsey Abbey;
Romsey Rapids; Southampton.
Location Romsey, a market town in
Hampshire's Test Valley **Food**
breakfast, lunch, dinner; afternoon
tea, tapas
Price ££–£££
Rooms 31; all with shower, TV and
wi-fi
Facilities brasserie, private dining
area, 2 sitting rooms, 24-hour room
service, conference facilities
Credit cards MC, V
Children welcome
Disabled access to restaurant but
not to rooms
Pets accepted
Closed never
Proprietors The Bereweeke Trust

The White Horse
Town inn

Our series editor Fiona Duncan
writes: 'The White Horse's brasserie
is one of my favourite eating places in
Hampshire – and that's not an idle compliment because I know that in recent years
the competition has warmed up.

'If you need a bed for the night, it offers
29 recently redone rooms, all my idea of
comfy, charming and fairly priced. Some of
the doubles are quite cottage-like – snug
and intimate; at the other end of the scale
is an enormous penthouse in the main
building.

'The main building is just what you'd
expect of a coaching inn with its roots in
the Middle Ages. It's somewhat rambling,
levels change unpredictably, and the layout
seems illogical. The private dining area is
on the street, there are sitting rooms in
the middle of the ground floor and then a
corridor takes you to the brasserie at the
rear. This is the part that works best: it has
tall windows that let you look out on to
the internal courtyard and the feeling is of
well-designed, restrained elegance. There
are often special offers here.

'There's a 'horse' theme throughout –
witness the the Lewis and Wood wallpaper
in reception, and the bedrooms each get a
famous racehorse's name.'

Rushlake Green, East Sussex

Rushlake Green, Heathfield,
East Sussex TN21 9QJ

Tel (01435) 830553
Fax (01435) 830726
email stonehousehotel@aol.co.uk
website
www.stonehousesussex.co.uk

Nearby Battle; Glyndebourne.
Location just off village green 3
miles (4.5 km) SE of Heathfield, in
large grounds with ample car parking
Food breakfast, lunch by arrange-
ment (summer only), dinner
Price £££ (special offers in spring
and autumn)
Rooms 7 double and twin, all with
bath; all rooms have phone, TV,
hairdryer, wi-fi
Facilities sitting room, library, din-
ing room; billiards, snooker; gar-
dens, croquet, fishing, shooting
Credit cards MC, V
Children welcome over 9
Disabled access difficult
Pets accepted in bedrooms only
Closed Christmas to 5 Jan
Proprietors Peter and Jane Dunn

Stone House
Country house hotel

Our latest reporter enthusiastically
agrees with everything we have said
about Stone House in the past. It is a glorious 16thC manor house, the ancestral
family home of the late Peter Dunn. His
wife, the delightful Jane Dunn ('old world
and lovely manners') continues to do what
she enjoys most – cooking, and looking
after her guests individually. Her relaxed
and friendly demeanour belies a very sure
touch, and Stone House is run with great
competence – which means it's much in
demand for Glyndebourne visitors (luxury
wicker picnic hampers can be prepared),
shooting weekends, house parties and
even small executive conferences. A few
years ago they created a Victorian walled
vegetable garden and an 18thC-style rose
garden. Wine is a hobby for Jane, and she
is justly proud of the their wine list.

Bedooms are beautifully decorated; two
have fine antique four-posters and are particularly spacious (the bathrooms can double as sitting rooms). An excellent place in
which to sample authentic English country
living at its most gracious – log fires and
billiards, woodland walks and croquet –
together with the atmosphere of a home.
A favourite of the guide for many years, we
have had consistently good feedback.

98 High Street, Rye, East Sussex
TN31 7JT

Tel (01797) 222114
Fax (01797) 224065
e-mail stay@thegeorgeinrye.com
website www.thegeorgeinrye.com

Nearby Camber Sands, Rye
Harbour Nature Reserve, Great
Dixter Gardens, Bodiam castle,
Hastings Old Town, Sissinghurst
castle gardens
Location off A259 in centre of town;
use public car park 5 mins walk away.
Food breakfast, lunch, dinner
Price ££££
Rooms 34; 6 Queen; 11 Superior;
11 Luxury and 6 junior suites; all
have copper bath and power shower,
TV, DVD, hairdryer, wi-fi
Facilities ballroom, restaurant, pri-
vate dining room, bar; courtyard
garden
Credit cards MC, V
Children accepted
Disabled access difficult, no lift
Pets not accepted
Closed never
Proprietors Alex and Katie Clarke

The George in Rye
Town hotel

The George is a Rye institution enjoying
a new life. Back in 2005 it was bought
by Katie Clarke and her husband Alex. They
lived with swirly carpets and partition walls
for a year "to get the feel of the place" then
attacked, closing for eight months and
reopening with stunning results.

At one end of the entrance hall, panelled
walls and a huge hearth create a cosy sitting area, while the other side shows the
hotel's contemporary face, with psychedelic
portraits of the Beatles adding warm splashes
of colour. By contrast, the sprawling bar at
the back is somehow less inviting – the
panelled sitting room perhaps has a better
ambience for pre-dinner drinks.

Katie, a set designer, is responsible for
the 34 delicious bedrooms, designing
much of the furniture herself. A warren of
stairs and corridors leads to the rooms,
each different, demonstrating her confident eye for colour as well as comfort.

The dining room underwent a slick
refurbishment in 2011 resulting in the
hotel's 100-seat restaurant. The George
Grill's food is memorable. If the 2003 Pinot
Noir from Sandhurst Vineyard in Kent is
on the winelist, try it. They're making every
effort to provide quality at affordable
prices here – long may it last.

Rye, East Sussex

Mermaid Street, Rye, East Sussex
TN31 7ET

Tel (01797) 222828
e-mail jeakeshouse@btinternet.com
website www.jeakeshouse.com

Nearby Great Dixter; Ellen Terry
Museum, 1066 country.
Location in centre of Rye; private
car parking nearby (3 minute walk)
Food breakfast
Price ££
Rooms 11; 8 double and twin, 2
family rooms, 1 suite; 9 rooms with
bath, 1 with private bath across hall;
all rooms have TV, phone, wi-fi
Facilities dining room, sitting room,
bar, wi-fi
Credit cards MC, V
Children accepted over 8
Disabled access difficult
Pets by arrangement
Closed never
Proprietor Jenny Hadfield

Jeake's House
Town house bed-and-breakfast

This splendid 16thC house – or rather three houses turned into one – has been lovingly restored to make a delightful small hotel: a verdict confirmed by many readers, who return time after time. It is the domaine of Jenny Hadfield, who used to be an operatic soprano, and although the place is essentially a charming small hotel, she has lent it a certain theatrical quality. Originally built as a wool store in 1689, it later became a Baptist school and, earlier this century, the home of American writer Conrad Potter Aiken, when it played host to many of the leading artistic and literary figures of the time.

The beamed bedrooms, which come in various shapes and sizes, overlook either the old roof-tops of Rye or Romney Marsh. Bedsteads are either brass or mahogany (some are four-poster), bedspreads lace, furniture antique. There are plenty of thoughtful extras in the rooms. Downstairs, a galleried ex-chapel makes the grandest of breakfast rooms. A roaring fire greets guests on cold mornings, and Jenny will serve you either a traditional breakfast or a vegetarian alternative. There is a comfortable parlour with a piano and a bar, with books and pictures lining the walls. 'Situated on the street in Rye (the cobbled Mermaid Street) within walking distance of all the sights,' says our reporter. This will suit our older readers.

Taynards Lane, Winchelsea, Rye,
East Sussex TN36 4JT

Tel 01797 226276
email info@thestrandhouse.co.uk
website www.thestrandhouse.co.uk

Nearby Rye, Romney Marsh
churches and miniature railway,
Hastings battle site, National Trust
properties and gardens.
Location in own grounds, with off-
road car-parking
Food breakfast, dinner; afternoon
tea **Price** ££-£££
Rooms 13; 12 double and 1 twin; all
rooms except 1 have bath or shower,
TV, free wi-fi, DVD player
Facilities sitting room, honesty bar,
garden
Credit cards DC, MC, V
Children accepted, but not especial-
ly suitable (steep stairs, open fires,
pond)
Disabled access difficult
Pets welcome by arrangement
Closed weekdays in winter
Proprietor Mary Sullivan and Hugh
Davie

Strand House
Country house hotel

Is it an upscale B&B? Or is it a small hotel?
We like places which occupy the grey area
between these types, especially when run by
dedicated on-the-spot owner-managers.
Mary Sullivan and Hugh Davie are just that
– she mainly in the kitchen, and he front of
house. They are just as happy with guests
who treat the place as a B&B, keeping themselves to themselves, as with those who eat
Mary's dinners (good, daily changing menu
with choices) in the intimate dining room
and engage with other guests and the hosts.
Which is only a start.

The thing here is the building: mainly
Tudor, with some medieval elements and as
quirkily charming as they come. We rarely
see such low ceilings (one door way is five
foot five in height) or so many blackened old
beams. The country cottage interior decoration is in keeping. Bathrooms tend to be
smallish, carved out of corners, as you'd
expect in a building of this age. To appreciate
Strand House you need to be happy stoop-
ing for the low ceilings, and to 'get' what
Mary and Hugh do (essentially, to provide a
home from home). Three contemporary
bedrooms (with normal-height ceilings) are
available in a cottage in the garden.

9 Eversfield Place,
St-Leonards-on-Sea, East Sussex
TN37 6BY

Tel (01424) 460109
e-mail info@zanzibarhotel.co.uk
website www.zanzibarhotel.co.uk

Nearby Hastings old town, Hastings
Fort
Location on seafront near Warrior
Square, just off A21; underground
secure parking 2 mins from hotel - a
limited amount so book in advance.
Food breakfast; all room rates
include a champagne breakfast
Price £££
Rooms 8 double, all with
shower/bath; all rooms have
flatscreen TV with freeview, DVD,
hairdryer, ironing board, iron, tea
and coffee making facilities, fridge
with milk/water
Facilities cafe, sitting room, garden,
honesty bar
Credit cards DC, MC, V, Amex
Children no children under 5
Disabled access difficult **Pets** small
dogs only, with a fee **Closed** never
Proprietor Max O'Rourke

Zanzibar
Seaside town house hotel

The somewhat run-down seaside town
of St Leonards-on-Sea is not over-
whelmed with hotels worth writing about,
but this stylish and relaxed place stands out.
Zanzibar occupies a Victorian seafront
town house which has been restored and
modernised by its enthusiastic and hands-
on owner, Max O'Rourke. On arrival, along
with your complimentary glass of champagne you are given a parking permit, a
key, and advice on where to go if you want
to explore. The ethos here is very much
'make yourself at home', though the
friendly staff are always on hand.

Zanzibar's eight rooms are individually
themed around a region of the world and
the decoration and furniture subtly reflect
this, adding a unique character to each without going over the top. Every bathroom has
a special feature – in 'Antarctica' where our
inspector stayed, it was a combined show-
er/sauna. Breakfast is ordered the previous evening and delivered hot to your
room, or the grand salon. Choices include
kippers, poached eggs, smoked salmon and
a 'full English' – all fresh and delicious.

Max says: "the best thing about Hastings
and St Leonards is that there isn't that much
to do", and the steady stream of (mostly)
Londoners coming to Zanzibar for a refreshingly calm, relaxing break, seem to agree.

Sandwich, Kent

Knightrider Street, Sandwich, Kent,
CT13 9EW

Tel (01304) 619919
e-mail enquiries@the-
salutation.com
website www.the-salutation.com

Nearby Roman Fort at
Richborough, Deal old-town (10
mins), Walmer Castle, Broadstairs,
Canterbury **Location** in heart of
Sandwich, in 3.7 acres of grounds
Food breakfast (inc), lunch, dinner,
afternoon tea **Price** ££-££££
Rooms Main House (8 double/
super-king/twin); Coach House (2
bedroom); Gardeners Cottage (3
bedroom); Knightrider (4 bedroom)
Facilities restaurant, gardens, Tea
Room, plant nursery, shop, 3.7
acreage **Credit cards** all major
Children welcome
Disabled facilities in restaurant
Pets The Coach House &
Gardeners Cottage suitable for dogs
(£35 surcharge per dog)
Closed never
Proprietor John Sutherngill

The Salutation
Country hotel

This magnificent Lutyens house has been a presence in Sandwich since it was built in 1912, recently taken on by John and Dorothy Fothergill with the aim of making it a top boutique hotel. They have a while to go, but the location in a historic medieval town, one of the Cinq Ports, is interesting; the garden exceptional and the food very good – more than just a bed for the night.

People drive miles just to visit the Lutyens-designed 3.7-acre garden, run by talented head gardner Steve Edney. The garden's symmetrical 'rooms' range from traditional to experimental. The effect is endlessly unfolding space and perhaps the crowning feature is the walk bordered by huge cylindrically-pruned holm oaks.

The interior is a masterful development of the Queen Anne style, full of surprises, such as the unusually sited staircase and the twisted columns on the ground floor. Our bedroom had a lovely view over the garden and church but the lighting, the bathroom and the bed itself were average.

Kitchens with windows or see-through partitions are commonplace, but this one takes the concept of seeing the chef and his team at work a step further: you actually walk through the kitchen via glass doors to reach the main dining room. Shane Hughes's inventive modern European dishes have subtle, clean flavours.

Hungerford, Berkshire

Ermin Street, Shefford Woodlands, Hungerford. RG17 7AA

Tel 01488 648284
e-mail info@thepheasant-inn.co.uk
website www.thepheasant-inn.co.uk

Nearby Wickham House (4km), Hungerford (6km), North Wessex Downs (9km), Marlborough (21km), Highclere Castle (22km), Avebury Stone Circles (31km)
Location less than 1km north of M4 in small village, with own car park
Food breakfast, lunch, dinner, snacks, room service **Price** ££
Rooms 11; 10 doubles of varying sizes and 1 twin. All have en suite bathroom, free wi-fi, flatscreen TV, radio with MP3 player connection, tea and coffee making facilities
Facilities sitting room, dining room, bar, laundry
Credit cards MC, V
Children welcome, 2 fold-down beds for children under 12 are available (£10 surcharge), no cots available **Disabled** not suitable **Pets** allowed **Closed** never **Proprietor** Jack Greenall

The Pheasant Inn
Village inn

Sophisticated, intimate and affordable: The Pheasant Inn is the perfect weekend bolt-hole, says our series editor Fiona Duncan. An old sheep drover's inn surrounded by the unspoiled countryside of the Berkshire Downs, it has uninterrupted views and a feeling of wonderful seclusion, while being only minutes from the M4.

Young owner Jack Greenall has refurbished the inn with the help of interior designer, Flora Soames. The result is stylish and cosy down to the last detail. The bar and restaurant have a rustic feel, with red leather banquette benches and wooden tables. Greens and blues in the decoration remind you that this is racing country: trainers and jockeys are historic patrons of The Pheasant, as saluted to by the game of Bullring at the bar. In the 11 immaculate bedrooms upstairs beds stand out for their comfort and quality with luxurious fabric headboards and attractive toppers. The bathrooms, while on the small side, are marble-clad with top-quality products.

Andy Watt's kitchen is packed every night, catering to guests and locals alike with his highly superior pub grub. We enjoyed the Scotch eggs and salt-baked saddle of lamb – flavoursome and unpretentious cooking. The atmosphere in the restaurant is animated, but there are also comfy corners for quiet dining.

Sidlesham, West Sussex

Mill Lane, Sidlesham
West Sussex, PO20 7NB

Tel (01243) 641233
e-mail enquiries@crab-lobster.co.uk
website www.crab-lobster.co.uk

Nearby Chichester, Selsey Bill,
Bosham, Pagham harbour walk and
nature reserve
Location on B1245 south of
Chichester
Food breakfast, lunch, dinner
Price £££
Rooms 4 double; 1 with shower
only, 3 with bath; 2-bed self-catering
cottage
Facilities bar, dining room, terrace,
garden; internet connection
Credit cards AE, MC, V
Children accepted
Disabled access possible to restau-
rant only
Pets not accepted
Closed never
Proprietor Sam and Janet Bakose

The Crab and Lobster
Restaurant-with-rooms

The landscape surrounding The Crab and Lobster is enchanting: salt marsh and woodland interlaced with watery creeks stretching across Pagham Harbour to the distant sea. Despite its spanking new interior, this 350-year-old building offers, with its slate floors, cream painted or bare brick walls and open fire, sophisticated charm.

There are four attractive bedrooms – all stylishly decorated with pastel or beige walls, and fresh flowers – in the main build-ing, plus a delightful two-bedroom cottage for self-catering next door. We stayed in a deluxe room under the eaves, a cosy hide-away with binoculars for a closer look at that wonderful view – a thoughful touch. The elegant bathroom had a velvet *chaise longue* (great touch), but was lacking in shelf space.

The Crab and Lobster is a stylish water-side hideaway, with slate floors, exposed brick walls and an open fire in the dining room and bar downstairs, and what's more the food is excellent. Dinner was a great success: local crab from Selsey and lobster, superbly dressed, plus a wild sea bass that had been brought to the door that day by a local fisherman, and a bottle of Sancerre – perfect. The Halfway Bridge in nearby Petworth is under the same ownership (page 171).

Sissinghurst, Kent

The Street, Sissinghurst, Kent,
TN17 2JG

Tel 01580 720200
e-mail fresh@themilkhouse.co.uk
website themilkhouse.co.uk

Nearby Sissinghurst Castle &
Gardens, Hole Park Gardens, Great
Dixter, Pashley Manor Gardens.
Scotney Castle, Hever Castle,
Bodiam Castle. Vineyards: Chapel
Down, Herbert Hall, Biddenden,
Location Near Staplehurst station;
Channel tunnel & Dover within an
hour's drive; Gatwick 1 hr away
Food breakfast, lunch, dinner, pizza
available from spring-autumn
Price ££ Rooms 4: 1 large double; 1
family room (sleeps 4); 1 double; 1
twin/double. All have bath and/or
shower, flat-screen TV, hairdryer,
kettle, iron & ironing board on
request, cot on request **Facilities** wi-
fi, beer garden, parking on site, bar
& dining areas **Credit cards** all
major **Children** welcome **Disabled**
not suitable **Pets** dogs in bar only
Closed never **Proprietors** Dane &
Sarah Allchorne

The Milk House
Village Inn

Contemporary inn The Milk House
opened its doors in 2013. Set within a
traditional 16thC hall, the open-plan pub
interior has been given quite a contemporary redecoration, with a creamy green-and-
white colour scheme, faux bookcase wallpaper and a wicker bar at its centre. It's sophisticated and inviting, if perhaps a touch modish and lacking in character. The place draws
in hordes of locals at all times of day, who
congregate around the bar or come in to
sample the menu of chef (and owner) Dane
Allchorne. Both the Dining and Classic menu
offer fresh British fare (from pan-fried John
Dory to beer battered cod), uncomplicated
but well done. Service from the young (mainly local) staff is swift and cheerful.

The dairy theme is carried through to the
bedrooms (named Dairy, Byre, Buttery and
Churn), helped along by milky colour
palettes and country furniture. Our series
editor Fiona Duncan much enjoyed her stay
here, reclining in an expansive four-poster
bed, opposite an original brick fireplace
Some noise carries through from the high-
street, but it is not insistent.

This is a useful address for exploring
Bodium Castle and Kent Weald, and considering what's on offer it's good value, with
rooms running from £140-£180.

8 Western Esplanade, Southampton,
Hampshire SO14 2AZ

Tel 0845 0779494
website www.pighotel.com

Nearby Southampton Docks, historic Southampton, museums and the city's modern high street and shopping centre are within walking distance.
Location within Southampton's historic medieval walls, near cruise terminal and city centre. Private car park in hotel.
Food breakfast, snacks, dinner at The Pig (free shuttle service)
Price £££
Rooms 12; most with shower only, 3 with bath, some rooms have larders full of snacks and drinks, TV and DVD player
Facilities deli, wi-fi throughout
Credit cards AE, DC, MC, V
Children welcome, cot and additional bed available
Disabled no special facilities
Pets not accepted
Closed never
Proprietor Jamie Banner

The Pig - in the wall
Town house hotel

The Pig in the wall was opened in October 2012 by the same team that created The Pig at Brockenhurst (page 97) – one of the most acclaimed of new hotel's in the last ten years. Its description – a 'Boutique B&B' – might tempt you to suspect it's a triumph of form over content – but it's not.

They've made this pleasing Georgian house in the medieval walls of Southampton near Town Quay feel as if it's always been a happy place to stay. You step off the wide pavement through the front door straight into the downstairs public space – a long sitting room, bar and bistro dining area. It smells pleasantly of wood smoke and herbs, which are grown in pots as table decorations and for the kitchen. At both ends are log fires with guests relaxing in chairs upholstered in smart fabrics that could be in your home. Warm, friendly, relaxed.

Simply decorated connecting corridors lead to the bedrooms. The cheapest room is artfully shoehorned into the attic. Mid-price and superior rooms are spacious enough – perhaps not especially so, but this is a town house. Colours are soothing browns, whites, greys with splashes of purple velvet. See other Pig hotels on pages 30, 50, 75 and 97.

Stockbridge, Hampshire

31 High Street, Stockbridge,
Hampshire SO20 6EY

Tel 01264 810833
website www.thegreyhoundon-
thetest.co.uk

Nearby Mottisfont Abbey,
Winchester Cathedral, Salisbury
Cathedral, Stonehenge, New Forest,
Beaulieu Motor Museum
Location on village High Street in
Stockbridge, ample car-parking at
rear of building
Food breakfast, lunch, dinner
Price ££-£££
Rooms 10; 6 doubles 3 can be twin,
1 single, all have bath/shower, all
with TV, tea/coffee facilities
Facilities restaurant, pub, honesty
bar, fly fishing
Credit Cards all major
Children accepted
Disabled no special access
Pets well-behaved dogs welcome
Closed Christmas day and Boxing
Day
Proprietor Lucy Townsend

The Greyhound
Country inn

An atmospheric Hampshire pub run by
Lucy Townsend, who used to be at The
Peat Spade (see opposite) and The Anchor
at Lower Froyle (page 93). She bought it in
2011 with an investment partner, and since
then she's run it hands-on.

The eight first-floor rooms are better
than similar country offerings in the area at
the same price. They are all different styles,
enhanced by painted panelling in Farrow &
Ball colours; upholstered bedheads; pretty
fabrics; chaises longues; country furniture,
big mirrors and colourful paintings. In ours,
there wasn't much room for a laptop, and
we would have liked fuller information on
what to do and see in the area. Six of the
rooms have a shower only, but at £110 as
we went to press, in the heart of plutocratic
Hampshire, they are fair value.

Downstairs, the dining room, with OKA
chairs at rustic tables set with prettily
coloured glassware, offers top-end pub fare.
The Test is right at the back – ask about fishing deals, and barbecues in the fishing hut.

Stockbridge, Hampshire

Village Street, Longstock,
Stockbridge, Hampshire SO20 6DR

Tel (01264) 810612
e-mail info@peatspadeinn.co.uk
website www.peatspadeinn.co.uk

Nearby Stockbridge, Romsey,
Winchester, Test Valley fishing and
fisheries
Location in sleepy village centre
with off road car parking
Food breakfast, lunch, dinner
Price ££
Rooms 8 doubles, 2 can be twin, all
with bath shower; all rooms have
phone, TV and DVD player,
hairdryer, wi-fi, minibar, tea/coffee
facilities
Facilities bar, dining room, court-
yard, terrace, in-house sporting
agents
Credit cards MC, V
Children over 10
Disabled access difficult
Pets accepted in twin room
Closed never
Proprietor Upham Brewery
Manager Shelley Diaf

Peat Spade Inn
Village inn

'A charming mix of traditional and new,
rustic and efficient' says our reporter.
The bar-dining area is one long room, and
is rustic-smart. It has warm green walls,
which continue into The Rod Room, which
opens on to the garden. The decoration in
here is more faithful to its status as a fishing
inn, and features cane fly rods, mounted
trout, reels, gilt-framed mirrors, period
shooting and fishing prints. There are clean
white napkins on scrubbed pine tables; the
food OK – ambitious but given the prices perhaps in some respects not quite there. The
Mayfly Mess upstairs accommodates private
lunch and dinner parties.

Our reporter's room – restful browns
and greens and wide oak floor boards in the
bathroom, excellent cotton sheets on a
thoroughly comfortable bed – homely, comfortable. Ask about their fishing weekends
for novices and experts, individuals and
companies. Ghillies and tutors to order.

151 Mitchell Avenue, Ventnor, Isle of Wight PO38 1DR

Tel 01983 852271
e-mail mail@hillsideventnor.co.uk
website www.hillsideventnor.co.uk

Nearby St Boniface Down, Ventnor beach, botanical gardens, Roman villa
Location on Mitchell Avenue, just off the B3327 towards Ventnor
Food breakfast and dinner at Hillside restaurant; further lunch and dinner at sister Bistro
Price ££-££££
Rooms 12; 7 doubles, 1 can be twin, 2 twins, 2 singles; 2 apartments sleeping up to 4 in each
Facilities restaurant, terrace, sitting room, Bistro
Credit cards MC, V
Children welcome over 12
Disabled no special facilities
Pets not accepted, kennels nearby
Closed never
Manager Gert

Hillside
Country hotel

Gert has recently re-invented the imposing 18thC house at Ventnor on the south coast of the Isle of Wight. The exterior remains unchanged – thatched roof and stone walls – but inside it's now contemporary, mostly white, and with a distinctly Scandinavian feel. The colour scheme – or lack of – initially feels impersonal, but Gert is a friendly host who knows how to create a relaxing, welcoming environment.

Downstairs, the public areas are large and furnished with Scandinavian pieces, while colourful modern paintings adorn most walls. The bedrooms, although rather uniform, are stylish, comfortable and provide everything you need.

Recent developments include Hillside Stables (adjacent to Hillside) with similar decoration and furnishings. The restaurant is open five days a week, and there's a 'continental' bistro a five-minute walk away.

St Boniface Down – the highest point of the Isle of Wight – has tremendous views over the island and is a brisk walk away. The Boniface cliffs give Ventnor its sheltered, mild maritime climate.

West Hoathly, West Sussex

Queen's Square, West Hoathly, West Sussex RH19 4PP

Tel 01342 810369
e-mail thecatinn@googlemail.com
website www.catinn.co.uk

Nearby The Priest House, Standen, Penshurst, Hever Castle, Bluebell Railway, golf courses, wine tasting, walking
Location West Hoathly village, parking at the inn and in the village
Food breakfast, lunch, dinner
Price £££
Rooms 4 doubles, all have bath/shower and TV, wi-fi, tea/coffee facilities
Facilities pub, dining room
Credit cards MC, V
Children over 7 in pub, no special rooms
Disabled ramp to pub, but no access to rooms
Pets dogs welcome in guest rooms
Closed never
Proprietor Andrew Russell

The Cat Inn
Village freehouse

Andrew Russell, formerly general manager of nearby Gravetye Manor, recently took on this formerly run-down pub. His management skills, concentrated on a more compact operation, are achieving almost everything we look for. Step into the bar, and it's comfortable and genuine, buzzing with locals; try the food, and it's simple but better than you would expect; go to your bedroom and you find it instantly comfortable, unflashy but pretty. A balance of form and content.

Back downstairs, we noticed how he has cleverly combined airy and cosy dining areas, and made an old-fashioned bar with huge inglenook fireplace work alongside other, gently upmarket modern features. Breakfast is well above average. West Hoathly is an interesting, historic village with views – if you can, spend time strolling the sites.

14 Southgate Street, Winchester, Hampshire SO23 9EF

Tel 0844 748 9267
website www.hotelduvin.com

Nearby Cathedral; Venta Roman Museum; Winchester College.
Location in the town centre, a minute's walk from the cathedral; limited car-parking onsite
Food breakfast, lunch, dinner; room service
Price £££
Rooms 24; 23 double and twin, 1 suite, all with bath; all rooms have phone, TV, minibar, hairdryer
Facilities sitting room, dining room/breakfast room, private dining room, bar, wine-tasting cellar; garden, boules
Credit cards AE, DC, MC, V
Children welcome
Disabled 1 disabled access room (The Garden Room)
Pets some dog friendly rooms
Closed never
Manager Hazel Galloway

Hotel du Vin
City hotel

There is still an alluring buzz in the air at this stylish, affordable Georgian town house, once the flagship of the Hotel du Vin mini-chain — even though it's now been taken over by Malmaison, a large hotel group. This was the original Hotel du Vin and it's got panache. The wood-floored, hop-garlanded Bistro sets the tone: staffed by a charming bunch of mainly youngsters, it has the intimate, slightly chaotic yet professional air of the genuine article. Start with a bucket of champagne in the voluptuous mirrored and muralled bar, then choose a bottle from the inventive, kindly priced wine list to go with the inventive, sunny, Modern French food.

The bedrooms and bathrooms are every bit as appealing, with fresh Egyptian cotton bedlinen, CD players, capacious baths and huge showers. For maximum quiet, ask for a Garden Room, or splash out on one of the principal suites (see top picture), with hardwood floors, roll-top baths and panoramic floor-to-ceiling windows. 'Breakfast in Bed' is available as part of the room service.

We also recommend the Hotel du Vins in Bristol (page 88) and Brighton (page 165). There are also Hotels du Vin in Harrogate and Tunbridge Wells (pages 281 and 26) — see www.hotelduvin.com.

Yarmouth, Isle of Wight

Quay Street, Yarmouth, Isle of
Wight PO41 OPE

Tel (01983) 760331
Fax (01983) 760425
e-mail info@thegeorge.co.uk
website www.thegeorge.co.uk

Nearby Yarmouth Castle (adjacent);
Newport 12 miles; ferry terminal.
Location in town, close to ferry port
overlooking Solent; long stay car
park 3-min walk
Food breakfast, lunch, dinner; room
service
Price £££
Rooms 17; 13 double and twin, 2
suites, 2 single, all with bath; all
rooms have phone, TV, hairdryer,
many with sea or harbour views.
Facilities sitting room, restaurant,
brasserie; garden, private beach, 36 ft
motor yacht available for charter
Credit cards AE, MC, V
Children welcome
Disabled 1 disabled room down-
stairs **Pets** not accepted
Closed never
Proprietors Dianne Thompson

The George Hotel &
Restaurant **Seaside town hotel**

In many ways the George is a perfect
hotel: an atmospheric building in the centre of a breezy and historic harbour town,
with welcoming rooms, a buzzing brasserie
with tables spilling across the waterfront
garden, and a quieter, more formal restaurant where good, inventive food is served.
A former governor's residence, the property has been restored and renovated
with sympathy. A panelled and elegantly
proportioned hall sets the scene, leading
to a cosy wood-panelled sitting room with
thick velvet drapes at the windows, an
amusing mid-Victorian evocation of the
George above the fireplace and a roaring
log fire in winter. Across the hall is Isla's,
their elegant fine dining restaurant, and
beyond the central stairs, the Conservatory and
garden, where you can dine by the waters
edge in fine weather.

Upstairs, the bedrooms are all inviting
and all different: one has a four-poster;
another is a light and pretty corner room;
two have wonderful teak-decked balconies
with views across the Solent. 'It's a sheer
pleasure,' writes a satisfied reader, 'to hop
on the ferry at Lymington, alight at
Yarmouth, and settle in to the George for
two or three days.'

Braye, Alderney

Braye Street, Alderney, GY9 3XT

Tel 0800 2800550
Fax 01481 824301
email holiday@brayebeach.com
website www.brayebeach.com

Nearby St Anne's Church, 'The
Cathedral of the Channel Islands',
Mannez Lighthouse at Quesnard
Point.
Location Alderney island
Food breakfast, lunch, dinner
Price ££
Rooms 27; all with wi-fi, bathrobes,
refrigerator, flat screen television,
choice of classic films on in-room
box office, hairdryer, complimentary
decanter of sherry, tea and coffee
making facilities, personal safe, fresh
seasonal fruit on arrival
Facilities free wi-fi throughout, cin-
ema, renovated bar, private dining
room, restaurant
Credit cards AE, MC, V
Children welcome
Disabled 1 specially adapted room
Pets dogs in bar but not in rooms
Closed never
Manager Richard Proctor

Braye Beach
Beach hotel

Much needed renovation has breathed
new life into Braye Beach Hotel.
Thoughtfully and tastefully redesigned, it is
a welcome retreat for guests, and a great
base from which to explore the little
island of Alderney.

The old public areas have been opened
up to create a big open space, including an
award-winning restaurant and bar. Outside,
the wraparound terrace gives plenty of outdoor seating, and allows you to follow the
sun. There's a little cinema for rainy days.

The bedrooms are comfortable and cosy,
and exceptional value for money. Bright patterned covers and cushions give a homely,
welcome feel and offset neutral walls and
furniture. There are rooms with views and
rooms without, but the ones with views on
to the beach are the best, and are available
on a first come first serve basis. However,
our reporter did comment that the windows needed cleaning – sea salt spray
obscured the view – but this was after a
storm and we are assured that they are normally cleaned regularly.

Deserted and charming, Braye Beach
itself is ideal. Located on the edge of the
beach, the hotel has great views across the
bay and beyond the harbour.

Castel, Guernsey

Kings Mills, Castel, Guernsey GY5 7JT

Tel (01481) 257996
Fax (01481) 256834
e-mail info@fleurdujardin.com
website www.fleurdujardin.com

Nearby Vazon and Richmond beaches for surfing and sea fishing trips.
Location Castel
Food breakfast, lunch, dinner
Prices ££-£££
Rooms 11; all rooms have phone, TV, hairdryer
Facilities restaurant, bar, health suite; outdoor solar-heated swimming pool, car and bike hire
Credit cards all major
Children welcome
Disabled not suitable
Pets allowed in the 2 Garden Rooms
Closed never
Proprietors Ian and Amanda Walker

Fleur du Jardin
Village hotel

A voluptuous bouquet of flowers greets you in reception, teetering on a table next to a vintage suitcase. Thus, the tone is set for Fleur du Jardin – it is a quirky, eccentric and comfortable place that welcomes all guests as if they are returning travellers.

Throughout the hotel we were met with jokey signs ('duck or grouse' over a low ceiling), beautiful furniture and lovely decoration in each room – a mixture of natural elegance and seaside charm. Owners Ian and Amanda Walker were keen to combine design influences seen on their own travels around the world, as well as ensuring Fleur du Jardin's Guernsey heritage.

The award-winning restaurant is charming and homely, and uses as much locally bred beef, pork and fresh fish as possible. Real effort has been spent on thoughtful decoration – a dainty vase of fresh flowers is placed on each table – making the dining room one of the most charming and relaxing places to be in the whole hotel. The adjoining bar is also award-winning, and has a changing selection of real ales.

The bedrooms are spacious and charming, decorated in a seaside theme. Big white lampshades, fluffy bedding and rustic walls make them feel cosy and peaceful.

St Peter Port, Guernsey

Fermain Lane, St. Peter Port,
Guernsey GY1 1ZZ

Tel 0800 316 0314
e-mail
reservations@fermainvalley.com
website www.fermainvalley.com

Nearby St. Peter Port.
Location close to St Peter Port
town centre, Guernsey
Food three restaurants (The Rock
Garden Steakhouse, Ocean Bar &
Grill, Buho) serving breakfast, lunch,
dinner
Price £££-££££
Rooms 43; all with free wi-fi,
bathrobes, refrigerator, flat screen
TV, hairdryer, personal safe
Facilities computer room with
internet access, indoor heated swim-
ming pool and sauna, poolside ter-
race, cinema with 3D, 2 lounges, 2
restaurants, gardens
Credit cards all major
Children welcome
Disabled lifts, 1 fully-equipped
room **Pets** not accepted
Closed never
Proprietors Derek Coates

Fermain Valley
Seaside town hotel

It's larger than our preferred size, but
Fermain Valley's focus on individuality
and unique design give it charm and origi-
nality. Situated high over popular Fermain
Bay, its views over the surrounding
Channel Islands and, on clear days, as far as
France, are spectacular.

The style and ambience is modern, with
neutral colours that will appeal to a wide
cross-section of people. However, it is the
thoughtful little touches that we like the
most, such as fresh flowers and seasonal
fruit in the bedrooms to make you feel at
home. Bedrooms are all individually
designed, many with sea or garden views,
and thoughtful touches such as matching
headboard cushions or curtain covers and
chunky bedspreads give a lovely greeting.

The facilities you find here are typical of
most large-scale, successful hotels. Its
three restaurants, private cinema and
indoor swimming pool/sauna have all
helped this place to achieve its four stars,
but we especially value the hard work that
goes into providing a calm and relaxing
atmosphere. One guest commented that it
was a 'relaxed atmosphere for such a
plush place'.

The hotel is justifiably proud of its land-
scaped gardens, which won the Floral
Guernsey Horticultural Award for
Horticultural Excellence in 2008.

Sous L'Eglise, St Saviour, Guernsey
GY7 9FX

Tel (01481) 263862
e-mail bookings@aubergedu-
valguernsey.com
website www.aubergedu-
valguernsey.com

Nearby Guernsey Woodcarvers, St
Apolline's Chapel, Castle Cornet,
Hauteville House, Saumarez Manor,
local beaches
Location St Saviour, near Guernsey
airport
Food breakfast, lunch, dinner
Price ££
Rooms 9; 2 family, 4 double, 3 twin,
all en-suite with central heating, tel-
evision, telephone, tea and coffee
making facilities
Facilities restaurant, bar, 3 acre gar-
dens
Credit cards MC, V
Children welcome
Disabled no special facilities
Pets not accepted
Closed Feb
Proprietor Fernando

Auberge du Val
Town bed-and-breakfast

A friendly, quaint establishment in St
Saviour, Auberge du Val is a 150-year-
old converted farmhouse. Manager Fernando
has been there for 16 years and has retained the
busy-but-cosy feel of a traditional farmhouse.

Our room was clean and comfortable,
with wonky walls and little bay windows
sympathetic to the old-fashioned building.

The grounds are impressive – three acres
of lush countryside complete with a trout
stream and woodland valley. In keeping with
its farmhouse heritage, the garden supple-
ments the local supplies of vegetables and
herbs for the restaurant.

The focal point of this little hotel, however, is
the award-winning restaurant, commandeered by head chef Anthony Hobson.
Reminiscent of a homely hunting lodge, it is
wonderfully cosy and hearty. The menu is
chalked erratically on blackboards in the bar,
and the locally caught fish on the 'Specials' is
always changing. It was busy when we were
there, full of guests and non-residents, who
grew noisier and happier with each excellent dish; the wine is reasonably priced. A rustic
retreat.

Herm, VIA Guernsey GY1 3HR

Tel (01481) 750075
Fax (01481) 710066
e-mail reservations@herm.com
website www.herm.com

Nearby Shell Beach (200 yds/180 m); wildlife: puffins, dolphins and seals; coastal walks.
Location Herm Island
Food breakfast, lunch, dinner
Prices ££-£££
Rooms 40; 18 in cottages, some on ground floor
Facilities 3 sitting rooms, 2 restaurants, 2 bars, conference room; garden, tennis, croquet, heated swimming pool; beach
Credit cards DC, MC, V
Children welcome; over 9 only in restaurant for dinner
Disabled not suitable
Pets dogs accepted in 1 room
Closed Oct to Mar
Proprietors John and Julia Singer

The White House
Island hotel

Herm is 'an enchanting, self-sufficient time warp' says Fiona Duncan, our series editor. Its sole hotel, The White House, is like a step back in time. There are no televisions, clocks or telephones in the hotel, as they have been deemed inappropriate to the atmosphere of the island – Herm is car-free. You will hear the occasional tractor or the piping of oystercatchers but not much else.

The hotel has a great sea view, and is in a prime location. When the tide goes out over nearby Shell Beach, it really goes out, leaving a vast and fascinating waterless expanse of sand. Coastal walks in this area are lovely. If visiting from May to July keep an eye out for puffins.

The interior of the hotel has an attractive staircase and light, spacious rooms. There's a beautiful conservatory with a swimming pool surrounded by palms.

Since John and Julia Singer took over in 2008 there have been improvements to the bedrooms and bathrooms. We'd be interested to hear reports.

St Aubin, Jersey

Clifden 1, Mont Les Vaux, St Aubin
JE3 8AF

Tel 01534 741350
email clifden@hotmail.co.uk
website
www.jerseyyurtholidays.com

Nearby St. Aubin village: bank, post
office, supermarket, beauticians, taxi
hire, bike hire, art and craft shops,
restaurants; the Railway Walk,
beaches.
Location situated on terraced cotils,
overlooking St Aubin's bay
Food self-catering – condiments
available to buy **Price** ££ **Rooms** 3
yurts, 1 double bed, 2 with king sized
beds, all with wood-burning stove,
BBQ, picnic table, sunloungers
Facilities bathroom has 3 showers –
one for each yurt – a toilet and 2
wash basins; hairdryer and natural
toiletries available, books, games and
toys to borrow, hot tub
Credit cards not accepted **Children**
welcome **Disabled** unsuitable **Pets**
not accepted **Closed** never
Managers Cath and Andy Mesch

Clifden Yurts
Beach yurts

'Glamping' is the new camping –
appealing to young and old alike –
and these yurts are one of many local visitor attractions that show how wrong it is to
think of the Channel Islands as old-fashioned.

Set into the hill opposite St Aubin these
three luxury yurts bring hotel comfort to
lovers of the outdoors. The circular tents
are comfortable and cosy, with double
beds, furniture and a log-burning stove for
chilly nights. Each one, and its fittings, is
designed to be eco-friendly, making the
whole experience as 'green' as possible.

Matching their names, Ship Ahoy, Forest
Green and Harbour Retreat, the yurts are
kitted out with vintage and home-made
accessories. Decorations such as hand-
made lavender bags adorn the walls, apple
crates become bedside tables, ladders are
turned into towel rails and potato boxes
make quirky mirror frames.

The lavatory and shower block is
thoughtfully designed, and gleaming clean,
as is the communal kitchen 'The Lookout',
which has home-grown ingredients to purchase, and a panoramic window with views
of the sea. There is an eco-friendly but
romantic hot tub installed at the top of the
site, again with views over St Aubin.

Many guests are often avid walkers and
cyclists, as Clifden is situated perfectly for
exploring Jersey's amazing coastline.

St Brelade, Jersey

Le Boulevard, St Aubin's Harbour,
St Brelade, Jersey JE3 8AB

Tel (01534) 741585
Fax (01534) 499460
e-mail
wakeup@harbourviewjersey.com
website
www.harbourviewjersey.com

Nearby Railway Walk to Corbiere
Lighthouse; airport (10 mins); St
Helier (15 mins).
Location overlooking St Aubins
Harbour; 10 minute drive from air-
port **Food** breakfast, lunch, dinner
Prices £-££
Rooms 16; 12 double/twin, 2 sin-
gles, 2 suites for up to 5; all rooms
have central heating, satellite TV,
hairdryer, most have harbour views
Facilities breakfast room, wi-fi; sun
terrace
Credit cards AE, DC, MC, V
Children accepted (half price for
under 10s) **Disabled** annex rooms
suitable for disabled access
Pets well-behaved dogs accepted
Closed never
Proprietor Kelly Keadell

Harbour View
Harbourside guesthouse

Modest prices, plus the view of St
Aubin's Harbour basin and, beyond,
the expansive bay, combine to make this
possibly Jersey's most charming budget
place. From the long, thin garden out front,
you can watch the rise and fall of the tide
and the comings and goings of the boats.
The garden is eclectically – perhaps eccentrically – planted and furnished by owner
Kelly, who is not just a people-person, but
a bit of a character. Through an unassum-
ing entrance you find a similarly unassum-
ing reception area, which is unlike any
hotel, B&B or anything else we can think
of. The formerly uninviting staircase and
hallway is now lovely and bright after a
refurbishment. These lead to the bedrooms. They offer fair space and comfort
for the price charged, with cheery stripped
bedspreads.

Adjacent is the Muddy Duck restaurant
where the focus is on flavour. Chris the
chef works hard to be imaginative with his
bistro-style food and the place was
buzzing when we visited. One jolly celebration continued with squeals of laughter
until some time after eleven – not a problem for residents, we were assured,
because diners are always eased out
before midnight. Of course, this place
comes into its own during warm summer
weather, when you can loll in the garden.

La Neuve Route, St Brelade, Jersey
JE3 8BS

Tel (01534) 741426
Fax (01534) 745501
e-mail office@lehaulemanor.com
website www.lahaulemanor.com

Nearby La Lande d'Ouest; Portelet
Common; St Catherine's Wood;
Jersey War Tunnels.
Location St Aubin's Bay, close to
airport and Elizabeth ferry terminal
Food breakfast
Prices ££-£££
Rooms 16; all rooms have TV,
hairdryer, wi-fi, most have views; 1
self-catering apartment
Facilities outdoor swimming pool,
Jacuzzi, hot tub
Credit cards AE, MC, V
Children accepted
Disabled no special facilities
Pets not accepted
Closed never

La Haule Manor
Village manor hotel

A grand, sturdy exterior combined with a romantic, stylish interior gives La Haule its special charm. Overlooking St Aubin's Bay and Fort and originally dating back to the early 15th century, it was restored once in 1796 and again a few years ago. The owners have succeeded in combining the traditional manor with typically French style and decoration. The mood is romantic and relaxing, and, unsurprisingly, La Haule is popular with honeymooners.

The spacious bedrooms have high ceilings and are decorated in neutral colours, with ornate vintage furniture. We liked the mirrors in the bathrooms, the elegant baths and the impressive chandeliers. All bedrooms are different and most have sea views. The recently refurbished dining room is modern, with an award-winning breakfast bar that caters to all appetites.

There's a lovely, lush sunken garden, where guests can play games or just relax and enjoy the view. A peaceful, spacious place.

Bray, Berkshire

Ferry Road, Bray, Berkshire SL6
2AT

Tel 01628 620691
e-mail reservations@waterside-inn.co.uk **website** www.waterside-inn.co.uk **Food** lunch, dinner
Price £££ **Closed** Monday, Tuesday;
from 26th Dec for 4 weeks
Proprietor Alain Roux (Chef
Patron)

The Waterside Inn
Riverside restaurant-with-rooms

The world-famous cuisine of Michel Roux is the thing at this elegant Thames-side restaurant, these days run by Michel's son Alain — so much so that people tend to overlook the existence of 11 superb bedrooms upstairs and in cottages nearby. They are individually designed, in a French style, feminine and elegant rather than glitzy. Midweek package prices for a room and dinner are, relatively speaking, value for money, given the quality. This is a half-page entry only because super-luxury dining is a little, but only a little, outside our usual territory. It would be easy to fill several pages describing the charm, the service, and of course the sublime food.

Brighton, East Sussex

Ship Street, Brighton, East Sussex
BN1 1AD

Tel (01273) 718588
Fax (01273) 718599
email reception.brighton@hotelduvin.com
website www.hotelduvin.com/locations/brighton **Food** breakfast,
lunch, dinner **Price** £££
Closed never
Manager Ben Haynes

Hotel du Vin
Town hotel

Down a narrow cobbled street, tucked back from the seafront, a collection of part-gothic-styled buildings make up this member of the stylish du Vin micro-chain. In the main building, bizarre gargoyles watch over a double-height hall and a heavily carved staircase. Through glass windows and doors, you can see the Bistro, done out in wine-related pictures, floor-to-ceiling windows and bunches of dried hops. Bedrooms facing the central courtyard have chalky blue-green wood siding, a beach-house style, and inside, are decorated in soft blue and sand tones. In the bathrooms, scroll top baths are mounted in driftwood and old railway sleepers.

Faversham, Kent

Macknade Manor, Canterbury Road, Faversham, Kent ME13 8XE

Tel 01795 535344 Fax 01795 591200 e-mail enquiries@reads.com website www.reads.com Food breakfast, lunch, dinner Price £££ Closed 2 weeks in Sept, Christmas/Boxing Day, a week in Jan Proprietors Rona and David Pitchford

Read's
Restaurant-with-rooms

We felt relaxed and content as we pulled up in front of this elegant Georgian house. At the door, bags are taken and you are ushered immediately to your room.

Ours was large, elegant and traditional with graceful bay windows, but we thought the decanter of cream sherry and the repro Sheraton furniture somewhat old-fashioned. The bar/sitting room, where guests gather for drinks before dinner, could also do with judicious updating.

However, Read's has integrity. Rona and David Pitchford bought the house 11 years ago and David, the chef, has had a Michelin star for 20 years. Consistent quality and attention to detail: a well-run place.

Gurnard, Isle of Wight

31 Marsh Road, Gurnard, Isle of Wight PO31 8JQ

Tel 01983 200299 e-mail info@thelittlegloster.com website www.thelittlegloster.com Food breakfast, lunch, dinner Price £££ Closed 1st Jan – 8th Feb Proprietors Cooke family

The Little Gloster
Restaurant-with-rooms

Gurnard is curious: suburban roads; contemporary houses and Edwardian villas; seaside chalets and beach huts. In among them, right on the sea, next to the sailing club, is The Little Gloster – quite a new venture (opened 2010). Chef-proprietor Ben Cooke's grandparents once owned The Gloster in Cowes.

The modern, purpose-designed building is based around the restaurant with Ben hands-on in the kitchen. It's an open, clean white space, with large windows maximising views over the Solent. The menu focuses on fresh, local seafood. Holly, front of house, creates a friendly atmosphere.

In an annexe with a separate entrance are three immaculate white bedrooms, done in Scandinavian chic.

Herstmonceux, Sussex

Wartling Place Country House **Country guesthouse**

Rowena and Barry Gittoes run their upmarket B&B in a substantial former four-bedroom rectory – room for guests and hosts to be separate – guests have the first floor, and their own drawing room and dining room, and there's a 3-acre garden. There is also a cottage with two extra rooms. Tasteful country house decoration and furnishing, including some genuine antiques. This is solid, unflashy quality, with personal but not intrusive attention, backed by 17 years of experience as we went to press. Wartling is a small, peaceful village on the edge of the Pevensey Levels nature reserve and there's much else of interest nearby – this is '1066 country'.

Wartling, Herstmonceux, East Sussex BN27 1RY

Tel 01323 832590
email accom@wartlingplace.co.uk
website www.wartlingplace.co.uk
Food breakfast, dinner by prior arrangement
Price ££ **Closed** never
Proprietors Barry and Rowena Gittoes

Kintbury, Berkshire

The Dundas Arms **Village inn**

At first, we were distinctly under-whelmed by our awkwardly shaped room, its sombre furnishings and clock that told the wrong time. In the cramped bath-room, the basin was so shallow that water bounced off the porcelain and on to the floor. But next morning we were charmed by the sunshine on our private terrace bordering the River Kennet.

Much of the emphasis is on the food, served in two comfortable dining rooms, but it's still the quirky original bar that acts as the focal point – this is an upgraded pub that can still bring in the locals. The Dundas Arms is not perfect, but the team is cheer-ful, and its heart is definitely in the right place. We're also told an extensive refur-bishment is imminent, which will no doubt enhance this address – reports welcome.

53 Station Road, Kintbury, Berkshire RG17 9UT

Tel 01488 658263
e-mail info@dundasarms.co.uk
website www.dundasarms.co.uk
Food breakfast, snack lunch, dinner
Price ££
Closed never
Proprietor James Waterhouse

11 Cadogan Gardens
City hotel

Our series editor Fiona Duncan was initially thrown by the dark and sultry interior of 11 Cadogan Gardens, seemingly out of step with its homely Chelsea address. However, its glossy opulence – all shadowy lighting and black wood pannelling – began to grow on her, while the impeccable service from William, and legendary concierge Richie was Chelsea through and through.

Where other top hotels standardize bedrooms, these are all individual: both stately and homely, with beautiful marble bathrooms. Downstairs you'll find the Mirror Room – a genius concoction of gilt-and-glass – as well as their glossy bar. The restaurant, Tartufo, is a welcome surprise of cream hues and natural light, serving delicious Italian food.

11 Cadogan Gardens, Chelsea, London, SW7 2RJ

Tel 020 7730 7000
email reception@11cadogangardens.com
website 11cadogangardens.com
Food breakfast, lunch, dinner, afternoon tea **Price** ££££ **Closed** never
Proprietors Cadogan Estate
Management Iconic Luxury Hotels

The Franklin
City hotel

Contemporary designer-chic in Knightsbridge. The sign at the entrance is discreet, presenting it (almost) as a private house. It's owned by an Italian hotel group whose mission is to bring Italian hospitality and design standards to London hotels. Redesigned in 2016 by Anouska Hempel, creator of Blakes in South Kensington, the style could only be hers, says our series editor Fiona Duncan: sophisticated, urban, innovatative and international, you'll find mirrored surfaces and moody lighting (perhaps a little dark for some).

The regular bedrooms are small – if you want space you have to pay for a suite. The restaurant is for residents only, so feels private, and serves a mixture of sophisticated and simple dishes – Italian cooking at its best, directed by a Michelin starred chef.

24 Egerton Gardens, Knightsbridge, SW3 2DB

Tel 020 75845533
email reservations.thefranklin@starhotels.com
website www.starhotelscollezione.com
Food breakfast, lunch, dinner
Price ££££ **Closed** never
Management Star Hotels

London

The Mayflower Hotel
City hotel

Trudging past the dire Earl's Court budget hotels en route to The Mayflower, you will feel relief at the sight of its smart, freshly painted façade. No disappointment, either, once inside: to the left, an airy bar/sitting room; to the right, a spacious, calm, sophisticated reception area.

Our reporter's room was tiny, but perfectly formed. In a clever move that makes this budget address feel both hip and characterful, the rooms have been enlivened with Oriental artefacts, carved wooden cupboards and mirrored bedheads, silk cushions and velvet bedspreads, plus attractive wooden blinds and sweeping curtains.

Our reporter reflected that the Mayflower stands out 'like an Aladdin's lamp in a junk shop amongst budget central London hotels.'

26-28 Trebovir Road, London SW5 9NJ

Tel 020 7370 0991
Fax 020 7370 0994
e-mail info@mayflower-group.co.uk
website www.themayflowerhotel.co.uk
Food breakfast **Price** ££-££££
Closed never
Manager Frank Davies

London

The Sumner
City hotel

The previous owners, the Palgan family, completed renovations of this Georgian town house in 2006, when it opened as The Sumner. The results of their £1.5m investment are impressive – the place is immaculate and stylishly done.

The sitting room is particularly striking – its high Georgian ceilings and original cornicing are complemented by a beautiful wooden floor, chunky dark wood furniture and inviting, deep sofas.

Bedrooms are generously proportioned, particularly those on the ground and first floors, which have very high ceilings. Bathrooms are spotless: white-tiled, with a block of turquoise colour.

This hotel is now under new management, and we would welcome reports.

54 Upper Berkeley Street, Marble Arch, London W1H 7QR

Tel (020) 7723 2244
Fax (0870) 705 8767
e-mail reservataions@the sumner.com
website www.thesumner.com
Food breakfast **Price** £££
Closed never
Manager Rashid

London

Twenty Nevern Square
City hotel

Peace and tranquility aren't two words usually associated with London but, just around the corner from bustling Earl's Court, Twenty Nevern Square is suprisingly calm and cosy.

Decorated in a colonial, Anglo-Indian scheme, rooms have a feeling of understated luxury. Natural fabrics have been used throughout; silk curtains, wooden floors and hessian carpets blend nicely with smart patterned bedspreads. One hundred metres of silk has been used in decorating the Chinese room, with oriental-print cushions and floor-to-ceiling white and navy drapes. Bathrooms are brick, smart and done out entirely in marble.

Breakfast is served downstairs in the conservatory-style restaurant.

Twenty Nevern Square, London
SW5 9PD

Tel (020) 7565 9555
Fax (020) 7565 9444
e-mail twenty@mayflowercollec-tion.com **website** www.20nevern-square.co.uk
Food breakfast, 24 hour room service for tea and coffee **Price** ££
Closed never
Manager Imran Saloojee

Lymington, Hampshire

Stanwell House
Town hotel

On Lymington's attractive High Street, an Italianate stone-flagged courtyard stretches the length of this building, affording inviting views from the street of a glass-roofed sitting room; on one side of the entrance is a country clothing shop, on the other a seafood restaurant in 17thC style.

This quite stylish hotel has been run by Robert Milton and Victoria Crowe for ten years. During their tenure they've individually designed 29 bedrooms; introduced a nautical-inspired cocktail bar; and launched Burcher & Co – an informal tapas restaurant showcasing local produce.

The bedrooms in the main house are theatrical. Dramatic walls, rich hangings and piles of colourful cushions vie for attention. The place attracts a youngish clientèle.

14-15 High Street, Lymington,
Hampshire, SO41 9AA

Tel (01590) 677123 **e-mail**
enquiries@stanwellhousehotel.co.uk
websitewww.stanwellhousehotel.co.uk
Food breakfast, brunch, lunch, afternoon tea, dinner **Price** £££ **Closed** never **Proprietors** Robert Milton and Victoria Crowe

Petersfield, Hampshire

JSW
Restaurant-with-rooms

An award-winning restaurant in a bustling Hampshire town, JSW also has four double rooms which follow the kitchen's 'stylish yet simple' mantra. Rooms are comfortable with character, both light enough to be attractive in summer and cosily well-heated in winter. The Egyptian cotton sheets and towels are a treat.

After the high point of dinner, breakfast is a simple continental affair served in your room, with an emphasis on fresh fruit and breads, as well as pastries from the renowned Rungis Market in Paris.

20 Dragon Street, Petersfield, Hampshire GU31 4JJ

Tel 01730 262030
email jsw.restaurant@btconnect.com
website www.jswrestaurant.com
Food breakfast included; lunch (Thur-Sat), dinner (Wed-Sat).
Price ££
Closed 23rd Dec-7th Jan, 2 weeks in April, 2 weeks in Aug
Proprietor Jake Watkins

Petworth, West Sussex

The Halfway Bridge
Restaurant-with-rooms

Sam and Janet Bakose hit the spot with the Crab and Lobster at Sidlesham (page 148) and did it again when they reinvented this restaurant-with-rooms between Petworth and Midhurst. It's ideal for a South Downs walking weekend, for browsing the antique shops in Petworth, or for visiting Cowdray Park.

The pleasing 17thC coaching inn was immaculately restored by Sam and Janet six years ago, making it contemporary-stylish but relaxed. The seven bedrooms, all different, are smart, comfortable and spacious. There are quirky design features such as a row of old beams upended to form panelling. When we visited, the food was as expected for the price: local fish and game alongside Mediterranean dishes.

Lodsworth, Petworth, West Sussex, GU28 9BP

Tel (01798) 861281
website www.halfwaybridge.co.uk
Food breakfast by appointment, lunch, dinner
Prices £££
Closed never
Proprietors Sam and Janet Bakose

Petworth, West Sussex

Petworth, West Sussex GU28 0JF

Tel (01798) 342346
email info@old-station.co.uk
website www.old-station.co.uk
Food breakfast, cream tea
Prices ££-£££
Closed Christmas
Proprietors Gudmund Olafsson
and Catherine Stormont

The Old Railway
Station Bed-and-breakfast

If you've ever dreamed about stepping back in time and taking a great rail journey, now you can do just that – in West Sussex. The Old Railway Station provides unique accommodation in either the original Petworth Railway Station building or in one of four Pullman carriages.

The station building, Grade II listed, is impressive and welcoming. The former waiting-room now contains the breakfast room and sitting-room, and has vaulted ceilings and original ticket office windows

Bedrooms and bathrooms are narrow, but very long. Original furnishings, marquetry in the walls and antique luggage and clocks all add to the charm.

Inside the main building the bedrooms are spacious and well-fitted out.

Seaview, Isle of Wight

High Street, Seaview, Isle of Wight
PO34 5EX

Tel (01983) 612711
Fax (01983) 613729
e-mail reception@seaviewhotel.co.uk
website www.seaviewhotel.co.uk
Food breakfast, lunch, dinner; room
service **Price** ££
Closed Christmas day
Proprietor Martin Gardener

Seaview Hotel
Seaside hotel

If you like breezy, old-fashioned English seaside resorts, you will love sailing-mad Seaview. When Brian Gardener bought this hotel in 2003 he had it completely redecorated and refurbished – adding a further seven rooms and greatly improving the disabled facilities. Bedrooms are a class-act with clean nautical lines and soothing colour schemes.

Since Brian's passing in 2015, the running has been handed over to his brother Martin. The hotel's restaurant has also been newly commandeered by Liam Hayes, who's earned a Michelin Bib Gourmand for his creative and affordable menu (£28 for 3 courses). Alternatively guests can eat more traditional pub food in one of their two public bars, or sit out on their terrace.

Totford, Hampshire

The Woolpack
Village inn

It stands in the smallest hamlet in Hampshire, possibly in England, in the Candover Valley. Built around 1880, the Grade I-listed brick-and-flint building is simple but full of character.

Inside, it's as appealing as outside, with room for armchairs and a pool table in the spacious bar. Next to it is a dining room with a raised open fire. Or you can choose to eat in the extension that cleverly encases the exterior walls of the pub and is designed to look like stables.

The rooms, found at the back of the inn in converted outbuildings, could be improved. In ours, Snipe, the exposed brick-and-flint walls also included swathes of ugly concrete and the furniture was basic.

Totford, near Northington,
Alresford, Hampshire SO24 9TJ

Tel 0845 2938066/01962 734184
email info@thewoolpackinn.co.uk
website www.thewoolpackinn.co.uk
Food breakfast, lunch, dinner; bar snacks, picnic hampers, Sunday lunch **Price** £££ **Closed** evening of Christmas Day **Proprietor** Andrew Cooper

Ventnor, Isle of Wight

The Hambrough Hotel
Seaside hotel

Ventnor is a pretty Victorian cliff-top town with winter gardens, an esplanade, a sandy beach and a shack selling crab and lobster. The Hambrough stands between the High Street and the seafront, overlooking the Cascade Gardens and the harbour. It has seven spacious bedrooms, a restaurant and a bar. It doesn't aim to do too much, but what it does, it hopes to do well and, by and large, it succeeds.

The restaurant continues to make waves locally and the five-course, tasting menu comes with well-chosen wines. A serious kitchen opens off an all-white dining room.

Our inspector had absolute quiet in her spacious room. Her only quibbles: the service lacked warmth; and the overall feel is stylish rather than characterful.

Hambrough Road, Ventnor,
Isle of Wight, PO38 1SQ

Tel (01983) 856333
e-mail info@thehambrough.com
website www.thehambrough.com
Food breakfast, lunch, dinner
Price £££-££££ **Closed** never
Manager Danielle Anderson

Wickham, Hampshire

The Square, Wickham, Hampshire
PO17 5JG

Tel (01329) 835870
e-mail info@bb-wickham.com
website www.bb-wickham.com
Food breakfast, lunch, dinner
Prices ££-£££ **Closed** never
Proprietor James Guess

Old House
Village hotel

The Old House possesses much that we look for: an interesting setting – at a corner of the main square of one of the finest villages in Hampshire; a superb building; a delightful garden; an immaculately kept interior; an intimate bar; and attractive dining rooms, created from the original timber-framed outhouse and stables.

Bedrooms vary – some palatial, others with magnificent beams, many with original features, one or two rather cramped – but again a mood of civilized comfort prevails. Times are changing for the Old House, and it has changed hands several times in recent years. Their restaurant has been reopened, with a new Italian menu, while the hotel's decorations and ambience have happily stayed largely the same – and so, it seems, does the warmth of welcome.

Winchester, Hampshire

75 Kingsgate Street, Winchester,
Hampshire SO23 9PE

Tel (01962) 853834
email wykehamarms@fullers.co.uk
website www.wykehamarmswin-
chester.co.uk
Food breakfast, lunch, dinner
Price ££
Closed never
Managers Jon Howard

The Wykeham Arms
Town pub-with-rooms

'Enormously charming; tons of personality,' confirms our latest reporter. Tucked away in the oldest part of the city, with Winchester College yards away and the Cathedral close by, this is a well-frequented pub, and it's first-rate: 250 years old with two bars furnished with old school desks. Quirky character runs to the bedrooms, which are small and low-ceilinged, but each furnished in its own style, and accommodating all the usual facilities.

Breakfast is served downstairs in the restaurant with Windsor chairs and a fine collection of silver tankards. Hearty food at lunch time and an *à la carte* menu in the evenings; real ales and an impressive list of around 100 wines, changed regularly.

Winkfield, Berkshire

Winkfield Street, Winkfield,
Windsor, Berkshire SL4 4SW

Tel 01344 882242
email
info@winningpostwinkfield.co.uk
website www.winningpostwink-
field.co.uk **Food** breakfast, light
lunch, lunch, dinner **Price** £££
Closed never
Proprietor Upham Pub Brewery

The Winning Post
Country inn

During the week, this pub attracts people on business, but the majority of
people drinking at the bar or dining are to
do with the worlds of polo and racing –
this is polo heartland, with major polo
clubs and Ascot racecourse close at hand.

From the outside, the pub looks like a
modest cottage but its interior is surprisingly spacious, cosy and characterful.
Bedrooms are in a purpose-built nineties
addition at the back of the building, and
need to be more alluring to justify their
price. Happily, there are plans to renovate
these these next year.

Staff are friendly and local. Food arrived
swiftly and was a cut above the norm for
such a place. Cooked breakfast (continental is included in the room price) is an
extra £4.

Yattendon, Berkshire

The Square, Yattendon, Berkshire
RG18 0UF

Tel 01635 201325
e-mail
info@royaloakyattendon.com **web-
site** www.royaloakyattendon.co.uk
Food breakfast, lunch, dinner
Price ££
Closed New Year's Day (evening of)
Proprietors Rob McGill

The Royal Oak
Village hotel

The Royal Oak is easy to find in the centre of the village of Yattendon.

Lest you mistake it for a mere pub, the
sign on the front of this cottage, mellow
red-brick inn announces Hotel and
Restaurant. Certainly, the Royal Oak is no
longer a common-or-garden local (as it was
when Oliver Cromwell reportedly ate
there). Its two dining areas have a style and
elegance not usually associated with ale
and darts. But there is still a small bar
where residents and non-residents alike
can enjoy a choice of real ales.

Bedrooms are prettily decorated and
equipped with every conceivable extra.
Another attraction is the walled garden, full
of colour and a delight during the summer.

St Peter Port, Guernsey

South Esplanade, St Peter Port,
Guernsey GY1 1AN

Tel 01481 715488
e-mail info@theyacht.gg
website www.theyacht.gg
Food breakfast, lunch
Price £-£££
Closed Christmas Day, Boxing Day
Proprietor Andy Roberts

The Yacht Inn
Seaside town hotel

In a great location for exploring busy St Peter Port, overlooking the Albert Marina. Inside, it's cosy and informal, decorated well in a contemporary style. The dining room has (tasteful) brown leather chairs and – like the rest of the hotel – a distinctly pleasant nautical feel.

Clean, contemporary bedrooms – again with brown leather and light walls – have all the latest fittings. Sea-facing rooms are more expensive, but worth it.

The downstairs bar is the highlight, appealing to young business people who like its relaxed feel and the in-house DJ. Recently re-styled, the tables are curvy, and a copper bar compliments the nautical theme. The restaurant is popular with non-residents.

Area introduction

The ancient kingdom of Wales, the Midlands industrial heartland and the mostly flat counties of Cambridgeshire, Norfolk and Suffolk are the main ingredients of this section. It also includes the fashionable counties of Gloucestershire and Oxfordshire, and the home countries to the west and north of London (Buckinghamshire, Hertfordshire, Essex and so on). Wales and East Anglia have always been important tourist regions, as are Oxfordshire and Gloucestershire because they contain Oxford and the Cotswolds. But imaginative tourist developments in Midland industrial cities (for example, Birmingham) and historic centres such as Ironbridge Gorge in Shropshire now also means that the Midlands, far from being tourist deserts, are increasingly important. Our selection of special places to stay in all of these has grown accordingly since the last edition.

Below are some useful back-up places to try if our main selections are fully booked:

Wales

The Bear Hotel
Country hotel, Crickhowell
Tel 01873 810408
www.bearhotel.co.uk
Comfortable hotel in the heart of the Brecon Beacons.

Fairyhill
Restaurant-with-rooms,
Reynoldston Tel 01792
391468 www.fairyhill.co.uk
Peaceful retreat with award-winning restaurant.

England

The Riverside Inn
Country inn, Cound
Tel 01952 510900
www.theriversideinn.net
Charming inn with great views of the River Severn.

Barnsdale Lodge
Farmhouse hotel, Exton
Tel 01572 724678
www.barnsdalelodge.co.uk
Extended farmhouse on the shore of Rutland Water.

Old Swan & Minster Mill **Town hotel, Minster Lovell** Tel 01993 774441
www.oldswanandminster-mill.co.uk Traditional and contemporary rooms.

Lion + Pheasant
Townhouse hotel,
Shrewsbury Tel 01743
770345 www.lionandpheasant.co.uk
Historic inn.

Crazy Bear
Village hotel, Stadhampton
Tel 01865 890714
www.crazybeargroup.co.uk/stadhampton
Off the wall.

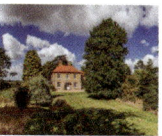

Godwick Hall
Town hotel, Godwick
Tel 01328 701948
www.godwickhall.co.uk
Country house with The Great Barn for events.

Bruisyard Hall
Country house, Saxmundham
Tel 01728 639000
www.bruisyardhall.co.uk
Countryside bed-and-breakfast, perfect for events.

Linden House
Restaurant-with-rooms,
Stansted Tel 01279 813003
www.lindenhousestansted.co.uk
Smart, trendy restaurant and stylish rooms.

Aberaeron, Ceredigion

Pen Cei, Aberaeron, Ceredigion
SA46 0BA

Tel (01545) 570 755
Fax (01545) 570 762
e-mail info@harbour-master.com
website www.harbour-master.com

Location off A487 in centre of town
on the quay; with ample car parking
Food breakfast, lunch, dinner
Price ££
Rooms 13; 1 suite, 10 double, 2 can
be twin, 2 single all with bath and
shower (1 with
hand held); all rooms have TV,
DVD player, hairdryer, some have
phone and wi-fi, others have broad-
band
Facilities dining room, bar, bikes
Credit cards all major suppliers
Children accepted in the cottage
Disabled 1 room is adapted, and 3
others acessible by lift
Pets not accepted
Closed Christmas day
Proprietors Menna and Glyn
Heulyn

Harbourmaster
Seaside inn

Back in the 1950s, an eccentric resident of Aberaeron decided to give each of her five properties a different brightly coloured coat of paint. The idea caught on, and today the purpose-built Regency harbour town is an uplifting riot of colour, where The Harbourmaster Hotel makes a splash all its own with a brilliant cobalt blue external livery. Opened in 2005, it is, as you would expect, a former harbourmaster's residence.

The ground floor is given over to eating and drinking, with a curving bar, informal dining room and inventive menu featuring local produce, including the day's catch, Welsh black beef and tapas. At breakfast, freshly baked bread or Welsh laverbread.

The light, tasteful interior decoration manages to be contemporary 'cool' as well as homely; an eyecatching feature is the listed spiral staircase. Upstairs there are seven bright, modern bedrooms, fine for a stopover. Best is the one at the top, from where the harbourmaster once kept an eye on all three harbours under his control in Cardigan Bay. No children under five.

Bontnewydd, Gwynedd

Bontnewydd, Caernarfon, Gwynedd
LL54 7YF

Tel (01286) 830214
e-mail info@plasdinas.co.uk
website www.plasdinas.co.uk

Nearby Caernarfon Castle;
Portmeirion; Welsh Highland
Railway; Snowdon.
Location 2.5 miles from
Caernarfon, ample parking
Food breakfast, dinner (Tue to Sat
only – book in advance)
Price £££
Rooms 9 double/twin, all with
bath/shower; all rooms have TV, wi-
fi **Facilities** dining room, sitting
room, bar, fireplace; gardens
Credit cards MC, V
Children not accepted
Disabled 1 ground-floor room
Pets dogs accepted in Buckley or
South rooms
Closed Christmas to New Year
Proprietors Neil and Marco

Plas Dinas
Country house hotel

It could easily be overbearing, but this elegant, Regency-style gentleman's house (though some parts date back 400 years) is the kind of place where you can be yourself. Neil and Marco have owned the property since 2013, and are responsible for the opening of The Gun Room restaurant, headed by a local award-winning chef.

Downstairs both the atmospheric drawing room and The Gun Room are decked in royal memorabilia, while upstairs, the mostly spacious bedrooms are decorated in either traditional country house style, or modern 'boutique' style, with bold wallpaper. All combine antiques with contemporary comforts. Each has its own character, with the kind of individual touch we look for, including the amusingly masculine Bachelor Room. Views are of the 15 acres of grounds to the Menai Strait, or over the unspoilt countryside.

The house, down a 100-m long drive, once belonged to the Armstrong-Joneses, the family of Lord Snowdon, who married the Queen's late sister, Princess Margaret. She stayed here, and Prince William has visited for a private lunch in the Gun Room.

Brechfa, Carmarthenshire

Brechfa, Carmarthenshire
SA32 7RA

Tel (01267) 202332
e-mail info@wales-country-hotel.co.uk **website** www.wales-country-hotel.co.uk

Nearby Brecon Beacons, National Botanical Gardens of Wales; National Trust Dinefwr Park and Castle, Abergalsney Gardens.
Location 10 miles (16 km) NE of Carmarthen, on B4310, in village; with ample car parking
Food breakfast, dinner
Price ££ Rooms 6; 3 superior super king-size double, 3 twin, all with bath and shower; all rooms have TV, hairdryer, tea and coffee facilities.
Facilities sitting room, dining room, breakfast room, bar/reception; garden
Credit cards MC, V, Amex
Children welcome over 10
Disabled not suitable
Pets welcome
Closed rarely
Proprietors Stephen and Annabel Thomas

Ty Mawr
Country hotel

Firmly at right angles to the main street of this tiny village on the fringe of Brechfa Forest, and by the River Marlais, Ty Mawr has a pretty garden and fine views of the surrounding wooded hillsides. It was bought in 2004 by Stephen and Annabel Thomas, who completely refurbished it while preserving the oak beams, stone walls and tiled floors that proclaim the building's three and a bit centuries' tenure of this glorious spot.

The public rooms are cosy and cheerful and include an immaculate bar with smart pine fittings, and a comfy sitting room with an open log fire. The long slate-floored restaurant looks out on to the garden and, candle-lit in the evenings, is where the chef's skill in the kitchen shows in earnest: fresh, usually Welsh, ingredients are assembled without undue fuss but with plenty of imagination. The wines are well-chosen and offered at eminently reasonable prices.

Upstairs, the bedrooms are bright, comfortable and pleasantly rustic, and breakfast in the morning answers to appetites ranging from the merely peckish to the downright ravenous. The flowers in the garden tubs are quite impressive, but it's worth remembering that the National Botanical Garden of Wales is nearby.

Builth Wells, Powys

Cwmbach, Newbridge-on-Wye
Builth Wells, Powys, LD2 3RT

Tel (01982) 552493
e-mail post@the-drawing-room.co.uk
website www.the-drawing-room.co.uk

Nearby Elan Valley walks; Brecon Beacons; Cambrian and Black Mountains
Location off A470 in Builth Wells with ample car parking
Food breakfast, dinner
Price ££££
Rooms 3 doubles, 2 with bath, 1 with shower
Facilities dining room, 2 sitting rooms, garden
Credit cards MC, V
Children not accepted
Disabled not suitable
Pets not accepted
Closed Mon except bank holidays – best to ring and check
Proprietors Colin and Melanie Dawson

The Drawing Room
Restaurant-with-rooms

This is one of Wales's growing group of exceptional restaurants with rooms, where commitment and attention to detail are second to none. Colin and Melanie Dawson have converted a Georgian house into a small restaurant, two sitting rooms and three bedrooms. The rooms are contemporary in style, one decorated bright red and quite masculine, the other two more feminine. They are not large, but perfectly formed and whilst lounging in the bath (one of them is a slipper bath) you can watch the hill sheep grazing opposite.

Colin and Melanie have decorated this property beautifully and with great attention to detail. Although the sitting rooms are small you don't mind because they are immaculately furnished with comfy sofas, chairs, roaring fires and interesting *objets d'art*. However, the emphasis here is on the food – pleasant as it is to get good bedrooms too. Both Colin and Melanie are chefs, and their food wins many plaudits. When we visited the menu included a ragout of sea bass, salmon and black bream with langoustine, fennel and leeks as well as a fillet of local Welsh beef. Make sure you book well in advance as this place gets booked up quickly.

Capel Garmon, Conwy

Capel Garmon, near Betws-y-Coed,
Llanrwst, Conwy LL26 0RE

Tel 01690 710507
Fax 01690 710 681
e-mail
stay@tanyfoelcountryhouse.co.uk
website www.tanyfoelcountry-house.co.uk

Nearby Conwy Castle; Caernarfon
Castle; Bodnant Gardens; Llanberis
Location just off the A5, head
towards Capel Garmon/Nebo, 1.5
miles (2.5 km) up the hill, Tan-y-
Foel is on the left
Food breakfast
Price ££
Rooms 6 doubles all with bath and
shower; all rooms have TV, hairdrier,
phone
Facilities sitting room, dining room;
garden
Credit cards MC, V
Children welcome over 12
Disabled not suitable
Pets not accepted
Closed Dec and Jan
Proprietors Mr and Mrs Pitman

Tan-y-Foel
Bed-and-breakfast

Parts date back to the 16thC; parts are highly contemporary and it pulls it off remarkably well. The interior is a riot of vibrant colours cleverly kept in check with beautiful furnishings and distressed paint work.

The intimate reception rooms are decorated in peaceful earth tones, for relaxing in with a drink before dinner. The gardens are secluded and well looked after, but not too manicured, perfectly in keeping with the ruggedness of the country beyond.

The breakfasts are exceptional, and Maria and Chris are exemplary hosts: full of genuine warmth and interest in their guests, and mines of information about the stunning local area. Situated in the Conwy Valley, there are plenty of great walks.

All the rooms are individually decorated, comfortable, out of the ordinary. Interesting objets d'art are placed on shelves or hang on the walls making you feel as if you should be somewhere more exotic, certainly farther afield than Wales. A highly original hotel for people who want something out of the ordinary in Wales.

Crickhowell, Powys

Crickhowell, Powys, NP8 1RH

Tel (01874) 730371
Fax (01874) 730463
e-mail calls@gliffaeshotel.com
website www.gliffaeshotel.com

Nearby Brecon Beacons National Park, River Usk, Abergavenny
Location off A40 in own large grounds with ample parking
Food breakfast, lunch, dinner, afternoon tea,
Price £££
Rooms 23; all doubles, 10 can be twinned, all rooms have shower, some have bath, all rooms have phone, TV, hairdryer, some have DVD player **Facilities** dining room, sitting room, drawing room, conference room, conservatory garden, terrace, fishing
Credit Cards MC, V
Children accepted
Disabled one room suitable for disabled access
Pets accepted
Closed Jan
Proprietors James and Susie Suter, and Peta Brabner

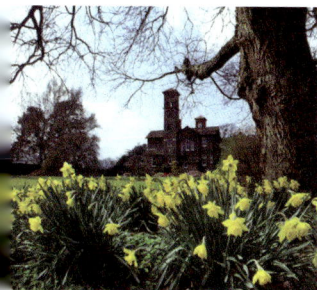

Gliffaes
Country house hotel

We've known about Gliffaes for many years and hesitated to put it in the guide despite its fine reputation because it seemed a little large (23 bedrooms), a little imposing (quite a grand Victorian-Italianate country pile); but above all not especially relaxed or personal. Then we dropped in by chance one day and changed our minds.

It's a superb example of a family-run (now third generation) country house hotel: a stunning location; caring, hands-on management; unpretentious yet with high standards. You will probably take away memories of the lovely views from the terrace, grounds falling steeply to the rushing Usk; and of the large grounds with exotic plantings. You might also catch a fish: the hotel has a mile and a half of highly regarded salmon and trout fishing on the Usk.

The decoration is traditional yet stylish. Most of the homely-smart country house style bedrooms are spacious, and one has a four-poster bed. Dinner is a smartish occasion – guests change, but into 'country casual' clothes, not black tie. The food is good, much of it from local suppliers. Tea is the most lavish spread you are likely to see for a while.

Denbigh, Denbighshire

Llandyrnog, Denbigh LL16 4LA

Tel 01824 790732
e-mail info@pentremawrcountry-house.co.uk **website** www.pentremawrcountryhouse.co.uk

Nearby Denbigh castle; Horseshoe Pass; Chester; Snowdonia.
Location from Denbigh take Llandyrnog turn-off. Exit for Bodari at roundabout, then take lane on left after 50 yds. **Food** breakfast hampers **Price** £-£££ **Rooms** 3 suites, all with TV, DVD player, iPod dock, hairdryer, private terrace and hot tub; 6 safari lodges, all with king size beds, en suite bathrooms, private hot-tubs. **Facilities** restaurant, drawing room, study, conservatory, swimming pool, hot tubs, fishing, parking, DVD library **Credit cards** MC, V **Children** accepted over 12 **Disabled** wide-doored rooms in lodges **Pets** welcome, owners have dogs **Closed** Christmas **Proprietors** Bre and Graham Carrington-Sykes

Pentre Mawr Country House **Country house**

Pentre Mawr offers a great mix of two things we love: old-fashioned, excellent service and individual character. It's an elegant white house which has been in the family for over 400 years, surrounded by 200 acres of woodland and meadows. Owners Bre and Graham greet every arrival with Buck's Fizz and afternoon tea: providing a mere hint at how 'spoilt rotten' you'll feel after a stay here.

The place has a feeling of being tirelessly worked at. A modern, minimalist style can be found in the suites, but the attention to detail is impressive everywhere.

Outside, there's an ultra-fashionable 'glamping' option: six safari lodges which look military from the outside, but are truly opulent within, with king-size beds, en suite bathrooms and hot-tubs: the works. A breakfast hamper with croissants and preserves is delivered to your suite or lodge, for added decadence. The restaurant is largely closed these days, but food can be had at any one of the excellent pubs nearby.

Despite all of this perfection, the atmosphere at Pentre Mawr is friendly, not formal. A guest describes it as a 'home from home' and the personalities of Bre and Graham shine through: they are thoughtful, welcoming and overall excellent hosts.

Eglwysfach, Powys

Eglwysfach, Machynlleth, Powys
SY20 8TA

Tel (01654) 781209
e-mail info@ynyshir.co.uk **website**
www.ynyshir.co.uk

Nearby Llyfnant valley;
Aberystwyth.
Location 11 miles (18 km) NE of
Aberystwyth, just off A487; ample
car parking
Food breakfast, lunch, dinner
Price ££££
Rooms 10; 6 in main house, 4
ground floor outside; all with bath
and shower, phone, TV, hairdryer,
tea and coffee trays; garden rooms
have log burners and balconies
Facilities Michelin-starred restau-
rant, bar, large gardens
Credit cards AE, DC, MC, V
Children 12+ accepted
Disabled 1 ground-floor room
Pets not allowed
Closed 23 Dec-8 Jan
Proprietors John and Jenny Talbot,
Gareth Ward (chef patron)
Manager Amelia Eriksson

Ynyshir
Restaurant with rooms

Since our last edition, Ynyshir has changed its identity. Now resolutely a restaurant-with-rooms instead of a country house hotel, with a full-scale refurbishment in 2017 to prove it. The restaurant, run by Gareth Ward, has achieved an avalanche of success since he came to helm in 2013, swiftly earning a Michelin star, and and becoming Chef Patron in 2016.

It still has ten well-appointed guest rooms. Each is individually decorated and stylishly furnished with contemporary touches, whilst being cosy and comfortable, with king-size beds, excellent bathrooms and views across the Cumbrian mountains.

The main event, however, is the food, served in their intimate restaurant with 26 covers and a chef's table seating six. Gareth serves what he calls, in his Northern parlance, 'Alternative British Snap' – sourced from the Welsh larder and British Isles, with Japanese influences: an exemplary crossover is his use of Welsh Wagyu Beef. As the guide went to press Ynyshir could list a slew of awards and plaudits to its credit.

The breakfast is as you'd expect from a top chef, with home-cured salmon, cream cheese, sourdough crumpets and home-soaked muesli.

Felin Fach, Powys

Felin Fach, Brecon, Powys
LD3 0UB

Tel (01874) 620111
e-mail
enquiries@felinfachgriffin.co.uk
website www.eatdrinksleep.ltd.uk

Nearby Hay Bluff; Pen y Fan;
Brecon Beacons and Black
Mountains; Brecon; Hay-on-Wye;
Llangorse Lake (sailing and wind-
surfing).
Location edge of village with off-
road car parking
Food breakfast, lunch, dinner
Price ££-£££
Rooms 7 double and twin; all rooms
have bath, phone, and Roberts Radios
Facilities bar, dining area; grassed
outdoor drinks area, croquet
Credit cards MC, V
Children accepted
Disabled no special facilities
Pets accepted
Closed Christmas Day and 1 week a
year, usually in Jan
Proprietors Charles and Edmund
Inkin

The Felin Fach Griffin
Country inn

The location is uninteresting, beside a busy-ish road, and you might think this is any old Welsh pub. But there's a clue it may be something different: the exterior is painted a mellow ochre, the colour seen all over Tuscany. Inside, you'll be struck by the layout: right by the bar is a pair of squashy leather sofas where you flop with the papers. A log fire is raised above floor level, radiating heat in two directions, into the bar and the adjacent dining room. Tongue-and-groove panelling is painted a brilliant blue. Nooks and crannies are filled with books: we spied *Debrett* and *Who's Who*. Upstairs are seven fresh, but perhaps boxey bed-rooms with homey decoration, again using bright colours. One has a four-poster bed and another extra beds for children.

The food is distinctly above average for the price. Home-made soda bread arrives on a simple wooden board. There's a large choice of interesting wines by the glass, including *prosecco*. The Griffin can claim to be Wales's original gastropub. Off the main dining room there's another smaller one with two tables seating eight (great for a party) in front of the AGA, where the day's fresh stocks simmer.

The Inkins also run The Gurnard's Head (page 86) and The Old Coastguard (page 60).

Ganllwyd, Gwynedd

Ganllwyd, Dolgellau, Snowdonia,
Gwynedd LL40 2HP

Tel 01341 440273
Fax 01341 440640
e-mail info@dolly-Hotel.co.uk
website www.dolly-hotel.co.uk

Nearby Cymer Abbey; Snowdonia;
Lake Vyrnwy. **Location** in country-
side, on A470 5 miles (8 km) N of
Dolgellau; ample car-parking
Food breakfast, lunch by arrange-
ment, dinner **Price** ££
Rooms 10; 9 double, 1 single, all
with bath; all rooms have phone, TV,
hairdrier
Facilities sitting room, dining room,
breakfast room, conservatory bar;
garden, fishing **Credit cards** AE,
DC, MC, V
Children welcome over 8
Disabled not suitable
Pets accepted in 2 bedrooms
Closed Nov to Mar
Proprietors Alan and Julie Pulman

Plas Domelynllyn
Country hotel

Alan and Julie Pulman, who took over
the hotel ten years ago, run it with
considerable style. Parts of it are more
than half a millennium old but there was
still work going on when we visited. It sits
in on its own terrace above Ganllwyd,
near Dolgellau, taking in the beautiful
views across the valley, and, in the princi-
pally Victorian interior, antiques mingle
equally comfortably with more modern
furnishings to create a warm, friendly
atmosphere. China and crystal twinkle on
all sides.

The drawing room is elegant but the
Old Hall Restaurant – the oldest part of
the house, with stone walls and slate
floors – is obviously where the team gets
down to real business. Visitors mention
the quality and choice of breakfast, served
in The Shelley Room which dates back to
the ninth century and has stained glass
windows. Locally sourced meats are used
for their dinner menu of 'British classics',
and there are homemade pâtés and
sausages on offer.

Bedrooms are named after local rivers
and individually furnished and decorated.
There is excellent walking from the door
and all guests have access to that essential
room in a Welsh hotel – the drying room.
This a passionately non-smoking hotel.

Llanarmon Dyffryn-Ceiriog, Wrexham

Llanarmon Dyffryn-Ceiriog
Nr Llangollen, Wrexham
LL20 7LD

Tel (01691) 600 665
Fax (01691) 600 622
e-mail info@thewestarms.co.uk
website www.thewestarms.co.uk

Nearby Chirk Castle, Ceiriog
Valley, Rhaeadr waterfall, Erdigg
Hall, Llangollen
Location on B4500, 7 miles SW of
Llangollen situated in centre of
hamlet, surrounded by countryside
with ample car parking at the rear
Food breakfast, lunch, dinner
Price ££-£££
Rooms 15; 2 suites, 1 four poster, 11
doubles, 1 twin, all with bath, some
with shower; all rooms have phone,
flat-screen TV, hairdryers, wi-fi
Facilities dining room, bar; garden
Credit cards MC, V
Children welcome
Disabled 1 accessible room
Pets accepted **Closed** never
Proprietors Mark and Nicola
Williamson

The West Arms
Country inn

A traditional, unspoilt inn with above average food and simple but comfortable bedrooms (try one of the character rooms which have pretty brass or four poster beds.) They are perhaps a little feminine, but decorated in a comfortable, unpretentious country style. You should get a warm welcome, and the mood will be helped along by flagstones and roaring inglenook fires surrounded by old blackened beams with traditional brasses on display. Our inspector found the dining room quite lacking in atmosphere, however the bar seemed the place to be for informal eating and drinking with the locals or alternatively the beer garden which has truly spectacular views over the Welsh hills and valleys.

Heartening food comes from the reputable head chef Grant Williams, who had been there 20 years as we went to press – a long time in this business, so there's probably a happy team here.

The West Arms is located in a natural spot for an inn, where three cattle drovers' tracks converge on the way to the markets at Oswestry, Chirk and Wrexham. Wonderful walking in the Berwyn Hills or Ceiriog Valley is a must if staying here.

Llanbrynmair, Powys SY19 7DY

Tel 01650 521479
Mobile 07766 312508
e-mail terrym@barlingsbarn.co.uk
website www.barlingsbarn.co.uk

Nearby Snowdonia; Aberdovey beach
Location 2 miles (3 km) NE of Llanbrynmair at end of private lane off road to Pandy; with ample car parking
Food self-catering
Price ££-£££
Rooms barn sleeps between 14-16 people
Facilities garden, indoor swimming pool - heated all year round, 20 acres of bluebell wood - a Plantation of Ancient Woodland, garden, BBQ, campfire, sauna, squash court, table-tennis, badminton, Sky TV, wi-fi and piano in the Wanws. **Credit cards** not accepted **Children** welcome
Disabled 2 ground-floor rooms
Pets accepted by arrangement
Closed never
Proprietors Terry and Felicity Margolis

Barlings Barn
Self-catering barns

The only sounds to disturb the peace in this corner of Powys come from the sheep on the surrounding hillsides, and from the nearby brook. Barlings Barn is a rural idyll in Llanbrynmair, in the heart of Wales, with a garden full of roses and honeysuckle: a picturesque setting for the outdoor activities, such as walking, bird-watching, fishing and golf, that you can enjoy in the surrounding Powys countryside.

Established in 1984, it is the perfect peace of the place that keeps it in the guide despite the move a few years ago towards a self-catering set-up. Home-made cakes await your arrival in the secluded barns adjacent to Felicity and Terrys Welsh farmhouse, one with an oak-beamed stone fireplace and wood-burning stove.

Since first featuring in the guide they have expanded from 2 to 22 acres with the purchase of beautiful surrounding woodland. They've also added an all-year-round heated pool, and a sunny new dining room with views over the valley to accomodate large parties of up to 28. The barns are well-equipped with range cookers, fridges, dishwashers, microwaves and barbecues. Though it's basically self-catering, the local caterer can deliver food to the door, and even provide waitresses to serve and wash up if you're feeling spoilt. There's a colourful market every Wednesday in Machynlleth.

Llandrillo, Denbighshire

Llandrillo, near Corwen,
Denbighshire LL21 0ST

Tel (01490) 440264
e-mail info@tyddynllan.co.uk
website www.tyddynllan.co.uk

Nearby Bala Lake and Railway;
Snowdonia.
Location 5 miles (8 km) SW of
Corwen off B4401; with ample car
parking
Food breakfast, lunch, dinner
Price ££££ (half board)
Rooms 12 double and twin, 10 with
bath, 2 with shower; all rooms have
phone, TV, radio, plus ground floor
suite
Facilities sitting room, bar, restau-
rant; croquet, fishing
Credit cards MC, V, Amex
Children welcome **Disabled** 1 suite
suitable
Pets accepted in bedrooms by
arrangement **Closed** 2 weeks in Jan
Proprietors Bryan and Susan Webb

Tyddyn Llan
Restaurant-with-rooms

A firm favourite with readers since our
first edition, this Georgian stone
house near Llandrillo is decorated with
elegant flair, period antiques and fine paintings, creating a serene ambience. Tyddyn
Llan is very much a home, despite the
number of guests it can accommodate.
There is a major extension to the building,
cleverly complementary to the original,
using slate, stone and cast-iron.

A reader writes: 'No intrusive reception
desk; spacious sitting rooms furnished
with style; dining room shows great flair;
bedrooms well equipped with original
pieces of furniture; small but modern and
very pleasing bathrooms; peaceful, comfortable stay, warm atmosphere provided
by attentive hosts'. When Fiona Duncan,
our series editor, visited a few years ago,
she felt that Bryan deserved a Michelin star
'for his instinctive cooking' and we were
delighted to hear that he was awarded one
not long after, in 2011.

Bryan and his wife Susan offer diners
with a new angle on Welsh country house
food with inventive and well-planned small
menus using quality local ingredients, plus
an impressive wine list.

The place is surrounded by large, beautiful grounds.

Llandudno, Conwy

Promenade, 17 North Parade,
Llandudno, Conwy LL30 2LP

Tel (01492) 860330
e-mail sales@osbornehouse.co.uk
website www.osbornehouse.co.uk

Nearby dry ski slope; Conwy Castle;
Bodnant Gardens; Snowdonia
Location on seafront opposite pier
and promenade gardens; off-road car
parking
Food breakfast (in room), lunch,
dinner
Price £££
Rooms 7 suites (1 family room), all
with phone, bath, walk-in shower,
TV, DVD, fridge, wi-fi
Facilities bar, 'bistro' restaurant,
cafe area, sitting area in reception,
terrace
Credit cards AE, DC, MC, V
Children welcome, but no children's
menu
Disabled access via a ramp
Pets not accepted
Closed one week at Christmas
Proprietors Maddocks family

Osborne House
Town hotel

There's virtually no mobile signal in the charmingly old-fashioned resort of Llandudno, but that's part of its appeal. Between the unspoilt beaches and the backdrop of mountains, life goes at a gentle pace. Summer here means strolling along the Promenade with an ice-cream cornet, pausing to watch Punch and Judy. In a plum position on the Prom, Osborne House fits its surroundings perfectly.

The Maddocks family have lavished attention on it. The public rooms are glamorous enough, but it's the seven gorgeous suites, six with sea views and private parking spaces, that really impress, and are kindly priced considering the wealth of antiques, pictures and porcelain in each one, and the marble bathrooms with splendid roll top baths. Some might find it all a bit over the top, certainly very Victorian, but downstairs the public spaces have plenty of modern touches including a sleek bar with two large plasma TV screens competing for attention. 'The Café,' a bistro-café, reckons on serving good food in a rather grand Victorian surroundings, but in an informal style – no set hours, okay to have just one course, and eat at the bar, a table or on a sofa.

Llanthony, Gwent

Llanthony, Abergavenny, Gwent
NP7 7NN

Tel (01873) 890487
website
www.llanthonyprioryhotel.co.uk

Nearby Offa's Dyke; Brecon
Beacons; Hay-on-Wye.
Location off A465 from
Abergavenny to Hereford, take
mountain road heading N at
Llanvihangel Crucorney; with ample
car parking
Food breakfast, lunch, dinner
Price £
Rooms 7 double and twin
Facilities dining room, bar; garden
Credit cards accepted
Children children under 10 unable
to stay in tower rooms
Disabled access not possible
Pets not accepted
Closed Nov-May only open on
weekends, but fully open 27th Dec-
New Year
Proprietor Geoffrey Neil

Llanthony Priory
Country inn

Far into the Black Mountains, on the west bank of the Afon Honddu and overlooked by Offa's Dyke to the east, Llanthony Priory lies high and remote in the Vale of Ewyas. The most spectacular approach is southwards from the sloping streets and busy bookshops of Hay-on-Wye.

One of the earliest Augustinian houses in Britain, it was endowed by the de Lacy family, but by the time of Henry VIII's dissolution of the monasteries had fallen into disuse. The Prior's quarters survived amongst the ruins and are now used as the hotel. Gothic horror enthusiasts will be delighted not only by the setting but also when they learn that the highest of the bedrooms can only be reached by climbing more than 60 spiral steps up into the south tower.

This is not a hotel for the fastidious or the faint-hearted: it is a long way from anywhere and much used by walkers attracted to the stunning country that surrounds it. Its isolation – not to mention lack of wi-fi and signal – is suited to those willing to switch off and relax, unharassed by the bleating of their mobile phone. The chance to sleep in this unique piece of history (with a four-poster and half-tester available) and to wake up to the view from the tower also comes with a very modest price tag.

Nant Gwynant, Gwynedd

Nant Gwynant, Gwynedd,
LL55 4NT

Tel (01286) 870211 (telephone for
bookings and cancellations)
website www.pyg.co.uk

Nearby Bodnant Gardens;
Caernarfon, Beaumaris and Harlech
Castles; Isle of Anglesey; Blackrock
Sands. **Location** take the A5 to
Holyhead, as you enter Capel Curig,
turn left on to the A4086. 4 miles (6
km) on the hotel is on a T junction
with the lake in front of it
Food breakfast, lunch, dinner, tea
Price £ **Rooms** 18 double and twin,
1 single; 7 premium rooms with private bathroom, 5 public bathrooms
Facilities sitting room, dining room,
smoke room, bar, sauna, natural
swimming pool, games room, beer
garden, lake
Credit cards MC, V **Children** welcome **Disabled** 1 ground-floor room
Pets by arrangement **Closed** mid-
week during Nov to Dec; Jan to 2nd
week of Mar
Proprietors Nick and Rupert
Pullee

Pen-y-Gwryd Hotel
Climbing hostel

A pilgrimage place for climbers: this is
the home of British Mountaineering,
where Edmund Hillary and his team set up
their training base before the assault on
Everest in 1953. Still in the same friendly
family after 58 years, the charming old
coach inn, set high in the desolate heart of
Snowdonia, is just the sort of place you
dream of returning to after a day outdoors: simple, unsophisticated, warm and
welcoming, with good plain home cooking,
including wickedly calorific puddings (dinner is £25 per head).

In keeping with the purpose of the place
the bedrooms are simple with no frills, not
all of them have private bathrooms, but
they all have fluffy towels and warm
embroidered bedding and linen; the best
room is in the annexe and has a grand four-
poster bed. One of the bathrooms houses
a vintage Victorian bath that looks deep
and inviting. For the less intrepid walkers
there is still plenty to see in the vicinity, as
it is littered with castles and gardens.

After a hard day on the hill you can soak
your aching muscles in the natural pool in
the garden or unwind in the sauna. For children (or playful adults) there is a games
room with a dart board and table tennis.

Molleston, Narberth,
Pembrokeshire SA67 8BX

Tel 01834 860915
email
reservations@grovenarbeth.co.uk
website www.thegrove-
narberth.co.uk

Nearby walks through Cannaston
Wood to the Blackpool Mill;
Stackpole Estate Coastal Walk;
Tenby; St David's; Porthgain; the
Blue Lagooon; galleries; craft shops
Location Narbeth with shops,
restaurants and boutiques, close to
the beautiful Preseli Hills
Food breakfast, lunch, dinner
Price £££
Rooms 26: all en-suite with cast iron
bath and shower, rooms have flat-
screen television and Sky TV; some
have fireplaces.
Facilities restaurant, sitting room,
bar, kitchen garden **Credit cards** all
major **Children** welcome **Disabled**
accessible **Pets** only in selected
rooms **Closed** never **Proprietors**
Neil Kedward and Zoe Agar

The Grove
Country hotel and restaurant

Neil and Zoe Kedward acquired this
place as a wreck and after nine months
of blood, sweat and tears – they worked on
a shoestring – got a beautiful result. The former somewhat quirky mansion is now a
unique boutique hotel and restaurant that
gets a big vote of confidence from our
series editor, Fiona Duncan. Its magic
worked on her as soon as she arrived. The
exterior is unusual, with two facades: one
tall and Georgian, painted brilliant white, the
other with gables and Arts and Crafts elements that also crop up inside.

She could not fault her bedroom. The
rooms are spread out across the house, a
cottage and an old long house.

Inside the house public spaces include a
relaxing library with chessboard, books and
games. We especially like the light breakfast
room. Chef Allister Barsby uses local Welsh
ingredients to memorable effect and has his
sights on a Michelin star.

Penally, Pembrokeshire

Penally, near Tenby, South
Pembrokeshire SA70 7PY

Tel (01834) 843033
e-mail info@penally-abbey.com
website www.penally-abbey.com

Nearby Tenby; Colby Woodland
Garden; Upton Castle, Pembroke
Castle
Location in Penally village 1 mile
from Tenby; with ample car parking
Food breakfast, dinner, afternoon
tea **Price** £££
Rooms 11 (7 rooms in the Main
House and 4 in the Coach House),
all double and double-twin. All
rooms have hairdryer, Nespresso
machine, bathrobes, Noble Isle toiletries **Facilities** Drawing Room,
Sun Room, dining room, bar, private
courtyard events space with bar and
garden **Credit cards** MC, V
Children accepted **Disabled** access
possible to 2 ground-floor bedrooms
Pets dogs accepted by arrangement
in Coach House rooms, at extra cost
Closed January **Proprietors** Lucas
and Melanie Boissevain

Penally Abbey
Country house hotel

Ever since the Middle Ages this has been
recognized as one of the spots from
which to appreciate the broad sweep of the
Pembrokeshire coast and National Park
from Tenby to Giltar Point. The links golf
course wasn't there, but the ruins of the
medieval chapel which gave this Gothic
country house its name are still in the
secluded and well-tended gardens. Many of
the windows and doors all have the characteristic double curve ogee arches. There is
a comfortable and well furnished drawing
room with an open fire, a welcoming bar far
from the world's woes and weather, and a
tall, candle-lit dining room. The restaurant
serves up a menu inspired by local
Pembrokeshire ingredients. An atmospheric
courtyard can be used for small weddings
and celebrations.

Bedrooms are comfortable, and well
equipped with fresh linen: some you could
play cricket in and are furnished traditionally, some in quite a grand style. St Deiniol's
Lodge now houses a further five rooms,
decorated in more contemporary style.

The Boissevains took over Penally in
2014. Melanie, an interior designer, has set
about putting her unique mark on the decoration, while Lucas aims to put Penally on
the culinary map. We imagine the atmosphere has the same *bonhomie* as under its
previous owners – reports welcome.

Penmaenpool, Gwynedd

Penmaenpool, Dolgellau, Gwynedd
LL40 1YB

Tel (01341) 422129
Fax (01341) 422787
e-mail relax@penhall.co.uk
website www.penhall.co.uk

Nearby Mawddach Estuary;
Snowdonia; Cader Idris,
Portmeirion.
Location off A493 Dolgellau-Tywyn
road; with ample car parking
Food breakfast, lunch, dinner
Price £££
Rooms 14 double and twin with
bath; all rooms have phone, TV,
iPod dock, hairdryer, minibar, wi-fi
Facilities sitting rooms, library, 2
dining rooms, bar; garden, helipad,
trout and salmon fishing
Credit cards DC, MC, V
Children babes-in-arms and chil-
dren over 6 accepted
Disabled only restaurant accessible
Pets accepted in 1 room by arrange-
ment
Closed 8 days in Dec, 10 days in Jan
Proprietors Mark Watson and
Lorraine Fielding

Penmaenuchaf Hall
Country house hotel

Not far from the market town of Dolgellau, Penmaenuchaf Hall's drive winds steeply up a wooded hillside from the south bank of the Mawddach Estuary to this sturdy grey stone Victorian manor house. Set on terraces in 21 acres of grounds, the views across Snowdonia must have been top of the list of reasons that brought the original builder – a Lancashire mill owner – to this peaceful spot at the foot of Cader Idris. A rose garden and a water garden add a charm of their own to the beautiful setting.

Indoors, Mark Watson and Lorraine Fielding have saved but also softened the Victorian character of the house so that, from the imposing main hall you are drawn to the warmth and light of the ivory morn-ing room, the sitting rooms and the library. The same sympathetic treatment carries through to the bedrooms – fine fabrics are married with fine furniture and only the beds are baronial. If you are not tempted by the excellent walking in the surround-ing hills, you can doze in the sunny con-servatory, or eat in the oak-panelled gar-den room restaurant, Llygad yr Haul.

Pwllheli, Gwynedd

Pwllheli, Gwynedd, North Wales
LL53 5TH

Tel (01758) 612363
email gunna@bodegroes.co.uk
website www.bodegroes.co.uk

Nearby National Trust walks,
Snowdonia, Bodmant Gardens
Location 1 mile west of Pwllheli on
the A497 Nefyn road; in own
grounds with ample car parking
Food breakfast, dinner (lunch on
Sundays)
Price ££-£££
Rooms 10 doubles; all have bath and
shower; all rooms have phone, tv,
hairdryer
Facilities restaurant, garden
Credit cards MC, V
Children welcome, though only
over 10s in the dining room
Disabled not suitable
Pets accepted
Closed Sun-Mon; 3 days off for
Christmas, open for New Year, then
shut from 2nd Jan to 8th Feb
Proprietors Chris and Gunna
Chown

Plas Bodegroes
Restaurant-with-rooms

Plas Bodegroes means Rosehip Hall – a
fittingly romantic name. It's a small
Georgian manor with a delicate frill of a
veranda, whose slim cast-iron columns are
smothered in wisteria, roses and wild
strawberry. The grounds feature a heart-
shaped swathe of lawn and a 200-year-old
avenue of beech trees. To one side, a long
red-and-white Danish pennant on a tall
flagpole flutters in the wind. Still run by
Chris Chown and his elegant wife, Gunna
(who is Danish/Faroese), though a new
head chef – Hugh Bracegudle – has taken
over from Chris in the kitchen.

Plas Bodegroes is emphatically a restaurant-with-rooms. The ten bedrooms are
cosy and pretty, in Scandinavian style, all
shapes and sizes (two of the bathrooms
are about to receive an upgrade). The dining room is romantic, too, with its clever
use of mirrors, its elegant French doors on
to the veranda and its beautifully lit duck-
egg blue walls. Welsh lamb and Black beef
feature prominently on the unpretentious
menu, though equal emphasis is given to
fresh fish. The wine list is interesting with
gentle prices and breakfast is exceptional.
Plas Bodegroes is off the beaten track on
the Lleyn Peninsula, with mystical Bardsey
Island at its tip, in almost completely
unspoilt countryside. Food and a setting of
this quality are hard to find at these prices.

Skenfrith, Monmouthshire

Skenfrith, Monmouthshire,
NP7 8UH

Tel (01600) 750235
Fax (01600) 750525
e-mail enquiries@skenfrith.co.uk
website www.skenfrith.co.uk

Nearby Brecon Beacons National
Park; Ross-on-Wye; Hereford; Hay-
on-Wye; Abergavenny; Monmouth.
Location beside river, off minor
road on edge of village in own
grounds; ample car parking
Food breakfast, lunch, dinner, afternoon tea
Price £££ **Rooms** 11 double, all
with bath; all rooms have phone, TV
Facilities bar, dining room, function
room; terrace, garden, bakery.
Credit cards MC, V
Children welcome, but not for
evening meals unless over 8. Special
menu available for under 12s.
Disabled disabled loo downstairs,
upstairs not suitable
Pets accepted (supervised at all
times; £5 per night) **Closed** Tue in
winter **Proprietors** Sarah Hudson
and Richard Ireton

The Bell at Skenfrith
Country inn

Though contemporary and cosy rarely
coincide, this is one place that con-
vincingly combines the two. Tucked into
the fold of a hill in the Welsh Marches, it
has all the ingredients for a winter break
that metropolitans could wish for: a huge
inglenook radiating heat, surrounded by
sofa, settle and rocking chair; a candle-lit,
flagstone dining room serving locally
sourced modern British dishes – planned
around seasonal vegetables and fruits,
some grown in The Bell's kitchen garden –
along with a well-organised wine list; and
11 delightful, simple-sophisticated bedrooms. Sarah also opened a bakery on the
premises in 2017.

Formerly a 17thC coaching inn, The Bell
stands on the Monnow River close to
Skenfrith Castle in an unchanged village.
There are wonderful walks in the area; six
circular routes leaving from the door have
been created by the hotel, with picnics
provided. They include the 18-mile Three
Castles Walk, which is demanding, but possible in a single day. When you get back,
you could have a Welsh cream tea while
easing your sore feet.

The Bell has regular special offers. As we
went to press you could enjoy two nights
dinner, bed and breakfast for two people
from £380.

Tal-y-llyn, Gwynedd

Tal-y-llyn, Tywyn, Gwynedd LL36 9AJ

Tel 01654 761247
e-mail info@dolffanogfawr.co.uk
website www.dolffanogfawr.co.uk

Nearby Cadair Idris, Snowdonia National Park, sandy beaches at Aberdyfi, Tywyn and Barmouth, Coed y Brenin Forest, Tal-y-llyn railway, Ynys Hir RSPB reserve, Dyfi Osprey Project **Location** Tal-y-llyn Valley at the foot of Cadair Idris mountain and overlooking Tal-y-llyn lake. **Food** breakfast, dinner **Price** £ **Rooms** 4; 3 double/twin, 1 double; all with shower and/or bath, Sky TV, wi-fi, hairdryer, L'Occatäine toiletries **Facilities** guest sitting room with log fire, dining room, garden, private off-road parking, spa, secure storage for mountain bikes or fishing tackle, fishing on over 13 miles of local rivers and a mountain lake. **Credit cards** MC, V **Children** accepted over 7 **Disabled** no special facilities **Pets** by prior arrangement **Closed** Nov-mid Mar **Proprietors** Alex Yorke and Lorraine Hinkins

Dolffanog Fawr
Country guesthouse

Recommended by a trusted reporter, this unpretentious Welsh farmhouse, has four bedrooms done up in contemporary-traditional style, with restrained good taste. All the basics are spot on: Egyptian cotton sheets, best quality beds. Three of the rooms have window seats for pondering the views across the Tal-y-Llyn valley, with the superb Cadair Idris almost on the doorstep. A top-end, modern B&B, run by friendly Alex and Lorraine, and their son Morgan, who live in a separate wing. Guests can feel private in their own sitting room and dining room. A set-menu dinner is prepared four days a week by Lorraine, who spent years working alongside top chefs. Ingredients are largely taken from Welsh larder, including its renowed black beef and wild Dysynni sea trout – and served 'dinner party style' around a large oak table (with the option to eat separately.)

Think about coming here to enjoy the coast as well as the mountains – it's only half an hour from the sea. The scenery around here, north of the Dovey estuary, is exceptionally wild and beautiful, and less overrun than Snowdonia. While the main route up Cadair Idris starts from nearby Minfford, a non-standard route to the top begins within half an hour's walk of Dolffanog Fawr.

Three Cocks, Powys

Three Cocks, near Brecon, Powys
LD3 0SL

Tel (01497) 847215
Fax (01497) 847339
e-mail info@threecockshotel.com
website www.threecockshotel.com

Nearby Brecon Beacons; Hay-on-Wye; Hereford Cathedral; Black Mountains.
Location in village, 11 miles (18 km) NE of Brecon on A438; ample car parking
Food breakfast, lunch, dinner
Price £-££
Rooms 7 double and twin, 6 with bath/shower, 1 with shower
Facilities sitting room, reception room with TV, dining room, breakfast room; large garden
Credit cards MC, V
Children welcome over age of 12
Disabled access difficult
Pets not accepted
Closed Jan
Proprietors Roy and Judith Duke

Three Cocks
Coaching inn and restaurant

The building is a charming ivy-covered 15thC coaching inn in the Welsh hills, constructed around a tree (still in evidence in the kitchen) and with its cobbled forecourt on the most direct route from Hereford to Brecon. Inside, carved wood and stone walls continue the natural look of the exterior, with beams and eccentrically angled doorways serving as proof positive of antiquity. The charmingly friendly and enthusiastic Roy and Judith continue to draw people great distances to the warm welcome and roomy restaurant with its lace-covered tables. There are plenty of places where you can sit in peace, and residents have a drawing room of their own, in keeping with its public oak-panelled counterpart but with more light, stone and fabric in evidence. There is now also a coffee shop and bar, leading on to the extensive gardens, serving refreshments and light lunches.

Bedrooms are modest but comfortable and well equipped, with dark oak furniture and pale fabrics. The food is honest, hearty British fayre, making full use of the wealth of local sources, including the Black Mountain Salmon Smokery, as well as local cheeses and meats. Roy uses local merchant Tanners as his wine cellar, importing an eclectic range of wines from around the world.

Abergavenny, Monmouthshire

The Angel Hotel/The Walnut Tree Inn/restaurant

15 Cross Street, Abergavenny,
Monmouthshire NP7 9AA

Tel 01873 857121
Fax 01873 858059
e-mail reservations@angelaber-gavenny.com **website** www.ange-labergavenny.com
Food breakfast, brunch, lunch, dinner, afternoon tea
Price ££ **Closed** Christmas Day
Proprietor Caradog Hotels Ltd

The Angel Hotel and The Walnut Tree restaurant are closely associated – the Griffith family, owners of The Angel, also have an interest in The Walnut Tree, which is run by Shaun Hill. The two places mark out Abergavenny as a useful gourmet base for exploring the Black Mountains.

Inside The Angel there's plenty of stylish architecture and pristine white walls, with bars and sitting rooms that are contemporary but still welcoming. The bedrooms are calming, with cream walls, wooden furniture and smart bathrooms; for more privacy there are two nearby cottages.

It's a ten-minute taxi ride from The Angel to The Walnut Tree restaurant (which has two cottages), where Shaun presents a menu of uncomplicated yet sublime dishes.

Abergavenny, Monmouthshire

The Hardwick
Restaurant-with-rooms

Old Raglan Road, Abergavenny,
Monmouthshire NP7 9AA

Tel 01873 854220
e-mail info@thehardwick.co.uk
website www.thehardwick.co.uk
Food breakfast, lunch, dinner
Price ££
Closed one week in Jan, Christmas Day, Boxing Day
Proprietor Stephen Terry

Run by well-known chef Stephen Terry, whose CV is as impressive as a chef's can be, including La Gavroche with Michel Roux and The Canteen at Chelsea Harbour (where he got his first Michelin star aged 25). The list is long, spanning Europe and America, and together with his grounding in classic French cooking adds up to quality and depth. Shame then that guests query the speed of service and value for money. We think it's worth the price when things are running smoothly, but perhaps the tough economics of the restaurant trade in places such as Abergavenny make it hard to afford enough hands to achieve consistency. The rooms are smart and modish, but some would say formulaic.

Dolydd, Gwynedd

Y Goeden Eirin
Country guesthouse

Set in what was originally a granite cow-shed, Y Goeden Eirin (The Plum Tree) is a cosy, charming guesthouse situated in the little hamlet of Dolydd in Gwynedd. Run by welcoming host Eluned Rowlands, the place offers a comforting blend of tradi-tional and contemporary.

The well-designed bedrooms are attractive and homely, with slate floors and underfloor heating, and include all the necessary mod-ern amenities to make for a supremely com-fortable stay. The breakfast/dining room (also with slate floor) is wonderfully tradi-tional, with its wooden beams and exposed granite walls. The atmosphere is laidback and intimate. Food is home-cooked on the AGA and is locally sourced wherever pos-sible.

Dolydd, Caernarfon, Gwynedd
LL54 7EF

Tel 01286 830942
Mobile 07999528414
e-mail eluned.rowlands@tiscali.com
website www.ygoedeneirin.co.uk
Food breakfast
Price £ **Closed** Christmas to New Year **Proprietors** Eluned Rowlands

Llyswen, Powys

Llangoed Hall
Country house hotel

With 23 bedrooms this (on the face of it) large and conventional country house hotel is a little outside the guide's territory, but our series editor Fiona Duncan rates it very highly. The house is imposing and beautifully restored by the late Sir Bernard Ashley, and wife Laura, of wallpaper and fabric fame. It houses his notable collection of 20thC British paintings.

Despite its formality, it's the type of place where guests are encouraged to be themselves – to curl up on the sofa, even play the piano.

The rooms are charmingly done with antiques and pictures, fine linen, new bath-rooms – guests will want to linger.

The food by Nick Brodie (ex-Olive Tree in Bath) is imaginative yet sensible.

Llyswen, Brecon, Powys, Wales LD3 0YP

Tel 01874 754525
Fax 01874 754545
e-mail enquiries@llangoedhall.com
website www.llangoedhall.co.uk
Food breakfast, lunch, dinner, after-noon tea
Price £££-££££ **Closed** never
Manager Calum Milne

Milebrook, Knighton, Powys LD7 1LT

Tel 01547 528632
e-mail hotel@milebrookhouse.co.uk
website www.milebrookhouse.co.uk
Food breakfast, lunch, dinner
Price ££
Closed Sunday and Monday between Dec-Feb
Proprietors Marsden family

Milebrook House Hotel **Country house**

Inside it's homely and chintzy rather than 'boutique' and minimalist: curtains are floral, walls are lined with paintings and bunches of flowers spring from vases. Bedrooms however, are calmly uncluttered, with bright walls and white linen. Certain things here are to everyone's taste: the food and the service.

Owners the Marsden family have built up a loyal following thanks to the genial atmosphere and high standards: Beryl, Rodney and Joanne run the hotel. This is also open to non residents and serves breakfast, lunch and dinner. The quality of the food is a recurring theme of guests' comments.

In the grounds there's a wildlife pond and a riverbank; and wildlife enthusiast Rodney is on hand with advice about where to point binoculars.

Ashbourne, Derbyshire

Mappleton, Ashbourne, Derbyshire
DE6 2AA

Tel (01335) 300900
Fax (01335) 300512
e-mail info@callowhall.co.uk **web-site** www.callowhall.co.uk

Nearby Chatsworth House; Haddon Hall; Hardwick Hall.
Location 0.75 mile (1 km) N of Ashbourne off A515; with ample car parking
Food breakfast, lunch, afternoon tea, dinner **Price** £££
Rooms 16; 15 double and twin, 1 suite, all with bath or shower; all rooms have phone, TV, hairdryer
Facilities sitting room, dining rooms, bar; garden, fishing **Credit cards** AE, DC, MC, V **Children** welcome **Disabled** 1 specially adapted room **Pets** accepted by arrangement **Closed** Christmas Day, Boxing Day, New Year's Day
Proprietors Hardman Family

Callow Hall
Country house hotel

The legacy of old owners the Spencers (master bakers in Ashbourne) is that one of the highlights of staying at this fine Victorian country house hotel is its excellent dining room. In the restaurant they serve many of their home-grown ingredients. There's a flavourful *á la carte* menu – some might think it old-fashioned.

Set in extensive grounds at the entrance to the Peak District National Park, the hotel overlooks the stunning landscape of the Dove valley. Public rooms and bedrooms are done out in an appropriate and not too flamboyant country-house style. The walls of the entrance are guarded by stags' heads and the flag-stoned floor is scattered with Persian rugs. In winter an open fire crackles, while guests dine in the glow of the deep-red dining room, and in the drawing room, comfy sofas and chairs provide plenty of space for relaxing. Carved antiques and family heirlooms mingle with period repro furniture. Ask for a decent-sized room when you book: one or two are on the small side for the price. Staff are helpful yet unobtrusive.

Still firmly a family affair, the Hardmans (owners of East Lodge in Rowsley) took over in 2011. Reports welcome.

Ashford-in-the-Water, Derbyshire

Fennel Street, Ashford-in-the-Water, Bakewell, Derbyshire, DE4 1QF

Tel (01629) 814275
Fax (01629) 812873
e-mail riversidehousehotel@btconnect.com
website
www.riversidehousehotel.co.uk

Nearby Chatsworth; Haddon Hall; Bakewell.
Location 2 miles (3 km) NW of Bakewell off A6, at top of village, next to Sheepwash Bridge; with ample car parking
Food breakfast, lunch, dinner
Price £££
Rooms 14; 1 executive suite, 13 double/twin, all with bath/shower; all rooms have phone, TV, hairdryer
Facilities 1 sitting room, conservatory, bar, 4 dining rooms; garden
Credit cards AE, DC, MC, V
Children welcome over 16
Disabled access possible to 4 rooms
Pets not accepted **Closed** never
Proprietor Penelope Thornton

Riverside House
Country hotel

Nestling in one of the Peak District's prettiest villages, this stone-built, ivy-clad house, has an idyllic setting in its own secluded grounds, bordered by the river Wye. The village is aptly named – on our inspector's visit during a spate of heavy rain, the river was threatening to encroach, but the hotel's manager was coping admirably, sandbags at the ready, with the possibility of a flood alert.

Penelope Thornton (of the Thornton chocolate family), who took over the hotel in 1997, has instituted a refreshingly plain style, entirely in keeping with the house's Georgian origins. A large plant-filled conservatory leads into a cosy snug with a recessed carved-oak mantelpiece and open fire. There is an elegant, comfortable sitting room and a variety of well-equipped bedrooms of different sizes. Rooms in the newer Garden wing overlook the river.

Crucial to Riverside is its reputation for fine food, which is served in two intimate dining rooms. Chef John Whelan creates imaginative dishes such as *mille-feuille* of marinated salmon with beetroot confit, and celery and wild mushroom strüdel; he also offers an intriguing selection of cheeses – Lincolnshire Poacher, Belineigh Blue and Gubbeen.

Barnsley, Gloucestershire

Barnsley, Cirencester,
Gloucestershire GL7 5EF

Tel 01285 740421
e-mail info@thevillagepub.co.uk
website www.thevillagepub.co.uk

Nearby Cotswold Water Park, riding, Cirencester, Daylesford Organics
Location Barnsley village with free parking
Food breakfast, lunch, dinner
Price £££
Rooms 6, all have bath/shower
Facilities restaurant, bar as well as access to spa and cinema at Barnsley House (across the road)
Credit cards AE, DC, MC, V
Children welcome
Disabled no special facilities
Pets welcome
Closed never
Proprietors Calcot Health & Leisure TA Calcot Hotels, MD Mr Richard Ball

The Village Pub
Country pub

Don't come here for authenticity or the laid-back village pub atmosphere. This is nearby Barnsley House's sister establishment, and you'll like it if you are after something of chic, contemporary Barnsley House's luxury and style at half the price. Still, it's a classic Cotswold haven: warm and inviting, with low wooden ceiling beams and deer-heads mounted above its fireplaces.

It would be worth coming for the food alone. The menu consists of imaginative variations on classic English dishes, beautifully presented.

The bedrooms are not large, but have creamy, sophisticated good looks and top bathrooms. The cheapest cost from £104 – at Barnsley House they start at £219.

And you can buy into some of the benefits of Barnsley House, such as the Barnsley House spa (check this is included in your deal). On Sunday you can relax in front of a film in their private cinema with free popcorn, followed by a two-course dinner in The Potager. A two-course supper and film costs £24 – not bad for the overpriced Cotswolds.

Chevin Road, Belper, Derbyshire,
DE56 2UN

Tel (01773) 822328
e-mail
enquiries@chevingreenfarm.com
website www.chevingreenfarm.com

Nearby Belper, Chatsworth, Peak
District scenery, Haddon Hall,
Kedleston Hall, Buxton spa town
Location 5min from Belper
Food breakfast
Price £-££
Rooms 4 double; all have TV/DVD,
wi-fi, radio, hairdryer, homemade
cake, drinks tray, shower/bath
Facilities sitting room, kitchen/din-
ing area
Credit cards AE, DC, MC, V
Children 16+ welcome
Disabled access difficult
Pets not accepted
Closed enquire before
Proprietors Sarah and David
Marley

Chevin Green Farm
Bed-and-breakfast

In order to hang on to this 350-year-old stone-built farmhouse, which had been in the family since 1929, Sarah bought it off her parents in 2013. Together she and her journalist husband David carried out a major refurbishment, converting their home into a boutique bed-and-breakfast. The redecoration has been hugely success-ful: quaint and cosy, with floral frills and pleated sofas, and a charming tea theme throughout, including hanging tea lamps and blue and white china.

Guests get a warm welcome: tea and bis-cuits of course, as well as home-made cake delivered to their bedrooms. The rooms are extremely comfortable and individually designed by Sarah.

Breakfast is delicious, involving a full English alongside yoghurt and fruit. Special dietary needs are looked after, and the selection of teas is large, as you'd expect. Sarah can also make lunch on request.

The setting is a delight. Surrounded by the beautiful Derbyshire countryside there are opportunities for great walks, whilst being a stones throw from the historic mill-town of Belper. The farm has a real sense of history: 350 years old, with the older parts lovingly restored, while in the garden there's a Roman well, and two apple trees planted in 1903 to celebrate twins born in the house.

Bishop's Castle, Shropshire

The Square, Bishop's Castle, Shropshire SY9 5BN

Tel 01588 638403
e-mail stay@thecastlehotelbishop-scastle.co.uk
website www.thecastlehotelbishop-scastle.co.uk

Nearby Ludlow, Shrewsbury, Clun, Welshpool, Welsh borders, Offa's Dyke, South Shropshire Hills, Bishop's Castle centre, arts and crafts shops
Location overlooking Bishop's Castle, around 30 mins away from Ludlow and Shrewsbury
Food breakfast, lunch, dinner
Price £
Rooms 12; double, single and twin (Master, Standard, Smaller) all with en-suite bath or shower, tea and coffee making facilities and TV
Facilities 3 bars, restaurant, garden, terrace
Credit cards MC, V **Children** welcome **Disabled** not suitable
Pets welcome **Closed** never
Proprietors Henry & Rebecca Hunter

The Castle Hotel
Town hotel

Built in 1719 by Lord Carnarvon, on the site of an old motte and bailey, the Castle Hotel stands overlooking the town of Bishop's Castle, in the midst of the Shropshire countryside. They do things traditionally here: wooden panelling, roaring open fires, chalk board menus, bar billiards and a fine selection of real ales.

The twelve rooms are spacious, pretty and unpretentious, with wooden furniture, original features and views right over the gardens, town and countryside. Some have high, gabled ceilings.

With Ludlow only down the road, the kitchen has a fine range of suppliers from which to choose, and makes good use of them. The menu has the same traditional feel as the hotel, but with a modern twist. Meals are hearty, healthy and fresh. Guests can dine in one of the three bustling bars or more serenely in the oak-panelled restaurant, The Oak Room. In the summer, many eat outside on the vine-covered terrace, overlooking the fishponds. At least five real ales are usually on tap, and a comprehensive wine list is also on hand.

Ludlow, Shrewsbury and mid-Wales are all within easy reach, and the South Shropshire hills offer some excellent walking. Bishop's Castle is a pretty little town with plenty of antique shops and tea rooms.

Bourton-on-the-Hill, Gloucestershire

Bourton-on-the-Hill, Moreton in Marsh, Gloucestershire GL56 9AQ

Tel 01386 700413
e-mail
enquiries@horseandgroom.info
website www.horseandgroom.info

Nearby Chipping Campden, Daylesford, Stratford-upon-Avon.
Location follow A44 from Moreton-in-Marsh and Horse & Groom is at top of hill on left-hand side
Food breakfast (included in price of room), lunch, dinner
Price ££-£££
Rooms 5 double; all with TV, Bramley produces, tea/coffee, wi-fi
Facilities TV, DVD, hairdryer, wi-fi, garden, restaurant
Credit cards MC, V
Children welcome **Disabled** no access **Pets** welcome in main bar area, and most bedrooms (enquire when booking)
Closed never
Proprietors Epicurean Inns

Horse & Groom
Pub-with-rooms

While long-term regulars might pine after the affable welcome from previous owners Will and Tom Greenstock, they won't find much else changed. Now run by Epicurean Inns, the pub-with-rooms is now a more low-key and countrified affair (it's dog-friendly, with a more neutral colour scheme) but it's still full of character.

The fun starts in the kitchen and its seasonal, daily changing menu, with offerings often changing in the course of service as one successfully finished dish becomes replaced with a fresh alternative. Atmosphere in the dining room is laid-back and the service energetic and friendly.

Each of the five bedrooms is light and spacious and abounds with finesse and modern finery. While some may find the shapes and colours in the rooms a little too eclectic for their taste, many will think it's rather invigorating to offer chequered chairs in one room or vibrant metallics in another. A pristine view of the Cotswolds helps to compensate for some noise from the road and the downstairs pub that affects one or two rooms.

A hearty breakfast is served and, like dinner, offers fresh ingredients and local produce. Prices are very reasonable, and visitors come away saying the Horse & Groom is an 'imaginative' but 'unpretentious' place which won't stand still.

Bourton-on-the-Water, Gloucestershire

High Street, Bourton-on-the-Water, Gloucestershire, GL54 2AN

Tel (01451) 822 244
e-mail info@dialhousehotel.com
website www.dialhousehotel.com

Nearby Burford, Blenheim, Upper and Lower Slaughter
Location in the heart of the village with large hotel car park
Food breakfast, lunch, tea, dinner
Price £££-££££
Rooms 13 rooms
Facilities bar, sitting-room, garden
Credit cards all major
Children over 12
Disabled a garden room is accessible by wheelchair
Pets well-behaved dogs allowed in bar area, but not in rooms
Closed one week in Jan
Proprietor Haley Davies

Dial House
Country hotel

The Dial House attracts a certain type of client (the upwardly mobile *Daily Telegraph* reader) and that type of client will like it very much. This is a place to forget boardroom worries, and enjoy being 'pampered'. In the summer, Bourton-on-the-Water can be crowded, so the neat garden behind the hotel gives guests a place to escape the hordes.

The place is spotless. Rooms are furnished comfortably, and a number of them have been recently refurbished. Bathrooms have roll-top free-standing baths, Elemis toiletries and piles of thick white towels.

A small bar downstairs caters for all tastes, including a selection from a local brewery. A sitting-room for residents has a log fire in winter and brightly coloured modern chairs, for the owners are careful not to let this honey-coloured 17th century house become too old-fashioned. The two recently refurbished dining rooms are cosy and relaxed, serving breakfast, afternoon teas, and dishes combining both English and Mediterranean influences, with classical and modern techniques. Try the spicy meatballs with *linguine*.

Burford, Oxfordshire

99 High Street, Burford,
Oxfordshire OX18 4QA

Tel (01993) 823151
Fax (01993) 823240
e-mail stay@burford-house.co.uk
website www.burford-house.co.uk

Nearby Cotswold Wildlife Park;
Blenheim Palace; Broadway.
Location middle of Burford High
Street; parking in street or free car
park nearby
Food breakfast, lunch, dinner
Price ££
Rooms 6 doubles with bath and
shower; all rooms have TV, wi-fi,
hairdryer
Facilities Bar area, dining room,
courtyard garden
Credit cards AE, MC, V **Children**
welcome
Disabled no ground floor rooms
Pets not accepted in rooms, but wel-
comed in bar and garden
Closed Christmas
Proprietors Steven and Karen
Nolan
Manager Scott Hoare

Burford House
Town house hotel

Without disturbing its historical integrity, you'll find 21stC comforts in the 15thC Cotswold stone and black-and-white timbered house in the heart of Burford. The whole place positively gleams with personal care and attention, with fresh flowers, books and magazines in the smartly decorated, dark-beamed bedrooms, and their own belongings dotted amongst the public furniture. The Italian-inspired restaurant and bar area are a real hit with the locals and tourists, bringing a relaxed and informal atmosphere for the downstairs bit. There is also a garden room looking out on to the lovely court-yard garden.

Upstairs there are six bedrooms, three with four-posters and a few of these also have huge free-standing baths. Each thoughtfully organized room is full of char-acter, and each has an immaculate bath-room. Breakfast (included in the price of the room) is an excellent production, taken in the dining room looking out on to the High Street.

Sheep Street, Burford, Oxfordshire
OX18 4LR

Tel (01993) 823155
Fax (01993) 822228
e-mail info@lambinn-burford.co.uk
website www.cotswold-inns-
hotels.co.uk/lamb-inn/

Nearby Minster Lovell Hall;
Cotswold villages; Blenheim Palace.
Location in village; with car parking
Food breakfast, lunch, dinner
Price £££
Rooms 17 double and twin with
bath or shower; all have phone, TV,
hairdryer, wi-fi
Facilities 3 sitting rooms, dining
room, bar; garden
Credit cards AE, MC, V
Children welcome
Disabled 1 ground-floor bedrooms
Pets dogs in room by prior arrange-
ment
Closed never
Proprietors Cotswold Inns and
Hotels
Manager Bill Ramsay

The Lamb
Town inn

If you want some respite from Burford's
summer throng, you won't do better than
The Lamb, only a few yards behind the High
Street, but a veritable haven of tranquillity –
particularly in the pretty walled garden, a
view endorsed by a recent inspection.

Inside the creeper-clad stone cottages,
you won't be surprised to find traditional
pub trappings (after all, The Lamb has been
an inn since the 15th century), but you
may be surprised to discover 17 spacious
beamed bedrooms decorated with plush
fabrics and antiques. All are different –
'Shepherd', for example, has a vast antique
four-poster bed and a little attic-like bathroom, 'Malt' (in what was once the neighbouring brewery) has a lavish canopy over
the bed and large stone mullion windows.

Head chef Piotr Galski produces the
daily-changing meals. These are served in
the dining room, looking on to the gerani-
um-filled patio. Coffee can be taken in
here, or one of the sitting rooms, both of
which have comfortable chairs and sofas
grouped around open fires

The Lamb Inn has been part of the
Cotswold Inns and Hotels collection since
2005. Reports welcome.

10 New Street, Chipping Norton, Oxfordshire OX7 5LJ

Tel 01608 645060
e-mail enquiries@wildthymerestaurant.co.uk
website www.wildthymerestaurant.co.uk

Nearby Oxford, Gloucester, Banbury. **Location** Chipping Norton, in a row of terraced houses opposite Sainsburys car park
Food lunch, dinner, continental breakfast in rooms
Price £-££
Rooms 3 doubles, all have bath/shower, with TV, DVD players, radio alarms, hairdryers
Facilities restaurant, courtyard garden **Credit cards** DC, MC, V
Children welcome, the Pink room and Lilac room are ideal for families with older children
Disabled wheelchair access to restaurant, not for rooms
Pets not accepted **Closed** open for lunch Thurs-Sat, open for dinner Tues-Sat; closed Sat-Mon
Proprietors Nick and Sally Pullen

Wild Thyme
Restaurant-with-rooms

Natural, honest and charming. This diminutive spot in Chipping Norton shows that the Cotswolds can do things simply and well, and isn't just there for the trendy and the rich.

It's owned by Nick Pullen, chef, and his wife Sally, front-of-house and in charge of rooms. Sally is a natural hostess who creates an easy-going ambience. The 400-year-old terraced house is as pretty (pale blue) on the outside as it is inside – the small, interconnecting dining rooms are painted soft grey, with beautiful cushions scattered on banquette seats, plain wooden tables and white-painted chairs.

"Nick cooks from the heart," says Sally. His food is essentially home-made, unaffected and moreish, and his menu changes with the advent of seasonal produce.

The rooms are as charming as the rest of Wild Thyme – pretty, cosy and well equipped. Blue, the largest, has gently sloping floors and walls and a small bath and shower. Pink and Lilac are snug, the latter with views of the countryside.

If you want a really good-value weekend away in the Cotswolds – and enjoyable food – this is the place.

Clearwell, Gloucestershire

Clearwell, Royal Forest of Dean,
Gloucestershire, GL16 8JS

Tel 01594 833046
Fax 01594 837093
e-mail info@tudorfarmhouse-
hotel.co.uk
web www.tudorfarmhousehotel.co.uk

Nearby Clearwell Caves &
Puzzlewood within 2km, Monmouth
11km, Chepstow 18km, Bristol
50km, Cardiff 700km
Location Clearwell village, in the
Forest of Dean and Wye Valley
Food breakfast, lunch, afternoon tea,
grazing menu, dinner
Price ££-££££
Rooms 20 double (4 can be twin); all
have TV, wi-fi, hairdryer, coffee/tea
facilities inc. a Nespresso machine,
bathrobes **Facilities** gardens (and 14
acres SSSI land) - walks, sitting
room with log burner
Credit cards MC, V, AM
Children welcome
Disabled ground floor rooms available **Pets** accepted in 3 rooms, £10
per night **Closed** never **Proprietors**
Colin and Hari Fell

Tudor Farmhouse
Country hotel

Clearwell is a small west Gloucestershire village near the Welsh border
surrounded by fields, so this place feels
countrified and peaceful even though you
enter from the village high street. Until
recently it was a farm and although trans-
formation has been achieved in several
stages, it all hangs together. The 20-plus
rooms, cottages and suites are placed
around various buildings – a relatively large
number for this guide but the feel is small
and intimate, even cosy. Old stonework and
timber has been preserved in the public
areas, there are log burning stoves, country
antiques and freshly cut rustic flowers.

The bedrooms are stylish yet homely
using whites, greys and greens – contemporary but not wannabee-trendy. Our bathroom was spacious, with a freestanding roll
top tub and a pleasing expanse of grey
'brickwork' tiling. Hari and Colin Fell have
paid attention to the basics – pocket sprung
mattresses, good linen, thick towels, duck
down pillows – and achieved an imaginative,
unstuffy but stylish overall decorative effect.

Chef Rob Cox uses locally sourced
ingredients where possible in his traditional dishes with a modern twist: a popular
dish is Gloucester Old Spot pork belly. The
menu has a sensible range of offerings from
light lunchtime bites to full celebration dinners. It's becoming a local food destination.

Clipsham, Rutland

Main Street, Clipsham, Rutland
LE15 7SH

Tel (01780)410355
Fax (01780) 410000
e-mail info@theolivebranchpub.com
website
www.theolivebranchpub.com

Nearby Burghley, Belvoir Castle,
Rutland Owl and Falconry Centre
Location in the centre of Clipsham
Food breakfast, lunch, dinner
Price ££-££££
Rooms 6 en-suite; all rooms have
TV, radio, tea and coffee making
facilities; most have DVD player,
broadband
Facilities DVD/CD library,
patio/gardens
Credit cards MC, V
Children welcome
Disabled fully wheelchair-accessible
room **Pets** accepted in ground floor
rooms **Closed** Christmas night,
Boxing day, New Year's day
Proprietors Sean Hope and Ben
Jones

Beech House
Country Inn

The Beech House is where you sleep, but
the Olive Branch began it all and the
two, though divided by the road, are really
indivisible. So good was the food in the pub
(named to mark the end of a quarrel with a
farmer; this is not an ordinary place) that
rooms were needed to house those who
had travelled to enjoy it. What looks like a
pretty doll's-house was bought and six en-
suite rooms were made, decorated with
fashionable modern colours and furnished
with a mix of rather striking antique and
modern pieces. It is a thoughtful management that provides a fully wheelchair-accessible bathroom in the ground floor room
and attention to the guests' needs and
attention to detail are probably what won
the combined establishments the Michelin
Pub of the Year award in 2007. There are
four types of tea in the bedrooms and fresh
coffee for the cafetière; a Roberts digital
radio (*de rigueur* in smart inns these days);
DVDs and a choice of duvets or sheets and
blankets. So far so homely. But the extra
factor which this place seems to have in
spades is what Michelin's men call 'star quality', the willing, informal, kind and efficient
service you get from people who have put
their hearts (and their savings) into a venture like this.

Corse Lawn, Gloucestershire

Corse Lawn, Gloucestershire,
GL19 4LZ

Tel (01452) 780771
Fax (01452) 780840
e-mail enquiries@corselawn.com
website www.corselawn.com

Nearby Tewkesbury Abbey; Malvern Hills.
Location 5 miles (8 km) W of Tewkesbury on B4211; ample car parking
Food breakfast, lunch, dinner
Price £££
Rooms 18; 16 double and twin, 2 suites, all with bath; all rooms have phone, TV, hairdrier
Facilities 3 sitting rooms, bar, restaurant, 2 meeting rooms; garden, croquet, tennis, indoor swimming pool
Credit cards AE, DC, MC, V
Children accepted if well-behaved
Disabled 5 ground-floor bedrooms
Pets accepted in bedrooms
Closed 24 to 26 Dec
Proprietor Baba Hine & Giles Hine

Corse Lawn House
Country hotel

This tall, red-brick Queen Anne house, set back across common land from what is now a minor road, must have been one of the most refined coaching inns of its day. Should you arrive in traditional style, you could still drive your coach-and-four down the slipway into the large pond in front of the house, to cool the horses and wash the carriage.

Baba Hine has been here since the late 1970s, first running the house purely as a restaurant, later opening up four rooms and in recent years adding various extensions (carefully designed to blend with the original building) to provide more bedrooms as well as more space for drinking, eating and sitting. Baba Hine is now front of house running the hotel with her son Giles, having handed over the kitchen to Martin Kinahan who, she says, produces dishes just as good as hers. The menu is an eclectic mix of English and French, modern and provincial dishes, all carefully prepared and served in substantial portions; there are fixed-price menus (with a vegetarian alternative) at both lunch and dinner as well as *a la carte*, all notably good value.

Bedrooms are large, with a mixture of antique and modern furnishings and the atmosphere of the house is calm and relaxing. Breakfasts are a home-made feast. A recent visitor was enchanted.

Fairford, Gloucestershire

The Market Place, Fairford,
Gloucestershire, GL7 4AA

Tel (01285) 712535
Fax (01452) 780840
e-mail
info@thebullhotelfairford.co.uk
website thebullhotelfairford.co.uk

Nearby Tewkesbury Abbey; Malvern
Hills.
Location on River Coln, 6m east of
Cirencester, 4m west of Lechdale
Food breakfast, lunch, afternoon tea,
dinner
Price ££££
Rooms 21; 3 standard double, 3
superior double, 6 luxury double, 6
twin, 2 family; all rooms have phone,
TV, hairdryer, ironing facilities,
shower
Facilities 24hr reception, wi-fi, on
and off-site parking, restaurant, bar,
sitting room, baggage store
Credit cards AE, DC, MC, V
Children welcome
Disabled no special facilities
Pets not allowed **Closed** never
Proprietor Sebastian and Lana
Snow

The Bull
Country hotel

The latest addition to Sebastian and
Lana Snow's family of Cotswold pubs,
The Bull is a bigger, more bustling affair, situated in Fairford's pretty Market Square in
a building dating back to the 15thC. Inside,
they've executed their signature shabby-
chic style with extra flair. There are the
usual Alpine touches, such as cow-skin
rugs and mounted antlers. There's also a
muraled sitting room, and an elegant mustard morning room. Guests can eat in the
intimate restaurant, or the sultry burnt-
orange Stables (horse rails intact). Or, if
they're feeling fancy, the magisterial Bull
Room, with its own bar, chandeliers, and a
long table seating 40 – ideal for raucous
dinners. Like any good pub, it's cosy, with
several roaring hearths and rich fir-green
walls, with flashes of original stone.

Upstairs, the 21 rooms, decorated by
Joe Titchener and Lana Snow, are proper
Costwold affairs, complete with Wold
Garden toiletries and Costwold Woollen
Weavers throws – painted in soothing
greys with judicious splashes of colour
(some noise penetrates from the square).

With stiff competition from trendy pubs
in the area, their forte is, undoubtedly, the
food. Professional chef Sebastian oversees
a menu of exceptional pub fare, full of
robust flavours: his twice baked Double
Gloucester cheese soufflé is a speciality.

Faringdon, Oxfordshire

Faringdon, Oxfordshire SN7 8RF

Tel 01367 870382
e-mail info@troutinn.co.uk
website www.troutinn.co.uk

Nearby Vale of the White Horse;
Kelmscott Manor; Chimney Nature
Reserve; Blenheim Palace; Bampton;
20 mins from Oxford town centre
Location on the River Thames in
the Cotswolds
Food breakfast, lunch, dinner
Price ££
Rooms 6; all with TV, DVD player,
radio
Facilities bar, dining room, garden
Credit cards DC, MC, V
Children welcome
Disabled 4 accessible rooms
Pets welcome **Closed** Christmas
and Boxing Day
Landlord Simon Young

The Trout at Tadpole Bridge **Bed-and-breakfast**

In this little-known, idyllic spot in Oxfordshire, the river flowing under Tadpole Bridge's diminutive span is, in fact, the Thames. Many customers arrive by boat, for a pint of ale or a night ashore. The Trout's garden runs down to the water, where there are moorings for patrons using the pub.

The old brick inn has the hallmarks of a modernised pub-with-rooms, but in landlord Simon Young's hands they add up to an unpretentious, family-friendly place to stay. There are lovely bedrooms that make you stop in surprise, a clutch of faithful regulars propping up the bar. Staff are local and cheerful.

The Trout, where the infant Thames is at its most peaceful, trickling under Tadpole Bridge, provides the most delightful base for a weekend away: downstream are the wildflower meadows and wading birds of the Chimney Nature Reserve; across the fields is Bampton, one of the oldest villages in the county; Blenheim Palace is within easy reach.

Filkins, Oxfordshire

Filkins, Lechlade, Gloucestershire, GL7 3JQ

Tel 01367 860875
e-mail info@thefiveallsfilkins.co.uk
website www.thefiveallsfilkins.co.uk

Nearby Cotswold Wildlife Park, Chastleton House, Kelmscott Manor, Buscot Park
Location Filkins, an hour and a half from London and approximately an hour from Bristol and Birmingham
Food breakfast (included), lunch, dinner
Price ££-£££
Rooms 4 double (no twin); all have TV, wi-fi, hot drinks on request from bar, hairdryer
Facilities pub, two dining areas, spa, restaurant, bar, garden, parking
Credit cards MC, V
Children welcome
Disabled no access
Pets welcome in bar, not roooms
Closed never
Landlord Sebastian and Lana Snow

The Five Alls

Village inn

Standing as a gatekeeper for the picturesque village of Filkins, The Five Alls was opened by Lana and Sebastian Snow in 2012. These two (former owners of The Swan in Southrop, and current owners of The Bull and The Plough on pages 217 & 226) have perfected the art of the gastropub, which might account for its glitzy clientéle, including Kate Moss and David Cameron.

Lana Snow and her sister-in-law, interior designer Miranda Snow, have decorated it in a rakish country pub style, replete with pine furniture and exposed beams. A large (often crowded) bar leads into delightfully 'hygge' Alpine sitting-room, with an open log fire, squidgy sofas and a stand selling infused olive oil and homemade fudge. The expansive interior includes two dining rooms: one country-casual, the other more formal, with chandeliers, oriental rugs and quirky postage stamp wallpaper. The food is tasty pub grub with a twist: tuna sashimi might be followed by game pie and finished with traditional apple, blackberry and almond crumble.

The four bedrooms are attractively decorated, with pretty details in the furnishings, though not as colourful as downstairs. Space has been ingeniously maximised by doing away with bulky wardrobes and replacing them with rows of pretty hooks.

Great Rissington, Gloucestershire

Great Rissington, Gloucestershire
GL54 2LP

Tel (01451) 820388
e-mail enquiry@thelambinn.com
website www.thelambinn.com

Nearby The Slaughters; Stow-on-the-Wold; Burford; Sudeley Castle.
Location 4 miles (6 km) SE of Bourton-on-the-Water, 3 miles (5 km) N of A40; with ample car parking
Food breakfast, lunch, dinner
Price ££
Rooms 14; 4 suites in The Lamb Inn, 2 garden suites, 5 pub rooms, 2 stable rooms, all with bath or shower; all rooms have TV, wi-fi
Facilities sitting room, bar; garden
Credit cards AE, MC, V
Children welcome
Disabled not suitable
Pets accepted in bedrooms by arrangement
Closed never
Proprietors Paul and Jacqueline Gabriel

The Lamb Inn
Country inn

If you follow the River Windrush as it rises westwards from Burford, and then roughly follow its curve from the north (where it has given Bourton-on-the-Water its name), you will arrive in Great Rissington, deep in the Cotswolds. Overlooking gently rolling farmland and built from the local stone, the original elements of this inn are 300 years old. Taken over in the year 2000 by Paul and Jackie Gabriel, The Lamb is still very much a pub, indeed it is enough of a pub to merit a recommendation in a national guide to good beer. But it also now has two elements that many other inns lack – good board and lodging. Board comes in the shape of a surprisingly large – and comfortingly busy – restaurant. It does a roaring trade in traditional dishes freshly prepared from the best of local produce, often with a modern twist.

The bedrooms are bright, fresh and individually designed, and more than half have space for sitting as well as sleeping. All bathrooms have recently been renovated, and updating the rooms of this 400 year-old property is an ongoing project.

Hambleden, Henley-on-Thames, Oxforshire RG9 6RP

Tel (01491) 571227
Fax (01491) 520810
e-mail enquiries@thestagandhuntsman.co.uk
website www.thestagandhuntsman.co.uk

Nearby Hell-fire caves, Clivedon, Henley-on-Thames, The Hughenden Manor
Location Hambleden village, just off Skirmett Road
Food breakfast, lunch, dinner
Price ££
Rooms 8 doubles with private bathrooms **Facilities** bar, restaurant, beer garden **Credit cards** all major
Children welcome
Disabled no disabled rooms.
Pets welcome in some rooms and all public areas apart from the restaurant **Closed** never
Manager Andrew Berridge
Proprietor Urs Schwarzenbach

The Stag & Huntsman

Village inn

The Stag and Huntsman, a Chilterns institution, recently reopened after a lavish makeover, paid for by its philanthropic owner, Urs Schwarzenbach, whose main aim was to create a welcoming hub for the community.

The makeover has succeeded, and the place thrives, even with a more sober appearance than other similar places. The handsome dark green livery may stray from contemporary colour palettes, but it's authentic and a refreshing change from the norm. It's said that architect Ptolemy Dean, who restored The Stag and Huntsman on behalf of the Culden Faw Estate, cried out "That's the colour!" as an innocent man strolled past in a dark green Barbour.

The whole place has echoes of elderly relatives – in a pleasing way – right down to the tessellated tile floors and the narrow staircase. But it has attitude – we were pleased to find a retro Roberts radio in our room.

The food is superior pub fare. The Stag and Huntsman recently appointed both a new Head Chef, Marius Pretorius, and a new manager, Andrew Berridge, who previously worked at The Oakley Court Hotel in Windsor. We would welcome reports on how they're getting on.

Hambleton, Rutland

Hambleton, Oakham, Rutland
LE15 8TH

Tel (01572) 756991
e-mail hotel@hambletonhall.com
website www.hambletonhall.com

Nearby Burghley House;
Rockingham Castle; Stamford,
Belvoir Castle.
Location 2 miles (3 km) E of
Oakham on peninsula jutting into
Rutland Water; with ample car park-
ing
Food breakfast, lunch, dinner
Price ££££
Rooms 17 double and twin with
bath; all rooms have phone, TV,
hairdryer
Facilities sitting rooms, 3 dining
rooms, bar; garden, swimming pool,
tennis, helipad; fishing, golf, sailing,
riding all nearby **Credit cards** AE,
DC, MC, V **Children** accepted
Disabled access possible, lift/eleva-
tor **Pets** by arrangement **Closed**
never **Proprietors** Tim and Stefa
Hart

Hambleton Hall
Country house hotel

If you're planning a second honeymoon, a break from work or a weekend away from the kids, this Victorian former shooting lodge in the grand hotel tradition is a sybaritic par-adise, from which only your wallet and your waistline will suffer. The location is unrivalled, standing in stately grandeur on a wooded hillock, surrounded by manicured lawns, sur-veying the expanse of Rutland Water. The interior is sumptuous. In her design of the rooms, Stefa Hart uses rich, heavy fabrics in some of the bedrooms, and showing a pref-erence for delicate colours. The rooms still have their original mouldings and are fur-nished with fine antiques and paintings. Bedrooms with a view over the water are the most sought-after and expensive.

Many people are drawn here by the wiz-ardry of Michelin-starred chef, Aaron Patterson. He works his magic on only the freshest of ingredients, whether Hambleton beef, sea bass or veal sweetbreads. One of the joys of staying here is that you can blow the cobwebs away with an exhilarating walk from the front door of the hotel as far as you want around Rutland Water, bird-watching as you go.

Some time ago the Harts opened a home bakery – Hambleton Bakery – that makes a variety of breads and cakes. We particularly like their Hambleton Sourdough loaf.

Hampton-in-Arden, Solihill

Shadowbrook Lane, Hampton-In-Arden, B92 0DQ

Tel 01675 446080
Fax 01675 443838
e-mail info@hamptonmanor.com
website www.hamptonmanor.com

Nearby Birmingham airport; Birmingham train station; Solihull; Stratford upon Avon; Royal Leamington Spa; Warwick; Birmingham City Centre
Location in 45 acres of woodland
Food breakfast, lunch, dinner, snacks, room service, afternoon tea
Price ££-££££
Rooms 15 doubles; of which 8 can be twinned. All come with fresh coffee to grind, bluetooth audio system, home-baked cookies, toiletries from 100 Acres **Facilities** bar; lounge; restaurant; 2 beauty treatment rooms; 45 acres of woodland
Credit cards AE, DC, MC, V
Children welcome
Disabled one room specially adapted **Pets** not accepted **Closed** Dec 23rd - Dec 28th **Proprietor** Joshua Oakes, House Manager

Hampton Manor
Manor house hotel

Original and refreshing. Owner, James Hill employs a young team: the general manager, Craig, is just 25. The result is rejuvenating. The feel of this grand, old 15-bedroom manor house is unexpectedly relaxed, but every bit as professional as you'd expect. Hampton Manor could well be leading the way for the next generation of independent hoteliers.

Each of the 15 rooms has been thoughtfully decorated and furnished with contemporary designer John Reeves' Louis Collection. Bathrooms are stunning and come with tasteful mosaics and monsoon showers. The bedrooms are opulent, with deep-wine hues, velour furnishings and oversized headboards.

The Michelin-starred restaurant, Peel's, is more than just the icing on the cake here. The seasonal and minimalist portions are served in the beautiful dining room, hung with hand-painted Fromental wallpaper. The service is personal and friendly; it almost feels more like a restaurant-with-rooms than a manor house hotel. Enjoy a drink before dinner in cosy Fred's Bar. The grounds are almost as grand as the house itself: 45 acres of majestic woodland. You'll often see James' father working on his tractor. The nearby village of Hampton-in-Arden is picturesque, and well worth the short walk.

Castle Street, Hereford
HR1 2NW

Tel (01432) 356321
email info@castlehse.co.uk
website www.castlehse.co.uk

Nearby Hereford Cathedral, chained library, Mappa Mundi, cider museum, Offa's Dyke
Location In Hereford city centre on Castle Street; valet parking
Food breakfast, lunch, dinner
Price £££
Rooms 24; 17 suites, 3 doubles, 4 singles; all with bath; all rooms have TV, phone, video player, mini hi-fi, fridge, safe
Facilities lounge, dining room, bar, gardens, terrace
Credit cards AE, DC, MC, V
Children welcome
Disabled one adapted room
Pets not accepted
Closed never
Proprietor David Watkins

Castle House
Town house hotel

Life goes at a slower pace in this rural part of England and Hereford is the ideal county town: tight-knit, accessible and tranquil, yet with world-class attractions in its fine cathedral and Chained Library. Castle House is an elegant Grade II listed town mansion whose charming gardens overlook the old Castle moat. The cathedral and shops are nearby, yet there is absolute quiet: no traffic noise, just birdsong and the quack of ducks. We can think of few lovelier, or better sited, city hotels in Britain.

Past the pillared entrance, you find an impressive hall, with wooden central staircase and reception tucked neatly out of sight. To one side: a panelled bar; to the other, a spacious restaurant and sitting room whose doors lead to the garden. All the rooms are full of light. Since the Watkins took over they've swept away the 'faux posh' lacquer and gilt of their predecessors, and created a restful, tasteful interior, where anyone can relax. The restaurant, hugely popular with locals, has been run by passionate chef Claire Nicholls for nearly ten years. Much of the produce is sourced from the Watkins' family farm, as is their beef and rare-breed lamb.

Like its home-county, this place is quiet and comfortable – a friendly local hub run by a close-knit team – and, we think, in a league of its own for the area.

Hough-on-the-Hill, Lincolnshire

Hough-on-the-Hill, Grantham Road, Lincolnshire NG32 2AZ

Tel 01400 250234
e-mail armsinn@yahoo.co.uk
website www.thebrownlowarms.com

Nearby Belton House, Lincoln Cathedral, Lincoln Castle, Belvoir Castle, Tattershall Castle
Location 5-10 minutes from A1, village of Hough on the Hill
Food breakfast, dinner (Tues-Sat), Sunday lunch
Price £-££
Rooms 5; 1 in the barn conversion, 4 in the pub, all with en suite, TV, DVD players, hairdryers, wi-fi, phone **Facilities** bar, restaurant, terrace **Credit cards** MC, V
Children accepted over 8
Disabled 1 room on ground floor in barn conversion, but some steps into the pub
Pets not accepted
Closed Christmas Day and Boxing Day, 1-14th Jan
Proprietors Paul and Lorraine Willoughby

The Brownlow Arms
Restaurant-with-rooms

Lorraine Willoughby has worked at The Brownlow Arms since she was 17; she and Paul now own and run it together.

The rooms are stylishly decorated under the acute eye of Paul. We entered our room through a wide lobby, beyond which our room opened out. The dramatic focal point of the room was a white bed framed by a huge antique oak mantelpiece on the wall behind, padded in the middle to create a headboard, with a capacious red sofa at the end of the bed. The other rooms in the inn and house next door are decorated in fresh checks and stripes, and displayed an equally impressive attention to detail (not to mention well-equipped with television, radio, and ironing board).

The restaurant makes a refreshing change from modern, wood-floored pub dining rooms – you get warm panelling, stone fireplace and high-backed, medieval-style striped pattern chairs. The dining room has recently been refurbished, as has the patio terrace, where you can eat and drink in the summer. We couldn't fault the food: all the dishes (such as bresaola with gazpacho jelly and parmesan crisp) were gracefully and swiftly presented.

This place gives value for money – the bedrooms could easily be in a luxury town house hotel at double the price.

Kelmscott, Oxfordshire

Kelmscott, Lechlade,
Gloucestershire, GL7 3HG

Tel 01367 253543
e-mail info@theploughinnkelm-
scott.com
website www.theploughinnkelm-
scott.com

Nearby cycling, horse riding, sail-
ing, indoor climbing, tennis,
Kelmscott House, festivals
Location Oxford, Cheltenham &
Cirencester are approx. 25 min
drive; based near stretch of Thames
Path
Food lunch & dinner Tue-Sun,
closed for food on Mon
Price £-££
Rooms 8; 7 double, 1 single, all with
wi-fi, TV, shower
Facilities bar, restaurant, free park-
ing, childrens menu, highchairs
Credit cards all major
Children welcome
Disabled no special facilities
Pets not allowed
Closed never
Proprietor Sebastian Snow

The Plough
Country inn

The most low-key of Sebastian and Lana
Snow's three Costwold pubs (a stones-
throw from the more party-centric Five Alls
and The Bull – pages 219 and 217), The Plough
is a quintessentailly cosy country inn, aptly situated in the idyllic village of Filkins. The decoration of its diminutive interior is wisely
understated, letting the 17thC features speak
for themselves: low beamed ceilings, flagstone
floors, and antique wooden benches set
before the toasty embrace of a wood-burning
stove. A few small but effective flourishes give
it the shabby-chic stamp of the Snow pubs,
such as a pair of oversized pheasant-feather
lamp shades mounted on old wheels, casting a
warm dappled glow on the dining area.

If the interior is understated, the food packs
a punch. Sebastian, who's worked as a chef for
30 years, has devised a menu that's both earthy
and sophisticated. We enjoyed chicken liver
pâté with spiced plum chutney and toasted
brioche, followed by succulent partridge, savoy
cabbage and red wine jus: boisterous, rich and
gamey, and lip-smackingly good.

Upstairs, eight cosy bedrooms have been
decorated by Sebastian's interior designer sister Miranda. They're proper country affairs,
with plaid throws and views over Cotswold-
stone houses. They're also well-equipped, and,
in this out of the way location, you couldn't
hope for a more peaceful sleep. An ideal base
for exploring nearby Kelmscott House.

Langar, Nottinghamshire

Langar, Nottinghamshire
NG13 9HG

Tel (01949) 860559
e-mail info@langarhall.co.uk
website www.langarhall.com

Nearby Belton House; Chatsworth;
Sherwood Forest; Lincoln
Cathedral, Belvoir Castle,
Nottingham.
Location in village behind church;
with ample car parking
Food breakfast, lunch, dinner
Price £££
Rooms 12 doubles; 1 room has
shower, all others have baths; all
rooms have phone, TV, hairdryer
Facilities sitting rooms, dining
rooms, bar; garden, croquet, fishing,
helipad **Credit cards** MC, V
Children welcome
Disabled 1 ground-floor bedroom
Pets accepted by arrangement
Closed never
Proprietor Lila Aurora

Langar Hall
Country house hotel

Since Imogen Skirving (who, upon her father's death, turned their family home into a hotel to prevent its loss) died last year, Langar Hall has been taken on by her grandaughter Lila, who has managed to preserve the unique experience created by Imogen. People who stay here feel more like guests in a beautiful Georgian stuccoed country house than customers in a hotel. The library appears to be totally unchanged, with hundreds of books available to leaf through with a drink or two before dinner. The food is superb and the wine list well judged.

The best bedrooms are airy, with furniture appropriate to the house that Imogen wanted to save, and enjoy glorious views of the Vale of Belvoir. For exercise, you can play croquet or stroll round the village church. Best of all is the friendliness of the hostess and her staff. Imogen wanders around the dining room, alighting at tables of single, bored businessmen and exchanging any sort of gossip, while nothing is too much trouble for the chef or staff. When our inspector realised, at 12.45 am, after an excellent dinner, that he had forgotten his sponge bag, an assortment of toothbrushes, toothpaste and razors was provided. We revisited recently and enjoyed the Imogen Skirving show as much as ever.

Little Malvern, Worcestershire

Little Malvern, near Malvern,
Worcestershire WR13 6NA

Tel (01684) 310288
e-mail
holdfastcottage@btconnect.com
website www.holdfast-cottage.co.uk

Nearby Eastnor Castle; Worcester;
Hereford; Gloucester.
Location 4 miles (6.5 km) S of
Great Malvern on A4104; with
ample car parking
Food breakfast, bar meals, dinner
Price £££
Rooms 8; 5 doubles, 2 twins, 1 sin-
gle all with bath or shower; all rooms
have phone, TV, hairdryer
Facilities sitting room, bar, dining
room, conservatory; croquet
Credit cards MC, V
Children welcome
Disabled access difficult
Pets not accepted
Closed Jan-March
Proprietors Steven and Julie
Thompson

Holdfast Cottage
Country hotel

'Cottage' seems to be stretching things somewhat – and yet, despite its size, this Victorian farmhouse does have the cosy intimacy of a cottage, and Steven and Julie Thompson create an atmosphere of friendly informality.

Inside, low oak beams and a polished flagstone floor in the hall conform to cottage requirement; beyond, headroom improves – though flowery, Laura Ashley decoration emphasizes the cottage status. Bedrooms are light and airy, with carefully co-ordinated fabrics and papers; some bathrooms are small. Outside, the veranda with its wistaria keeps the scale of the house relatively intimate. The garden – scarcely cottage-style – adds enormously to the overall appeal of the place, with its lawns, shrubberies, fruit trees and delightful 'wilderness'. Beyond are spectacular views of the Malvern Hills.

The daily-changing menu is based on continental as well as traditional English dishes, using the best local and seasonal produce, as well as freshly prepared home-baked rolls and hand-made ice cream. Herbs are gathered from the garden to compliment the English fare, which is sometimes found alongside more unusual dishes such as guinea fowl.

Malvern Wells, Worcestershire

Holywell Road, Malvern Wells,
Worcestershire WR14 4LG

Tel (01684) 588860
e-mail reception@cottageinthe-
wood.co.uk
website
www.cottageinthewood.co.uk

Nearby Malvern Hills; Eastnor
Castle; Worcester Cathedral.
Location 2 miles (3 km) S of Great
Malvern off A449; with ample car
parking
Food breakfast, lunch, dinner
Price £££
Rooms 30 double and twin with
bath or shower; all rooms have
phone, TV, hairdryer
Facilities sitting room, dining room,
bar; garden
Credit cards AE, MC, V
Children welcome
Disabled ground-floor rooms in
annexe **Pets** accepted in ground-
floor rooms, £10 per night
Closed never
Proprietors Nick and Julia Davies

The Cottage in the
Wood **Boutique country hotel**

Three buildings form this glossy little
hotel perched, very privately, in seven
wooded acres, high above the Severn valley and with a superb vista across to the
Cotswolds thirty-something miles away
(binoculars provided). There are bedrooms in all three buildings, taking the
hotel over our usual size for this guide; but
the smartly furnished Georgian dower
house at its heart is so intimate, calm and
comfortable that we decided to relent.

A short stroll away is the rebuilt Coach
House, where rooms are smaller but have
the best views, and Beech Cottage with
four cottage-style bedrooms. Apart from
its food, the restaurant (modern English
cuisine) has two other substantial qualities: windows that let you see the view and
a wine list that lets you roam the world.
Walkers can get straight out on to a good
stretch of the Malvern Hills and for tour-
ers the hotel provides leaflets giving con-
cise notes on everything that's worth visiting for 50 miles (80 km) around. For the
rest of us, there's a very well stocked bar
and a free video library.

This place is no longer family run. We'd
be interested to hear how the hotel is far-
ing under new ownership. Bedrooms have
recently been refurbished – reports welcome.

Telford, Shropshire

Bridgnorth Road, Norton, Near
Shifnal, Telford, Shropshire,
TF11 9EE

Tel (01952) 580240
e-mail reservations@hundred-
house.co.uk **website** www.hundred-
house.co.uk

Nearby Telford, Ironbridge Gorge
Museum, Severn Valley steam way,
The Long Mynd (walk).
Location just off the M54 from
junction 4, on the A442 between
Telford and Bridgnorth, with car-
parking **Food** breakfast, lunch, dinner **Price** £–£££ (min 2 night stay)
Rooms 9; 8 doubles, 1 single, all
with bath; all have TV, phone, tea
and coffee making facilities, hairdryer **Facilities** dining room, bar,
brasserie; herb garden, beer garden,
conference rooms **Credit cards** AE,
MC, V **Children** welcome
Disabled some access in public
rooms **Pets** well behaved dogs (£10
charge) **Closed** Christmas day/
night, Boxing Day night, New
Years's day/night **Proprietors**
Phillips family

Hundred House Hotel
Country hotel

"Quite extraordinary, a pleasant surprise around every corner" says one
recent reporter. From the moment you pull
in to the car park you don't quite know what
to expect next. The building itself dates back
to the 1500's, when it was the local court
house, and the remains of the stocks and the
whipping post can still be seen opposite.
Push open the stained glass doors, and the
atmosphere hits you: dim lighting, mellow
wood floors, panelled walls, bouquets of
dried herbs and flowers hanging from ceilings. The dining areas are spacious – the
Hundred House caters for non-residential
guests, but the tables are cosy and intimate,
some in front of a large open fire, others
tucked in various nooks. The menu is impressive and unusual, but cooked well with no
corners cut. The bar/brasserie area offers an
impressive range of ales.

The bedrooms are, well, eccentric: swings
in the 'superior' rooms; lively, floral decoration; and some very spacious bathrooms. The
one single room in the house is a little
cramped. The award-winning herb garden,
tended to by owner Henry Phillips and an
expert team of gardeners, is magical.
Elsewhere, you'll find relaxing sitting areas
and a small pond. Weddings are held in the
refurbished 17thC barn. It's family run, with
parents and sons working together to create
a memorable experience.

92-94 High Street, Oxford
OX1 4BN

Tel (01865) 799599
e-mail info@oldbank-hotel.co.uk
website www.oldbank-hotel.co.uk

Nearby Oxford colleges; Botanical Gardens; Sheldonian Theatre.
Location in city centre, with ample car parking
Food breakfast, lunch, dinner; room service
Price £££-££££
Rooms 42; 40 double and twin, 1 suite, 1 Junior Suite; all rooms have phone, flat-screen TV, complimentary wi-fi, Bluetooth DAB radio, fresh flowers, tea and coffee making facilities, treat filled mini-bar with complimentary mineral water, air-con and safe. **Facilities** restaurant, bar, courtyard **Credit cards** AE, DC, MC, V **Children** accepted
Disabled 1 room is specially adapted, most other rooms have lift/elevator access
Pets not accepted
Closed never
Proprietor Jeremy Mogford

Old Bank Hotel
City hotel

Hardly a quintessential charming small hotel because of its size, but we still think Old Bank Hotel is a good central Oxford address. What was, until the 1990s, a venerable bank with a fine Georgian façade, is now a cool, sophisticated hotel with a buzzing restaurant. It has kept up its high standards since we last visited.

The building has much to recommend it. The best bedrooms are graced with floor-length windows or, in the Tudor part, beams and deep window seats under lattice windows – the Junior Suite (room 45), in this style (see above), is particularly charming. All the bedrooms feature hand-made beds and marble bathrooms – with striking artwork from the owners' private collection decorating rooms, corridors and restaurant.

As well as a hotel, the Old Bank has become the 'in' place to eat in Oxford. The Quod Reataurant & Bar stretches across the former banking hall. Most guests will enjoy the buzz and bonhomie that emanates from this always packed meeting place (service can be slow), with a wide-ranging menu. Staff are welcoming, helpful and knowledgeable.

Oxford

1 Banbury Road, Oxford OX2 6NN

Tel (01865) 310210
e-mail info@oldparsonage-hotel.co.uk **website** www.oldparson-age-hotel.co.uk

Nearby Oxford colleges; Botanical Gardens; Sheldonian Theatre.
Location 5 minutes' walk from city centre, at N end of St Giles, close to junction of Woodstock and Banbury Roads; limited car parking
Food breakfast, lunch, dinner; room service and afternoon tea
Price £££ **Rooms** 35; 30 double and twin, 1 single, 4 suites, all with bath; all rooms have phone, TV, hairdryer, wi-fi **Facilities** sitting room, dining room, bar, garden library; terrace, roof garden **Credit cards** AE, DC, MC, V **Children** welcome
Disabled disabled access at entrance and some accessible rooms
Pets not accepted **Closed** never
Proprietor Jeremy Mogford

Old Parsonage Hotel
City hotel

Talk about contrast. The two best hotels in Oxford, Old Bank House (see opposite), and this one are in the same ownership – Jeremy Mogford. The Old Parsonage is much more typical of our guide, occupying a characterful, wistaria-clad house that has been owned by University College since 1320. Compared to its sleek, hip younger sibling, it seems at first quaint and old-fashioned, yet there is no themed olde worlde charm here, despite the great age of the building.

In early 2014, there were major renovations to the hotel. In addition to five new bedrooms, a garden library has been added for guests. The development of these new areas is in line with the rest of the hotel – wool, linen and velvet have been used in the rooms, and a colour scheme that centres on plum, deep red and grey. There is a brand new Old York stone floor downstairs.

Since then the restaurant has been rebranded as The Parsonage Grill, but reports tell us it's retained the intimate and Bohemian atmosphere that marked it out before, even with new furniture and decoration. We would welcome reports on the new look.

Painswick, Gloucestershire

Tibbiwell Street, Painswick,
Gloucestershire GL6 6XX

Tel (01452) 814006
Fax (01452) 812321
e-mail info@cardynham.co.uk
website www.cardynham.co.uk

Nearby Cheltenham; Chedworth
Roman Villa; Cirencester,
Gloucester, Sudeley.
Location in village, 3 miles (5 km)
N of Stroud; car parking on street
Food breakfast, Tues to Sat dinner
and Sun lunch
Price ££-££££
Rooms 9; 6 double, 3 family, all with
bath or shower; all rooms have
phone, TV
Facilities sitting room, breakfast
room
Credit cards AE, MC, V
Children accepted
Pets not accepted
Disabled not suitable
Closed restaurant only, Sun eve,
Mon eve
Proprietor John Paterson

Cardynham House
Village bed-and-breakfast

Built with money from wool and from pale gold stone out of a local quarry, Painswick is a classic Cotswold town perched rather precariously on (and over the brink of) a steep hillside. If you're not paying attention you might quite easily walk past Cardynham House – a discreet sign above the venerable front door of this Grade II-listed building, right on the street, is hardly enough to focus your attention when everything else around is so worth looking at. The real fun starts once you get inside. A cavernous open fireplace, flanked by a bread oven, warms a cosy drawing room which seems to metamorphose at some point into a conservatory.

Somehow, nine totally unique bedrooms have been created in this apparently modest-sized house, and each one is a triumphal exercise of imagination. Dotted with antiques and murals, each is decorated to a different theme and, even side by side in the same building, they all work unusually well. The most eccentric of all, air-conditioned because it hasn't a window to its name, has been got up like a desert pavilion. Another has its own private patio largely taken up with a covered plunge pool (heated, and with a powered current to swim against). Lunch and dinner can be taken in their Bistro Restaurant (when it's open), serving simple European food.

Radnage, Buckinghamshire

Horseshoe Road, Bennett End,
Radnage, Buckinghamshire HP14
4EB

Tel (01494) 482440
e-mail hello@themashinn.com
website www.themashinn.com

Nearby Saunderton station 15 min
Location in hamlet of Bennett End
(40 min drive from London)
Food breakfast (delivered to room),
restaurant
Price £££-££££
Rooms 6 double; 3 with hip bath, 3
with shower, 2 with private patios; all
have L:A Bruket toiletries and
Roberts Radios
Facilities bar, restaurant, garden
Credit cards all major
Children accepted
Pets welcome in bar
Disabled not suitable
Closed 24 Dec - 2nd Jan
Proprietor John Nash

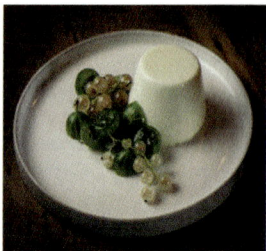

The Mash Inn
Country inn

With its red brick exterior and higgeldy rooftop, this diminutive pub (formerly The Three Horseshoes) is as cosy on the inside as it looks on the outside: original carved settles tucked into corners, and a tiny bar leading into the breezy dining area.

New owner John Nash has brought a dose of professionalism, as you'd expect from his years owning gastropubs in London, as well as a unique no-nonsense attitude. A bustling open kitchen, groaning with croquery, sits in the centre of the dining room, so diners can watch the talented Jon Parry whip up their food. Our series editor Fiona Duncan almost felt compelled to get up and help – barriers are broken down, adding to a relaxed and no-frills atmosphere. The high-class food is the real draw, consisting of hearty but sophisticated mains such as Cornish blue lobster stew with gnudi and nasturium, and a fancy tasting menu for £55 a head.

Rooms are compact but well-equipped, with Roberts Radios and exceptional Hypnos beds (no TVs). They've even squeezed freestanding hip baths into the tiny bathrooms – all in all, a fair offering for the price. Breakfasts are served in bed: expect a continental spread rather than cooked dishes, with croissants, jam and homemade granola with yoghurt.

Rhydycroesau, Shropshire

Rhydycroesau, Near Oswestry,
Shropshire, SY10 7JD

Tel (01691) 653700
e-mail stay@peny.co.uk **website**
www.peny.co.uk

Nearby Erdigg; Llanrhaedar waterfall; Powys Castle; Pistyll Rhaedar
waterfall
Location 3 miles (4.5 km) West of
Oswestry on the B4580. Hotel is 3
miles (4.5 km)down on that road on
the left
Food breakfast, dinner, afternoon
tea of clotted cream, jam and scones;
light lunch on request.
Price ££
Rooms 12 double; all with bath and
shower; all rooms have TV, hairdry-
er, modem point, tea and coffee
making facilities, phone
Facilities dining room, sitting room,
bar, reading room; garden
Credit cards AE, MC, V
Children welcome
Disabled 1 ground-floor room
Closed 21st of Dec for 4 weeks
Pets by arrangement
Proprietors Mr and Mrs Hunter

Pen-y-Dyffryn
Country hotel

Driving through the windy lanes cutting through the Shropshire hills from Oswestry, you can easily miss this attractive Georgian House tucked away off the main road. It nestles serenely among trees and green fields and you will be taken aback by the views that stretch (on a clear day) to the Welsh mountains. The dining room and sitting areas are decorated in warm colours; open log fires for the chilly winter evenings are perfect. If you prefer to drink or dine outside, there's a delightful little patio stretching round the side of the hotel. Look closely and you'll see modern touches about the place, such as abstract art.

The bedrooms are large, spacious and comfortable, with large fluffy towels provided in all the en suite bathrooms (some with spa baths and Jacuzzis) and fresh flowers on arrival. Four of the bedrooms are in the coach house, which is ideal for guests with animals. They each have spectacular views and their own private little patio. Chef Dave Morris has been here for 15 years and his cooking is perfect for the place – we enjoyed goats' cheese and maple syrup mousse and rose veal with Madeira cream sauce. The small bar by the entrance is staffed by helpful staff who can advise you on sightseeing, walking, or shopping in Wales or Shropshire.

Rowsley, Derbyshire

Rowsley, Derbyshire DE4 2EB

Tel (01629) 733518
Fax (01629) 732671
e-mail reception@thepeacocka-trowsley.com **website** www.thepea-cockatrowsley.com

Nearby Haddon Hall, Chatsworth, rivers Wye and Derwent
Location beside A6, between Matlock and Bakewell
Food breakfast, lunch, dinner; room service
Price ££-£££
Rooms 15; 14 doubles and 1 suite, 2 with four-poster, all en suite; all rooms have phone, TV, DVD player, tea and coffee making facilities, hairdryer **Facilities** bar, conference rooms, private dining and restaurant, fishing, golf nearby **Credit cards** AE, DC, MC, V **Children** accepted, but not on Friday or Saturday
Disabled not suitable **Pets** dogs £10 per night, not in public rooms
Closed 9th-26th Jan **Proprietor** Lord Edward Manners
Managers Laura Ball

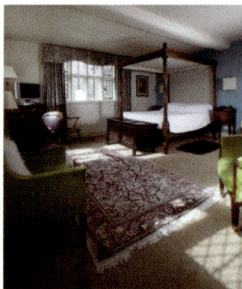

The Peacock at Rowsley
Country hotel

Just inside the door of the Peacock is a bowl of water and a basket for your dog. This is a sportsman's hotel, though an aesthete would be just as happy here; the pictures are outstandingly good. The River Wye – the only water in the country where wild rainbow trout breed naturally – is what the sportsmen come for. It is said to be the finest dry fly trout fishing in the land and the Head River Keeper from Haddon Hall is on hand to help you enjoy it. The Hall (Thornfield in BBC TV's *Jane Eyre*) is a nearby outing for days when the fish won't bite.

The Peacock, built in the 17th century, was once Haddon's dower house. Now it has all the comforts and convenience (wi-fi, DVDs) that modern visitors expect. Furnished with a mixture of old pieces and comfortable modern upholstery, there is an aura of antique furniture wax and wood smoke. In the bedrooms, fresh flowers, mahogany dressing tables and top-notch beds will make you feel at home. Uniformed staff are attentive and friendly – occasionally a little too much so for old-fashioned tastes. A great ledger in the hall records the fishermen's daily successes and disappointments. Whatever their luck on the river bank, they will not be disappointed in this handsome, well-run hotel.

92 Brocco Bank, Sheffield, S11 8RS

Tel 0114 2661233
e-mail hello@brocco.co.uk
website www.brocco.co.uk

Nearby close by are the city centre,
Weston Park Museum, Millennium
Gallery and the Winter Gardens; a
short drive away are Chatsworth
House, Bakewell and the Peak
District; 45km Robin Hood Airport
Location just off Ecclesall Road,
opposite Endcliffe Park
Food breakfast, lunch, dinner,
snacks, afternoon tea (pre-booking
and at weekends only)
Price £-££££
Rooms 8; 6 double and 2 twin. All
with wi-fi, Nespresso machine, ket-
tle, organic cosmetics, hairdryer.
Facilities wi-fi, restaurant, heated
terrace, guest lounge, free parking.
Credit cards AE, MC, V
Children accepted
Disabled one specially adapted
room **Pets** on terrace only; not
allowed in hotel or restaurant area
Closed never
Proprietor Tiina Carr, Owner

Brocco on the Park

City hotel

Picasso and Sheffield: you wouldn't pre-
dictably link the two, but the artist had a
direct influence on the interior design at
Brocco. Picasso is thought to have stayed
here in 1950 while attending the Peace
Congress in Sheffield. Its emblem was
Picasso's dove, and Tiina Carr, the friendly
Finnish owner, has put a series of avian
touches on each of the eight bedrooms.
Doves adorn bedroom walls, some baths are
egg-shaped and room keys fit into miniature
birdhouses near the door: touches which
create a warm and personal atmosphere.

When Tina purchased Brocco it was in a
state of near disrepair. Since then, she has
worked tirelessly, overseeing a stylish trans-
formation. Brocco now accommodates a
near-perfect fusion of Scandinavian charm
and solid British character.

There's another reason for Tina's avian
design: the 'park' in 'Brocco on the Park' is
Endcliffe Park, which lies directly opposite
the hotel, and is a city-centre haven for birds.
Many of the bedrooms overlook the 'living
roof' and beyond to the grassy park. The 'living roof' is exactly that: a flat roof imaginatively carpeted with grass and other plants.

The food at the all-day restaurant is popular and the atmosphere relaxed, friendly
and contemporary without trying too hard.
We think prices are fair for a city-centre
establishment of this standard.

South Leigh, Oxfordshire

Station Road, South Leigh, OX29
6XN

Tel +44 (0) 1993656220
e-mail oxford@artistresidence.co.uk
website
www.artistresidenceoxford.co.uk

Nearby Oxford:15 min drive away,
The Cotswolds: 15 min drive, 1.5
hrs from London
Location the peaceful village of
South Leigh.rear of building
Food breakfast, lunch, dinner,
Sunday lunch
Price ££-££££
Rooms 5: 3 farmhouse loft suites, 1
farmhouse suite, 1 single. Farmhouse
Loft rooms can accommodate chil-
dren with cot (additional fee). wi-fi,
flat screen TV, organic Bramley toi-
letries, Roberts radio, mini fridge,
Nespresso coffee machine
Credit Cards all major **Children**
below 12 not allowed in dining room
Disabled access to pub only
Pets allowed in pub, restaurant and
farmhouse rooms (extra fee)
Closed never **Proprietor** Charlotte
and Justin Salisbury

Artist Residence Oxford **Village inn**

Young artists no longer actually decorate this place, but their work hangs on the walls, and the creativity and originality of founders Justin and Charlotte are still intact here at their fourth hotel. A thatched gin-gerbread house, with five bedrooms tucked away in its eaves, it's a 16thC inn bursting with authenticity and original features: flag-stone floors, open hearths, a wooden bar and settles, complemented by William Morris wallpapers (breaking the Farrow & Ball mould, we were gratified to see). As with the other Artist Residences, there are lively hints of contemporary quirk, from Connor Brothers artworks to neon prints by Andy Doig.

The Connor Brothers were also respon-sible for designing the restaurant – Mr Hanbury's Mason Arms – curiously named after a fictional former owner of the inn. The talented chef and passionate forager, Leon Smith, serves dishes that are both satisfying-ly rustic and sophisticated.

The bedrooms are decked out with reclaimed furniture, Volga furnishings and hung with eclectic paintings. Our series edi-tor, Fiona Duncan, stayed in The Farmhouse Suite – a rustic bolt-hole built into the rafters, with exposed beams, slanted walls and a freestanding copper bath. So lovely, she thought she'd never want to leave.

Tetbury, Gloucestershire

Near Tetbury, Gloucestershire
GL8 8YJ

Tel (01666) 890391
Fax (01666) 890394
e-mail reception@calcotmanor.co.uk
website www.calcotmanor.co.uk

Nearby Chavenage; Owlpen Manor; Westonbirt Arboretum.
Location 3 miles (5 km) W of Tetbury on A4135; with ample car parking
Food breakfast, lunch, dinner
Price ££££
Rooms 35; 22 double and twin, 7 family suites, 6 family rooms, all with bath or shower; all rooms have phone, TV, hairdryer
Facilities 2 sitting rooms, dining room; garden, swimming pool, croquet, 2 all weather tennis courts; playroom, crèche, Spa, gym.
Credit cards AE, DC, MC, V
Children welcome (crèche)
Disabled 4 ground-floor bedrooms
Pets by arrangement
Closed never
Proprietor Richard Ball

Calcot Manor
Country house hotel

This 15thC Cotswold farmhouse has been functioning as a hotel since 1984. Richard Ball took over Calcot Manor from his parents when they retired, and with a team of dedicated staff continues to provide the highest standards of comfort and service while preserving a calm and relaxed atmosphere. The lovely old house itself was a sound choice – its rooms are spacious and elegant without being grand – and the setting amid lawns and old barns, surrounded by rolling countryside, is all you could ask for.

Furnishings and decorations are carefully harmonious, with rich fabrics and pastel colours throughout. A converted cottage provides seven family suites, designed specifically for parents travelling with young children. There's an Ofsted registered crèche and babsitting service to take the children off your hands.

Richard Davies is head chef of both the Conservatory Restaurant and the adjoining Gumstool Inn, which is more informal and moderately priced. In the restaurant, you might dine on champagne poached halibut with sea vegetables and a mussel saffron nage, or Calcot organic beef with a *béarnaise* sauce, French beans and artichokes.

Titley, Herefordshire

Titley, Kington, Herefordshire HR5 3RL

Tel 01544 230221
e-mail reservations@thestagg.co.uk
website www.thestagg.co.uk

Nearby Offa's Dyke, The Mortimer Trail, Ludlow, Hay-on-Wye, Hereford.
Location Titley village on B4355
Food breakfast, lunch, dinner
Price ££-£££
Rooms 6; 3 in The Vicarage, 3 in the pub; all have bath/shower and wi-fi, tea/coffee facilities
Facilities bar, dining room, garden
Credit cards AE, MC, V
Children accepted, but no special facilities
Disabled not suitable
Pets dogs welcome to stay in the pub, not the Vicarage **Closed** Mondays and Tuesdays, Christmas and Boxing Day, 2 weeks in Nov, 1 week in Jan or Feb
Proprietors Stephen and Nicola Reynolds

The Stagg Inn

Country inn

In 2001 this was the first gastropub to receive a Michelin star. Alas, they have not held on to it, but The Stagg Inn continues to be (deservedly) recognised for its menu (it was named Dining Pub of the Year in the 2018 Good Pub Guide). Chef Steve Reynolds creates straightforward country dishes with a focus on using locally sourced ingredients – served in their delightfully rustic and cosy bar.

But the food, though good, is only part of the story. There are six rooms, three in the pub and three in the Old Vicarage: a charming Grade II-listed property a 4 minute walk away. The pub rooms are beamy and comfortable, but the vicarage ones are exceptional: large, with high ceilings, elegant shuttered windows, wooden floors and great bathrooms. The furniture is unpretentious and pleasing – in fact the whole effect is that of a well-loved family home. And, starting at £125, they are notable value. Guests can also use The Vicarage garden down the road – it's Steve's pride and joy.

Winchcombe, Gloucestershire

High Street, Winchcombe,
Gloucestershire, GL54 5LJ

Tel (01242) 602 366
Fax (01242) 604360
e-mail enquiries@wesleyhouse.co.uk
website www.wesleyhouse.co.uk

Nearby Sudeley Castle, Cheltenham
race course, Hailes Abbey (NT)
Location in the centre of the town,
parking in the street about 200m
away
Food breakfast, lunch, dinner; after-
noon tea
Price ££
Rooms 5 doubles, 1 can be twin,
shower only; all with TV; one with a
small roof terrace/balcony
Facilities restaurant **Credit cards**
AE, MC, V
Children welcome
Disabled access not possible
Pets small to medium dogs accepted
with £10 charge per night
Closed Boxing Day; restaurant is
closed on Monday's and Sunday
evenings
Proprietor Matthew Brown

Wesley House
Restaurant-with-rooms

You don't go to Wesley House for spacious rooms, for fine antique furniture
or for its facilities. There are no telephones
in the bedrooms; no spas or conference
rooms. It doesn't even have a place to park
your car. As the smiling owner put it, "We
were built before the internal combustion
engine." And the five rooms, which are small
and furnished with old (not antique) pieces,
are squeezed into the old town house
where the original Methodist once stayed.
You go for the food, which is excellent. The
restaurant serves a short fine-dining menu
that would not disgrace a more pretentious
London restaurant. Portions are generous,
the price is modest (£35 for three courses),
the kitchen is skilled and the wine list exemplary. Recorded music (Louis Armstrong,
Edith Piaf) was slightly intrusive. For breakfast there were outstanding croissants, a
full English and good *cafetière* coffee. You
will have slept well because the beds are
comfortable and the town is quiet at night,
but don't expect luxury. Our inspector's
shower room, hardly larger than the loo
on a train. The rooms are *vin ordinaire*, that
is to say, inexpensive and fine for everyday,
but not for an occasion.

Winteringham, North Lincolnshire

Winteringham, North Lincolnshire
DN15 9PF

Tel (01724) 733096
Fax (01724) 733898
e-mail enquiries@winteringham-fields.com **website** www.winteringhamfields.co.uk

Nearby Normanby Hall; Thornton Abbey; Lincoln.
Location in centre of village on S bank of Humber, 4 miles (6 km) W from Humber bridge off A1077; with ample car parking
Food breakfast, lunch, dinner; room service **Price** £££ **Rooms** 15: 4 in the manor house, 7 in courtyard, 4 in the dovecots (100m off main site); all rooms have phone, TV, hairdryer
Facilities 2 sitting rooms, 2 dining rooms, conservatory; garden, helipad
Credit cards AE, MC, V **Children** welcome for lunch **Disabled** restaurant and public rooms accessible but not bedrooms **Pets** welcome in named rooms **Closed** 3 weeks at Christmas, but open New Years Eve; 3 weeks in August **Proprietors** Colin and Bex McGurran

Winteringham Fields
Manor house hotel

Halfway between Scunthorpe and the Humber bridge is one of Britain's gastronomic hotspots. Furthermore, you can sleep in great comfort no more than a few paces from the table. The hotel is in the middle of Winteringham, a quiet country village on the south bank of the Humber estuary. Colin and Bex McGurran are in charge, and Colin, the chef, is relishing the challenge of maintaining the very high culinary standards this hotel has always been known for. Having lived and worked in such diverse places as Zambia, the UAE and France, Colin's influences are eclectic.

The rambling 16thC house is full of nooks and crannies and still has many original features such as exposed timbers and period fireplaces. These are set off by the warm colours of walls and fabrics and the antique furniture. The bedrooms are all uniquely decorated and have recently been renovated, and the bathrooms modernised. There are four in the main house (with not a single right-angle between them), three in the courtyard, one in a cottage round the corner, and two more made from a dovecote a couple of minutes away.

Woodstock, Oxfordshire

Market Street, Woodstock,
Oxfordshire OX20 1SX

Tel (01993) 812291
Fax (01993) 220799
e-mail enquiries@feathers.co.uk
website www.feathers.co.uk

Nearby Blenheim Palace; Oxford.
Location in middle of town; with limited car parking
Food breakfast, lunch, dinner; afternoon tea
Price £££
Rooms 21; 16 double and twin, 5 suites all with bath or shower; all rooms have phone, TV
Facilities 2 sitting rooms, bar, dining room, restaurant; courtyard garden
Credit cards AE, DC, V
Children welcome
Disabled access difficult
Pets accepted by arrangement
Closed never
Proprietor Dr Munir

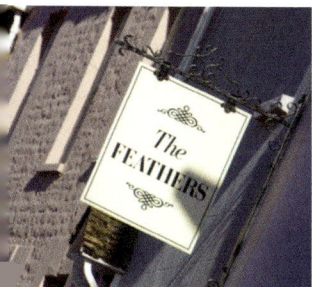

The Feathers
Town hotel

The Feathers is an amalgam of four tall 17thC town houses of mellow red brick in Woodstock. It makes an exceptionally civilized town hotel: one visitor was full of praise for the way the staff managed to make a weekend entirely relaxing, 'without intruding in the way that hotel staff so often do.

There is a cosy study for reading the papers or drinking tea. If you want fresh air, there is a pleasant courtyard garden and bar. Bedrooms are spacious (on the whole) and beautifully decorated, comfortable yet still with the understated elegance that pervades the whole hotel. Five further bedrooms are to be found in the building next door, renovated a few years ago. The elegant panelled dining room serves excellent food from Dominic Chapman's rustic, easy-going menu. Recent visitors have been impressed by both the food and service in the lively restaurant.

The upstairs Drawing Room is available for conferences of up to 30 people. It has the relaxed atmosphere of a well-kept English country home rather than a hotel, with antiques, and plenty of fresh flowers and a refreshing absence of 'Olde Worlde'.

Technically, this has all the trappings of a smart business hotel, but don't be put off it has character and a very home-like atmosphere.

Worfield, Shropshire

Worfield, near Bridgnorth,
Shropshire WV15 5JZ

Tel (01746) 716497
e-mail
admin@oldvicarageworfield.com
website
www.oldvicarageworfield.com

Nearby Ludlow; Severn Valley
Railway; Ironbridge Gorge Museum.
Location in village, 8 miles (12 km)
W of Wolverhampton, 1 mile off
A454 , 8 miles (12 km) S of junction
4 of M54; in own grounds with
ample car parking
Food breakfast, lunch, dinner
Price ££
Rooms 14 double, 1 family, all with
bath and/or shower (some have
jacuzzi baths and private patio
access); all rooms have phone, TV,
minibar, hairdryer
Facilities 2 sitting rooms, 3 dining
rooms, 1 with bar **Credit cards** AE,
DC, MC, V **Children** welcome
Disabled 1 specially adapted bedroom **Pets** accepted in bedrooms
Closed never **Proprietors** David
and Sarah Blakstad

Old Vicarage
Country house hotel

When this substantial red-brick vicarage was converted into a small
hotel in 1981, every effort was made to
retain the Edwardian character of the
place – restoring original wood block
floors, discreetly adding bathrooms to
bedrooms, furnishing the rooms with
handsome Victorian and Edwardian pieces,
carefully converting the coach house to four
'luxury' bedrooms (one of which, 'Leighton',
has been specially designed for disabled
guests). Readers have praised the large, comfortable bedrooms, named after Shropshire
villages and decorated in subtle colours, with
matching bathrobes and soaps.

Attention to detail extends to the sitting
rooms (one is the conservatory, with glorious views of the Worfe valley) and the
three dining rooms. The award-winning
Orangery restaurant has a daily-changing
menu and an impressive cheeseboard. It's
top-class English cuisine, ambitious and not
cheap. It's served at polished tables by
cheerful staff, with views over the rolling
Shropshire hills (it makes a lovely wedding
venue). There is a reasonably extensive
wine cellar.

Baslow, Derbyshire

Baslow, Derbyshire, DE45 1SP

Tel (01246) 582311
e-mail info@cavendish-hotel.net
website www.cavendish-hotel.net
Food breakfast, lunch, dinner
Price £££
Closed never
Manager Philip Joseph
Proprietor Chatsworth Estate

The Cavendish
Country house hotel

The name doesn't suggest a personally-run small hotel, but 'Cavendish' is appropriate because the hotel is on the glorious Chatsworth Estate of the Dukes of Devonshire, surname Cavendish. Until this edition it was a whole-page entry but following a disappointing experience there we now include it as a half page. No mistake, it's a good place, with charm, even grace and good taste, but with getting on for 30 bedrooms and more planned it is becoming a little large for the guide, bearing in mind its country location. The restaurant serves ambitious, but highly priced food.

Biggin-by-Hartington, Derbyshire

Biggin-by-Hartington, Buxton,
Derbyshire SK17 0DH

Tel 01298 84451
e-mail enquiries@bigginhall.co.uk
website www.bigginhall.co.uk
Food breakfast, lunch, dinner
Price ££-£££
Closed never
Proprietor James Moffett

Biggin Hall
Country house hotel

A gaggle of geese may follow you up the path to this friendly 17thC house. Popular with walkers, it's ideal to come back here after a day's trek: sink into a well-worn chair by a crackling fire and enjoy a drink in a relaxed, cosy atmosphere. Rooms are attractively decorated, with personal touches and stone mullioned, leaded windows. The roofs slope steeply. Breakfast is generous. Dinner (set menu with vegetarian options, changing daily) is excellent for the price – like home dining, but at the house of a very good cook.

Bledington, Oxfordshire

The King's Head Inn
Village inn

The Green, Bledington, Oxfordshire OX7 6XQ

Tel 01608 658365
Fax 01608 658902
e-mail info@kingsheadinn.net
website www.thekingsheadinn.net
Food breakfast, lunch, dinner
Price £££ **Closed** Christmas Day
Proprietors Archie and Nicola Orr-Ewing

A revamped village pub, but special because its character has been correctly preserved. A warren of cosy rooms circle the central bar. It's popular at weekends, and almost all the public space is devoted to dining tables — we often wish there could be more flopping space (armchairs and sofas) in pubs-with-rooms. The bedrooms are simple and unpretentious, but well decorated, with some amusing junk shop finds, books, pictures, pretty fabrics and rugs.

The food is top-quality pub fare, locally raised beef a speciality. The location, on the village green, is unspoiled, with a stream nearby and swings for the children. Owners Archie and Nicola Orr-Ewing give a friendly welcome and have happy staff.

Chipping Campden, Gloucestershire

Cotswold House Hotel & Spa **Town hotel**

The Square, Chipping Campden, Gloucestershire GL55 6AN

Tel (01386) 840330
e-mail reservations@cotswold-house.com **website** www.bespokehotels.com/cotswoldhouse
Food breakfast, lunch, dinner; afternoon tea **Price** ££££
Closed never **Proprietors** Bespoke Hotels **Manager** Craig Webb

Described by one reader as 'the place to stay' in Chipping Campden, Cotswold House can claim to be a very popular hotel and Spa. Set in a fine street, the building, dating from 1650, was renovated in 1999, with new rooms and the new coach house, where clean modern lines, gas log fireplaces and broad exposed beams definitely add to the place. In the main hotel, an impressive spiral staircase leads to well-appointed rooms, which are a similar standard to those in the coach house.

You have the choice of two restaurants: the relaxed Bistro on the Square and the formal Fig Restaurant. Alongside the coach house, a Mediterranean-style garden, attractively lit in the evening, is perfect for an after-dinner stroll.

Chipping Campden, Gloucestershire

Noel Arms
Town hotel

This new entry automatically gains points for location. It's in one of the Cotswold's most charming towns at the foot of the Cotswold Way, with great opportunities for walks. We hear that it oozes charm and historic atmosphere — the honey-stone building dates back to the 14thC. One bedroom has a four-poster in which the future Charles II allegedly slept when on the run during the Civil War.

The Noel Arms also has a reputation for excellent brasserie food. Talented chef Indunil Sanchi cooks high-quality pub fare alongside dishes inspired by his Sri Lankan heritage: the curries have won numerous plaudits. For £10 you can use the spa at Costwold House (opposite page) down the road.

High Street, Chipping Campden, GL55 6AT

Tel (01386) 840317
e-mail reception@noelarmshotel.com
website www.noelarmshotel.com
Food breakfast, lunch, dinner
Price £££–££££
Closed never
Proprietors Bespoke Hotels

Ilmington, Warwickshire

The Howard Arms
Village inn

Equidistant between Stratford-upon-Avon and Moreton-in-Marsh, this is useful for Stratford and the Cotswolds.

It's laid back: locals drink at the bar and the place has an easy-going charm. But there's professionalism too: our bags were carried upstairs and when the television didn't work in our room, it was dealt with at once.

The food is exactly what one wants in a 400-year-old stone-built inn, with pretty arched windows, a mix of old furniture and giant polished flagstones. Expect comforting dishes such as steamed suet pudding and sticky toffee pudding — all at sensible prices.

There are three rooms above the pub and five in a low-key garden wing. They are excellent, if somewhat formulaic.

Lower Green, Ilmington, Warwickshire CV36 4LT

Tel 01608 682226
email info@howardarms.com
website www.howardarms.com
Food breakfast, lunch, dinner
Price ££–£££
Closed never
Manager Robert Jeal

Ironbridge, Shropshire

Severn Bank, Ironbridge, Near Telford, Shropshire TF8 7AN

Tel 01952 432299
e-mail info@libraryhouse.com
website www.libraryhouse.com
Food breakfast, lunch, dinner
Price ££
Closed never
Proprietors Sarah and Tim Davis

Library House
Townhouse hotel

Reliable B&B (rooms from £75) with high standards in the heart of the Ironbridge World Heritage Site, opposite the Ironbridge itself and centrally located for the shops, pubs and restaurants. Smart decoration and authentically Georgian features and furniture throughout. The three bedrooms are more homely, and well equipped. The hosts Tim and Sarah Davis welcome guests personally, with afternoon tea and homemade cake served on arrival, and are strong on advice on where to eat and what to see – ask for their Ironbridge walks. Free passes to the local car parks are a genuine bonus.

A church bell rings nearby, day and night, but it's a light sound which doesn't disturb.

Kingham, Oxfordshire

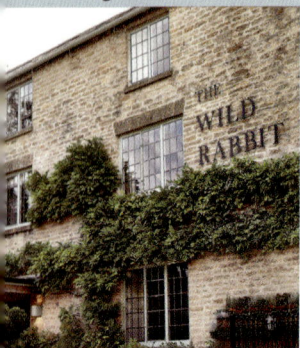

Church Street, Kingham, Oxfordshire OX7 6YA

Tel 01608 658389
e-mail theteam@thewildrabbit.co.uk
website www.thewildrabbit.co.uk
Food breakfast, lunch, dinner (no food served Sunday night and Monday) **Price** ££ **Closed** no specific dates **Proprietors** Lord and Lady Bamford

The Wild Rabbit
Country inn

Two endearing flop-eared topiary bunnies flank the entrance to this place – Lady Bamford's latest creation – fashioned from a former inn close to her Daylesford farm shop, café and Bamford Haybarn Spa

Our room, The Boar, was chilly, but it did have aromatic Bamford toiletries, attractive beams and scrubbed stone walls, a desk and a big bed. Downstairs there's a big buzzing dining space and, adjacent, a generous bar area with comfy seating for those who simply want a drink at the bar. Carol Bamford was determined to make this a casual meeting place for locals, and she has succeeded.

The food has also vastly improved since the kitchen has been taken over by Michelin-starred chef Tim Allen. Overall a useful address.

Leamington Spa, Warwickshire

The Lansdowne
Town house bed-and-breakfast

The Lansdowne is a creeper-covered Regency house in the heart of Leamington Spa – just as well there is double-glazing, says our reporter, who liked it not for its location but its food – though now only breakfast is served.

The public rooms are elegantly decorated in vibrant colours; the bedrooms, comfortable and cosy with pine furniture and pretty fabrics. Readers comment on the friendly atmosphere.

Leamington's heyday as a popular spa town might be over, but the Royal Pump Rooms were reopened to visitors in 1999 as a cultural complex, and there is still much to see in the neighbourhood. The Lansdowne makes an ideal base from which to explore Warwickshire sights. Reports welcome

87-89 Clarendon Street, Royal Leamington Spa, Warwickshire CV32 4PF

Tel 01926 450505
e-mail reservations@thelansdowne.co.uk
website www.thelansdowne.co.uk
Food breakfast **Price** ££
Closed after Christmas-Jan
Proprietor Mr Ross

Leintwardine, Herefordshire

Upper Buckton Farm
Bed and breakfast

A B&B and working farm set in 400 acres of unspoiled Teme Valley, this is a quintessentially charming small place to stay. Run by friendly owners Hayden and Yvonne Lloyd, you'll receive a personal welcome and the benefit of their local knowledge. The farmhouse itself is packed with homely comforts. The bedrooms are quaint and understated, and decorated with antique furniture, while neutral shades and thick fabrics dominate. The dining room has an open fireplace – used in winter – and decorated with Georgian period furnishing and 19thC oil paintings.

Yvonne does the cooking, which can be described as 'real home cooked food', from locally sourced ingredients, that are well matched with Hayden's extensive wine list.

Leintwardine, Craven Arms, SY7 0JU
Tel (01547) 540634
e-mail ghlloydco@btconnect.com
website www.upperbuckton.co.uk
Food breakfast
Price £
Closed occasionally
Proprietors Hayden & Yvonne Lloyd

Nether Westcote, Oxfordshire

Nether Westcote, Oxfordshire OX7 6SD

Tel 01993 833030 **e-mail** info@the-featherednestinn.co.uk **website** www.thefeatherednestinn.co.uk **Food** lunch, dinner, afternoon tea **Price** £££-££££ **Closed** Mondays, Christmas Day **Proprietor** Tony and Amanda Timmer

The Feathered Nest Country Inn **Country inn**

Another converted Cotswold inn, less formal but just as comfortable as some country house hotels.

Tony and Amanda Timmer's four bedrooms may be coyly named (eg. Cuckoo's Nest, Cockerel's Roost), but they are a blend of the practical, the luxurious and the countrified.

The food in the homely but elegant dining room is as impressive as the bedrooms. The pub fare served in the bar (where the stools are fashioned from riding saddles) is also above average. The wine list features unsung 'boutique' growers from around the world.

The Feathered Nest wouldn't work everywhere, but in the Cotswolds it does.

Northleach, Gloucestershire

West End, Northleach, Gloucestershire GL54 3EZ

Tel 01451 860244 **e-mail** reservations@cotswoldswheatsheaf.com **website** http://theluckyonion.com/property/the-wheatsheaf/ **Food** breakfast, lunch, dinner **Price** £££-££££ **Closed** never **Proprietors** Julian Dunkerton

The Wheatsheaf Inn **Country inn**

Welcome to the Cotswolds: Chelsea tractors in the drive; leggy blondes in designer country-wear sipping martinis at the bar; landscaped gardens leading up to a Farrow & Ball-painted inn. But we were won over by the interiors: an attractive dining area, gleaming with polished wood; the relaxed Game Bar; the treatment room. The location is not special, but the bedrooms are fabulous: imaginative wallpapers and fabrics, zinc bath, comfortable beds. This is the third establishment to be bought by Julian Dunkerton, who has a number of plans for the place. The food from chef Ronny Benetti (formerly of the Soho group) doesn't miss a beat. Breakfast was superb, including wonderful devilled kidneys.

Shipton-under-Wychwood, Oxfordshire

The Shaven Crown
Country house hotel

The Shaven Crown Hotel, as its name suggests, has monastic origins; it was built in 1384 as a hospice to nearby Bruern Abbey, and many of the original features remain intact – most impressively the medieval hall, with its beautiful double-collar braced roof and stone walls decorated with tapestries and wrought ironwork. The hall forms one side of the courtyard garden, which is decked with flowers and parasols, and on a sunny day is a lovely place in which to enjoy wholesome pub lunches. Some of the bedrooms overlook the courtyard, others are at the front of the house and suffer from road noise – though this is unlikely to be a problem at night. Phil and Evelyn carried out an extensive refurbishment to the ground floor and bedrooms in 2014, which complements the historic setting well.

High Street, Shipton-under-Wychwood, Oxfordshire OX7 6BA

Tel 01993 830500
e-mail relax@theshavencrown.co.uk
website www.theshavencrown.co.uk
Food breakfast, lunch, dinner
Price ££
Closed Christmas day - 4th/5th Jan
Proprietors Phil and Evelyn Roberts

Shrewsbury, Shropshire

Brompton Farmhouse
B&B Bed-and-breakfast

This gentrified farmhouse in National Trust-owned Attingham Park offers an unusual package. The Bean family run both – B&B in the farmhouse and a cookery school in the smart farm buildings across the yard. Marcus Bean, who has appeared in several television cooking programmes, is an excellent chef and a good cookery teacher. He produces dinner to order in the farmhouse. When we stayed we enjoyed beautifully done scallops and tender lamb.

The bedrooms are comfortable and furnished with Edwardian antiques, but lacked personal touches; the reception area and sitting rooms are also a touch impersonal.

An ideal place for exploring nearby Shrewsbury and learning about everything from cupcakes to currymaking.

Brompton, Near Cross House, Shrewsbury, Shropshire SY5 6LE

Tel 01743 761629
e-mail info@bromptonfarmhouse.co.uk
website www.bromptonfarmhouse.co.uk
Food breakfast **Price** ££ **Closed** Christmas **Proprietors** Marcus and Jenny Bean

Stamford, Lincolnshire

The Bull and Swan
Town inn

Quaint is an over-used description for inns in old buildings, but here it really does fit. This historic inn on the High Street of Stamford's St Martins district is mainly 17thC and has been sympathetically made over in the usual quirky-luxurious style of the Hillbrooke mini chain, of which it is a part.

Well-chosen antiques rub shoulders with top-quality beds and pristine white linen in the nine bedrooms. Most of the rooms are a fair size. There is a pleasasnt kitchen garden where they host film and pizza nights during the summer.

Food is better-than-average country inn fare using local ingredients. A drinking club for a 17thC Earl of Exeter and friends was based here, and members' nicknames eg The Badger are used for the rooms. Burghley House can be reached on foot.

St Martins, Stamford, Lincolnshire PE9 2LJ,

Tel 01780 766 412
email enquiries@thebullandswan. co.uk **website** http://www.hill-brookehotels.co.uk/the-bull-and-swan/ **Food** breakfast, lunch, dinner **Price** ££-£££ **Closed** never **Proprietors** Hillbrooke **Manager** Peter Brighouse

Stamford, Lincolnshire

The William Cecil
Town hotel

With 27 rooms this is somewhat out-side our usual size, but the unstuffy staff make it feel like a smaller place. The atmosphere is relaxed but gracious, as you would expect from a house on this scale.

They've got the basics right here, including the quality beds, the Egyptian cotton linen and the intelligent use of space. Design and furnishings are nicely in keeping with the building, and the overall effect is perhaps more harmonious than other Hillbrooke hotels.

It's just along the road from The Bull & Swan (see above), and part of the same group. This guide doesn't normally favour chains, but the Hillbrooke philosophy shares much with ours: no managers in suits, no staff uniforms, no name badges.

St Martins, Stamford, Lincolnshire PE9 2LJ

Tel 01780 750070
e-mail enquiries@thewilliamcecil.co.uk **website** www.thewilliamcecil.co.uk **Food** breakfast, lunch, dinner **Price** ££-£££ **Closed** never **Proprietors** Hillbrooke **Manager** Peter Brighouse

Bildeston, Suffolk

High Street, Bildeston, Suffolk IP7
7EB

Tel 01449 740510
e-mail reception@thebildeston-
crown.co.uk
website
www.thebildestoncrown.com

Nearby Lavenham, Long Melford,
Constable Country, Wool Town
Walks **Location** 10 mins on
A1141/B115 from Hadleigh
Food breakfast, lunch, afternoon tea,
dinner, snacks **Price** ££
Rooms 11 double, 1twin; all have
bath/shower, TV, wi-fi, hairdryer,
bathrobes, iron & board, MusicCast
system, Noble Isle toiletries
Facilities bar, lounge, 2 dining
rooms, courtyard, 2 function rooms;
fishing, riding, shooting, tennis
Credit cards AE, MC, V
Children welcome **Disabled** lift,
Room 2 has access, 'drop off' point
with step-free access to hotel **Pets**
dogs accepted, £10 per night **Closed**
Christmas Eve, Christmas Day and
New Year's Day evenings
Proprietors Chris & Haley Lee

The Bildeston Crown
Village inn

This refurbished inn in sleepy Bildeston
is in fact, first and foremost, a rather
expensive and sophisticated restaurant,
with the entire ground floor given over to
tables and smart dining chairs in a series of
rooms with attractive, boldly painted
walls. However, changes have been afoot
since Chris and Hayley Lee returned here
in 2015 (having spent two years setting up
a Suffolk-based hospitality company) after
former owner James gave them an offer
they couldn't refuse. The restaurant is no
longer run separately, meaning guests can
now order from any menu wherever they
want in the hotel – a welcome transition
to a more inn-like feel. During the ten
years this pair formerly worked here as
Head Chef and manager, the hotel earned
a slew of foodie awards, so with free reign
their focus continues to be on quality seasonal produce, often locally sourced.

The rooms are lovely, with pretty fabrics
and charming touches. Ours had a great
bathroom, with a rolltop bath and large
shower. Their weekend rates, in particular,
are steep, but the Sunday-night dinner, bed
and breakfast package (from £140-185 for
two, depending on the room) is a good
deal.

Brancaster, Staithe, Norfolk
PE31 8BY

Tel (01485) 210 262
e-mail reception@whitehorsebran-caster.co.uk
website
www.whitehorsebrancaster.co.uk

Nearby Holkham Hall, Brancaster beach, Norfolk lavender, Burnham Market, Sandringham Estate Peddars Way
Location on A149 coast road with ample car parking
Food breakfast, lunch, dinner
Price ££-££££
Rooms 15; 5 family rooms, 10 doubles (4 can be twin), all with bath and shower; all rooms have phone, TV, hairdryer, wi-fi
Facilities dining area, sitting room, conservatory, restaurant, bar, garden, terrace, courtyard **Credit cards** MC, V **Children** accepted **Disabled** 1 room with low-rise bath and ground floor access (enquire before) **Pets** well behaved dogs in 8 ground room floors **Closed** never **Proprietor** Nye family

The White Horse
Village inn

Cliff Nye, proprietor of The White Horse at Brancaster, is tired of reading in guides that from the outside, his building is not exactly charming – and rightly so, because as soon as you're inside, it's something else. First you walk into a bar area for non residents, with a local community atmosphere; this melts seamlessly into a more 'residential' area with reception desk and seating; and this gives way to the big, airy conservatory dining room with its scrubbed pine tables and extraordinary view out over a network of creeks and marsh across Brancaster Staithe to Scolt Head Island – surely one of England's most distinctive coastal panoramas. You could easily while away most of a morning or afternoon here, followed by lunch or dinner, and still not be tired of the view.

Your room, either upstairs or in the Garden Rooms, will be comfortable and cleanly decorated and furnished in a modern style with seaside colours and Lloyd Loom chairs. The food is good – no more or less than you'd expect for the price – though you might hope to find a somewhat wider range of seafood on the menu. A lesson in how to transform what was a horrible old pub in a fabulous situation into thriving 21st century operation.

The Green, Burnham Market,
North Norfolk, PE31 8HD

Tel (01328) 738777
Fax (01328) 730103
e-mail reception@thehoste.com
website www.thehoste.com

Nearby Houghton Hall; Holkham
Hall; Sandringham House;
Titchwell, Holme, Holkham and
Cley nature reserves.
Location in centre of Burnham
Market; with ample car parking
Food breakfast, lunch, afternoon tea
and dinner
Price £££
Rooms 61; 36 doubles in main
house, 8 in Railway House hotel, 8
in Vine House, 9 in 3 cottages, all
with bath or shower; all rooms have
phone, TV, hairdryer
Facilities traditional bar, conserva-
tory, lounge, sheltered walled gar-
den, restaurants, beauty spa and lux-
ury 20-seat cinema **Credit cards**
MC, V **Children** accepted **Disabled**
ground-floor bedrooms **Pets** not
accepted **Closed** never **Proprietors**
Bee and Brendan Hopkins

The Hoste Hotel
Village hotel

Overlooking the green in a village
whose main claim to fame is that it
was Admiral Nelson's birthplace, this handsome yellow-and-white 17thC inn has won
a clutch of awards for its bedrooms, bar and
restaurant. Downstairs, it positively buzzes
with life in the evenings, when locals come
here to drink and eat – in that order. The
brasserie-style menu includes British,
European and Oriental-inspired dishes.

The man responsible for this reputation, Paul Whittome, bought The Hoste in
1989 and died tragically young, in his 50s,
in July 2010. We happened to revisit the
day after his funeral and found business as
usual, just as he would have wished.
Despite being deaf, Paul was a chatty, affable proprietor, who made The Hoste into
a local institution – and helped spread its
fame as far afield as the Home Counties.

Since Bee and Brendan Hopkins took
over changes over the years have included
a stylish garden room which accommodates up to 110 people, and a lodge for 16
to 30 people. The Hoste kitchens have
doubled in size and they also now have a
rather large spa. Further rooms are on
offer across the road in peaceful Vine
House hotel, which is a one-minute walk
away, and The Railway House hotel, situated seven minutes from the main hotel.

Northgate Street, Bury St Edmunds, Suffolk IP33 1HP

Tel 01283 339604
e-mail info@thenorthgate.com
website www.thenorthgate.com

Nearby Abbey gardens (350 yards); St Edmunds Cathedral (350 yards); Theatre Royal (1232 yards)
Location 350 yards from city centre
Food breakfast, lunch, cream tea, dinner
Price ££
Rooms 10; 8 double, 1 suite (2 linked bedrooms); all have TV, wi-fi, hairdryer, tea/coffee
Facilities chef's table, private dining room, restaurant, bar, conservatory
Credit cards AE, MC, V
Children welcome
Disabled access difficult
Pets not accepted
Closed never
Proprietors Steven Mariott

The Northgate
Town hotel

Formerly Ounce House – run by the Potts family – it was recently taken over by The Chestnut Group (headed by ex-banker Philip Turner). While there certainly have been changes, its excellence hasn't been compromised. Perhaps this is why Genevieve, the Potts' daughter, has chosen to stay on as host and receptionist. Staffed by sneaker-wearing youths and frequented by metropolitans, it's no longer a guesthouse, but the experience is relaxing and the service instant. The swishing drapery of Ounce House have given way to a glitzier style, complete with a moody cocktail bar and glamorous dining room. Turner's aim was to avoid hotel labels such as restaurant-with-rooms, guesthouse and so on, preferring it to be "simply eponymous with a great experience."

The nine bedrooms are decorated in neutral colours combined with luxurious fittings – both classic and glamorous. Bathrooms are very smart, and you'll find home-made shortbread on arrival. The food generally is a great draw, with an option to sit at the chef's table and watch Daniel Grigg (formerly chef at Gilpin Lodge, Langley Castle and Linthwaite House) in action. Our series editor Fiona Duncan especially enjoyed cauliflower risotto for dinner, and grapefruit granita with orange and thyme at breakfast.

Cley-next-the-Sea, Norfolk

Cley-next-the-Sea, Holt, Norfolk
NR25 7RP

Tel (01263) 740209
e-mail info@cleywindmill.co.uk
website www.cleywindmill.co.uk

Nearby Sheringham Hall; Cromer
Lighthouse; Holkham Hall.
Location 7 miles (11 km) W of
Sheringham on A149, on N edge of
village; with ample car parking
Food breakfast, dinner on request
Price ££
Rooms 9 double, all with
bath/shower
Facilities sitting room, dining room,
garden **Credit cards** MC, V
Children welcome
Disabled access difficult
Pets accepted in some rooms
Closed bed-and-breakfast closed for
Christmas and New Year; self-cater-
ing let available during this time
Proprietor Dr Julian Godlee
Manager Simon Whatling

Cley Mill
Converted windmill B&B

Imagine staying in a 'real' windmill. That is the sense of adventure that Cley Mill can induce even in the most world-weary. Memories of Swallows and Amazons or the Famous Five crowd in as you climb higher and higher in the mill, finally mount-ing the ladder to the look-out room on the fourth floor. Superb views over the Cley Marshes, a Mecca for bird-watchers.

The sitting room on the ground floor of the Mill is exceptionally welcoming – it feels well used and lived-in, with plenty of books and magazines, comfortable sofas, TV and an open fire. Bedrooms in the Mill feel rather like log cabins – much wood in the furniture and fittings. They are pretty rooms, with white lace bedspreads, and bathrooms ingeniously fitted in to the nooks and crannies.

Since our last edition, Cley Mill has changed hands. The new owner is Julian Godlee, a GP from Hertfordshire with roots on the Norfolk coast – the only bid-der who wanted it to continue as a B&B. There has been maintenance and restora-tion recently, but the basic formula remains unchanged. A new bedroom has been added right at the very top of the windmill – reached by a steep ladder, it is only for the adventurous and fit, but the view makes it worthwhile. Try to book well in advance. See also our other windmill (page 35).

Dedham, Essex

Stratford Road, Dedham,
Colchester, Essex CO7 6HN

Tel 01206 322367
e-mail maison@milsomhotels.com
website
www.milsomhotels.com/maisontal-
booth

Nearby Sir Alfred Munnings
Museum at Castle House,
Colchester, Ipswich, Constable
Country, Suffolk Heritage Coast
Location bypass Colchester A12
northbound, take left signposted
Dedham, follow signs for Maison
Talbooth **Food** breakfast, lunch at
hotel **Price** ££££ **Rooms** 12; all double, 7 can be twin, all have
bath/shower, one has additional
bunk beds; terrace; all have free soft-
drinks, mini bar, hairdryer, wi-fi, Sky
HD TV **Facilities** sitting rooms,
garden room, day spa, pool, tennis
court **Credit cards** all major
Children welcome **Disabled** 5
downstairs rooms **Pets** dogs welcome **Closed** never **Proprietors**
Milsom family

Maison Talbooth
Country house hotel

A welcome addition to our Essex section – under an hour and a half drive
from London – this smart, rather plain-
looking Victorian house is hard to beat for
lavish comfort. It's recently undergone
some impressive embellishments: two new
suites, a spa, pool, and tennis court.
The 12 poet-themed suites have a decadent Sixties feel: quilted fabrics and luxury
drapes; charcoal greys and muted greens;
and patterned wallpaper that contradicts
the all-new modern bathrooms.

Down the road, Le Talbooth, also under
the Milsom ownership, is the gastronomic
hotspot of the area. It remains a popular
place to eat even after 50 years, and still
exudes the feel of its 'Sixties heyday'.
There's an exceptional wine list and a
blend of old-and-new style cooking. If you
don't feel like going out, light snacks can be
served in your room at Maison Talbooth.
The hotel's Range Rover takes you to and
from the restaurant, or anywhere else
nearby.

Dedham, Essex

High Street, Dedham, CO7 6DF

Tel 01206 323351
e-mail
office@thesuninndedham.com
website www.thesuninndedham.com

Nearby Dedham Vale Area of
Outstanding Natural Beauty (near-
by), Flatford Mill (1m), Constable's
Haywain (1m), Beth Chatto Garden
(5m), Colchester (7m), Manningtree
and Mistley (7m)
Location in village centre, opposite
St Mary's Church **Food** breakfast,
lunch, dinner, cream tea **Price** ££
Rooms 7; 6 doubles and 1
double/twin. All have TV, radio, tea
and coffee making facilities, wi-fi,
hairdryer
Facilities bar, lounge, restaurant,
terrace, garden, bikes
Credit cards AE, MC, V
Children welcome
Disabled not suitable **Pets** dogs
allowed in bar and oak room, and in
rooms by arrangement - enquire
before **Closed** 24-27th Dec
Proprietors Charlotte Green and
Dominique St Rose

The Sun Inn
Village inn

On the Essex/Suffolk border, in
Constable country, a buttercup yellow coaching inn stands at the centre of
the village of Dedham. Piers Baker took
over the scruffy old building in 2003 and
filled it with antiques, upmarket furniture
and paintings. The result is homely and
authentic. The reception is at the front elm
bar, where patrons sip local ales. There is a
split-level sitting room with a cosy open
fire, and a beamed dining area with parquet floors and fresh flowers.

Most of the seven bedrooms face
Dedham High Street and the huge windows of St Mary's church opposite, with
the periodic chiming of bells reminding
you of the quaintness of this rural village.
One room faces the back of the inn, offering more peace to light sleepers. There are
painted, wardrobes, Robert radios, and
paintings that carefully match the colour
schemes. The four-poster and half tester
beds are the most remarkable, but all
rooms are comfortable and well equipped.

In good weather, The Sun Inn does jus-
tice to its name: at breakfast, tables are
draped in white linen, brightening the dining room. At lunch and dinner the menu
includes local fish and game, and many
items have a Mediterranean twist (you
might find pappardelle with lamb ragu, but
also poached salt cod among the choices).

Fritton, Norfolk

Church Lane, Fritton, Norfolk
NR31 9HA

Tel (01493) 484008
e-mail
frittonarms@somerleyton.co.uk
website www.frittonarms.co.uk

Nearby Somerleyton House and
Estate; Norfolk Broads; Gorleston
beach, Beccles, Southwold,
Aldeburgh, Walberwick
Location in own grounds with
ample private car parking
Food breakfast, lunch, dinner
Price £££
Rooms 9; all double, two can be
twin; all with bath or shower, TV,
wi-fi
Facilities bar, dining room, sitting
room, private dining room
Credit cards MC, V
Children welcome **Disabled** no spe-
cially adapted rooms **Pets** small,
well-behaved dogs **Closed** never
Proprietor Hugh Crossley

Fritton Arms
Country hotel

This former 15thC smuggler's inn was
turned into a hotel some years back by
30-something Hugh Crossley, heir to the
Somerleyton Estate of which it is a part.
Interior design is by Hugh's wife Lara, with
many an old beam exposed to contrast
with the mainly contemporary, easy-going
feel of the place. It's as relaxed as a hotel
gets, the tone set by the manager David
Smith, and Hugh himself, who keeps a close
eye on everything and is always hatching
new plans.

Downstairs there's a cosy sitting room,
but the hub is the bar and restaurant,
where locals come to eat. 'Simple food, well
cooked' is the aim of the menu devised by
James Santillo and his team. The wine list
has an unusual selection of bottles for
around £12.

Fritton House stands on the edge of a
country park whose main feature is
Fritton Lake, with rowing boats and other
amusements. It's open to the public from
April to October; for the rest of the year,
and after five in summer, guests at Fritton
House have the run of the place, free of
charge. A great place to bring children.

Great Waldingfield, Suffolk

Great Waldingfield, Sudbury,
Suffolk CO10 0TL

Tel 01787 372428
e-mail bookings@theoldrecto-
rycountryhouse.co.uk
website www.theoldrectorycountry-
house.co.uk

Nearby Lavenham, Long Melford,
Bury St Edmunds, Sudbury
Food breakfast, dinner only by
arrangement when booking the
whole house
Price ££-££££
Rooms 7; all double, two ground
floor, all have bath/shower; 3 in the
main house, 4 in The Old Stables
annex
Facilities drawing room, honesty
bar, swimming pool, tennis court,
free wi-fi
Credit cards MC, V
Children welcome
Disabled access difficult
Pets clean dogs accepted
Closed rarely
Proprietor Frank Lawrenson

The Old Rectory
Country house hotel

Much of the charm of this tucked-away
rectory lies in the way owner Frank
Lawrenson has thoroughly restored its
original character – it's in superb condition, but uncompromised by trendy, contemporary add-ons. All the rooms have
bathrooms and are individually decorated:
subtle pastel shades reign, with delicately
floral cushions and curtains. There is a
sense of space everywhere, but especially
in the drawing room, and to complete the
gracious but relaxed atmosphere guests
get a high level of unobtrusive but personal attention from Frank and his team,
including a butler. The books, the honesty
bar and copious, well presented information on what to see and do in the area
make you feel at home. One concession to
contemporary design is the swimming
pool's curved roof, open on one side, making it
an indoor-outdoor pool – used mainly in
the summer-time.

We sense that this place is always on
the move. Major refurbishments of the
bedrooms are expected between
November 2017 to January 2018. It's also
making a foray into environmentally
friendly technology, including a Biomass
boiler and a conservation programme in
partnership with local artisans. Staying
here means you have the satisfaction of
making a contribution to their cause.

Harwich, Essex

The Quay, Harwich, Essex
CO12 3HH

Tel (01255) 241212
Fax (01255) 551922
e-mail pier@milsomhotels.com
website
www.milsomhotels.com/thepier

Nearby Harwich sights including
Electric Palace Cinema, Ha'penny
Pier, Redoubt fort, golf **Location** on
quayside in old town; own off-road
car parking for 25 cars
Price ££ **Food** breakfast, lunch, dinner **Rooms** 14; all doubles with own
shower or bath, phone, TV, wi-fi,
minibar **Facilities** 2 restaurants, bar,
terrace, sitting room, private dining
facilities, house party service, sailing
arranged on yacht or traditional
Essex craft **Credit cards** AE, DC,
MC, V **Children** accepted **Disabled**
specially adapted room and WC on
ground floor, access at rear of building; lift to first and second floors
Pets dogs allowed (in bedrooms and
in the NAVYARD bar and terrace)
Closed never
Proprietor Milsom family

The Pier

Seaside town hotel

Here's a good place for a weekend – if
you like the sea, ships, and industrial
seascapes. Picture-book pretty it isn't;
atmospheric, absorbing and 'real' it most
certainly is. The Pier, with its distinctive blue
and white façade, designed to resemble a
Venetian *palazzo*, was built in 1864 to
accommodate overnight passengers from
Harwich to the European mainland. It was
from here, too, in 1620, that the Mayflower
set sail for the New World.

The Pier restaurant on the first floor is
relaxed and informal, specializing in locally
caught seafood – with the option to dine
on the balcony with views over the harbour. There's also the continental-styled
NAVYARD bar, with 115 gins (and counting) to choose from (open from 9am).
Check-in is at the bar, and bags are prompt-
ly taken to your room.

All the rooms are several cuts above
what you would expect for the price (deep,
white-sheeted beds, natural sea colours on
tongue-and-groove panelling), but with only
£10 each between a 'standard', a 'superior'
and a 'deluxe' it pays to go for the largest –
and get the view.

The Pier has been owned for nearly 30
years by the Milsom family. Like their other
establishments, Maison Talbooth (page 258)
and Milsoms, it's a close-knit operation,
with long-serving locals on the happy team.

Park Road, Holkham, Norfolk
NR23 1RG

Tel (01328) 711008
e-mail victoria@holkham.co.uk
website www.holkham.co.uk/thevic-
toria

Nearby Holkham Hall, Holkham
beach, Pensthorpe, Norwich.
Location just off the B1105 on th
A149 near Wells; with ample car
parking
Food breakfast, lunch, dinner
Price £££
Rooms 20 double and twin, all en
suite with shower; all rooms have
TV and DVD, hairdryer, tea/coffee
facilities
Facilities 2 dining rooms, 2 sitting
rooms, 1 bar; garden
Credit cards MC, V, AE
Children welcome **Disabled** 1
ground-floor room with wet room
Pets dogs in some bedrooms at
£10/night
Closed never **Proprietors** Viscount
and Viscountess Coke

The Victoria at Holkham **Country hotel**

Part of the Holkham Estate owned by the Earl of Leicester, The Victoria (named after Queen Victoria, a year after she became queen) is an eclectic and stylish blend of colonial furniture and fabrics. Built in 1837 by Coke of Norfolk, the hotel is a five-minute stroll from the beautiful white sands of Holkham beach where there are water sports. Viscount Coke, a descendent of Coke of Norfolk, and his wife Polly acquired the hotel some time ago and undertook a major refurbishment. One of its many successful outcomes is the new conservatory.

Everywhere you turn your attention is caught by some curious object or another. Rooms contain items from the attics and basements of Holkham Hall, as well as furnishings and ornaments that have been flown in from Rajasthan. All of the bedrooms are decorated individually with flare and good taste. Although the rooms may look old they have modern comforts such as seriously comfy beds, big warm duvets and deep baths for a serious soak.

The restaurant and bar area is very much in keeping with the colonial feel, slightly hard chairs, but beautiful wall hangings and views. The food is cooked and presented to a high standard (don't overlook the fish and chips); and there's a long wine list.

Huntingdon, Cambridgeshire

1 High Street, Huntingdon,
Cambridgeshire, PE29 3TQ

Tel (01480) 458410
e-mail oldbridge@huntsbridge.co.uk
website www.huntsbridge.com

Nearby Cambridge (18m), London
(1hr)
Location central, on Huntingdon
High Street
Food breakfast, lunch, dinner
Price ££–££££
Rooms 24; 12 double, 8 single, 1
twin, 3 four-poster. All have power-
shower, bath, TV with DVD player,
Noble Isle toiletries, wi-fi
Facilities dining room (can be used
for wedding parties), wine shop, bar,
sitting room, morning room, buis-
ness centre
Credit cards all major
Children welcome
Disabled no 'accessible' bedrooms,
one disabled toilet located outside
main building
Pets welcome in bar, lounge and
bedrooms **Closed** never
Proprietors John and Julia Hoskins

The Old Bridge

Town hotel

Legend has it this is the place that
inspired Robin Hutson and Gerrard
Basset to open their acclaimed Hotels du
Vin, after being impressed by a hotel so
packed full of locals. But while Hotel du Vin
ended up as a chain, The Old Bridge preserves its individual character to the hilt.
The charm offensive begins the moment
you step inside the handsome ivy-clad
townhouse, with Julia Hoskin's fabulous
decoration: sumptuous swags of material
and well chosen antiques are styled with
contemporary flair, with playful prints and
visual surprises at every turn.

The individually decorated bedrooms
combine decorative quirk with modern
comforts, such as smart TVs, luxurious
beds and roll-top baths. Three of the bedrooms have stunning four-posters.

Head chef Jack Woolner describes his
food as 'robust, British and very honest'.
There's an *á la carte* menu with pub classics, alongside scones, snacks and cocktails
to keep guests going throughout the day.
The hotel's still a huge hit with locals, who
spread themselves *laissez faire* across its
cosy bar, panelled morning room and beautifully refurbished restaurant.

John Hoskin became a 'Master of Wine'
in 1994 – the same year he and his wife
took over – hence the lovely wine shop at
reception.

King's Staithe Square, King's Lynn, Norfolk PE30 1RD

Tel 01553 660492
e-mail info@thebankhouse.co.uk
website www.thebankhouse.co.uk

Nearby the Custom House, King's Lynn Minster, The Corn Exchange **Location** on the quayside, accessible via the A10, A17 and A47; ample parking.
Price ££-£££
Food breakfast, all day food, afternoon teas, Sat and Sun brunch
Rooms 12; singles, doubles, large doubles all with TV, radio, telephones, wi-fi, tea and coffee making facilities and guidebooks **Facilities** bar, brasserie, terrace, sitting area, parking **Credit cards** MC, V
Children welcome; under 5s free, £10 per night for cot, £20 per night for children under 12 in parents' room **Disabled** ramps both inside and out, and fully accessible WC
Pets allowed on request
Closed never **Proprietor** Anthony and Jeanette Goodrich

Bank House Hotel
Town house hotel

This is the sister hotel of The Rose & Crown in Snettisham (page 272). It's just as quirky and historic as its sibling. The Grade II listed Georgian townhouse started life as the home of a rich King's Lynn merchant, but in the 1780s was set up as the first branch of what is now Barclays Bank. A dent in the wooden floor is still visible, maybe left behind by the nervous shuffling of 18thC account holders. C a r e f u l design brings out the history of the building, but this place is far from old fashioned. Traffic-light bright chairs decorate the waterside terrace outside, whilst inside the armchairs are bright green and magenta. Rooms are airy and modern, although some are a little small. Most have river views; a few look out on to King's Staithe Square.

The brasserie and bar are relaxed and welcoming, made up of a number of different areas from which you can choose according to how formal you're feeling. We think that the most sympathetic area is the former counting house – all dark, polished wood and original flooring. Dishes vary from the standard (burgers, fish and chips) to the exotic, and are prepared using local ingredients whenever possible. Bank House is brilliantly situated for exploring this historic town. The Corn Exchange theatre is nearby and pre-and post-theatre dining can be arranged.

King's Lynn, Norfolk

Lynn Road, Grimston, King's Lynn, Norfolk PE32 1AH

Tel (01485) 600250
Fax 01485 601191
e-mail
info@conghamhallhotel.co.uk
website www.conghamhallhotel.co.uk

Nearby Sandringham; Ely; Norwich.
Location 6 miles (10 km) NE of King's Lynn near A148; with parking for 50 cars **Food** breakfast, lunch, dinner **Price** ££££
Rooms 26; 15 in the main house, 11 garden rooms, 11 double, 2 suites, all with bath, 1 single with shower; all rooms have phone, TV, DVD player, room larders with small fridges, Nespresso machines **Facilities** 2 sitting rooms, bar, dining room; garden, spa, indoor swimming pool, tennis, croquet, putting
Credit cards DC, MC, V
Children welcome (over 7 in restaurant) **Disabled** easy access to restaurant **Pets** dogs allowed in some rooms **Closed** never
Proprietor Nicholas Dickinson

Congham Hall Hotel & Spa **Country house hotel**

'Quintessentially English' is how some guests describe their stay here. Practically everything about this white 18thC Georgian house, set in 40 acres of lawns, orchards and parkland, is impressive. The spacious bedrooms and public areas are luxuriously furnished and our reporter found the service to be solicitous and efficient and the staff helpful and welcoming. Cooking (in the modern British style) is adventurous and excellent, making much use of home-grown herbs. The restaurant is a spacious, airy delight, built to look like an orangerie, with full-length windows overlooking the wide lawns of the parkland, where the herb gardens are an attraction in their own right. Visitors stop to admire the array of 600 herb varieties and to buy samples, from angelica to sorrel. The restaurant doors open on to the terraces for pre-dinner drinks and herb garden strolls.

Personal attention is thoughtful. The hotel keeps a book of special walks, devised by the previous owners, the Forecasts, and can arrange clay pigeon shooting on site, subject to availability. Taken over in 2012 by Nicholas Dickinson, a seasoned hotelier. Reports welcome.

Lavenham, Suffolk

Market Place, Lavenham, Suffolk
CO10 9QZ

Tel (01787) 247431
Fax (01787) 248007
e-mail info@greathouse.co.uk
website www.greathouse.co.uk

Nearby Little Hall Museum;
National Trust Guildhall
(Lavenham); Melford Hall;
Gainsborough's House; Sudbury.
Location 16 miles (26 km) NW of
Colchester, in middle of
village; car parking
Food breakfast, lunch, dinner
Price £££
Rooms 5; 3 double with bath, 2 lux-
ury suites with bath/shower; all
rooms have phone, TV, minibar, wi-
fi, some have espresso machine,
hairdryer
Facilities dining room; patio, gar-
den; bicycle hire
Credit cards MC, V
Children welcome
Disabled access difficult
Pets not accepted
Closed Jan **Proprietor** Régis Crépy

The Great House
Restaurant-with-rooms

The old timber-framed houses, the fine 'Wool Church' and the high street full of antiques and galleries make Lavenham a high point of any visitor's itinerary of the pretty villages of East Anglia.

The Great House in the market place was built in the heyday of the wool trade but was extensively renovated in the 18th century and looks more Georgian than Tudor – at least from the outside. It was a private house (lived in by the renowned artist Humphrey Spender and his brother, the poet Stephen Spender, in the 1930s) until Régis and Martine Crépy turned it into a hotel in 1985. The food (predomi-nantly French) is the best for miles, with a well-chosen wine list – 'stunningly good', enthuses one visitor (a fellow hotelier).

If you can secure one of its five bed-rooms it is also a delightful place to stay. All are different, but they are all light and elegant, with the same charm as the rest of the house. Four have their own sitting area or sitting room, with sofa or upholstered chairs. The beds (one a king-size Jacobean four-poster) are dressed with Egyptian linen and eiderdown duvets. The compli-mentary fruit and decanter of sherry are a welcoming touch.

In summer, the dining room French doors open on to a pretty stone-paved courtyard for drinks, lunch or dinner.

Long Melford, Suffolk

The Green, Long Melford, Suffolk
CO10 9DN

Tel (01787) 312356
e-mail info@theblacklionhotel.com
website www.blacklionhotel.net

Nearby Long Melford church;
Melford Hall; Kentwell Hall.
Location in village 3 miles (5 km) N
of Sudbury, overlooking village
green; with car parking
Food breakfast, lunch, afternoon tea,
dinner
Price £££
Rooms 10; 8 double, 1 suite, 1 fami-
ly room; all have bath/shower, TV,
tea and coffee making facilities,
superfast wi-fi, Noble Isle bath prod-
ucts **Facilities** sitting room, 2 dining
rooms, bar
Credit cards AE, MC, V
Children welcome
Disabled no special facilities
Pets dog-friendly
Closed never
Proprietor Philip Turner

The Black Lion
Country hotel

Long Melford is a famously attractive Suffolk village, and The Black Lion is at the heart of it, overlooking the green. Since becoming the latest member of the Chestnut Group the hotel – set in an elegant 19thC building – has undergone an extensive renovation.

The new interiors are smart yet warm, retaining The Black Lion's signature antique style with a more elegant feel: roaring fires, oil paintings and mounted antlers create a pleasant, countrified atmosphere. The set-up features a new conservatory, which can be used as a space for private parties, and leads on to their new terrace where guests can dine *al fresco*.

Bedrooms, either 'snug' or 'luxury' are soothing, in pastel olives and creams, with pleated headboards and wool throws.

Their already delicious food has gone up a notch with new chef, Nick Traher. The focus is on pub classics, full of flavour whilst being refined. Dinner might include twice baked soufflé with braised celery, salt baked beetroot and walnut granola, and is served in their restaurant, conservatory, bar or lounge.

We'd be interested to hear reports on how the new management are getting on.

High Street, Mistley, Essex CO11 1HE

Tel 01206 392821
e-mail info@mistleythorn.co.uk
website www.mistleythorn.co.uk

Nearby Colchester 7 miles, Ipswich 8 miles, Stour Estuary
Location Mistley High Street, car park for 5 cards and street parking
Food breakfast, lunch, dinner, afternoon tea
Price ££-£££
Rooms 12; all have television, DVD player, iPod dock, tea/coffee facilities, wi-fi; 3 rooms have small kitchen facilities
Facilities restaurant, bar, separate dining area that can be used for private functions (up to 30 people)
Credit cards AE, MC, V
Children welcome
Disabled a ramp can be used
Pets well-behaved dogs in some rooms
Closed Christmas day
Proprietor Sherri Singleton and David McKay

The Mistley Thorn
Village inn

In the 1700s, a wealthy, local landowner had plans to turn Mistley into a fashionable saltwater spa, but his scheme never came off. Be prepared for a place that's semi-industrial and rough at the edges.

Two 18thC towers rise from a churchyard on the edge of the town, and the High Street has prettily painted Georgian terraces. The Mistley Thorn is a former Victorian public house, outside of which you get the smell of Horlicks emanating from the Edme Maltings factory along the road. Opposite is the Stour Estuary, upstream from Harwich. We liked The Mistley Thorn as much for its setting as for the food and accommodation.

It's run with panache by Californian Sherri Singleton. Her menu majors on local seafood, including Mersea oysters and Colchester natives when in season. There's Suffolk Red Poll beef and Sutton Hoo chicken.

Our top-floor room, with a view of the Stour, was somewhat cramped, but it was freshly decorated and had a well-equipped, airy bathroom. Other rooms are larger, and all of them have views across Stour Estuary, as well as homely touches such as home-made cookies and dressing gowns. We heard some traffic noise in the morning.

Morston, Norfolk

Morston, Holt, Norfolk
NR25 7AA

Tel (01263) 741041
Fax (01263) 740419
e-mail reception@morstonhall.com
website www.morstonhall.com

Nearby Sandringham; Felbrigg
Hall; Holkham Hall; Brickling.
Location 2 miles (3 km) W of
Blakeney on A149 coastal road
opposite entrance to quay and seal
trips; ample car parking
Food breakfast, Sun lunch, dinner
Price ££££
Rooms 7 double and twin in main
hotel, plus 6 pavilion suites; all
rooms have phone, TV, CD player,
hairdryer **Facilities** sitting room,
sun lounge, conservatory, dining
room, orangery; garden, croquet
Credit cards AE, DC, MC, V
Children welcome
Disabled 1 ground-floor bedroom
Pets accepted in bedrooms **Closed**
Jan, Christmas Eve, Christmas day,
Boxing Day
Proprietors Galton and Tracy
Blackiston

Morston Hall
Country hotel

Don't be put off by the rather severe-looking flint exterior of this solid Jacobean house on the North Norfolk coast. Inside, the rooms are bright and airy, painted in summery colours and overlooking a sweet garden, where a fountain plays in a lily pond and roses flourish. The *raison d'être* of Morston Hall is its dining room, the responsibility of Galton Blackiston, who shot to fame as a finalist in ITV's 'Chef of the Year'. He has since won huge acclaim for his outstanding modern European cuisine and, the icing on the cake, a Michelin star in 1999. His set four-course menu changes daily and might feature: confit of leg of duck on sautéed Lyonnaise potatoes with thyme-infused jus or grilled fillet of sea bass served on fennel duxelle with sauce vierge. The carefully-stocked wine cellar offers a comprehensive selection of (not overpriced) wines from all over the world. Galton and his wife, Tracy, also organize wine-tasting dinners and cookery lessons. He gives a number of half-day cookery demonstrations and runs two three-day residential courses each year. Most of the large bedrooms are decked out in chintz fabrics, with armchairs and all the little extras, such as bottled water, bathrobes and large, warm, fluffy towels.

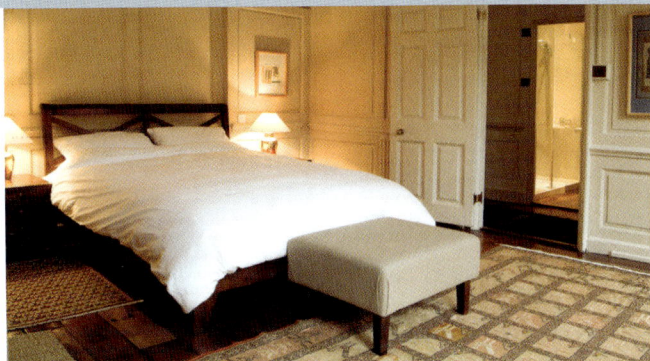

38 St Giles Street, Norwich, Norfolk
NR2 1LL

Tel 01603 662944
e-mail bookings@38stgiles.co.uk
website www.38stgiles.co.uk

Nearby Norwich Castle, Norwich
Cathedral, shops, bars, restaurants
Location Norwich town centre
Food breakfast
Price ££-£££
Rooms 8; all have bath/shower, wi-
fi, smart TV's, hairdryer, tea and cof-
fee making facilities
Facilities wi-fi
Credit cards MC, V
Children welcome, family room
available
Disabled 1 ground-floor room, but
no special access
Pets not accepted
Closed Christmas
Proprietor Dennis and Holly Bacon

38 St Giles
Town bed-and-breakfast

This sophisticated bed-and-breakfast in the heart of Norwich can claim to be one of the best in the city.

The breakfasts here are particularly acclaimed – imaginative jams, fresh pancakes and homemade granola feature on the wide-ranging menu – and all ingredients are locally sourced. The Norfolk breakfast is a particular favourite with guests – one recent visitor describing it as 'the best British breakfast' around.

They've made the most of the breakfast room as a public space. White walls and lofty ceilings enhance the feel of Georgian grandeur – the pretty crockery adds a contrasting, feminine touch.

Bedrooms are an interesting marriage of traditional and contemporary design. Period features such as large fireplaces and generous bay windows give a lovely old-fashioned feel, while contemporary chaise longues, colourful silk curtains and modern wooden furniture make each room feel chic and cool. Welcome treats, such as homemade brownies, are left for guests.

Snettisham, Norfolk

Old Church Road, Snettisham, Norfolk PE31 7LX

Tel (01485) 541 382
Fax (01485) 543 172
e-mail info@roseandcrownsnettisham.co.uk
website www.roseandcrownsnettisham.co.uk

Nearby Peddars Way, Houghton Hall, RSPB Snettisham, North Coast beaches, Holkham Hall, Sandringham, Norfolk Lavender, Burnham Market
Location off B1440, in centre of Snettisham village with ample car-parking
Food breakfast, lunch, dinner
Price ££ **Rooms** 16; 1 twin, 15 doubles (4 can be split for twins); all rooms have phone, TV, wi-fi, air-conditioning, hairdryers, irons
Facilities 3 dining rooms, walled garden, bar, sitting room **Credit cards** V **Children** welcome **Pets** accepted **Disabled** 2 rooms have access **Closed** never **Proprietors** Anthony and Jeanette Goodrich

Rose and Crown
Village inn

We like the way this inn keeps both locals and visitors happy. There are plenty of activities nearby, it is situated near an area of outstanding natural beauty, and it is far better value for money than its grander neighbours in nearby villages. The oldest part of the inn is the bar, originally built for workers who erected the local church, and where locals and visitors enjoy the beer and a wide selection of sandwiches whilst sitting by the open fire, then totter off to their rooms, minding the wonky old flagstones on the way.

On the way to your room, admire owner Anthony Goodrich's sporting prowess: his old school photos adorn the walls. The bedrooms are smallish, but done out in a fresh, sea-sidey way, with all the creature comforts you would expect. If you need a substantial lunch or dinner, head downstairs to one of the three dining rooms that provide fresh, locally sourced food, including beef from the salt marshes at Holkham, seafood from Brancaster and game from the gentlemen in wellies in the back bar.

Parents can rest assured that their children will be safe in the walled garden, sporting an impressive climbing frame and play area. They can be watched from the terrace or the attached dining room/sitting room. The Goodriches thoroughly deserve their Publicans' Pub of the Year award.

Stoke by Nayland, Suffolk

Stoke by Nayland, Suffolk,
CO6 4SA

Tel (01206) 263245
e-mail info@angelinnsuffolk.co.uk
website www.angelinnsuffolk.co.uk

Nearby Guildhall; Dedham Vale; Flatford Mill; East Bergholt.
Location in village centre, on B1068 between Sudbury and Ipswich; small car park for 20 cars
Food breakfast, lunch, dinner
Price ££
Rooms 6 double, 2 twin, 4 with bath; all with TV, hairdryer, wi-fi
Facilities sitting room, 2 dining rooms, bar; garden, herb garden, beer garden
Credit cards MC, V
Children travel cots in 4 rooms
Disabled not suitable
Pets accepted in pub only
Closed never
Proprietors Suffolk Country Inns

Angel Inn
Village inn

A proper inn rather than a pub, with spick-and-span bedrooms off a long gallery landing upstairs, the Angel Inn has been in business since the 16th century. There are plenty of nooks and crannies in the bar and a variety of seating in the series of interconnecting public rooms. You'll find sofas and chairs grouped together in the lounge; and a dining room with its ceiling open to the rafters, rough brick-and-timber-studded walls and a fern-lined well-shaft 52 feet (16 m) deep. The bedrooms are a fair size, individually and unfussily decorated, and are ideal for a one- or two-night stop on a tour of Suffolk. Since the last edition, they have renovated these, re-painting them and adding new baths.

The public rooms downstairs have great character, with interesting pictures and low lighting, and are filled with the hum and buzz of contented lunch and dinner conversation. The food is excellent, with local produce used where possible, including fresh fish and shellfish from nearby ports, and game from local estates. Dishes might include griddled hake with red onion dressing, or stir-fried duckling with fine leaf salad, Cumberland sauce and new potatoes. Service is informal, friendly and helpful. Children are not allowed in the bar, and though flexible, check when booking what the rules are.

Swaffham, Norfolk

Ash Close, Swaffham, Norfolk
PE37 7NH

Tel (01760) 723845
e-mail enquiries@strattonshotel.com
website www.strattonshotel.com

Nearby Norwich; North Norfolk
coast.
Location down narrow lane between
shops on main street; with car park-
ing
Food breakfast, lunch, dinner
Price £££
Rooms 14; 7 doubles, 7 suites, all
with bath or shower; all rooms have
phone, TV/DVD, hairdryer, mini-
bar, iron
Facilities 2 sitting rooms, dining
room, bar, cafe/deli
Credit cards MC, V
Children welcome
Disabled access difficult **Pets** wel-
come in specific rooms **Closed**
Christmas
Proprietors Vanessa and Les Scott

Strattons
Town hotel

Strattons has long summed up everything we are looking for in this guide.
When Les and Vanessa Scott bought
this elegant listed villa in 1990 they had a
very clear vision of what they wanted to
create, decorating it with their unique
artistic flair (they met as art students).
Bedrooms are positively luxurious. Plump
cushions and pillows jostle for space on
antique beds, books and magazines fill the
shelves. Their style extends to the smart
bathrooms – one resembling a bedouin's
tent. The two beautifully furnished sitting
rooms, *trompe l'oeil* hallway and murals
painted by a local artist are equally impressive. A reader writes: '20 out of 20 for staff
attitude, value for money, quality of accommodation… An absolute delight.'

Les and Vanessa's daughter Hannah has
been running the hotel with her husband
for the past ten years – keeping it very
much a family affair. They've expanded the
hotel to include extra bedrooms, and an
on-site cafe – with a lifestyle/interiors
shop is in the pipeline. The food is special
too. They now have a resident head chef,
although Vanessa (an acclaimed cookery
writer) continues to oversee its opera-
tions. The seasonal menu plucks produce
from their nearby orchard and allotment,
and is cheerfully served by the small team
of staff in the cosy basement restaurant.

Thorpe Market, Norfolk

Cromer Road, Thorpe Market,
Norwich, Norfolk NR11 8TZ

Tel 01263 832010
e-mail office@theguntonarms.co.uk
website www.theguntonarms.co.uk

Nearby Cromer, Holt, Holkham
Hall, Houghton Hall, The Sainsbury
Centre of Art
Location just off the A149 on
Elderton Lane
Food breakfast, lunch, dinner
Price ££-££££
Rooms 8 double in the main build-
ing, all have bath/shower; 4 Coach
House rooms (next door) and 4 Barn
house suites **Facilities** restaurant,
sitting area, bar, The Stamp Rooms
Credit cards AE, MC, V
Children welcome, £15 per night
for additional bed
Disabled disabled lavatory, bar and
restaurant on one level. One fully
adapted room in the coach house on
the ground floor.
Pets 5/16 rooms allowed dogs, £10
per night (please ask on booking)
Closed Christmas Day
Proprietor Ivor Braka

The Gunton Arms
Country pub-with-rooms

One of the most impressive refurbished inns in East Anglia, possibly in
the country. It's a substantial, flint-walled
building in flat, spreading Norfolk parkland.
Money did not deter the owner, art dealer
Ivor Braka, from achieving the result he
wanted. Although cash does not guarantee
success, here it has come together to great
effect with Braka's vision and high standards, and designer Robert Kime's flair.

Downstairs is a series of rooms which
manage to feel traditional, cosy and stylish
– and are full of surprises. Cropping up
everywhere is outstanding contemporary
art, much of it amusingly sexual. Tracy
Emin's plates above the bar shocked one
straightlaced couple so much that they got
their solicitor to write a complaining letter.
Country folk and Londoners seem to mix
easily in the bar-dining area. The food is
quite straightforward, including steaks
cooked, memorably, on an open wood fire.
The bedrooms are enchanting. If you find
yourself in Ellis, look twice at the prints by
the dressing table, but not if you were
offended by Tracy Emin's plates.

Walberswick, Suffolk

Main Street, Walberswick, Suffolk
IP18 6UA

Tel 01502 722112 **e-mail**
info@anchoratwalberswick.com
website
www.anchoratwalberswick.com

Nearby local beach and river are
both a 2 minute walk, Minsmere
RSPB centre, golf courses at
Aldeburgh, Thorpeness and
Southwold, Dunwich forest is a 45
minute walk. **Location** 10 minute
drive from the A12 along the B1387,
15 minute drive from Southwold
Food breakfast, lunch, dinner
Price ££ **Rooms** 10; 6 garden rooms
(3 are dog-friendly), 4 rooms in the
main building; all en-suite with a
bath and/or shower, all rooms have
wi-fi, satellite television **Facilities** 2
sitting rooms, dining room, bar
Credit cards AE, MC, V **Children**
welcome **Disabled** one room accessible **Pets** accepted in 3 Garden
Rooms, 2 seating areas of pub and
outdoor terraces **Closed** Christmas
day **Proprietors** Mark and Sophie
Dorber

The Anchor
Village inn

A place that stands out because of the
hosts, says our series editor, Fiona
Duncan. Some twelve years ago the
Dorbers acquired this formerly run-down
pub in the village where Sophie Dorber
grew up. (She and Mark had run the popular White Horse pub in Parson's Green,
Fulham. Sophie did the food, he was the
landlord, with a special interest in wine
and beers from the world over.)

The Anchor is far from boring now: it's
a comfortable place, popular with the
locals. The staff are attentive (unless overrun at peak times), and sometimes funny
(watch out for Luke's unexpected quips).
Sophie's food is full of flavour and Mark
has done something unique with the wine
list: matched dishes with not just wines but
beers too. He'll even tell you what beer to
drink with you breakfast porridge.

Don't be misled by the building's nothing-
special exterior. The ten bedrooms (four in
the main building, six more spacious
chalets in the garden) aren't as inviting as
the colourful bar and restaurant – in fact
they're simple, but they are priced for what
they are. Bathrooms have underfloor heating.

It's a terrific weekend getaway, with
much of interest nearby – the town of
Southwold, and the famous Walberswick
reedbeds – a birder's paradise.

Coltishall, Norfolk

Church Loke, Coltishall, Norfolk,
NR12 7DN

Tel 01603 737 531
email info@norfolkmead.co.uk
website www.norfolkmead.co.uk
Food breakfast, lunch, dinner, after-
noon tea, picnic hampers
Price ££-££££
Closed very rarely   **Proprietors**
James Holliday and Ann Duttson

Norfolk Mead
Village hotel

The Norfolk Broads aren't known for their hotels, which is why we were gratified to come across this charming riverside address. The hotel comes with its own boat to ferry guests up the river Bure, spotting herons and otters whilst chugging past stretches of idyllic countryside. Back in the handsome Georgian house they can spoil themselves with an 'Aromassage' from Catherine's healing hands.

James Holliday and Anna Duttson, who bought and refurbished the hotel in 2013, make a kindly and hands-on team. The interiors are very smart, albeit a little bland for the taste of our series editor, Fiona Duncan, but the tranquility of location and spot-on hospitality more than compensate.

Lavenham, Suffolk

Water Street, Lavenham, Suffolk
CO10 9RW

Tel (01787) 247404
Fax (01787) 248472
website www.lavenhampriory.co.uk
Food self-catering
Price ££
Closed Christmas and New Year
Proprietors Sayed

Lavenham Priory
Self-catering guesthouse

This is a very special place: the beautiful Grade I-listed house dates from the 13th century when it was home to Benedictine monks, and has been restored in keeping with its later life as home to an Elizabethan merchant, complete with origi-nal wallpaintings, Tudor fireplace and sofas covered in cushions and throws.

The house is large, and as well as the Great Hall sitting room there's a smaller room so more than one party can use the public rooms. Each of the bedrooms has a superb bed, including a four-poster in the Painted Chamber. Since its new ownership the two suites have become self catering, with guests receiving a local food hamper on arrival, but there are a number of fine dining restaurants and pubs in the area.

Lavenham, Suffolk

High Street, Lavenham, Suffolk
CO10 9QA

Tel (01787) 247477
e-mail
info@theswanatlavenham.co.uk
website
www.theswanatlavenham.co.uk
Food breakfast, lunch, afternoon tea,
dinner Price ££-££££ Closed never
Proprietor TA Collection

The Swan Hotel
Village hotel

On the news that Lavenham Priory was to become self-catering, we include this large but characterful inn as a useful alternative. The Swan's exterior competes head-on with the quaintest, but the recently refurbished interior is the reason to stay.

The down-at-heel, pokey old coaching inn has been made to look fresh without losing its essential character. The brasserie, overlooking the garden, works especially well. The beamy bedrooms are not as interesting as the ground floor spaces, but you may enjoy the test of finding your way back to your room through the labyrinth of passages and quirky floor levels. The Gallery Restaurant's food, in a reconstruction of a medieval timbered hall, is enjoyable, the wine list expertly chosen. Since out last edition they've also opened a luxury spa.

Norwich, Norfolk

Lodge Lane, Old Catton, Norwich,
Norfolk NR6 7HG

Tel (01603) 419379
Fax (01603) 400339
e-mail enquiries@catton-hall.co.uk
website www.catton-hall.co.uk
Food breakfast
Price ££ Closed over Christmas
Proprietors Nicola and James
Waterman

Catton Old Hall
Country house bed-and-breakfast

An impressive 17thC gentleman's residence, built from reclaimed Caen stone, local flint and oak timbers, has been transformed with great success into this genteel, family-run guesthouse. With its mullioned windows, beamed ceilings, inglenook fireplaces, polished antiques and warm colour schemes, the interior feels intimate and inviting. Manager Paula is on-hand to welcome guests and look after them during their stay.

Named after former inhabitants of the house, the bedrooms have been decorated boldly, in-keeping with the age of the house in country-house style.

The breakfast menu is superb, making use of local produce as well as herbs and fruit from the garden.

Orford, Suffolk

Orford, Woodbridge, Suffolk, IP12
2LJ

Tel 01394 450205
email info@crownandcastle.co.uk
website crownandcastle.co.uk
Food breakfast, lunch, dinner
Price ££££
Closed never
Proprietor Ruth Watson

The Crown and Castle
Restaurant-with-rooms

There's been a hostelry here for eight centuries, but today's inn is a quirky, late-19thC building that has an immediately welcoming feel. The Trinity restaurant makes a beguiling place for an informal lunch or smarter dinner (an excellent breakfast, too). When Fiona Duncan visited she felt that there were some jarring notes, such as funky wall and ceiling lights. Her bedroom (in the outbuilding) was smart, with a pretty headboard, but lacked personality. Stock furniture, plain grey walls, and a 'no smoking' notice made it less of a welcoming sanctuary than rooms she has stayed in for the same price. Since then they've refurbished a number of rooms as well as the restaurant. We'd be interested to hear reports, as it's a useful address in an interesting area.

Southwold, Suffolk

High Street, Southwold, Suffolk
IP18 6DP

Tel 01502 722275
e-mail crown.hotel@adnams.co.uk
website
www.adnams.co.uk/hotels/the-crown
Food breakfast, lunch, dinner
Price £££-££££
Closed never
Proprietors Adnams

The Crown Hotel
Town hotel

The recently upgraded Crown is quite a characterful place, but with flaws. From the outside it looks like a substantial hotel, but inside it's more of a pub with rooms. It's on Southwold's High Street, as is its sister hotel, The Swan – see page 280, also owned and managed by Adnams, the Southwold Brewery.

On our latest visit, we noticed worn carpets on the narrow staircases and fire extinguishers rather prominent in the corridors. Our bedroom and bathroom were chilly and cramped for the price. But don't be put off. The bedrooms are well thought out and have some charming touches.

Downstairs is the vibrant bar-dining area, loved by locals, with great food, and the charming, tiny Back Bar.

Southwold, Suffolk

The Swan Hotel
Town hotel

Market Place, Southwold, Suffolk
IP18 6EG

Tel 01502 722186
e-mail swan.hotel@adnams.co.uk
website
www.adnams.co.uk/hotels/the-swan
Food breakfast, lunch, dinner
Price ££-££££
Closed never
Proprietors Adnams

Since our last edition The Swan, a Southwold institution like its sister hotel The Crown (see page 279), has had a bold and judicious refurbishment. Bedrooms have taken on a contemporary coastal look, with bright-coloured furnishings, bespoke modern lighting and furniture. They're also spacious, with sumptuous sitting areas, striking 'Tall Boy' beds and decent bathrooms.

The hotel is largish, and quite conventional for this guide, but the staff and on-hand butlers are helpful, giving individual attention, including a gin and tonic on arrival. There are also two restaurants, with short menus of interesting dishes. The newly refurbished Still Room has a special ambience.

Woodbridge, Suffolk

The Crown
Town hotel

Thoroughfare, Woodbridge, Suffolk
IP12 1AD
Tel (01394) 384242
Fax (01394) 387192
email
info@thecrownatwoodbridge.co.uk
website www.thecrownatwood-
bridge.co.uk **Food** breakfast, lunch,
dinner **Price** ££-£££ **Closed** never
Proprietor T A Hotel Collection
Ltd **Manager** Laura Miles

The Crown may have stood for more than 400 years on the Thoroughfare crossroads, but its latest reincarnation combines stylish interiors and modern comforts with the centuries of architecture and period charm. It's open for breakfast, lunch and dinner seven days a week, but reservations are recommended as the restaurant – award-winning and highly recommended – can get busy. It boasts ten gorgeous bedrooms – all created by an award-winning interior designer, with an emphasis on style and comfort.

Area introduction

The far north of England divides neatly into two areas: the north-west and the north-east. The north-west includes Cumbria, some of North Yorkshire, Lancashire and Merseyside. The north-east is a large band of territory stretching from the Humber Estuary up to the Scottish border, taking in most of the rest of North Yorkshire, the Yorkshire Dales and the large, wild county of Northumberland, together with County Durham and some heavily industrialized counties such as Teeside. Cumbria and the Yorkshire Dales have the richest crop of charming small hotels for the obvious reasons: their wonderful mountain and moorland scenery, terrific walking and many numinous ancient monuments and historic houses. For visitor numbers, Cumbria is up there with Devon and Cornwall, and getting there by train from London is much quicker.

Below are some useful back-up places to try if our main selections are fully booked:

Blakey Hall Farm
Bed-and-breakfast, Colne
Tel 01282 863121
www.blakeyhallfarm.co.uk
Interesting, luxury B&B on Leeds-Liverpool Canal.

Kelleth Old Hall
Country guesthouse, Kelleth
Tel 015396 23344
www.kelletholdhall.co.uk
Delightyful, idiosyncratic, one-room country retreat.

Seatoller House
Country guesthouse, Seatoller
Tel 017687 77218
www.seatollerhouse.co.uk
Sociable guest-house.

Goldsborough Hall
Country house hotel, Goldsborough
Tel 01423 867321
www.goldsboroughhall.com
Historic, luxurious hotel.

Hotel du Vin
Townhouse hotel, Harrogate
Tel 01243608121
www.hotelduvin.com
Richly furnished chain hotel overlooking The Stray.

42 The Calls
Town hotel, Leeds
Tel 0113 244 0099
www.42thecalls.co.uk
Converted riverside corn mill.

Haley's Hotel
Town house hotel, Leeds
Tel 0113 2784446
www.haleys.co.uk
Useful address for Leeds, with friendly, local staff.

The Wensleydale Heifer **Village hotel, West Witton** Tel 01969 622322
www.wesleydaleheifer.co.uk
Characterful, themed bedrooms in Yorkshire Dales.

Mount Pleasant Farm
Bed-and-breakfast, Whashton Tel 01748 822784
www.mountpleasantfarmhouse.co.uk Top-end B&B in 1850s farmhouse.

Askham, Cumbria

Askham, near Penrith, Cumbria
CA10 2PF

Tel 01931 712350
e-mail enquiries@askhamhall.co.uk
website www.askhamhall.co.uk

Nearby Askham village, River
Lowther, Penrith, Ullswater 20 mins
by car, walks from the door and fishing **Location** in own grounds, 10-
minute drive from Penrith and the
M6; ample car-parking
Food breakfast, lunch (café only),
dinner
Price £££–££££
Rooms 16; all with own bath or
shower **Facilities** restaurant, private
gardens, heated outdoor swimming
pool, spa, hot tub, cafe, converted
barn, medieval hall and garden pavilion for weddings **Credit cards** all
major **Children** welcome, catering
arrangements to be discussed
Disabled no special facilities
Pets dogs accepted by prior
arrangement **Closed** Jan and first 2
weeks of Feb **Proprietors** Charles
Lowther

Askham Hall
Country house hotel

One of the most exciting developments in Lake District accommodation for a long time. The young owner,
Charles Lowther (half brother of the present Earl of Lonsdale) and his family have
created a 'hometel' – a home from home
hotel out of Askham Hall, on the edge of
the Lake District. After driving through
Lowther Park and reaching the pretty village of Askham, the hall's gates are a little
way down the hill from the houses.

Charlie has given serious thought to
making this place super-relaxed, more like
staying in a private house than a hotel. Its
one-off location in a family home gives it
an added twist of originality.

Their eclectic, occasionally quirky country
house style decoration and furniture is all different. A professional kitchen produces sophisticated food from a small menu with an
impressive wine list, served in their recently
upgraded Conservatory dining room.

The Lowthers' other place to stay nearby is
The George and Dragon near Penrith (page 290).

Austwick, North Yorkshire

Austwick, Settle, North Yorkshire
Dales LA2 8BY

Tel 01524 251224
Fax 01524 251796
e-mail info@thetraddock.co.uk
website www.thetraddock.co.uk

Nearby the Yorkshire Dales
National Park, Settle Carlisle
Railway and 3 Peaks of
Ingleborough, Whernside and Pen-
Y-Ghent **Location** 1 mile off the
A65 between Skipton and Kendal;
with ample car-parking **Food** break-
fast, lunch, dinner, bar snacks, after-
noon & cream tea
Price ££-£££ **Rooms** 12; 3 shower
only, 9 bath and shower; 12 double
and suites; all with LCD TV, phone,
hairdryer, tea/coffee facilities
Facilities 2 dining rooms, 3 sitting
rooms, 1 bar; garden and patio
Credit cards MC, V **Children** welcome **Disabled** limited access **Pets**
£5 per dog **Closed** never **Proprietor**
Jane, Bruce, Paul and Jenny
Reynolds

The Traddock
Country hotel

'Traddock'? It means a trading pad-
dock, and this hotel stands in a field
that was forever used for just this purpose. It's a grey stone house on the edge
of a mostly pretty village, part of the
scenery and ideally located for the big
walks in the south-western Yorkshire
Dales. The feeling of being in its skin continues inside. Renovated by the
Reynoldses as a new venture in the last
ten years, original features and country
antiques sit comfortably alongside new
furniture and fabrics in confident 'country
house' taste. The three sitting rooms, one
spacious and well proportioned, are quirkily linked by the bar, the standing area in
front of it doubling as a passage.

Our reporter's room was again in good
country house taste – pine chest, pine
wardrobe, rusty-red wall paper nicely off-
setting cream-yellow paintwork. There
were two easy chairs, but no desk and
chair for writing. The shower, loo and wash
basin were in a somewhat cramped cube
built into the corner of the room; the
shower stream was feeble; but still, the
price at £140 at weekends was normal.
Since our last edition, every bedroom and
bathroom has been upgraded.

Worthy company for nearby Hipping
Hall (page 295), with friendly owner-managed atmosphere, and just-right food.

Bassenthwaite Lake, Cumbria

Bassenthwaite Lake, near
Cockermouth, Cumbria CA13 9YE

Tel (017687) 76234
Fax (017687) 76002
e-mail info@the-pheasant.co.uk
website www.the-pheasant.co.uk

Nearby Bassenthwaite Lake;
Keswick.
Location 5 miles (8 km) E of
Cockermouth, just off A66; with
ample car parking
Food breakfast, lunch, dinner, bar
snacks **Price** £££
Rooms 15; 11 double and twin, 3
suites and 1 single; all with bath and
shower; all rooms have flat-screen
TV, hairdryer, phone **Facilities** sitting rooms, dining room, bar; garden
Credit cards MC, V **Children**
accepted over 8, but not in the bar or
dining room at night
Disabled access possible to public
rooms, Garden Lodge and 3 en suite
rooms **Pets** accepted in public rooms
and Garden Lodge rooms **Closed**
Christmas Eve and Day **Manager**
Matthew Wylie

The Pheasant
Country inn

'Still a very special place,' says our most
recent inspector. Nestled away behind
trees just off the A66, the Pheasant was
originally an old coaching inn, and there
are many reminders of this within, particularly in the little old oak bar, which is full of
dark nooks and crannies – little changed
from its earliest days. The building is a long,
low barn-like structure that has been
exceptionally well maintained. There is a
small but well-kept garden to the rear and
grounds that extend to 60 acres.

The two sitting areas are one of the
main attractions of the place. The one to
the front is low-ceilinged, with small windows and plenty of prints on the walls. The
second has a serving hatch to the bar;
both have open log fires.

The grand refurbishment scheme was
undertaken in early 2000, and smaller, more
recent ones have seen the conversion of 20
old bedrooms into 15 larger, lighter, more
modern rooms. They are individually decorated, partnered by *en suite* bathrooms, and
some have spectacular views of the fells.
The original dining room has been re-
organized to make the best of its slightly
uncomfortable shape; there's also a new
restuarant (The Fell) at the back of the
hotel. The menu changes daily, and service is
outstandingly friendly.

Borrowdale, Cumbria

Borrowdale, Keswick, Cumbria
CA12 5UY

Tel (017687) 77247
Fax (017687) 77363
e-mail
reservations@leatheshead.co.uk
website www.leatheshead.co.uk

Nearby Derwent Water;
Buttermere; Castlerigg Stone Circle.
Location 3.5 miles (5.5 km) S of
Keswick, off B5289 to Borrowdale,
in 3 acres of grounds; car-parking
Food breakfast, afternoon tea, lunch,
dinner
Price ££ **Rooms** 11 double and
twin, all with shower, some with
bath; all rooms have phone, TV,
hairdryer, wi-fi
Facilities 2 sitting rooms, dining
room, bar; garden
Credit cards MC, V **Children** not
accepted **Disabled** 1 ground-floor
room **Pets** not accepted
Closed 3 weeks in Jan
Managers Laura Dadulak

The Leathes Head
Country hotel

In the beautiful Borrowdale valley near
Derwent Water, perched in its own
wooded grounds, this Lakeland stone
Edwardian house was originally built for a
Liverpool ship-owner. In recent years it's
undergone a refurbishment in line with the
hotel's general ethos: to use Cumbrian
products, skills and natural materials. The
bar has been dressed with Kirkstone
Brathay slate, Cumbrian oak, and a basket
light weaved with willow harvested near
Cockermouth. The hotel interiors have
been crafted stylishly by local artisans.
However, many of its period features, the
plasterwork and wood-panelled ceiling in
the hall, are still there. They have also
recovered original tile flooring in the main
reception area, found in stellar condition.

It is informal enough to attract the
walkers and climbers who return year
after year for the glorious fells ringing the
valley. All the bedrooms are comfortable
and individually furnished. Bathrooms are
modern and light. The three-acre grounds
include lawns big enough and level enough
to play boules or croquet – and flat areas
are few and far between in this region. The
real challenges are the fells beyond the
gate, and the hotel can help here too, with
its extensive collection of walking guides.
There are also lake cruises, water sports
and mountain biking in the area.

Bowness-on-Windermere, Cumbria

Bowness-on-Windermere, Cumbria
LA23 3JP

Tel (015394) 43286
Fax (015394) 47455
e-mail kennedy@lindethfell.co.uk
website www.lindethfell.co.uk

Nearby Windermere Steamboat
Museum; Lake Windermere (cur-
rently closed).
Location 1 mile (1.5km) S of
Bowness on A5074; with ample car-
parking
Food breakfast
Price ££
Rooms 14; 12 double and twin, 2
single, 9 with bath, 5 with shower; all
rooms have phone, TV, hairdryer
Facilities 2 sitting rooms, dining
room, bar; garden, lake, croquet,
bowling green
Credit cards MC, V
Children accepted
Disabled access possible to ground-
floor bedroom
Pets not accepted
Closed 3 weeks in Jan
Proprietors Kennedy family

Lindeth Fell
Country house bed-and-breakfast

To stay at Lindeth Fell is like visiting a well-heeled old friend who enjoys mak-
ing his visitors as comfortable as possible, and is justifiably proud of the view from his house. The Kennedys' establishment hits this mark (they are always there to see that it does), and, not unsurprisingly, their approach and warm courteous welcome have been duly rewarded with a faithful following.

Approached through trees, and set in large mature gardens glowing with azaleas and rhododendrons in spring, Lindeth Fell's wood-panelled hall leads to a pair of comfortable and attractive sitting rooms and a restaurant where large windows let in the tremendous view. Weather permitting, drinks and tea can be taken on the terrace, and the same warm weather might even allow for a game of croquet. Upstairs, the rooms vary in size and out-
look, and both qualities are reflected in their price. All the rooms are comfortably furnished and pleasingly decorated.

Crook Road, Bowness-on-
Windermere, Cumbria LA23 3JA

Tel (015394) 88600
Fax (015394) 88601
e-mail
reception@linthwaitehouse.com
website www.linthwaitehouse.com

Nearby Windermere Steamboat
Museum; Lake Windermere; Beatrix
Potter's Hilltop
Location 1 mile (1.5km) S of
Bowness off the A5074; with ample
car parking
Food breakfast, lunch, dinner
Price ££-£££
Rooms 36 double and twin with
bath; all rooms have phone, TV,
hairdryer; wi-fi
Facilities sitting rooms, conservato-
ry, dining rooms, bar; terrace, gar-
den, veranda
Credit cards AE, MC, V
Children accepted
Disabled one specially adapted
room **Pets** accepted **Closed** Jun to
Dec 2017 **Proprietor** Leeu
Collection

Linthwaite House
Country house hotel

Linthwaite House is undergoing extensive refurbishment, and is due to reopen
in March 2018, when this guide goes to
press – so we cannot vouch for its new
character. It's the latest addition to the Leeu
Collection, who are promising a slicker and
upgraded version, although we hope it will
retain its uniqueness: when Mike Bevans
was at the helm, service at this Edwardian
country house managed to be crisp and
amiable at the same time.

What we do know is that its new restaurant, Stella, will have a menu influenced by
Indian celebrity chef Ritu Dalmia, and her
passion for Italian cuisine – so expect excellence, international flavours, and a focus on
local Cumbrian ingredients.

Of the bedrooms, the best look directly towards Windermere, some are in a
modern annexe, and there is quite a variation in size. They all have style though, with
thoughtful use of fabrics and furnishings
and bathrooms that are attractive rather
than utilitarian. Beyond the terraces outside are 14 acres of lawn, shrubs, woods
and a small lake.

Reports welcome.

Brampton, Cumbria

Brampton, Cumbria CA8 2NG

Tel (016977) 46234
e-mail farlam@farlamhall.co.uk
website www.farlamhall.co.uk

Nearby Hadrian's Wall; Lanercost Priory; North Pennines (Area of Outstanding Natural Beauty)
Location 3 miles (5 km) SE of Brampton on A689, NE of (not in) Farlam village; with ample car parking
Food breakfast, dinner; afternoon tea (pre-booking essential)
Price ££££
Rooms 12 double with bath; all rooms have phone, TV, hairdryer
Facilities 2 sitting rooms, dining room, wi-fi; garden, croquet
Credit cards MC, V
Children accepted over 5
Disabled 2 ground-floor bedrooms
Pets welcome
Closed Christmas week
Proprietors Quinion family

Farlam Hall
Country house hotel

'Charming family, quiet surroundings, excellent food,' are the phrases that encapsulate Farlam Hall. Since 1975 the Quinion family has assiduously improved their solid but elegant Border country house. It has its roots in Elizabethan times, but what you see today is essentially a large, Victorian family home, extended for a big family and frequent entertaining. No coincidence that it makes such a good hotel.

The dining room and public rooms are discreet and the atmosphere is one of traditional English service and comfort. The bedrooms vary widely, with some decidedly large and swish. Nevertheless, all are luxurious and charmingly done out, and some have beautiful views of the grounds flocked with sheep.

The chef, being one of the family, takes pride in his food and it shows. The menu changes daily (so guests staying for longer than one night don't get bored) and there is an impressive wine list, not to mention the extensive English cheese board or a choice of deliciously unhealthy puddings.

Farlam Hall is well placed to explore Hadrian's Wall, Northumberland Coast as well as Hadrian's Wall.

Cartmel Fell, Cumbria

Cartmel Fell, Grange-over-Sands
LA11 6NW

Tel (015395) 68486
e-mail info@masonsarmsstrawber-
rybank.co.uk
website www.masonsarmsstrawber-
rybank.co.uk

Nearby Holker Hall, Hawkshead
Brewery, Blackwell Arts & Crafts
House
Location overlooking the Winster
Valley; access from A5074
Food breakfast, lunch, dinner
Price £-££
Rooms 2 cottages with kitchen and
sitting rooms, sleeping 4/6; 5 2-level
suites, with sitting areas; all have
welcome basket, hairdryer, towels,
Bath House toiletries, iron & board
Facilities bar, garden, restaurant
Credit cards MC, V
Children welcome
Disabled pub accessible but no
adapted rooms
Pets welcome (by pre-arrangement)
Closed never
Proprietor John Taylor

The Masons Arms
Country inn

Despite its peaceful setting on the edge
of two country lanes overlooking
Windermere, the Masons Arms is far from
quiet. Now something of a local institution, visitors and locals flock at all times of
year to enjoy its lively atmosphere. The
downstairs pub area is fairly cramped, in
classic British style. It's traditional and rustic with a roaring fire, and, more impor-
tantly, food that can't be faulted. The
extensive menu of their award-winning
kitchen specializes in hearty pub grub,
enhanced by strong flavour and local ingredients: for example, Lamb Cartmel – slow
roasted shoulder of lamb cooked on the
bone, served with garden peas, rosemary
and garlic mash and shallots. You can eat in
the lovely, heated outdoor seating area,
with views across Windermere (which
you'll find busy even in colder months).

The quality and spaciousness of the
bedrooms mark it out as more than a pub
with rooms. The Strawberry Bank Suite is
elegantly designed with a four-poster bed,
exposed ceiling beams and a freestanding
roll-top bath set in a marble niche. Several
of the rooms have their own private terraces. You can order breakfast hampers in
advance. There's a separate cottage with
its own kitchen and sitting area, and two
bedrooms on two levels with their own
seating areas.

Clifton, Cumbria

Clifton, Near Penrith, Cumbria
CA10 2ER

Tel 01768 865 381
e-mail enquries@georgeanddrag-
onclifton.co.uk
website www.georgeanddrag-
onclifton.co.uk

Nearby Ullswater; Lowther Castle
Location come off the M6 at junc-
tion 39 towards Shap, continue for
10 minutes and you will come to
Clifton; has its own car park
Food breakfast, lunch, dinner
Price ££-£££
Rooms 11, all have bath/shower, 6
with shower, 5 with bath, all have
TV, hairdyer
Facilities restaurant, bar, garden,
courtyard
Credit cards all major
Children welcome
Disabled public areas accessible but
not rooms
Pets welcome in rooms and bar but
not restaurant, small charge for dogs
Closed Christmas
Proprietor Charles Lowther

George and Dragon
Country inn

In 2008, The George and Dragon – then a rather shabby village tavern – was in need of a face-lift. It was taken over by Charles Lowther and his mother, Caroline, Countess of Lonsdale, who carried out a sensitive and intelligent restoration.

Rather than transforming the whole of the ground floor into a restaurant, they kept the bar as its focal point and allowed for a virtually uninterrupted view all the way to the far side of the slate-floored, duck-egg blue panelled restaurant. Come here for lunch, dinner or to while away the time amongst regulars with a pint of ale.

Bedrooms are homely, some a little awk-wardly shaped, but redeemed by luxury bath products and comfortable beds. It's a great, affordable base from which to explore the Lake District, or stopover when travelling between Northern and Southern England.

As for the food: it's tasty, uncomplicated and locally sourced. Venison and beef fea-tures large and most of the produce comes directly from the Lowther Estate – Charles breeds Beef Shorthorn cattle.

A true celebration of country life. Guests are taken hunting by the Estate's head stalk-er and there are one or two good fishing spots nearby. The George and Dragon is the little sister of Askham Hall, page 282, where Charles Lowther spent his childhood.

Crosthwaite, Cumbria

Crosthwaite, Lyth Valley
LA8 8HR

Tel (015395) 68237
Fax (015395) 68875
e-mail info@the-punchbowl.co.uk
website www.the-punchbowl.co.uk

Nearby Lake District National Park,
Grizedale Forst Park, Windermere,
Kendal
Location just N of the A5074
between Bowness and Levens
Food breakfast, luch, tea, dinner
Price ££
Rooms 9 doubles; all with bath and
shower
Facilities restaurant, bar, sitting
rooms
Credit cards AE, MC, V
Children welcome
Disabled not suitable
Pets not accepted
Closed never
Proprietors Richard Rose and
Amanda Robinson

Punchbowl Inn
Country inn

The Punchbowl has had new owners since 2005. They have done it up in contemporary style, using mushroomy off-white shades from heritage paint makers. Tiny high-intensity downlighters make the free-standing roll-top bath and expensive taps glitter. Little bottles of as-it-were home-made shampoo and body lotion have hand-written labels. The power shower is excellent. The bath towels are enormous. The tongued and grooved wainscoting is painted Cooking Apple Green. More original is the old-style Roberts radio beside the bed tuned to Classic FM and playing when you first come in: perhaps a bit self-conscious, but not disagreeable.

The kitchen team, headed by Arthur Bridgeman-Quin, draws people from far and wide to eat quite luxurious and very imaginative dishes, made with great flair. William Nicholson's woodcuts of Twelve Sports, a polished refectory table with a bowl of fashionable green foliage and a dish of used corks give the room the air of a smart London restaurant, though the waitresses at the Punch Bowl are much nicer than their big city counterparts. The same dishes are obtainable in the bar for those who want to eat more informally. The surrounding countryside is lovely, the welcome genuine. A truly charming small hotel.

Grasmere, Cumbria

Keswick Road, Grasmere, Cumbria,
LA22 9RN

Tel (015394) 35250
e-mail info@theforestside.com
website www.theforestside.com

Nearby Dove Cottage and the
Wordsworth Museum, Sarah
Nelson's Grasmere Gingerbread
Shop, Heaton Cooper Studio
Location on at foot of Butter Crag;
at end of a private drive approx.
300m off A591 Ambleside to
Keswick Road. In 43 acres
Food breakfast, lunch, dinner
Price £££-££££
Rooms 20; 12 double, 5 of which
can accomodate extra guests; 8 twin.
All have wi-fi, TV, tea and coffee
tray, hairdryer, toiletries
Facilities bar, restaurant, sitting
room. private dining room, 43 acres
of grounds **Credit cards** all major
Children over 12s welcome in
restaurant **Disabled** 1 adapted
rooom, with roll-in wet room **Pets** 6
dog-friendly rooms, 2 dogs max (£20
per day) **Closed** 7-12th Jan
General Manager Franck Deletang

Forest Side
Country hotel

Our series editor Fiona Duncan had
misgivings when she entered Forest
Side's slick interior, which seemed a little
out of step with the hotel's handsome
slate-built exterior and Lakeland setting.
These fears were quickly allayed by a
warm Northern welcome, and the hotel
soon stole her heart. Owner Andrew
Wildsmith has lavished £4 million as well
as his attention to detail, which made Hipping
Hall – his other hotel – such a success.

The interiors are beautifully done:
expect genuine Lincrusta walls, shimmery
velvet sofas and bird of paradise wallpapers. At first they may seem a little too
carefully composed and 'designer', but this
belies what is in fact a well-thought out
symbiosis between the hotel with its natural setting and local traditions: wool from
sheep in the surrounding fields is used for
carpets and beds, waiters are dressed in
Pendle Tweed hacking jackets, and local
pottery is used for dining.

The hotel's *raison d'être* is its food: a
stand out culinary experience commandeered by the young chef Kevin Tickle,
whose passion for foraging and processes
like pickling, distilling and curing, makes for
a menu that is both satisfyingly earthy yet
light and modern. You will be pleasantly
surprised by some unusual ingredients,
including scurvy grass and tree sap.

Hawkshead, Cumbria

Near Sawrey, Hawkshead,
Ambleside, Cumbria LA22 0JZ

Tel (015394) 36393
Fax (015394) 36393
e-mail mail@eeswyke.co.uk
website www.eeswyke.co.uk

Nearby Hill Top; Lake
Windermere; Grasmere.
Location in hamlet on B5285, 2
miles (3 km) SE of Hawkshead; with
car parking
Food breakfast, dinner
Price ££
Rooms 8 double and twin, 2 with
bath, 6 with shower; all rooms have
TV, hairdryer, hospitality tray
Facilities 2 sitting rooms, dining
room; garden
Credit cards MC, V **Children**
accepted over 12
Disabled not suitable
Pets not accepted
Closed never
Proprietors Richard

Ees Wyke
Country house

Esthwaite Water, to the east of
Windermere, has been kept safely in
private hands, so has escaped the development that has ravaged some of the other
Lakes. Ees Wyke, a gem of a white-painted
Georgian mansion, is perched above park-
like meadows that roll gently down to the
reed banks on the shore, punctuated here
and there by sheep and mature trees. As
well as unmarred views, Richard has happily
discovered the secret of making people
feel instantly at home.

This is a well-kept house, with everything just so, even down to a plentiful supply of games and books for those
inclement days. In the dining room are
beautiful large windows to show off the
view (these are new since Beatrix Potter
stayed here for her holidays), with crisp
white tablecloths. The dinners (Richard's
department, with an AA rosette) run to
three generous and unhurried courses and
the price/quality ratio of the wine list is
definitely tipped in your favour. The bedrooms are attractive and generously proportioned, most with small but well-
equipped bathrooms, and comfortable
enough to allow you to build up the
strength you need to tackle the truly hero-
ic, Lakeland breakfast.

Kirkby Stephen, Cumbria

Leacett Lane, Kirkby Stephen,
Cumbria, CA17 4DE

Tel 01768 341937
e-mail enquiries@stayinacastle.com
website www.stayinacastle.com

Nearby North Pennines, Lake
District, Yorkshire Dales, Eden
Valley
Location rural setting, 1 mile outside the nearest village down tree-
lined drive; accessible from A66
which links the M6 with the A1
Food breakfast, afternoon tea, dinner: house-party style weekends,
grazing style week days.
Price £££-££££
Rooms 15; 2 interconnecting, 2
suites; 8 in main house, the rest
attached.**Facilities** 15 acres grounds,
playground, tennis court, cinema,
bar, sitting room, library, dining
room, cookery school, hall
Credit cards V, A, M
Children welcome
Disabled suitable **Pets** by prior
arrangement **Closed** never
Proprietor Simon and Wendy
Bennett

Augill Castle
Castle hotel

A place with a sense of fun. You might find
a piano in your bathroom, a church
pew next to the loo, maybe even an
Indonesian blowpipe above your bed. The
hotel's setting, in a perfectly formed neo-
Gothic folly castle (built in the 1840s), amid
20 acres of grounds within the achingly
beautiful Eden Valley, compounds its charm.

It was bought on an impulse by former
restaurateurs Simon and Wendy Bennett,
who transformed the ailing castle into a
unique place to stay. The result, says our
series editor Fiona Duncan, is a 'home-
from-home' that is wonderfully family
friendly and relaxed. There are minimal
rules, and dinner is served communally on a
long oak table at the heart of the castle
(akin to having "a dinner party with friends
you haven't met yet" say its owners). You
can also dine privately in the Conservatory,
Drawing Room or garden terrace.

The bedroom decoration enhances the
sense of staying with a grand but eccentric,
and very hospitable, friend. Bold and well-
chosen antiques playfully rub shoulders
with contemporary pieces, and features
such as turrets for a wardrobe, stained glass
windows and magnificent views add up to a
romantic experience.

Your stay may be relaxed, but the housekeeping is far from it: enjoy a feeling of
order and of things running on the rails.

Kirkby Lonsdale, Cumbria

Cowan Bridge, Kirkby Lonsdale,
Cumbria LA6 2JJ

Tel (015242) 71187
e-mail info@hippinghall.com
website www.hippinghall.com

Nearby Yorkshire Dales; Lake
District; Settle to Carlisle railway.
Location on A65, 2.5 miles (4 km)
SE of Kirkby Lonsdale; in 3-acre
walled gardens with ample car park-
ing
Food breakfast, lunch (weekends
only), dinner
Price £££–££££
Rooms 15 double/twin; all rooms
have phone, TV, hairdryer, free wi-fi
Facilities sitting room, dining room,
private dining room, guest bar,
orangery, extensive gardens, croquet,
boules
Credit cards AE, MC, V
Children welcome; over 12 in
restaurant **Disabled** access possible
Pets accepted in the Stable rooms
Closed 2 weeks in Jan
Proprietor Andrew Wildsmith

Hipping Hall
Restaurant-with-rooms

This place, long in the guide but always
refreshing itself, underwent a major
refurbishment in 2017. This saw a redecoration of the main bedrooms, bar, restaurant and reception: plasterered in specially
created paint pigments, and bedecked with
tweed fabrics by Benjamin Thornber &
Sons, Miles-Moore ceramics, and local land-
scapes in pastel by the distinguished artist
Sandra Orme.

They also have a new head chef,
Lancashire born Oli Martin, who we hear is
maintaining the superlative standards of his
predecessor. His five and eight course tasting menus, made from local ingredients,
include dishes such as Fylde Coast sea vegetables with Lindisfarne oysters, and salt-
aged breast of Goosnargh duck with elder-
berries.

Parts of the Hall date back to the 15th
century when a hamlet grew up around
the 'hipping' or stepping stones across the
beck. After a strenuous day on the fells,
you can relax in the bar with a gin and
tonic.

There are seven bedrooms in the main
house and three 'cottage' rooms across
the courtyard, with a five further rooms in
the Stables. Bathrooms are tiled in natural
stone and have modern fittings. They've
got a lovely calm and relaxed atmosphere,
as has the rest of the hotel.

Wyresdale Road, Lancaster, LA1 3JJ

Tel (015224) 684600
e-mail stay@theashtonlancaster.com
website
www.theashtonlancaster.com

Nearby Lancaster Castle (1 km),
Morecambe Bay (5 km).
Location 1 km east of the city centre
next to Williamson Park
Food High Tea at weekends,
meat/fish/cheese platters in evenings
(by pre-order)
Price ££-£££
Rooms 6; all super king, some can
be twin; all have TV, freeview, tea &
coffee facilities, mini fridge, hairdry-
er, DVD player
Facilities sitting room
Credit cards AE, MC, V
Children not accepted
Disabled not suitable
Pets 2 dog-friendly rooms
Closed 2 weeks in Jan
Proprietor James Gray

The Ashton
Town bed-and-breakfast

Just off the main road, and slightly overlooked by a new housing development,
the location of this Lancaster B&B might
not be ideal, but the hospitality at The
Ashton is a lesson in perfection. As guests
arrive at the handsome Georgian manor
house, they are welcomed by James with
homemade cake, and the choice of a glass
of wine or hot drink, while bags are spirit-
ed up to the bedrooms. As your stay draws
on there isn't a need James won't fulfil.
There's no restaurant, but he readily supplies recommendations and books restaurants nearby, or (if pre-arranged) he'll bring
you a meat, fish or cheese platter with chutney and homemade bread. The cooked
breakfast is delicious and varied.

The house's old features are decorated
with a contemporary twist, giving it an air
of London chic. Stripped floorboards,
leather Chesterfield sofas and mismatched
furniture combine to create a hip but comfortable feel, while quirky and entertaining
touches can be found in every corner, from
bowler hats to old telephones. The five bedrooms, overlooking the beautiful herb garden, are spacious and very comfortable.

Lancaster may have few sites worth visiting, but we think The Ashton is worth a two
night stay.

Langho, Lancashire

Northcote Road, Langho,
Blackburn, Lancashire BB6 8BE

Tel (01254) 240555
Fax (01254) 246 568
e-mail reception@northcote.com
website www.northcote.com

Nearby Ribchester Roman remains
and museum; Forest of Bowland.
Location in own grounds, 9 miles
(15 km) from M6 junction 32, secure
car-parking
Food breakfast, lunch, dinner
Price £££-££££
Rooms 26, all double; 25 with bath,
1 with shower only; all have phone,
TV, Sky TV sports channels, sound
system with iPod dock, free wi-fi,
boards games, hairdryer, ceiling fans.
Credit cards AE, DC MC, V
Children accepted
Disabled two specially adapted
rooms
Pets guide dogs only
Closed never
Proprietor/Manager Nigel
Haworth and Craig Bancroft

Northcote
Country house hotel

A gourmet oasis ideally located in the
north-west (London 220 miles,
Perthshire 220 miles). Half close your eyes
and this solid 1880s Victorian mansion
could be a restaurant-with-rooms, though
in fact it offers all the comforts of a top
country hotel.

But the food is the thing here, Nigel
Haworth having won many local and
national awards, most recently BBC's
Great British Menu accolade. His cooking
is firmly rooted in local ingredients, but its
edge is the fresh, clean flavours and imaginative rather than trendy presentation. A
cheese-flavoured ice cream partnering the
summer pudding arrived in a cone on a
wooden rack. Nigel's famous Lancashire
hot-pot came in its own small oven-proof
dish. The service is charming, the atmosphere friendly and food- and wine-orient-
ed, much influenced by Nigel's long standing collaborator, Craig Bancroft, a great
enthusiast.

Bonhomie aside, these two are shrewd
marketeers and managers of staff who
have a formidable local reputation.
Recently re-done bedrooms are a designer's nirvana. The location is not ideal,
though the Forest of Bowland is minutes
by car.

Fair prices, and for kids, mini-gourmet
portions. Outstanding breakfast.

Near Sawrey, Ambleside,
Cumbria, LA22 0LF

Tel (015394) 36334
e-mail
enquiries@towerbankarms.com
website www.towerbankarms.com

Nearby Hilltop (NT), between
Esthwaite Water and Windermere.
Location beside B5285 near Sawrey;
some car parking
Food breakfast (residents only),
lunch, dinner
Price ££
Rooms 4; 2 doubles, 1 twin, 1 supe-
rior double, all with shower; all
rooms have TV, tea and coffee mak-
ing facilities
Facilities bar, restaurant
Credit cards AE, MC, V
Children welcome on premises until
9pm
Disabled not suitable
Pets accepted in bar and overnight
in rooms
Closed 1 mid-week in Dec and Jan
Proprietor Anthony Hutton

Tower Bank Arms
Country inn

Beatrix Potter pilgrims need look no
further. This simple inn, a short walk
from Hilltop (NT), where many of Miss
Potter's books were written, is surely
where Mr MacGregor allowed himself an
occasional dram and it is to be seen – dis-
tantly – in The Tale of Jemima Puddleduck.

It looks more like a cottage than a pub,
only the ticking clock over the porch sug-
gesting otherwise. The inn caters for many
people staying in B&Bs in the village and
the owner wants the exterior to look
unpretentious, feeling that walkers with
muddy boots or those on budgets might
otherwise be put-off. For £9.75 at
lunchtime they can enjoy dishes such as
Cumbrian Beef & Ale Stew ('with herby
dumplings and mashed potato'), in surroundings grander than one would expect
at that price, with Wedgwood china and
linen napkins. It is not a posh place or a
large one – three doubles and one twin
room – but it is clean and tidy and the flag-
stoned bar offers the comfort of a woodfired range and a number of good beers.
Don't come here expecting tea on the
lawn or room service. But if your imagination is fired by a view of the street where
Mrs Tabitha Twitchet or the Sandy-
Whiskered Gentleman strolled, this is for
you.

Ullswater, Cumbria

Ullswater, Cumbria, CA11 0PH.

Tel (01768) 482874
e-mail stay@glenriddinghouse.com
website www.glenriddinghouse.com

Nearby at centre of Lake District National Park, Helvellyn (3 m)
Location on shores of Ullswater. Free parking.
Food breakfast, packed lunch (pre-arranged), dinner (pre-booked)
Price ££££
Rooms 4; 1 suite-ensuite, 3 double-superior-ensuite; all Regency style with bathrobes, shower/wetroom or bathroom, toiletries, seating area, TV, wi-fi, refreshment tray, views
Facilities breakfast room, dining room, landscaped gardens, ample parking
Credit cards AE, MC, V
Children not allowed
Disabled where possible they've accomodated wheelchair access, enquire before
Pets not allowed
Closed enquire before
Proprietor Lynne and Stephen

Glenridding House
Boutique bed-and-breakfast

Darwin declared this place to be 'magnificently beautiful' when he holidayed here in 1881 – a sentiment that rings true today. The Grade II-listed villa, built in 1815, is bursting with classic Regency elegance. The current owners spent seven years carefully restoring it to former glory, starting with its striking wrap-around latticed balcony, complete with outdoor furniture and direct access to all the bedrooms. Their real *raison d'être*, however, is the location on the shores of Ullswater, with a path down to the lake for easy-access swimming. It's surrounded by the dramatic fells and crags of the Lake District, with opportunities for great walks.

The bedrooms continue the Regency theme, with oak floors, window shutters and brass Victorian bedsteads (many have four-posters). Egyptian cotton bedding and bathrobes are matched with exquisite showers, wetrooms or bathrooms.

Breakfast, served in the lovely Darwin Lakeview Room, includes a full English as well as choices such as Manx kipper fillets, and a simple but excellent dinner can be pre-arranged. This might include wild baked salmon with new potatoes, followed by sticky toffee pudding. Hospitality even extends to afternoon tea, with an array of scones and jams set up before the French windows in the sitting room, with views across the lake.

Ullswater, Penrith, Cumbria CA10 2ND

Tel (017684) 86514

Nearby Ullswater, Lake District National Park
Location just off B5320, near Pooley Bridge; located in city centre up a 500 yard beaten track, right on the shores of Ullswater.
Food breakfast, lunch, dinner and afternoon tea.
Price ££ (rate includes dinner and breakfast)
Rooms 11; 7 double, 4 twin
Facilities 2 sitting rooms, restaurant, tennis court, garden, surrounding mountains for walking.
Credit cards all major debit cards
Children welcome
Disabled access to dining room possible; not to rooms
Pets accepted in rooms for extra fee
Closed 1 Nov to Easter
Proprietor David W O Baldry

Howtown Hotel
Country hotel

Howtown Hotel is the Real Thing. It is a house that has been in the same family for well over a century. And little seems to have changed – except the bathrooms, which are modern and efficient. They are mostly not en-suite, but all are private and individual, usually just across a passage. Downstairs, Toby jugs, brass warming pans, the heads of foxes hunted in the 1930s, and oil paintings make the hall seem like a pre-war antique shop. Doors are wood-grained in the old-fashioned way (no Farrow & Ball paint here). The cosy little bar with stained glass in the windows might be the snug where the Swallows & Amazons' uncle, Captain Flint, met his friends. The Smoking Room opposite has succumbed to modern diktat. Other public rooms are grander, lighter, more like drawing-rooms. The bedrooms are equally comfortable and impressive. Presiding are the Baldrys, ably supported by a very capable management and uber-friendly Eastern Europeans. Nothing is too much trouble. The place is as clean as a museum. The scenery around is staggering. They sell wine for as little as £16 (almost unheard of), and they sound a gong before meals.

Mrs Baldry says she doesn't like publicity, and needs it still less. On the other hand, we feel that not a few readers of this guide will be just the right sort of guest for this unique place.

Wasdale Head, Cumbria

Wasdale Head, Seascale, Cumbria
CA20 1EX

Tel (019467) 26229
e-mail reception@wasdale.com
website www.wasdale.com

Nearby Hardknott Castle Roman
Fort; Ravenglass and Eskdale
Railway; Wastwater; Scafell Pike.
Location 9 miles (14.5 km) NE of
Gosforth at head of Wasdale; with
ample car parking
Food breakfast, bar and packed
lunches, dinner
Price ££
Rooms 18; 9 doubles, 3 suites, all
have telephone and TV; also 6 self-
catering apartments
Facilities sitting room, dining room,
2 bars; garden **Credit cards** MC, V
Children accepted **Disabled** 2
ground floor rooms
Pets accepted in 9 rooms, 5 self-
catered apartments and all public
areas except the restaurant
Closed never **Proprietors** Nigel
and Lesley Burton

Wasdale Head Inn
Mountain inn

The Wasdale Head is in a site unrivalled
even in the consistently spectacular
Lake District. It stands on the flat valley
bottom between three major peaks – Pillar,
Great Gable and Scafell Pike (England's
highest) – and only a little way above
Wastwater, England's deepest and perhaps
most dramatic lake.

Over the last decade and a half, the old
inn has been carefully and thoughtfully
modernized, adding facilities but retaining
the characteristics of a traditional mountain inn. The main sitting room of the hotel
is comfortable and welcoming, with plenty
of personal touches. The bedrooms are not
notably spacious but they are adequate,
with fixtures and fittings all in good condition. There are also six self-catering apartments in a converted barn, and three suites.
The dining room is heavily panelled, and
decorated with willow pattern china and a
pewter jug collection. There is also now a
children's menu. Food is considerably better
than you would expect of a mountaineering
inn, served by young, friendly staff. There are
two bars. The one for residents has some
magnificent wooden furniture, while tasty
bar food is served in the congenial surroundings of the public bar, much frequented by walkers and climbers.

Whitewell, Lancashire

The Inn at Whitewell, Forest of
Bowland, near Clitheroe, Lancashire
BB7 3AT

Tel (01200) 448222
Fax (01200) 448298
e-mail reception@innatwhitewell.com
website www.innatwhitewell.com

Nearby Browsholme Hall; Clitheroe
Castle; Blackpool.Location 6 miles
(9.5 km) NW of Clitheroe; with
ample car parking
Food breakfast, picnic lunch on
request, dinner, bar meals
Price ££
Rooms 23 double and twin, 1 suite,
all with bath and/or shower; all
rooms have phone, TV, CD; some
have minibar, hairdryer, peat fire
Facilities dining rooms, bar; garden,
fishing, cycling route, golf nearby,
wine tasting
Credit cards DC, MC, V
Children welcome
Disabled 2 ground-floor rooms
Pets welcome **Closed** never
Proprietor Charles Bowman

The Inn at Whitewell
Country inn

Past and present come together with
great effect at this welcoming inn with
a glorious situation, on a riverbank plumb
in the middle of the Forest of Bowland. In
the 14th century it was a small manor
house where the Keeper of the Forest
lived. Today, some of the original architecture survives and rooms are furnished
with antiques, but modern comfort is the
order of the day, with, for example, hi-tech
stereo systems in all the bedrooms. Most
of these are spacious and attractive, with
warm lighting and prints clustered on the
walls; many contain an extra sofa bed; a
couple have four-posters. To keep romance
alive, you can book one of the rooms with
a fireplace and snuggle up to a cosy peat
fire while your favourite CD plays on the
Bang and Olufsen, or wallow in the deep
vintage baths.

Food is an important consideration
here. English dishes feature predominately
on the menu – seasonal roast game or
grilled fish, followed by wicked home-
made puddings and a selection of farmhouse cheeses. Alternatively, bar meals are
on offer at lunchtime and in the evening.
Just past the bar is a small shop that sells a
great selection of wines, books, cheeses
and other bits and bobs. Be sure to check
the terms and conditions of the inn before
making a booking.

Windermere, Cumbria

Ambleside Road, Windermere,
LA23 1AX

Tel (015394) 448222
Fax (01200) 43192
e-mail stay@cedarmanor.co.uk
website www.cedarmanor.co.uk/

Nearby Windermere Lake,
Holehird Gardens, Blackwell House,
Hill Top (Beatrix Potter), Dove
Cottage (Wordsworth)
Location on A591 next to St Mary's
Church
Food breakfast, dinner, lounge and
room service **Price** ££ -££££
Rooms 10; 8 double (2 can be twin),
2 double suites with separate din-
ing/sitting room; all have tea/coffee
facilities, TV, wi-fi
Facilities 2 sitting rooms, bar, din-
ing room, garden and patio, giftshop
Credit cards MC, V, debit cards
Children welcome, 2 rooms have
sofa beds, only 10+ in dining room
Disabled no special facilities
Pets not allowed **Closed** 1 week for
Christmas, 3 weeks in Jan
Proprietor Jonathan Kaye

Cedar Manor
Boutique hotel

A short walk north of Windermere, hidden behind trees and greenery, stands
Cedar Manor with its grey brick façade
and mullioned windows – built in the
19thC by the same architect who designed
nearby St Mary's Church.

Its owners, Caroline and Jonathan Kaye
are a friendly, hands-on couple with an eye
for detail. There are two comfortable sitting rooms decorated with imaginative
wallpaper and harmonious colours. One
leads to a wooden carved bar, while the
other displays a collection of arts, crafts
and jewellery – all for sale, and made by
local artists. Bedrooms and bathrooms are
gracefully decorated, with canopied beds
and furniture made to fit by local craftsmen. The award-winning detached Coach
House Suite features a dining area and a
twin spa bath. In the evening, relax with a
drink in the patio by the great cedar tree.

Their candlelit restaurant offers a short
but excellent menu, focussing on modern
English cuisine – save room for dessert.

Jonathan, who used to manage the
exclusive Raffles nightclub in Chelsea,
hosts weekly backgammon nights, as well
as the yearly Lake District backgammon
championship. There is friendly banter,
relaxed organisation and informal mingling
– Cedar Manor in a nutshell.

Windermere, Cumbria

Crook Road, near Windermere, Cumbria LA23 3NE

Tel (015394) 88818
Fax (015394) 88058
e-mail hotel@thegilpin.co.uk
website www.thegilpin.co.uk

Nearby Windermere Steamboat Museum; Holker Hall; Sizergh Castle; Kendal; Grasmere.
Location on B5284 Kendal to Bowness road, 2 miles (1 km) SE of Windermere; with ample car parking
Food breakfast, lunch, dinner
Price £££ **Rooms** (Gilpin Hotel) 14 double and twin with bath; 6 Garden Suites with hot tubs; (Gilpin Lake House) 6 suites with bath, 2 double and twin with shower; all rooms have phone, TV, minibar, hairdryer.
Facilities (2 sitting rooms, 4 dining rooms; garden, swimming pool, sauna, hot tubs, jetty spa, boat house, private lake **Credit cards** AE, DC, MC, V **Children** accepted over 7
Disabled access limited, call to discuss
Pets not accepted **Closed** never
Proprietors Cunliffe family

Gilpin Hotel & Lake House **Country house hotel**

Just occasionally, whether by luck or judgement, you can arrive somewhere that tells you to congratulate yourself on your choice of hotel before you even step through the door: Gilpin Hotel & Lake House is one of these happy places. Barney Cunliffe's great grandmother lived in this Edwardian house for 40 years, and when his parents came 25 years later, it had become a rather ordinary B&B. Now, with manicured grounds and gleaming paint, quite substantially and wholly sympathetically enlarged and set on a peaceful hillside with moor beyond the boundary, you are to some extent prepared for the warm welcome and deep-pile comfort waiting for you inside. This is a highly professional and well-staffed operation, yet still driven by the enthusiasm of owners whose unmistakeable priority is the happiness of their guests.

If your tastes run to good pictures, fine furniture and immaculate service you will be happy; if they include excellent and imaginatively presented food with more than the occasional touch of outright luxury, you will be happier still; and if you want a large, thoughtfully decorated room, probably with its own sitting area, and a bathroom to talk about when you get home, then you're in luck. The Hotel now also has 5 detached Spa Lodges if you're keen for a pampering.

Windermere, Cumbria

Holbeck Lane, Windermere, Cumbria LA23 1LU

Tel (015394) 32375
Fax (015394) 34743
e-mail stay@holbeckghyll.com
website www.holbeckghyll.com

Nearby Lake Windermere.
Location 3 miles (5 km) N of Windermere, E of A591; with ample car parking
Food breakfast, light lunch, dinner
Price ££££
Rooms 23 double, all with bath; 4 suites; all have phone, TV, DVD, hairdryer
Facilities 2 sitting rooms, 2 dining rooms; garden, health spa, tennis, croquet, Jacuzzi
Credit cards AE, DC, MC, V
Children welcome
Disabled 3 lodge rooms
Pets accepted in the Lodge rooms
Closed 2 weeks Jan
Proprietors Private Investor

Holbeck Ghyll
Country house hotel

An award-winning hotel in a classic Victorian lakeland house, ivy-clad with steep slate roofs and mullioned windows – plus oak panelling and art noveau stained glass. Our latest reporter had a 'friendly welcome' and was impressed by its superb position, providing both privacy from the bustle of Windermere and grand lake views from the immaculate gardens; also indeed by the two comfortable sitting rooms, both homelike and beautifully furnished.

The buildings have been refurbished to very high standards in a traditional, slightly formal style – though proprietors and staff alike are friendly and relaxed. Bedrooms and bathrooms are beautifully and individually decorated, very spacious, some with their own sitting room. At the top of the house is a 'very special' four-poster room. In the Lodge nearby are six further rooms (four are self-catering), with breathtaking views. The food is a clear attraction: pre-dinner canapés are served while you select from the inventive daily-changing menu designed by head chef Jake Jones.

There is a jogging trail from which you can spot deer and red squirrels.

Arkengarthdale, North Yorkshire

Charles Bathurst Inn
Country inn

Arkengarthdale, nr Richmond,
North Yorkshire DL11 6EN

Tel (01748) 884567
e-mail info@cbinn.co.uk
website www.cbinn.co.uk
Food breakfast, lunch, dinner
Price ££
Closed Christmas Day
Proprietors Charles Cody

Charles Cody has turned this once derelict inn in Arkengarthdale into something special. It is very popular with Dales people, to whom it is important socially, and this may have made it a bit clannish, even self-satisfied. The bedrooms have glorious views. They are light and modern, with homely touches and some period furniture. Downstairs, the ambience is darker and more masculine. A large and tempting menu of locally-sourced dishes is painted on the vast mirror at one end of the room. The Inn is halfway along the Coast to Coast walk and those setting out from here can expect a hearty breakfast and good advice, well-made sandwiches for lunch and a Thermos of something warm.

Reports welcome.

Aysgarth, North Yorkshire

Aysgarth Falls
Country hotel

Aysgarth, Leyburn DL8 3SR

Tel (01969) 663775
e-mail info@aysgarthfallshotel.com
website www.aysgarthfallshotel.com
Food breakfast, lunch, dinner
Price £-££ **Closed** between 8th
Jan-2nd Feb it's closed Mon-Thurs
Proprietors Heather and Steve
Swan

This once old-fashioned, not-outstanding country inn which we've previously ignored has had a makeover downstairs and upstairs in recent years making it more than just a useful address. Downstairs it's essentially a big bar, eating and dining area, congenially decorated, with a pleasant atmosphere and well above-average food – try the chicken pie with its buckets of delicious, rich sauce.

Bedrooms are neat, newly refurbished in pleasant neutral colours and new bathrooms. It's well placed, of course, for the famous Aysgarth Falls but also for the many Wensleydale walks and sights.

Barngate, Cumbria

Drunken Duck Inn
Country inn

So named after a Victorian landlady who found her ducks lying on the nearby crossroads. Presuming them dead, she started to pluck them; but soon realized that they were actually blind drunk, and not dead in the slightest. This inn has real character and charm. The bar/pub is delightful and exactly as you would hope an old country inn should look and feel. The menu in the bar and dining room is extensive, yet not overambitious.

Ambling round the side of the inn you will come across the 'deluxe' and 'superior' rooms. Each is individually decorated with contemporary yet comfortable furniture and fabrics, and has the added perk of private garden sitting areas. The standard bedrooms in the main house are also tastefully done out, if a little cramped.

Barngate, Ambleside, Cumbria, LA22 0NG

Tel (015394) 36347
e-mail info@drunkenduckinn.co.uk
website www.drunkenduckinn.co.uk
Food breakfast, lunch, dinner
Price ££–£££
Closed Christmas Day (though open a couple of hours for drinks)
Proprietors Stephanie Barton

Great Langdale, Cumbria

Old Dungeon Ghyll
Country hotel

Neil and Jane Walmsley have been the proprietors here since 1983 and have continued to improve and develop this popular family hotel retaining as many old features as possible. Once, many a climber chose to stay here. They were a pretty uncritical bunch (any kind of a roof was a luxury), but now all bedrooms have bathrooms, most of which are en suite, there is a comfortable residents' sitting room with an open fire, a busy hikers' bar (open to the public) as well as the warm guests' bar, and a snug dining room offering wholesome, uncomplicated food. Neil and Jane hold occasional charity folk festivals, and there are music nights in the bar every Wednesday.

Great Langdale, Ambleside, Cumbria LA22 9JY

Tel (015394) 37272
e-mail olddungeonghyll1@btconnect.com **website** www.odg.co.uk
Food breakfast, packed lunch, dinner, bar meals **Price** ££ **Closed** 20 to 26 Dec **Proprietors** Neil and Jane Walmsley

The Racquet Club
Town hotel

A good-value place that defies the chain-hotel atmosphere of central Liverpool. Book in advance as weddings are prioritised at weekends – about 120 per year.

The design (devised by Martin Ainscough) is thoroughly quirky. For instance, stag heads line the stairs, leading up to an enormous moose head on the first floor. Throughout the corridors, there are prints of Georgian aristocracy as well as modern art – some local, some bizarre. Bedrooms are cosy and comfortable. Rooms two and three have hand-carved detail on the beds' headboards and polished antique furniture.

Sue, the bubbly general manager, has been here ever since the Ainscoughs bought the place, 11 years ago.

The Hargreaves Building, 5 Chapel Street, Liverpool L3 9AG

Tel 0151 236 6676 **e-mail** info@racquetclub.org.uk **website** www.ainscoughs.co.uk/Racquet-club/racquet-club-home.html **Food** breakfast, lunch, dinner; no lunch Sat, closed Sun **Price** ££ **Closed** 24th-26th Dec; weddings only until early Jan **Proprietors** Martin and Helen Ainscough

Aysgarth, Yorkshire

Aysgarth, Leyburn Yorkshire
DL8 3SR

Tel +44 1969663635
e-mail info@stowhouse.co.uk
website www.stowhouse.co.uk

Nearby Leyburn and Hawes,
Aysgarth Falls, Askrigg, Bolton
Castle, Dales trekking
Location in the heart of
Wensleydale
Food breakfast
Price £££
Rooms 7 double, all with
bath/shower and Dales views
Facilities living room, honesty bar,
snug, dining room - all with wood-
burners, 2 acres of grounds
Credit cards all major
Children welcome
Disabled no special facilities
Pets dogs welcome in all rooms
except Love is Blind and Badger
Manager Sarah and Phil Bucknall

Stow House
Bed-and-breakfast

A shot in the arm for Yorkshire Dales B&B: Sarah and Phil Bucknall have asked themselves what you don't get else-where in the national park and confidently provided it. First, a blend of old and new – often colourful, sometimes whacky fabrics and contemporary art co-exist with antiques in a 19thC vicarage. Second, chic modern bathrooms to a standard that travellers usually expect in city hotels. Third, their cocktails – which seem to aptly express Sarah and Phil's approach: friendly, hands-on, communicative hosts who make you feel better as you walk through the door. Their signature cocktail is the Corpse Reviver No.2.

Both worked in big London advertising businesses before launching Stow House in 2014, though their feel for what the cus-tomer wants is far from superficial. They've looked after the basics: the beds and linen are high quality; the rooms warm; break-fast well above average. As you'd expect of a vicarage, the seven rooms are spacious. Guests have the run of the house, with their own entrance, while Sarah and Phil live in an unobtrusive annexe. In other words, this is B&B-plus, with maximum pri-vacy and independence for the guest, a choice of two downstairs sitting rooms and dinner provided for groups if ordered in advance. Prices above average, but fair.

Bolton Abbey, North Yorkshire

Bolton Abbey, Skipton, North
Yorkshire BD23 6AJ

Tel (01756) 718100
e-mail res@devonshirehotels.co.uk
website
www.thedevonshirearms.co.uk

Nearby Castle Howard; Skipton
Castle; Brontë Parsonage; Harewood
House. **Location** on B6160 just N of
junction with A59; in grounds with
ample car parking **Food** breakfast,
lunch, dinner, afternoon tea **Price**
££££ **Rooms** 40; 37 double and twin,
1 family, 2 suites, with a combination
of bath/shower (requests for specific
bathrooms must be made); all rooms
have phone, TV, DVD, hairdryer
Facilities 3 lounges, conservatory,
restaurant, brasserie, 2 bars, gym,
sauna, steam room, solarium, indoor
swimming pool; garden, tennis, croquet, putting, helipad, fishing **Credit
cards** all major **Children** not under
7 in restaurant **Disabled** rooms on
the ground floor, and 1 specially
adapted **Pets** accepted, £10 per dog
Closed never **Manager** Adam Dyke

The Devonshire Arms
Hotel & Spa **Country hotel**

As your helicopter whirls towards its
helipad, you can see that the moorland
of the Dales proper comes to within a mile
or so of the 17thC Devonshire Arms.
Follow the path down the bank of the
Wharfe, which gives the valley its name, for
the half mile from Bolton Abbey village to
the stone bridge and you're there. Owned
by the Duke and Duchess of Devonshire,
the hotel is doubly graced since it contains
antiques and paintings from Chatsworth,
the family seat; the Duchess has master-
minded their placement and the design of
the interior. This is a hotel in two parts, old
and new. The elegant old wears its years
well and has happily grown out of exact
right angles. The extension, which brought
with it an indoor swimming pool, spa and
gym, is settling in well.

The dining alternatives cover a similar
spectrum. On the one hand is the quiet
comfort of the classical Burlington
Restaurant, and on the other a buzzy
brasserie with dishes to suit most moods
and a snappy wine list to go with them. The
bedrooms also come in old and new varieties: the older win on character and the
newer score better with their views. See
also The Devonshire Fell (page 311).

Burnsall, North Yorkshire

Burnsall, Skipton, North Yorkshire
BD23 6BT

Tel 01756 729000
Fax 01756 729009
e-mail res@devonshirehotels.co.uk
website www.devonshirefell.co.uk

Nearby Bolton Abbey Estate, Leeds,
Harrogate
Location Burnsall village, just off
the B6160
Food breakfast, lunch, dinner, after-
noon tea
Price £££-££££
Rooms 16 doubles (some can be
twin), all ensuite; 4 more planned
Facilities restaurant, bar, conserva-
tory, wine cellar, Devonshire Spa
located at The Devonshire Arms
Hotel & Spa **Credit cards** all major
Children welcome
Disabled no lift to bedrooms, but
wheelchair access points, trained
staff **Pets** dog friendly rooms avail-
able, £10 charge per night
Closed no specific closure dates
Proprietors Duke and Duchess of
Devonshire

The Devonshire Fell
Restaurant-with-rooms

Just outside picturesque Burnsall, the
Devonshire Fell sits above the village,
with great views across the River Wharfe.
Located very close to the Bolton Abbey Estate,
this is a less formal sister hotel to The
Devonshire Arms (page 310).

The ground floor leads seamlessly from
one room to the other with simple wood-
en floors, log fires and pretty shutters in
the dining room. No chintz here: the stair
carpets are pink-and-grey striped; the bedrooms have bedheads and Roman blinds in
bright colours. Prints, black-and-white
photographs and contemporary paintings
decorate the walls.

Bedrooms are very comfortable, with
good sheets. On a large tray you'll find
quality coffee and tea, cakes, soft drinks
and fresh milk. Our reporter appreciated
the large flat-screen TV, and the unusual
gels and shampoos.

Drinks are generally served in a cosy
conservatory, often a contradiction in
terms, but this one has a log fire at one
end and was 'blissfully comfortable'.
Dinner, from a small menu, was 'well
thought out with local fish and meat.
Presentation was elegant (don't expect
huge Yorkshire platefuls). Fish and chips
and homemade beefburgers were just
right after a day walking the fells.' A superb
place to stay for walkers, and dog friendly.

Byland, North Yorkshire

Byland, Coxwold, North Yorkshire
YO61 4BD

Tel 01347 868 204
e-mail abbey.inn@english-her-
itage.org.uk
website http://www.english-her-
itage.org.uk/daysout/properties/byla
nd-abbey/inn/

Nearby Byland Abbey
Location 2 miles from A170
between Thirsk and Helmsley
Food breakfast
Price ££-£££
Rooms 2 doubles, 1 twin, all
ensuite, with TV
Facilities breakfast room, tea room
in the summer
Credit cards MC, V
Children welcome
Disabled no special access
Pets not accepted
Closed never
Proprietor English Heritage

Byland Abbey Inn
Country bed-and-breakfast

The pairing of an isolated inn with stark-
ly beautiful Cisterican abbey ruins is
rare in Britain; sitting in the stone-walled
Wass Room, one could almost be in
France, in a *vieux logis* overlooking a *monument historique*. Hope to stay at full moon
when they look particularly majestic.
English Heritage, which maintains Byland
Abbey ruins, bought the small 19thC inn
some years ago and gave it a conscientious
makeover, and it is now a Tearoom, attracting walkers, cyclists and tourists.

The three bedrooms are prettily decorated. The Mouseman, is notable for its specially commissioned Mouseman furniture
made in nearby Kilburn. You can breakfast
in the Coxwold room whilst gazing at the
ruins, and then wander among them free of
charge, probably alone. The Black Swan at
Oldstead is Michelin-starred, and recommended for dinner, and the Stapylton Arms
is within walking distance.

However, our most recent reporter
found the prices too steep for what was on
offer. The breakfast (no longer served in
bed) was ample but basic, and the amenities in the rooms could have been
improved. We'd be interested to hear
reports on how English Heritage have
addressed these issues – an inventive project which perhaps hasn't yet reached its
full potential.

Main Street, Cornhill-on-Tweed,
Northumberland TD12 4UH

Tel 01890 882424
e-mail enquiries@colling-
woodarms.com
website www.collingwoodarms.com

Nearby golfing, fishing, riding,
cycling, sightseeing walks
Location near Berwick-Upon-
Tweed, Cheviot Hills, North
Northumberland, Scottish Border
Food breakfast, lunch, dinner
Price £££
Rooms 15 all with digital televisions
Facilities brasserie, dining room,
bar, library
Credit cards DC, MC, V
Children accepted
Disabled access possible, ground-
floor bedroom and bathroom
Pets not accepted, but kennels avail-
able **Closed** never
Proprietor Ronald Watson
Manager Kevin Kenny

The Collingwood Arms
Town inn

'A more relaxing, solid, reassuring and
unpretentious hotel would be hard
to imagine,' comments our series editor,
Fiona Duncan. A former coaching inn (the
words 'Post Horses' still appear above the
door), it sits on an old main road to
Edinburgh, with the River Tweed below.

A stone building with a plain Georgian
front, its name is from its original owners:
a local merchant family with strong ties to
the 19thC naval hero Vice-Admiral
Collingwood. They left in 1955, but current
owner Ronald Watson (who has two
other establishments on Bamburgh) clearly respects the place's heritage: each bedroom is named after a ship in the Admiral's
Trafalgar division. Colours and fabrics have
been kept muted, and Persian rugs and
antique furniture scattered throughout.

There are a few contemporary twists –
a trendy, wood-floored pub-brasserie; simple, almost minimalist, headboards on beds
– but these are thoughtful touches rather
than needless trend-following. Attention
to detail is evident, from the library-cum-
sitting room to each of the 15 bedrooms.

Food is widely praised. You eat in a stylish, relaxing, parquet-floored restaurant or,
if weather allows, out in the manicured
gardens. Ingredients are fresh and locally
sourced. When Fiona visited, she enjoyed
her grilled black pudding and leek starter.

34 Old Elvet, Durham DH1 3HN

Tel 01913 841037
e-mail info@thetownhouse-durham.co.uk
website www.townhousedurham.co.uk

Nearby Durham Cathedral; Durham University; city centre
Location on Old Elvet, just off A690 and New Elvet
Food breakfast, lunch, dinner
Price ££-££££
Rooms 11; all doubles, all ensuite, all have TV, hairdryer
Facilities dining room, bar, wi-fi on ground floor, terrace
Credit Cards AE, MC, V
Children accepted, travel cot can be put in most rooms
Disabled 1 room fully equipped
Pets not accepted
Closed Christmas Day, restaurant closed on Sundays
Proprietor Shepherd Cox Group

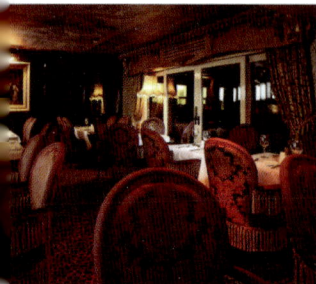

The Town House
Townhouse hotel

This used to be called The Fallen Angel, known for its (mostly irritating) themed bedrooms, but which could still claim to be the only interesting place to stay in Durham, a city badly in need of a characterful place to stay. Debbie and Nigel Gadd gallantly stepped up to the challenge, reincarnating this tired hotel with panache. Since our last edition it's been taken over by the Shepherd Cox group, but we hear things are ticking over just the same.

A trusted reporter tells us he entered the front door to see 'plastic replicas of Roman remains illuminated by a somewhat lurid, violet coloured chandelier'. But his worries disappeared rapidly. The reception staff were 'friendly and helpful in a practical way', and were just as helpful at check out.

He eulogises the food – 'one of the most excellent dinners we have had recently. Breakfast was well above average, too.'

'Our room was strange but interesting, and above all else clean, warm and comfortable.' The shower, between the bedroom and the bathroom, was open to view – encased in glass on three sides – but could be closed off with a curtain.'

The location, within walking distance (uphill) of the Cathedral and University, is fine. And it is 'very good value for money'.

Summers Fold, Grassington, near
Skipton, North Yorkshire BD23 5AE

Tel (01756) 752584
Fax (07092) 376562
e-mail sales@ashfieldhouse.co.uk
website www.ashfieldhouse.co.uk

Nearby Skipton Castle, Gordale
Scar, Janet's Foss, Ripon, Malham
Cove, Bolton Abbey
Location in Grassington, just off the
main square; with ample car parking
Food breakfast
Prices £-££
Rooms 8 double and twin with bath
or shower; all rooms have TV,
hairdryer, wi-fi
Facilities 2 sitting rooms, 1 with bar,
dining room; garden
Credit cards MC, V
Children welcome over 10
Disabled not suitable
Pets not accepted
Closed two weeks each year
Proprietors the Howard family

Ashfield House
Country bed-and-breakfast

Grassington, and Wharfedale in general, is a little-known Northern gem, especially for keen walkers. Tucked away off the main street is this small private stone and slate hotel, a peaceful sanctuary at the end of its own yard. What's more, and unlike anywhere else in Grassington, you can park your car there. Oak and pine furniture, bare beams and stone walls are combined with neat furnishings. The bedrooms are modestly sized with fresh, clean decoration and their own shower rooms.

The Howard family took over in 2016, with 30 years hotel experience already under their belt, and are incrementally putting their own stamp on the place. They've improved the car-parking facilities, decorated a couple of rooms and are in the process of improving the kitchen – so in the future, dinner might come into play again. In the meantime guests can enjoy a hearty breakfast laden with Yorkshire produce, and complimentary homemade cake on arrival.

Beyond the house, insulated from the bustle of the town, is a quiet walled garden with a table and chairs where you can simply sit and enjoy the sunshine if the prospect of a walk along the river seems too testing.

Harome, North Yorkshire

Harome, Nr Helmsley, North
Yorkshire, YO62 5JE

Tel (01439) 770397
website www.thestaratharome.co.uk

Nearby Helmsley market town,
Castle Howard, Duncombe Park.
Location 2.5 miles SE of Helmsley
off the A170, ample car parking
Food breakfast, lunch, dinner
(restaurant in the Inn closed on
Mon) **Price** £££
Rooms 9 doubles, 3 suites, all with
bath or shower; all rooms have TV,
DVD, CD, radio, hairdryer, phone,
tea and coffee making facilities
Facilities dining rooms, breakfast
room, bar, sitting room; garden
Credit cards MC, V **Children** wel-
come **Disabled** 4 ground-floor
rooms **Pets** accepted in a couple of
ground-floor rooms
Closed never
Proprietors Andrew Pern

The Star Inn
Country hotel

'One of the most comfortable, relaxing nights I have spent in a hotel' says a recent reporter. Wellies and umbrellas wait by the front door of Cross House (the Inn's guest house) in case you feel like having a stroll around the beautiful countryside. The opulent sitting room is kept warm by the grand fire in the centre and once sat on the sofas with tea and seriously good cakes you can hardly make it to your room. When you do, you'll discover that they are immaculate, balancing the contemporary and the rustic perfectly with fantastic bathrooms (some with whirlpool baths) and music, DVDs and chocolates and crisps to tide you over until supper.

Supper and lunch can be served in the Inn itself: just across the road. The pub and restaurant are bursting with charm and decorated in keeping with the 14thC thatched image, so expect old beams and secret little loft spaces in which to enjoy coffee; the rear terrace is a popular place to eat *al fresco* in the summer. The restaurant, serving Andrew's 'modern Yorkshire' dishes, recently regained its Michelin star. Upstairs the fairytale private dining room has been decorated by local artists.

Hawes, North Yorkshire

Hawes, North Yorkshire DL8 3LY

Tel (01969) 667255
Fax (01969) 667741
e-mail
enquiries@simonstonehall.com
website www.simonstonehall.com

Nearby Pennine Way; Wharfedale;
Ribblesdale.
Location 1.5 miles (2.5 km) N of
Hawes on Muker road; with ample
car parking
Food breakfast (residents only), bar
lunch, Sun lunch, dinner
Price £££
Rooms 18 double and twin with
bath and shower; all rooms have
phone, TV, wi-fi
Facilities bar, lounge, brasserie,
restaurant; garden, terrace
Credit cards AE, DC, MC, V
Children welcome
Disabled access possible to ground
floor only **Pets** welcome in bar area
and in certain bedrooms
Closed never
Managing Director Jake Dinsdale
General Manager Paul Ransome

Simonstone Hall
Country house hotel

Simonstone has undergone major refurbishment in the last few years, but still has the air of something special, helped by the friendliness of the staff. Outside, it is the same dignified, slightly forbidding, large Dales country house; but as you enter you will probably hear the lively chatter coming from the extensive bar area which is intended to re-create the hotel as a place that will attract local non-residents as well as overnight guests. To have this popular country pub within an essentially dignified old country hotel is something of a novelty – a pleasant one at that. The bar is handsomely done out; the meals and range of wines by the glass are imaginative; waiters in black tie and apron, French bistro-style, bustle about. It gives the place an injection of life, but if you've come here for peace, or a romantic twosome, just walk down the corridor to the sitting room, hidden at the far end of the hall to provide guests with peace and quiet. You can enjoy dinner in both The Brasserie and The Four Fells restaurants.

All bedrooms now have bathrooms with showers. The luxury and superior bedrooms are handsomely done out in country house style, some with sleigh beds, others with four-posters, many of them with fantastic views of the Dales.

Hawnby, North Yorkshire

Hill Top, Hawnby, near Helmsley, North Yorkshire YO6 5QS

Tel (01439) 798202
e-mail info@innathawnby.co.uk
website www.innathawnby.co.uk

Nearby Rievaulx Abbey; Jervaulx Abbey; North York Moors.
Location at top of hill in village 7 miles (11 km) NE of Helmsley; with car parking
Food breakfast, lunch, dinner
Price ££
Rooms 9 double and twin with bath; all rooms have phone, TV, hairdryer
Facilities sitting room, bar, restaurant, garden
Credit cards MC, V
Children welcome
Disabled access difficult
Pets accepted in 3 rooms
Closed Monday lunchtime; Christmas day
Proprietors Dave and Kathryn Young

The Inn at Hawnby
Country hotel

After a spectacular drive through rolling valleys and the unspoilt stone village of Hawnby, you come across Dave and Kathryn Young's country inn, formerly The Hawnby Hotel. The 'village pub' façade hides an exquisite small hotel which was decorated with obvious flair by Lady Mexborough. The hotel used to be part of the 13,000-acre Mexborough estate and Lady Mexborough gave it much personal attention, refurbishing the Inn's six bedrooms which are named after colour schemes (Cowslip, Coral, Jade and so on), choosing Laura Ashley wallpaper and fabrics throughout the cosy rooms and immaculate bathrooms. Three further bedrooms are available just over the road, these ones named after stables.

The Youngs have tidied up the outside of the Inn and the gardens, as well as giving the public rooms and bedrooms some attention, aiming to make them altogether brighter and more welcoming. They have also turned their attention to the kitchen, hiring a new head chef who produces a full *a la carte* menu, all from scratch and using fresh, local produce.

Reports continue to heap praise on the Inn at Hawnby: 'This charming country hotel … is an ideal base for touring North Yorkshire; a gem with fabulous views, home cooking and friendly service'.

Stonegate, Hunmanby, North
Yorkshire YO14 0NS

Tel (01723) 891333
Fax (01723) 892973
e-mail staciedevos@aol.com
website www.wranghamhouse.com

Nearby Scarborough Castle; North
York Moors National Park.
Location behind church in village, 1
mile (1.5 km) SW of Filey; ample car
parking
Food breakfast, lunch, dinner
Price ££
Rooms 12; Double, Twin, Super-
King, Four-Poster and 2 Executive
Suites available; 7 with bath, 5 with
shower; all have phone, TV, hairdry-
er and welcome tray **Facilities** sit-
ting room, dining room, bar; garden
Credit cards AE, MC, V
Children welcome **Disabled** 1
adapted room
Pets by arrangement
Closed Christmas and Boxing Day
Proprietors Peter and Stacie Devos

Wrangham House
Country house hotel

Wrangham House is a well-preserved and elegant Georgian former vicarage set in three acres of beautiful gardens. The main part of the house was built in 1700 and continues to be sympathetic to its period. The eponymous Francis Wrangham added a wing, now housing the restaurant, in 1810. Stacie and Peter Davos purchased Wrangham House in 2005, and set about restoring the house to its former glory – the pair are passionate about the house and its upkeep. Over the years this has involved refurbishing the kitchen, sitting room, dining room and most of the bedrooms, as well as giving the gardens some much-needed care and attention.

Peter, a talented cook, is in charge of the kitchen – and delights in using seasonal produce such as game and lobster – so there is always something new on the menu. Everything is freshly made and locally sourced. Peter and Stacie take pride in offering a personal and flexible service – guests on long stays have the opportunity to influence the menu by discussing their preferences with Peter, and early dinners will be arranged for families with young children. Reports welcome.

Lastingham, North Yorkshire

Lastingham, North Yorkshire
Y062 6TH

Tel (01751) 417345/417402
Fax (01751) 417358
e-mail reservations@lastingham-grange.com **website** www.lasting-hamgrange.com

Nearby North York Moors;
Scarborough; Rievaulx Abbey.
Location at top of village, 7 miles
(10 km) NW of Pickering; ample car
parking **Food** breakfast, lunch, dinner **Price** £££
Rooms 12 and 1 self-catering cottage – The Old Reading Room; 10
double, 2 single, all with bath; all
rooms have phone, TV, hairdryer,
wi-fi **Facilities** sitting room, dining
room; terrace, garden
Credit cards MC, V
Children welcome
Disabled access to restaurant and
garden **Pets** accepted in bedrooms
by arrangement, not in The Old
Reading Room **Closed** Dec to mid-
Mar **Proprietors** Jane, Bertie and
Tom Wood

Lastingham Grange
Country house hotel

Lastingham Grange – a wistaria-clad former farmhouse – nestles peacefully in a delightful village on the edge of the North York Moors. Unlike many country house hotels, it manages to combine a certain sophistication – smartly decorated public rooms, friendly unobtrusive service, elegantly laid gardens – with a large dash of informality, which puts you immediately at ease. From the moment you enter, you feel as if you are staying with friends. Recently, we had this reaction from an inspector: 'Family feeling; very child friendly; charming rooms.–'

The main attraction is the garden. You can enjoy it from a distance – from the windows of the large L-shaped sitting room (complete with carefully grouped sofas, antiques and a grand piano) – or, like most guests, by exploring. There is a beautifully laid rose garden, enticing bordered lawns and an extensive adventure playground for children.

Bedrooms are perfectly comfortable, with well-equipped bathrooms, and have been totally redecorated since our last visit, when a reporter felt that they were somewhat downbeat in places. Paul Cattaneo and Sandra Thurlow produce traditional English meals for the daily-changing menu, prepared from fresh, local ingredients. Reports welcome.

Millgate, North Yorkshire

Millgate, Richmond, North
Yorkshire DL10 4JN

Tel (01748) 823571
e-mail
oztim@millgatehouse.demon.co.uk
website www.millgatehouse.com

Nearby Cleveland hills; Swale val-
ley; the Dales; Richmond.
Location in Richmond town centre
Food breakfast, dinner for larger
parties
Price ££-£££
Rooms 3 double; self-catering
accommodation for up to 12 people
Facilities sitting room, dining room;
garden
Credit cards not accepted
Children accepted over 10
Disabled not suitable
Pets accepted (not in dining room)
Closed never
Proprietors Austin Lynch and Tim
Culkin

Millgate House
Town guesthouse

Millgate House dates back to the early
1700s and, despite its relatively unas-
suming exterior, is full of surprises. Behind
the street façade is a house of real charm
and character, tastefully furnished with
antiques and interesting pieces sourced
from from all over the world. Below, and
sloping away from the house, lies an award
winning garden with excellent views
across the river Swale towards the beautiful Cleveland Hills beyond.

What really sets Millgate House apart is
its garden. Since scooping first prize in the
National Royal Horticultural Society
Garden Competition, the grounds have
been featured in publications in the UK as
well as internationally. The gardens are
open all year round, and entry is free to
house guests.

Breakfast is very good at Millgate House
and dinners can be pre-arranged for parties of 16 and over. The accommodation
on offer is of a high standard. All bedrooms
are warm and spacious with fine views, and
each has its own large, airy bathroom with
great period details. All of this, together
with some outstanding care and service
from the owners, make Millgate House a
fine choice in this area. It was named B&B
of the Year 2011 by the Good Hotel Guide
and now holds the prestigious César
Award.

Pateley Bridge, North Yorkshire

Wath-in-Nidderdale, Pateley Bridge, near Harrogate, North Yorkshire HG3 5PP

Tel (01423) 711306
Fax (01423) 712524
email
sportsmansarms@btconnect.com
website
www.nidderdale.co.uk/sportsman-sarms

Nearby Wharfedale, Wensleydale; Fountains Abbey, Bolton Abbey. **Location** 2 miles (3 km) NW of Pateley Bridge, in hamlet; with ample car parking **Food** breakfast, bar lunch, dinner **Price** ££ **Rooms** 11; 9 double, 2 twin with bath or shower; all rooms have TV **Facilities** 3 sitting rooms, bar, dining room; fishing **Credit cards** MC, V **Children** accepted **Disabled** public rooms are ground floor **Pets** welcome by arrangement **Closed** Christmas Day, New Year's Day **Proprietors** Jane and Ray Carter

The Sportsman's Arms
Country hotel

Our latest inspection confirms that the Sportsman's Arms is going from strength to strength. The long, rather rambling building dates from the 17th century, and the setting is as enchanting as the village name sounds; the River Nidd flows across the field in front; Gouthwaite reservoir, a bird-watchers' haunt, is just behind; glorious dales country spreads all around.

Jane and Ray Carter have been running the Sportman's Arms, with the help of a young enthusiastic team, for over 30 years now, and continue to make improvements. Bedrooms (two with four-posters) are light and fresh, with brand-new bathrooms. Six more rooms, four with views across open countryside, are located in the barn and stable block.

And then there is the food. The Sportsman's Arms is first and foremost a restaurant, and the large dining room is the inn's focal point, sparkling with silver cutlery and crystal table lights. The lively menu embraces sound, traditional local fare, as well as fresh fish and seafood brought in daily from Whitby. To back it up, there is a superb wine list – and an extremely reasonable bill.

Ramsgill-in-Nidderdale, North Yorkshire

Ramsgill-in-Nidderdale, Pateley
Bridge, near Harrogate, North
Yorkshire, HG3 5RL

Tel (01423) 755243
e-mail enquiries@yorke-arms.co.uk
website www.yorke-arms.co.uk

Nearby Harewood House; Newby
Hall; Fountains Abbey; Ripon
Cathedral.
Location in centre of village; take
Low Wath Road from Pateley
Bridge bordering Gouthwaite
Reservoir; with car parking
Food breakfast, lunch, dinner
Price ££££
Rooms 15 twin/double (including 4
in the Courtyard), all with bath; all
rooms have mini bars, TV, coffee
making facilities.
Facilities sitting room, 2 dining
rooms, private dining room; garden
Credit cards AE, DC, MC, V
Disabled not suitable
Pets accepted in some public rooms
Closed Sundays and Mondays
Proprietors Frances and Gerald
Atkins

The Yorke Arms
Restaurant-with-rooms

On the green in a pretty Nidderdale village, the creeper-clad Yorke Arms was
a fully-functioning pub for 150 years. Now,
it is a Michelin-starred restaurant-with-
rooms. You are greeted as you enter by
flagged floors, beams and, in winter, open
fires. There is also a reassuring feeling of
order: what should have been polished has
been polished, and what should have been
swept has been. In the restaurant, wooden
tables and a carpeted floor strewn with
rugs are pleasantly rustic, and serve as a
showcase for Frances Atkins' Michelin-
starred daily changing menu: traditional and
modern English dishes are her starting-
point, but she also draws on other cuisines
from all over the world. Old favourites
such as Yorkshire hot-pot or slow-cooked
shoulder of lamb usually make an appearance. The wine list is comprehensive and
sympathetically priced.

The bedrooms, which have all been
thoroughly refurbished, with stylish modern bathrooms, are comfortably furnished
and range in size (and price) from cosy to
a modest suite, 'Gouthwaite', which boasts
a sofa and armchairs. A recent reporter
staying in one of the courtyard rooms
found them spacious but a little aseptic,
and in need of a few feminine flourishes.
There is also a two-bedroom cottage with
a private garden and terrace.

Reeth, North Yorkshire

On the Green, Reeth, Richmond, North Yorkshire DL11 6SN

Tel (01748) 884292
e-mail enquiries@theburgoyne.co.uk
website www.theburgoyne.co.uk

Nearby Richmond Castle; Middleham Castle Aysgarth Falls, Wensleydale Railway.
Location 10 miles (16 km) W of Richmond on B6270; with car parking **Food** breakfast, packed lunch on request, Sunday lunch on first Sunday of month, dinner; room service **Price ££ Rooms** 10 double and twin with bath; all rooms have phone, flat screen TV, DVD player, hairdryer, tea/coffee facilities **Facilities** sitting room, dining room; garden, fishing, drying facilities, lock-up for bicycles
Credit cards MC, V **Children** accepted **Disabled** access possible to ground-floor room **Pets** dogs accepted by arrangement **Closed** weekdays early Jan **Proprietor** Mo and Julia Usman

Burgoyne Hotel
Village hotel

The Burgoyne Hotel stretches its late-Georgian length along the top of the sloping green in Reeth. If you turn round and look the other way, you'll see why: the Swale valley is extremely pretty, and with only the green in front of it, the Burgoyne has an uninterrupted view. Inside, time, money and taste have conspired to produce something of a masterpiece to which has been added the magic ingredient of a warm welcome. There are two elegant and richly furnished sitting rooms on the ground floor with Medieval touches here and there: stone coats of arms on the fireplaces and 'Gothic' oak doors. The restaurant, where the snowy napkins, the crystal and the silver stand out against the cool blues of the decoration, is a kind of inner sanctum where head chef David Spencer offers old-fashioned dishes with modern twists. The daily-changing menu uses Yorkshire produce, and is complemented by an impressive wine list.

The bedrooms, most of which face the valley, are beautifully appointed and deeply comfortable. Window seats offer pleasant perches for people who just want to sit and enjoy the view. Rather than hack space for bathrooms out of the well-proportioned rooms, one or two bathrooms are across the corridor – voluminous robes and slippers are provided for the short journey.

Richmond, North Yorkshire

Easby, Richmond, North Yorkshire,
DL10 7EU

Tel 01748 826 066
Mobile 0776 967 3835
e-mail easby.hall@zen.co.uk
website easbyhall.com

Nearby The Yorkshire Dales, Easby
Abbey, the market town Richmond
with castle and Georgian Theatre
Royal; waterfalls **Location** 4 miles
from Scotch Corner (A1), 15 minutes from Darlington train station;
overlooks the Swale river and ruins
of Easby Abbey; ample private parking. **Food** breakfast, complimentary
afternoon tea on arrival **Price** £££-
££££ **Rooms** 3; super-king doubles
(can become twin), 2 with
bath/shower, 1 with shower, wi-fi,
hairdryer, log burner/open fire,
fridge, tea/coffee, radio/TV
Facilities drawing room, 3 gardens
with a summer house and winter hut
with open fire. **Credit cards** none
Disabled 1 ground floor room but
no special facilities **Pets** by arrangement **Closed** never **Proprietors**
John and Karen Clarke

Easby Hall
Country house hotel

Easby Hall stands on a country lane outside Richmond. Our first impression:
here's a well-proportioned and stylish
home, recently renovated. The kitchen garden is impressive, with much companion
planting and not a weed in sight.

Stroll into the elegant drawing room and
you will stop dead in your tracks: beyond
and below the 'infinity lawn' lie the tranquil,
romantic ruins of Easby Abbey, surrounded
by gently rolling woods and meadows.
Couples marry in St Agatha church and
walk up to Easby Hall for their reception.

The house is immaculately decorated
using bold wallpapers and soft paint
colours. The views, but each is exceptional, with
quite a tea tray: home-made biscuits, fresh
mint for infusions and fresh flowers. Dinner
is currently not provided, although a private chef can be brought in for groups by
prior arrangement.

Breakfast was special, with an emphasis
on organic produce largely sourced from
their kitchen garden. Each table had pretty
floral china and flowers from the garden.
Coffee from a silver pot; seasonal home-
made compote on offer (be it rhubarb with
cardamom, blackcurrant or poached pear);
poached eggs scattered with edible violas.
Had the room overlooked the abbey ruins,
it would have been even better.

Ripley, North Yorkshire

Ripley, Harrogate, North Yorkshire
HG3 3AY

Tel (01423) 771888
Fax (01423) 771509
e-mail boarshead@ripleycastle.co.uk
website www.ripleycastle.co.uk

Nearby York; Fountains Abbey and
Studley Royal Water Gardens;
Ripley Castle
Location in village centre, 3 miles (5
km) N of Harrogate on A61; with
ample car parking
Food breakfast, lunch, dinner
Price ££
Rooms 25 double and twin; 5 rooms
with shower only, 14 with shower
over bath, 2 with bath only; all
rooms have phone, TV, fax/modem
point, hairdryer; minibar on request
Facilities sitting room, dining
rooms, 2 bars; garden, tennis, fishing
Credit cards AE, MC, DC, V
Children accepted **Disabled** 1 specially adapted room, 8 ground-floor
rooms **Pets** accepted in some rooms
only **Closed** never **Proprietors** Sir
Thomas and Lady Ingilby

Boar's Head
Country house hotel

Anyone with a spare inn and enough
paintings and antique furniture to fur-
nish it could do worse than emulate Sir
Thomas and Lady Ingilby's successful renovation of the Boar's Head in Ripley. It is a
thriving establishment with helpful, pleasant staff who do not leave your comfort to
chance. There are bedrooms in the inn
itself, lighter more contemporary ones in
its cobbled courtyard, and across the road,
in the peace and quiet of Birchwood
House, are four of their six best rooms. All
have fresh flowers, pristine modern bathrooms and thoughtful decoration.

The public rooms are warm and welcoming, filled with period furniture;
seascapes and ancestors share the walls.
There is a choice for dinner: you can
either go to the relaxed bar/bistro (packed
when we visited) or the richer candle-lit
comfort of the restaurant to agonise over
a choice that includes 'Yorkshire
Cassoulet' – Yorkshire duck leg, Yorkshire
sausage and Easingwold pork belly – or
Ripley's Famous Mushroom Stroganoff.
Fresh vegetables and game make seasonal
appearances from the Ingilby estate,
presided over by their castle.

Romaldkirk, County Durham

Romaldkirk, Barnard Castle, Co
Durham DL12 9EB

Tel (01833) 650213
e-mail hotel@rose-and-crown.co.uk
website www.rose-and-crown.co.uk

Nearby Barnard Castle; Egglestone
Abbey; High Force.
Location in centre of village, on
B6277, 6 miles (9.6 km) NW of
Barnard Castle; with ample carpark-
ing **Food** breakfast, dinner, Sun
lunch **Price** ££
Rooms 14; 13 double and twin, 2
rooms in Monk's Cottage, 1 family,
11 with bath, 3 with shower; all
rooms have phone, TV, hairdryer,
Bose sound systems
Facilities sitting room, dining room,
bar, gun lockers, wi-fi
Credit cards AE, DC, MC, V
Children welcome **Disabled** access
possible to courtyard rooms
Pets accepted in 12 bedrooms
Closed Christmas Eve, Christmas
Day, Boxing Day
Proprietors Thomas and Cheryl
Robinson

The Rose and Crown
Country inn

The Rose and Crown was built in 1733
in this very pretty light stone village,
which owes its original layout to the
Saxons and its name to the patron saint of
the church. Recently refurbished by owners Thomas and Cheryl Robinson, this
place has gone from strength to strength.
It is set in the centre of the three-green
village. The bar is comfortingly traditional:
real ales, natural stone walls, log fire, old
photographs, copper and brass knick-
knacks. Excellent pub food is at the heart
of this inn, and can be enjoyed in either the
relaxed bar area or the charming oak-panelled room. The menu often features seasonal ingredients and organic produce.

There are seven comfortable bedrooms,
attractively decorated and furnished with
antiques, in the main building. Five more
have been added round the courtyard at
the back, and open directly on to it. Since
our last edition, the Monk's Cottage has
been opened to provide two extra bedrooms. It overlooks the Saxon church next
to the inn. This accommodation has an honesty bar and boot room – perfect for walkers.

Sheriff Hutton, North Yorkshire

High Sittenham, Sheriff Hutton,
York, North Yorkshire, YO60 7TW

Tel 01347 878386
e-mail
info@hallfarmhouseyork.co.uk
website
www.hallfarmhouseyork.co.uk

Nearby Bridlington, Robin Hood
Bay, Castle Howard, North
Yorkshire Moors, Scarborough and
Filey beaches, York, Whitby, Eden
Camp **Location** on a farm in the
Howardian Hills; ample parking
Food breakfast, evening meals on
request **Price** £-££
Rooms 3; 1 super-king/twin (also
has a sofa bed); 2 double. All have
bath/shower, TV, sofa, wi-fi,
hairdryer, coffee/tea facilities
Facilities on-site parking, lock up
facilities for bikes, garden
Credit cards cash or bank transfer
only **Children** welcome
Disabled not suitable
Pets dogs not allowed in main
house, but can sleep in porch/boot
room (£10 sur-charge)
Closed Jan (makes exceptions)
Proprietors Sally Hemingway

Hall Farm House
Bed-and-breakfast

North Yorkshire has a chilly reputation:
the North York Moors are bleak and
windswept, the Yorkshire Wolds to the
south a little less so, but still not exactly
cosy when the wind blows in from the
east. This Georgian farmhouse belies that
reputation, sitting on a hill between the
two in a relatively benign countryside, the
Howardian Hills Area of Outstanding
Natural Beauty. And once inside, the welcome is warm.

Owner Sally Hemingway goes out of
her way to make her guests feel at home
and have everything they need. Sally used
to be a chef, so the food is unusually good.
The full English breakfast is based on local
produce; croissants and muffins are home-
baked; jams and compotes are home-made
from berries grown in the garden; afternoon tea, with freshly baked cakes, scones
and biscuits is free. She will produce a
three-course dinner if asked in advance.

The bedrooms are individually decorated in fresh but neutral colours, mainly
creams and greys, with a few well judged
splashes of colour or pattern. A new garden bedroom, accessed from the garden, is
more extrovert.

The Ebor Way and Centenary Way long
distance trails go past the house, so this is
a walker's stopover as well as being convenient base for York and Castle Howard.

South Dalton, East Yorkshire

West End, South Dalton, Beverley,
East Yorkshire, HU17 7PN

Tel (01430) 810 246
e-mail email@pipeandglass.co.uk
website www.pipeandglass.co.uk

Nearby Dalton Estate, St Mary's
Church, Beverley Minster,
Location on the site of the original
gatehouse to Dalton Park, on edge
of the Yorkshire Wolds
Food breakfast (residents only),
lunch, dinner, afternoon
tea/savouries, Sunday lunch, chil-
drens menu **Price** £££-££££
Rooms 5; all have super king-size
bed, tea and coffee making facilities,
air-con, wi-fi, TV, radio, bathrobes,
Temple spa toiletries, hairdryer
Facilities restaurant, bar, garden,
private dining room
Credit cards AE, DC, MC, V
Children welcome
Disabled accessible restaurant, disabled toilet, one fully accessible
room **Pets** not allowed
Closed Mondays 2nd-17th Jan
Proprietors James and Kate
Mackenzie

The Pipe and Glass
Pub-with-rooms

The Pipe and Glass is based on a winning formula of rustic luxury: a cosy
country pub serving up Michelin food.
James Mackenzie (former head chef at The
Star at Harome, page 316) and his wife
Kate stress that it's first and foremost a
pub – so expect hearty pub classics at
their best, with an emphasis on local
flavours. This includes barbecued rump of
Yorkshire lamb, and Yorkshire rhubarb
with pistachio Bakewell tart (they're particularly good at puddings). Nor are they a
one-trick pony. Our hotel's editor, Fiona
Duncan, was especially impressed by their
five ground floor bedroom suites, individually decorated by local designer David
Bird. Bold patterned wallpapers combine
with sumptuous throws and walnut furniture make for a luxurious and comforting
effect. All the rooms are well-equipped,
and come with their own private garden
patios. You can also have breakfast in bed.

The main pub and private dining areas
have also been given the Bird treatment:
cosy sitting areas, open fires and soft pools
of lighting entice ramblers in from the
Yorkshire Wolds to warm their feet with a
pint. The pub's lack of pretension draws an
eclectic crowd: local drinkers mix with
smart diners who have driven some distance for the food, adding to the happy,
relaxed atmosphere.

17 Blosson Street, York, YO24 1QA

Tel 01904 643238
e-mail reception@bar-convent.org.uk **website** www.bar-convent.org.uk

Nearby York Minster, York Castle Museum, Yorkshire Museum, York city centre (1 km or less), York railway station (400 m) **Location** by the medieval gatehouse of Micklegate Bar, on the A1036 travelling E into York **Food** breakfast, light lunch, snacks, afternoon tea (book in advance) **Price** £-££ **Rooms** 20; 8 singles, 5 doubles, 5 twins, 2 triples; 16 have en-suite, 4 have shared bathroom; all have flat-screen TV, hairdryer, free wi-fi, tea/coffee making facilities **Facilities** sitting room, self-catering kitchen, garden, café, permanent exhibition, laundry **Credit cards** DC, MC, V **Children** welcome **Pets** guide dogs only **Disabled** there's a lift but some corridors may be unsuitable for wheelchairs **Closed** end of Dec to start of Jan, Easter **Proprietor** The Bar Convent Trust - James Foster (GM)

Bar Convent
City hotel

If you're looking for something different, the Bar Convent won't disappoint. It was founded in the 17thC by Frances Bedingfield as clandestine convent for the 'Ladies of the Bar', during a time of Tudor suppression. After a significant fundraising effort, it is now a 20-bedroom guesthouse, with a permanent exhibition celebrating its chequered past.

A Victorian winter garden sheltered by a glass roof is now the entrance hall, also accommodating the popular all-day café. A tangle of corridors and staircases lead up to the rooms, some with en-suites and some with shared bathrooms, offering great flexibility for single travellers and families alike. Two of the bedrooms, St Anna and St Joachim, are designed by famous hotelier Olga Polizzi, with tranquil blue and cream furnishings.

The white-and-gold Baroque chapel is a delight to the eyes, and the garden is a real oasis. Certainly no other place in York can offer the experience of staying in a Grade I-listed building where a Catholic order was founded, wounded soldiers were cared for during the war and where families and children were sheltered from persecution. Our series editor Fiona Duncan says: "As you might expect, it is memorable, tranquil and affordable; the sisters make Bar Convent a special place to stay."

Grays Court, Chapter House Street,
York YO1 7JH

Tel 01904 612613
e-mail office@grayscourtyork.com
website www.grayscourtyork.com

Nearby York Minster, St William's
College, Railway Museum, Jorvik
Viking Centre
Location Chapter House Street, off
St. Maurice's Road, car parking at
£15 per night
Food breakfast, lunch, dinner, after-
noon tea
Price ££££
Rooms 11 doubles, 1 can be twin, all
have bath/shower, with TV, safe,
tea/coffee facilities, telephone, wi-fi
Facilities The Bow Room
Restaurant, Long Gallery with bar,
function rooms, library, garden
Credit cards all major
Children welcome
Disabled no special facilities
Pets small dogs by prior arrange-
ment
Closed Christmas
Proprietor Helen Heraty

Grays Court
Town house hotel

We've never found a hotel in York that we liked enough for the guide but at last this could be it. Its strength is its young and enthusiastic staff, its hands-on owner Helen, and a wonderful old build-ing, which she lovingly converted with her late husband John.

You enter by a long, comfortable sitting room, with original 11thC walls forming one side. Above is a long, imposing gallery with wonderful oak panelling (not much enhanced by the hung pictures). There's a small bar at one end, and a peaceful sitting-room/library on the same floor. The com-fortable bedrooms have been done up in a classic style, mainly off-whites, with some show-stopper antiques in the mix, such as a William IV four poster bed (Willoughby room).

Before the hotel opened the building housed a tea shop, and there was some local opposition to its conversion. However, this has died down and they've compensated with their bountiful and popular afternoon tea open to non-resi-dents. A short, classic menu can be enjoyed in The Bow Room restuarant.

Since its opening the hotel has found its feet with an injection of atmosphere, and is on its way to becoming a real local gem. The location is good too, on a quiet street, with added peace and privacy from a small tree-lined courtyard for parking.

Area introduction

From the fertile southern uplands bordering England to the dramatic mountain ranges and sensational coasts of the Highlands and Islands, Scotland is varied and breathtakingly beautiful. Within a few hours' drive the scenery changes from gently rolling hills to craggy peaks. Visitors come to hike, climb, ski, play golf, fish, and to explore Scotland's fascinating historical heritage and lively cultural life. People describe Scotland as being either 'Lowland' or 'Highland'. The lowlands, which are not all low, lie south of a line drawn between Glasgow and Edinburgh. The Highlands, though not all high, are north of this line. Our selection includes converted castles, country manors, farmhouses and town houses. This edition has a number of interesting additions, thanks to the work of Jonathan Noble. Entries are indexed in alpha order by place name, regardless of whether they are on the mainland or on an island. *Below are some useful back-up places to try if our main selections are fully booked:*

One Devonshire Gardens Town hotel, Glasgow Tel 084473 64256
www.hotelduvin.co.uk
Glasgow's stylish Hotel du Vin in the leafy West End.

Ednam House Hotel Country house hotel, Kelso
Tel 01573 224168
www.ednamhouse.com
Traditional fishing hotel with great location on the Tweed.

Crolinnhe Bed-and-breakfast, Fort William Tel 01397 703795
www.crolinnhe.co.uk
Guesthouse with spectacular views of Loch Linnhe.

Dornoch Hotel Country hotel, Dornoch
Tel 01862 810351
www.bespokehotels.com
Overlooking Royal Dornoch Golf Course.

Closeburn, Dumfries and Galloway

Closeburn, Thornhill, Dumfries and
Galloway DG3 5EZ

Tel 01848 331211
e-mail info@trigonyhotel.co.uk
website www.trigonyhotel.co.uk

Nearby Drumlanrig Castle;
Caerlaverock Castle; Caerlaverock
Nature Reserve **Location** just north
of Closeburn before the village of
Thornhill; about 200 yards from the
main road. **Food** breakfast, lunch
Friday–Sunday, otherwise by reservation only **Price** ££-££££ **Rooms** 9;
4 doubles (2 can be twin), 4 superior
(3 can be twin), one garden suite
with heated conservatory and small
private garden; all have bath/shower,
TV, DVD and radio, hairdryer, tea
and coffee making facilities.
Facilities restaurant, gardens, bar,
terrace; activities include: falconry,
vintage car hire, land-rover safaris,
salmon fishing, spa **Credit cards**
MC, V **Children** welcome **Disabled**
no special facilities **Pets** dogs welcome **Closed** never **Proprietors**
Adam and Jan

Trigony House Hotel
Country bed-and-breakfast

Owners Adam and Jan bought Trigony
House Hotel 11 years ago after
deciding to quit the rat-race in York and
move to the Scottish countryside. They've
created a homely, family atmosphere
founded on simple, honest comforts.
Adam's food is a major draw. His unfussy
classic dishes can be enjoyed in the informal bar or the slightly more formal restaurant, both with cosy wood-burning stoves.

Inside and out, it's what you would
expect of a former Edwardian shooting
lodge: understated and handsome, ivy
creeps up the exterior and a large trim
front garden is perfect for dogs. The interiors don't try too hard and suit the building; muted colours are used throughout
for understated ambience and the whole
building is well maintained and a perfect
size for the operation. The Garden Spa is a
recent addition; kitted out with a Swedish
hot tub and sauna cabin, it offers a selection of pampering holistic treatments.

Although tucked away in the countryside, there are lots of things to do. Adam
and Jan have a wealth of suggestions for
the area and often arrange things to do
nearby and in the grounds. One of our
favourite activities was driving around the
winding Scottish country roads in a hired
vintage Austin 14. Low-key walks and
cycling routes are on hand, too.

Cupar, Fife KY15 5LH

Tel 01334 840206
Fax 01334 84053
e-mail stay@thepeatinn.co.uk
website www.thepeatinn.co.uk

Nearby Edinburgh; Piscottie; St
Andrews; golf courses; Dundee;
Perthshire; East Neuk; Falkland
Palace; The Secret Bunker **Location**
from the B940 and 941 follow signs
to the village of Peat Inn – in prominent position with parking **Food**
breakfast, lunch and dinner
Tuesday–Saturday inclusive
Price £££-££££
Rooms 8; double and family suites
Facilities private garden, restaurant,
safe, parking **Credit cards** AE, MC,
V **Children** welcome; under fives
are free, over fives: supplement for
sofa bed. Cots and high chairs available **Disabled** easy access to public
areas and an adaptable ground-floor
bedroom **Pets** not accepted
Closed Sun-Mon, Christmas and 10
days at the beginning of Jan
Proprietors Geoffrey and Katherine
Smeddle

The Peat Inn
Restaurant-with-rooms

This restaurant-with-rooms, a former
17thC coaching inn, has had a sterling
reputation for more than 30 years.
Originally owned by renowned chef David
Wilson, it was taken over in 2006 by
Geoffrey Smeddle and his wife Katherine,
who are, according to one guest 'creating
something quite special'.

A warm, professional welcome is
ensured by Katherine and the front of
house team, but the food is the big draw
here. Geoffrey's dishes, which use only the
best local and seasonal produce, are rack-
ing up awards. Typical dishes include
poached longoustines with coriander and
satay sauce, honey-glazed duck breast and
hot strawberry soufflé. This award-winning
restaurant isn't intimidating, though: it's
split into three small areas, which, helped by the
service, create a friendly, intimate atmosphere.

Upstairs, the eight suites are each individually designed, with the bedroom and
living room set on two separate levels and
bathrooms finished with Italian marble.
Carpets are deep, fabrics are rich, and
towels are thick and fluffy. Continental
breakfast (home-made, of course) is
served in your suite at a preferred time –
a touch that might feel intrusive to some,
decadent to others. It's almost impossible
to find any fault with this place.

15 Woodside Place, Glasgow G3 7QL

Tel 0141 332 1263
e-mail rooms@15Glasgow.com
website www.15glasgow.com

Nearby art galleries; all major attractions; shopping; bars; restaurants. **Location** city centre, in green area a 10 minute walk to city and West End attractions; free car-parking available on request
Food breakfast
Price ££
Rooms 5; 3 double (1 can be a twin), 2 suites, all have bath/shower, bath robes, TV, hairdryer, tea/coffee
Facilities guest sitting room, DVD collection, access to residents garden
Credit cards MC, V
Children welcome
Disabled not suitable
Pets not accepted
Closed Christmas
Proprietor Lorraine Gibson

15Glasgow

City bed-and-breakfast

Situated in a terrace of large, confident Victorian terrace houses near the city centre, 15Glasgow was converted from offices into a B&B in 2009 by Shane and Laura McKenzie, and taken on by Lorraine Gibson in 2016. She's made a few changes (the rooms now have Scottish themed names, such as Tartan, Thistle and Heather) but the period features – original shutters, fireplaces, ceilings – are preserved, alongside a tasteful, design-led style. The rooms are spacious, with swish bathrooms and underfloor heating. The Charles Rennie Mackintosh Suite, the original first floor reception room of the house, is enormous, stunning whatever your taste, with feminine touches of pink, and three floor-length sash windows overlooking the private garden – and priced at a friendly £150 a night in peak season.

Breakfast is delicious, and served in the spacious ground floor sitting room or brought to your bedroom. There's a good amount of choice, with gems such as clementine-and-whisky marmalade, as well as the full Scottish, complete with haggis.

With its West End location and good value, Lorraine offers a great alternative to staying in a Glasgow hotel.

Heiton by Kelso, Roxburghshire

Heiton by Kelso, Roxburghshire,
TD5 8JZ

Tel 01573 450331
e-mail hotel@roxburghe.net
website www.roxburghe.net

Nearby the Roxburghe Estate and
Floors Castle; The Roxburghe Golf
Course; Melrose Abbey; Abbotsford
Location on the Roxburghe Estate
just outside the village of Heiton, 4
miles from Kelso
Food breakfast, lunch, dinner, afternoon tea
Price £££-££££
Rooms 22; all rooms en suite, some
rooms have log fires, all have
flatscreen TV, iPod stations, wi-fi, a
selection of books, hospitality tray
Facilities drawing room, library,
dining room, conservatory, terrace,
private function room
Credit cards AE, MC, V
Children welcome
Disabled 3 ground-floor rooms,
easy access **Pets** welcome **Closed**
never **Proprietor** Duke and Duchess
of Roxburghe

The Roxburghe

Country house hotel

The Roxburghe, under general manager
Niall Keddy for the Duke of Roxburghe,
shows all those personal touches that we
love in privately owned estate hotels.

It's a typically solid Victorian house,
scented by wood smoke and whisky. There
are open fires, tartan carpets, tables piled
with books, and family photographs and
portraits. The drawing room, in particular,
owes everything to a combination of the
Duke and Duchess of Roxburghe, and a
particularly sensitive designer.

The bedrooms are just right too, in classic country house style. Though our room
was hardly trendy, it had character in
spades. A fire crackling in a freestanding
grate (logs in the basket, coal delivered on
request), completed the happy mood. Our
one criticism of the decoration is the oddly
bleak arrangement of furniture on the wide
first-floor landing.

It's also an ideal sporting hotel. Riding,
golf on a championship course, fly fishing
and clay-pigeon shooting (both with
renowned experts) are all close and at discounted prices. World-class salmon fishing
is possible on prime beats of the Tweed
and the Teviot. Even when bad weather
might make your visit seem in vain, the
Roxburghe's charms can make the journey
seem worthwhile.

Kilberry, Argyll

Kilberry, Argyll PA29 6YD

Tel (01880) 770 223
e-mail relax@kilberryinn.com
website www.kilberryinn.com

Nearby secluded beaches, distilleries, ferries to the surrounding islands
Location on the B8024 between Tarbert and Lochgilphead
Food breakfast, lunch, dinner
Price ££
Rooms 5 double with shower; all rooms have TV, hairdryer, tea and coffee, books
Facilities restaurant
Credit cards MC, V
Children over 12 welcome
Disabled access to restaurant and 1 bedroom
Pets dogs accepted by arrangement
Closed Dec-Mar
Proprietors Clare Johnson and David Wilson

The Kilberry Inn
Restaurant-with-rooms

This traditional whitewashed, red-roofed 'but'n'ben' cottage had long been run as an inn before David Wilson and chef Clare Johnson, who used to run the renowned Anchorage Seafood Restaurant in the nearby fishing village of Tarbert, took it on and set about transforming it into a modern restaurant with rooms. Gone is the former cluttered, rustic, 'twee' look. It has been replaced with minimal and contemporary decoration, with cosy log fires, beams and quarried stone-walls, hung with art from local painters. The inn has five comfortable, tastefully decorated double bedrooms with showers, in adjacent buildings.

The focus in the restaurant is on fresh, locally produced ingredients – crab, lobster, langoustine, scallops and fish are all caught within a few miles of the inn, and meat is all reared nearby. Dinner might be potted Kilberry crab, followed by Sound of Jura monkfish with pepperonata and piquillo pepper dressing, then Isle of Mull cheddar with biscuits and chutney to finish.

The inn is situated on a remote single track road on the Kintyre peninsula, with stunning views of the surrounding lochs and islands, and David thinks this remoteness makes arriving an adventure in itself. Reports welcome.

Kirkcolm, Dumfries and Galloway

Corsewall Point, Kirkcolm,
Stranraer, Dumfries and Galloway
DG9 0QG

Tel (01776)853220
Fax (01776) 854231
e-mail info@lighthousehotel.co.uk
website www.lighthousehotel.co.uk

Nearby Stranraer – ferry to Ireland,
Loch Ryan, Iron Age fort, pony-
trekking, golf.
Location remote; in own grounds
with ample private car parking, air
transfer arrangeable.
Food breakfast, lunch, dinner
Price ££
Rooms 10; 6 doubles, 4 suites, some
can be twin-bedded; all rooms have
phone, TV, DVD, hairdryer
Facilities 2 sitting rooms, restau-
rant, 20-acre grounds
Credit cards AE, MC, V
Children accepted
Disabled 1 accessible room
Pets allowed in 2 of the suites
Closed never
Proprietor Kay F Ward and Pamela
Stevenson

Corsewall Lighthouse
Lighthouse hotel

Remote – the last mile is down a track –
on a windswept promontory north of
Stranraer, this is a listed, 200-year old working lighthouse. The tower itself isn't part of
the hotel, but the structure at its foot, the
former lighthouse keeper's dwelling, houses
the restaurant, public areas and some of the
rooms. Other accommodation, including
the suites, are in separate buildings, none
more than three minutes from the hub.

Guests come here for a unique and
romantic experience, the generally light
rooms and dramatic seascapes, but not for
style. It's mostly done out comfortably, but
in a conventional, unpretentious way – you could
hardly be anywhere else but a hotel. Some
of the smaller rooms may not please perfec-
tionists – but bear in mind it's an old building.

The food ('tremendous' says a reporter)
wins general approval. Service is thoughtful
and the welcome personal. 'Truly magical'
says one reporter of their experience
there. 'Nothing beats going out after dinner
to walk the shore and hear the waves
exploding on the rocks' says another.
Porpoise, seals and basking sharks can be
seen off the coast. To climb the lighthouse
tower you need permission in writing from
the Northern Lighthouse Board. Reports
welcome.

Burts Hotel
Melrose, Scottish Borders TD6 9PL

Tel 01896 822285
e-mail enquiries@burtshotel.co.uk
website www.burtshotel.co.uk

Food breakfast, lunch dinner
Price £-££
Closed 6-12 Feb (2018)
Proprietors Henderson family

The Townhouse Hotel
Melrose, Scottish Borders TD6 9PQ

Tel 01896 822645
e-mail enquiries@thetownhouse-melrose.co.uk **website** www.thetownhousemelrose.co.uk

Food breakfast, lunch dinner
Price £-££
Closed 6-12 Feb (2018)
Proprietors Henderson family

Burts Hotel

Town hotel

Unusually for a Scottish border town, pleasant Melrose appeals to all sorts of visitor – it offers walking and fishing, as well as shopping, museums and Melrose Abbey. Similarly, the Hendersons' two places to stay, standing opposite each other in the town centre, accommodate a range of visitors' needs.

Burts (top) is secure in its reputation as a fishing hotel with great atmosphere. Jolly flowers tumbling out of every window at the front prepare you for an unstuffy atmosphere within. Upstairs, bedroom walls are decorated in an earthy range of colours, while a lively variety of fabrics and patterns in each room add bolder colours (four have been recently refurbished). Be sure to book dinner in advance, as the bistro is popular with locals – 'the hottest seats in town' we are told.

The Townhouse (bottom left) departs from the country sports ethos of its sister hotel. The rooms are similarly bold – intensely patterned walls, cushions and sofas, but more ambitious in colour scheme and size. Young city dwellers seeking a contemporary, uncluttered ambience will feel more comfortable here.

The menu offers local produce (as at Burt's), and is elegantly served, but we were underwhelmed by the drinking area in the lean-to conservatory at the back.

Portpatrick, Dumfries and Galloway

Portpatrick, Dumfries & Galloway
DG9 9AD

Tel (01776) 810471
Fax (01776) 810435
e-mail reservations@knockinaam-lodge.com
website www.knockinaamlodge.com

Nearby Logan; Ardwell and Glenwhan Gardens; Castle Kennedy.
Location 3 miles (5 km) SE of Portpatrick, off A77; in grounds; ample car parking
Food breakfast, lunch, dinner
Price ££££
Rooms 10; 3 double with bath, 7 double with bath and walk-in shower; all rooms have phone, TV, video and hairdryer **Facilities** 2 sitting rooms, bar, dining room; garden, croquet, helipad
Credit cards AE, MC, V
Children welcome
Disabled public rooms accessible (no ground-floor bedrooms)
Pets accepted, but not in public rooms
Closed never
Proprietor David Ibbotson

Knockinaam Lodge
Country hotel

Galloway is very much an area for escaping the hurly-burly, and Knockinaam Lodge complements it perfectly (as well as being the ideal staging post for anyone bound for the ferry at Stranraer to Northern Ireland). Succeeding proprietors of the Lodge have had a reputation for fine food and warm hospitality, and the tradition is still maintained with the help of an enthusiastic staff and the present owner, David Ibbotson.

The house, a low Victorian villa, was built as a hunting lodge in 1869 and extended at the turn of the century. It was used by Sir Winston Churchill as a secret location in which to meet General Eisenhower during the Second World War. The rooms are cosy in scale and furnishings, the bedrooms varying from the stylishly simple to the quietly elegant. A key part of the appeal of the place is its complete seclusion – down a wooded glen, with lawned garden running down to a sandy beach. Children are welcome, and well catered for, with special high teas.

Since taking over in 2003, David has brightened up the place considerably, completely redecorating, as well as turning his attention to the grounds and painting the exterior. The restaurant now has a Michelin star, and the wine list has more than 540 bins.

Sanquhar, Dumfries and Galloway

Sanquhar, Dumfries and Galloway,
DG4 6JJ

Tel (01659) 50270
e-mail ian@blackaddiehotel.co.uk
website www.blackaddiehotel.co.uk

Nearby Drumlanrig Castle 8 miles;
Dumfries House 18 miles; Dumfries
28 miles; Kilmarnock 30 miles; Ayr
32 miles **Location** on the banks of
the River Nith, just outside the village of Sanquhar
Food lunch and afternoon tea
(booking required), dinner (no booking required)
Price ££-££££
Rooms 7; all double, 3 can be twin,
2 are suites; all have wi-fi, tea and
coffee facilities, homemade shortbread, HD TV
Facilities restaurant, garden
Credit cards AE, MC, V
Children welcome
Disabled 1 suitable self-catering
cottage with a ramp up to the front
door and an extra large bathroom
Pets accepted, £10 surcharge
Closed never
Proprietor Ian McAndrew

Blackaddie House
Country hotel

Husband and wife Ian and Jane
McAndrew bought Blackaddie back in
2007. Since then, they have worked tirelessly to refurbish the property and now offer
seven bedrooms – of which two are classed
as suites – and two self-catering cottages.
The Grouse Suite, which is the largest of all
the rooms, has a jacuzzi and king-sized four-
poster bed. The River Suite features a set of
French windows that lead out on to the
patio, where you can sit by the River Nith as
it flows through the end of the garden.

Jane's detailed knowledge of the area
includes suggestions for some great walking
routes, not least Mennock Pass to
Wenlockhead, which is only a short drive
away. Ian, who is also the head chef, creates
some fabulously presented dishes using
locally sourced ingredients. The menu
changes daily and includes a locally famed
seven course tasting menu with matching
wines. Ian was the youngest British chef to
be awarded a Michelin star in 1980 and was
crowned Scottish Chef of the Year in 2016:
the food is that good.

If you're not too full after dinner, retire to
the bar – where there's a choice of single
malt whiskies – and relax by the log fire. Ian,
a chatty and affable man who loves to meet
his punters, can often be found mingling with
guests in the bar when the kitchen closes.

Edinburgh

Castlehill, The Royal Mile,
Edinburgh EH1 2NF

Tel (0131) 225 5613
Fax (0131) 220 4392
e-mail mail@thewitchery.com
website www.thewitchery.com
Food breakfast, lunch, dinner
Price ££££
Closed never
Proprietor James Thomson

The Witchery by the Castle **Restaurant-with-rooms**

It takes its name from the hundreds of witches burned at the stake nearby, but The Witchery by the Castle is, thankfully, not macabre. However, it is gothic and, above all, luxurious. It occupies a pair of 16thC buildings at the gates of Edinburgh Castle. Entering from a close off the Royal Mile, candle-light reveals painted ceilings and walls covered in tapestries and 17thC oak panelling rescued from a fire at St Giles Cathedral.

Suites, either above the restaurant or in an adjacent building, are plush and opulent, with antiques, historic paintings and dramatic colour schemes, and have views towards the Old Town or over the Royal Mile.

You can eat either in the award-winning restaurant of the same name; in the Secret Garden; or in The Tower.

Gullane, East Lothian

Muirfield, Gullane, East Lothian
EH31 2EG

Tel 01620 842144
Fax 01620 8422412
e-mail enquiries@greywalls.co.uk
website www.greywalls.co.uk
Food breakfast, lunch, dinner, afternoon tea **Price** ££££
Closed Jan to Feb
Proprietor ICMI Management

Greywalls
Country house hotel

Greywalls is a slick, expensive country house hotel, with – by our standards – quite a large number of bedrooms, but despite this we cannot resist including such a distinctive place. It is a classic turn-of-the-century house, and for golf enthusiasts – it overlooks the tenth green of the famous Muirfield championship course.

The feel of Greywalls is very much one of a gracious private house, although series editor Fiona Duncan felt it would have been cosier were it still family-run.

Dinner, served in a room overlooking the golf course, is superb – it's one of Albert Roux's Chez Roux outposts. Bedrooms are attractive and well-equipped, particularly those in the original house rather than the new wing.

Jedburgh, Roxburghshire

Jedburgh, Roxburghshire TD8 6PA

Tel (01835) 863011
e-mail
sheila.whittaker@btinternet.com
website www.accommodation-scot-
land.org
Food breakfast **Price** £
Closed Nov-Mar
Proprietors Mr and Mrs Whittaker

Hundalee House
Bed-and-breakfast

Set back in the hills, this 18thC limestone manor house has been home to the Whittakers for a decade. They created the fine large garden, putting in flowering shrubs, adding peacocks and digging a pond for koi carp. Inside, the taste is even more exotic, reflecting their time in Egypt. Egyptian motifs hang on the walls and Egyptian hounds guard the fireplace in the sitting room, which has fine views of the Cheviot Hills to the south. Bedrooms may not be luxurious but one has a four-poster bed. Two others share a bathroom; these offer notable value and are useful for a family. Sheila Whittaker does not serve dinner, but her breakfasts are 'cooked and copious,' according to one teenage visitor.

Auldearn, Nairn

Auldearn, Nairn, IV12 5TE

Tel (01667) 454896
Fax (01667) 455469
e-mail info@boath-house.com
website www.boath-house.com

Nearby Inverness, Nairn, Loch Ness, Balmoral Castle
Location off A96, near Nairn, ample parking
Food lunch, dinner, afternoon tea (served to guests and non-residents)
Price ££££
Rooms 8, all with bath/shower
Facilities 2 sitting rooms, restaurant; golf, fishing, riding, clay shooting all available nearby
Credit Cards MC, V
Children welcome
Disabled one ground floor cottage, restaurant is accessible
Pets accepted by arrangement
Closed never
Proprietors Don and Wendy Matheson

Boath House Hotel
Country House Hotel

This Grade A listed Georgian mansion was standing derelict until Don and Wendy Matheson found and fell in love with it in the early Nineties. Having restored the house to its former glory the Mathesons decided to open their home to guests, and have since made a great success of it.

Boath House has eight guest bedrooms, all individually decorated in rich colours in a mix of contemporary and traditional styles. All have private bathrooms, and two have four poster beds. It stands in 20 acres of grounds, including a 2-acre lake and Victorian walled garden.

The kitchen gardens provide many of the ingredients served in the award-winning restaurant, which ushers in guests and non-residents alike. Charlie Lockley is head chef, and the focus is on organic, locally–produced and seasonal food. Local seafood is delivered daily, and meat and cheese come from a nearby farm. Wild food items, such as wild mushrooms and herbs, are also on the menu when in season, and even honey comes from the hotel's own hives – organic food is a real passion here.

The Mathesons are keen to foster a friendly, informal atmosphere and want their home to be "somewhere guests can relax and feel at ease", despite the grandeur of the house. We have heard great things about Boath House. Reports welcome.

Balquhidder, Lochearnhead,
Perthshire FK19 8PQ

Tel (01877) 384622
e-mail monachyle@mhor.net
website monachylemhor.net

Nearby in the heart of Rob Roy
country.
Location on private estate; turn off
A84, 11 miles (17.5 km) N of
Callander at Kingshouse Hotel, then
follow single-track lane for 6 miles
(9.5 km); well-signposted; ample car-
parking
Food breakfast, lunch, dinner
Price ££-££££
Rooms 16 double, all with bath or
shower; all rooms have phone, TV,
hairdryer. Also The Cabin (sleeps 4)
with own kitchen, and The Wagon
(sleeps 4)
Facilities sitting room, bar, restaurant; terrace, garden, fishing, stalk-
ing **Credit cards** MC, V
Children well behaved children
accepted over 12
Disabled access easy
Pets accepted in 2 rooms
Closed Jan **Proprietors** Tom Lewis

Monachyle Mhor
Farmhouse hotel

A small, family-run farmhouse with a
charm all its own. The setting is both
serene and romantic: this was the home of
Rob Roy MacGregor, approached along
the Braes of Balquhidder and set beside
Lochs Doine and Voil.

Rob and Jean Lewis came here in 1983
from Monmouth to farm the 2,000-acre
estate, later opening it as a hotel. When
they moved to the South of France, their
enterprising son Tom took over and
expanded the buisness. There's now a total
of 16 rooms spread across the main house,
Courtyard and Farmhouse, all very stylishly
decorated with a medley of bold modernist
strokes and well-chosen antiques. The
Cabin and The Wagon – a 1950s Pilot
Panther wagon restored by artist Sarah
Kechington – are available for glamping.
Tom's unstoppable empire now includes a
fish shop, bakery, Mhor to Your Door (a
mobile restaurant) and Mhor 84 – a road-
side gastropub with seven rooms.

The award-winning restaurant takes
'locally sourced' to another level, shooting
the lamb, pork, venison and game on-site,
and foraging much of their vegetables and
herbs. It's situated in a light and airy conservatory overlooking the two lochs.

For a relaxing, country break in magnificent scenery and with memorable food,
Monachyle Mhor would be hard to beat.

Brachla, Loch Ness-Side, IV3 8LA

Tel 01456 459469
Fax 01456 459439
e-mail escape@loch-ness-lodge.com
website www.loch-ness-lodge.com

Nearby Loch Ness, Culloden, Isle of Skye, Glen Affric National Nature Reserve **Location** from Inverness follow signs for A82 Fort William/Loch Ness Road, Lodge is on the right after approximately 9 miles
Food breakfast
Price £££-££££
Rooms 7 double with flat screen TV and DVD, CD player, direct dial telephones
Facilities drawing room, spa, garden, wi-fi throughout
Credit cards AE, MC, V
Children welcome (over 12)
Disabled access possible
Pets not accepted
Closed Jan
Proprietor Scott Sutherland

Loch Ness Lodge
Highland bed-and-breakfast

Located just a stone's throw from the waters edge, this B&B offers unrivalled views across Loch Ness and the hills beyond. The lodge sits in its own cultivated gardens and acts as an ideal setting-off point to explore the surrounding highlands.

The emphasis at Loch Ness Lodge is on understated indulgence: it seems that nothing is too much for the staff (who will even provide you with satnav details for your excursions). Although dinner is no longer offered, the team are more than happy to recommend (and book) a restaurant nearby.

Breakfast is wide ranging and often centres on locally-sourced ingredients. The complimentary afternoon tea, with a variety of loose-leaf teas and home-made bakes, was a welcome addition and has proved popular with the regular guests.

Our room was particularly spacious, simply decorated in muted colours with dark wood furnishings, and came complete with sherry and our own view of the Loch – a luxury shared by all seven rooms.

Castle Street, Dornoch, Sutherland,
IV25 3SN

Tel 01862 811811
e-mail web@2quail.com
website www.2quail,com

Nearby Royal Dornoch Golf Course
and Club.
Location north of Inverness, en-
route to or from the Orkneys
Food breakfast, dinner (by prior
arrangment)
Price ££-£££
Rooms 3; all with bathrooms
Facilities library/lounge
Credit Cards AE, MC, V
Children not under 10
Disabled no access available
Pets not accepted
Closed never
Proprietors Michael and Kerensa
Carr

2 Quail
Town bed-and-breakfast

An exceptional B&B, and our only one in these parts. Dornoch, on the east coast of Scotland, north of Inverness, is a stopping point on the way to the far north and the Orkneys. It is also home to one of the largest golf courses in the world, but this unusual B&B should attract guests on its own merits.

When we stepped inside 2 Quail, a sandstone terraced house in the heart of town, we felt as though we had entered a time warp. Much of the furniture – dainty, brown and cream upholstered armchairs, lamps with fringed sides – are family pieces. The residence is neat and furnished in a way that says 'Edwardian' or '40s' or somewhere in between; idiosyncratic, well executed and refreshingly different. There are three bedrooms. Ours was soberly furnished, yet arresting, with its wrought iron bedstead and comfortable mattress.

Owners Kerensa and Micheal Carr used to run a tiny but well-regarded restaurant. After a spell of nearly seven years as head chef at the Royal Dornoch Golf Club Michael is now back cooking at 2 Quail, tailoring a two-three course set dinner to his guests. It's essentially a private dining experience with a professional edge, and a menu that might include baked cheese and chive soufflé followed by loin of venison with parsnips and a juniper port gravy.

Elgol, Isle of Skye

Elgol, Isle of Skye, IV49 9BL

Tel 01471 866330
e-mail info@coruiskhouse.com
website www.coruiskhouse.com

Nearby Bonnie Prince Charlie's
cave, boat trips take you to Loch
Coruisk, islands of Rum and Canna,
Cuillins, Neolithic settlements
Location Elgol village, 13 miles
down a single track road from
Broadford **Food** breakfast, dinner
Price ££-££££
Rooms 2 en-suites and 2 large suites
(one suite=2 adjoining doubles). All
have king-size beds, bathrooms,
hairdryer, tea/coffee facilities, fresh
fruit, bathrobes, White Company
toiletries.
Facilities parking, bar, sitting room
with wood burning stove and TV
Credit Cards all major except AE
Children uner 14s not allowed
Disabled not suitable
Pets not allowed **Closed** Christmas,
New Year, 20 Oct-28 Feb
Proprietors Clare Winskill and Iain
Roden

Coruisk House
Restaurant-with-rooms

On the wilder side of the 'dinosaur isle'
of Scotland (named for the fossils
and footprints discovered here), Coruisk
House can be found at the the end of a 13-
mile single track, running through the most
spectacular scenery in the Highlands. In
Clare and Iain's cosy and informal restaurant, guests choose from a short but sublime menu that lets the local ingredients
sing: shellfish such as langoustines, lobsters
and hand-dived scallops are served with
their perfectly appointed wine list, and an
array of Highland malt whiskeys and gins
(give advance notice for a delicious vegetarian option). Food writer Hattie Ellis
called this 'the best food on Skye', but perhaps the greatest testament to this tiny
restaurant on a far-flung isle is a booking
list stretching months in advance.

The five bedrooms are perfectly hygge
little havens, with sheepskin rugs and duck-
down bedding, and views across the Sound
of Sleat. Guests are welcomed into the
couple's embracing hospitality with a glass
of prosecco on arrival, and breakfasts that
include peat-smoked salmon, Scottish pancakes and homemade compotes.

And Skye's the limit when it comes to
activities: catch a boat from Elgol harbour
(where Bonnie Prince Charlie fled in 1745)
into the spectacular Loch Coruisk, to spot
orcas, puffins and golden eagles.

Fort William, Inverness-shire

Glenfinnan, Fort William,
Inverness-shire, PH37 4LT

Tel 01397 722235
e-mail availability@glenfinnan-
house.com
website www.glenfinnanhouse.com

Nearby Ben Nevis, Glenfinnan
viaduct railway bridge, Shiel Cruises,
Glenfinnan Monument, Fort
William, Highland activities.
Location pass through Fort William
and turn off the A82 to follow the
A830 'Road to the Isles', west for 15
miles to Glenfinnan. Turn left just
after the Glenfinnan Monument
Visitor Centre
Food breakfast, dinner, bar food
Price ££-£££ **Rooms** 12 including
some suites and family rooms
Facilities drawing room, playroom,
garden, function/wedding facilities,
bar, dining room **Credit Cards** AE,
MC, V **Children** welcome **Disabled**
no access **Pets** not accepted in
restaurant **Closed** beginning of Nov
to Mid-Mar
Proprietors Jane Macfarlane
Managers Manja & Duncan Gibson

Glenfinnan
Country house hotel

The owners of Glenfinnan House Hotel clearly value family time. That perhaps explains why children are so readily welcomed, why the hotel operates a no-TV policy, and why dogs are well and truly smothered when they stay. Rooms are comfortable rather than inventive, but the real charm lies elsewhere.

Chef/manager Duncan produces some outstanding things from the kitchen, using fine local produce such as salmon, mussels, beef or venison; some of his classic dishes, as well as various innovative options from the *a la carte* menu, can be enjoyed in both the dining room and the bar.

Most important, this is inspiring, mountainous country which adults and kids will love (the latter will enjoy the chance to visit famous scenes from the Harry Potter films). Loch Shiel cruises operate from nearby, with regular sightings of golden eagles, black-throated divers and red deer. In season, trips slightly further afield often bring you face-to-face with whales, dolphins, seals, puffins and otters.

Some reports suggest that staff can be a little over-zealous, but this can be explained by an earnest effort to keep things running smoothly; the consensus is that they know their stuff here, and do things rather well.

Fort William, Inverness-shire

Grange Road, Fort William,
Inverness-shirePH33 6JF

Tel (01397) 705516
Fax (01397) 701595
e-mail info@grangefortwilliam.com
website www.grangefortwilliam.com

Nearby Ben Nevis; 'Road to the
Isles'; Loch Ness. **Location** on outskirts; from town centre take A82
direction Glasgow, then turn left
into Ashburn Lane; hotel is at top on
left; ample car parking **Food** breakfast, tea and shortbread served on
arrival **Price** £££
Rooms 1 Superior Terrace Suite,
with lounge, king-size bed, french
doors leading to patio; 1 Garden
Suite; all rooms have bath/shower,
tea/coffee making facilities
 Facilities breakfast room, sitting
room; garden, sea loch close by
Credit cards by arrangement
Children not accepted **Disabled**
access difficult **Pets** not accepted
Closed mid-Nov to Easter
Proprietors Joan and John
Campbell

The Grange
Bed-and-breakfast

We were delighted to discover this outstanding bed-and-breakfast establishment on the outskirts of Fort William,
run with great flair by Joan and John
Campbell. A ten-minute walk from the fairly charmless town centre brings you to this
late Victorian house, set in pretty terraced
grounds overlooking Loch Linnhe. There's
the option of staying in the Terrace Suite in
the main building, or in their new Garden
Suite – both offering the visitor tranquil
privacy with lovely views over the garden
and Loch Linnhe.

A feminine touch is distinctly in evidence in the immaculate interior, which is
decorated with admirable taste and a flair
for matching fabrics with furnishings and
fittings. First glimpsed, you might expect a
stand-offish 'don't touch' approach from
the owners, but nothing could be further
from the truth at the Grange. Joan
Campbell, responsible for the decoration,
is naturally easy-going, with a great sense
of hospitality.

Both suites are superbly, and individually, decorated and furnished, their bathrooms lavish and luxurious – it all comes
as rather a surprise. A delightful place.

Harrapool, Isle of Skye

13 Harrapool, Isle of Skye IV49 9AQ

Tel 01471 820022
e-mail hopeskye@btinternet.com
website www.skyebedbreakfast.co.uk

Nearby Harrapool, Broadford, Eilean Donan Castle, Clan Donald centre, Broadford Bay, Broadford harbour, Elgol & Cuillins.
Location in Harrapool, off the A87
Food breakfast; evening meal available on request
Price £-££
Rooms 3 double, all with underfloor heating.
Facilities free wi-fi, sitting room, dining area, gardens, stretch of beach
Credit cards MC, V
Children welcome, but cots, highchairs etc not provided.
Disabled not suitable
Pets not accepted
Closed rarely
Proprietors Neil Hope and Lesley Unwin

Tigh An Dochais
Island bed-and-breakfast

Tigh An Dochais stands on a narrow strip of land overlooking Broadford Bay. It's not what immediately springs to mind when picturing a Skye B&B. Designed in 2005 by award-winning architects, it is completely contemporary: all plate glass and slate. The first-floor entrance is reached by a small wooden bridge. Stained larchwood lines the walls.

Inside, floor-to-ceiling glazing lets in the light and the landscape. Every room in the house overlooks the bay, and the views here are so stunning there's little need for further decoration: things are kept simple and uncluttered, except perhaps for a few traditional touches. Tartan fabric brightens up the bedrooms (a fair size, and with underfloor heating), and the booklined sitting room – with a part-glazed, gabled ceiling – is warmed by a log-burning stove and filled with squishy red sofas.

Breakfast is cooked by Neil, and is good old-fashioned fare. It's eaten with the other guests around the large breakfast table, which overlooks yet another breathtaking view. You can take on a full Scottish or sample the home-made bread, muffins and yoghurt: we've heard all are lovely.

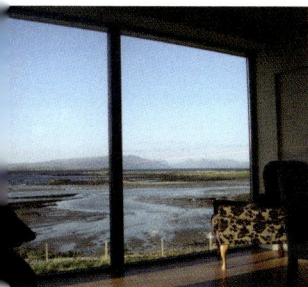

Isle of Eriska, Argyll

Isle of Eriska, Ledaig, Oban, Argyll
PA37 1SD

Tel (01631) 720371
Fax (01631) 720531
e-mail office@eriska-hotel.co.uk
website www.eriska-hotel.co.uk

Nearby Oban; Isle of Mull; Inverary
Castle; Glencoe.
Location on private island connected by road bridge; from Connel take
A828 toward Fort William for 4
miles (6 km) to N of Benderloch village, then follow signs; ample car
parking **Food** breakfast, lunch, dinner
Price ££££ **Rooms** 16 in main house
(deluxe and standard); 6 Hilltop
Reserves; 2 self-catering cottages
(each with 3 bedrooms) **Facilities** 3
drawing rooms, bar/library, dining
room, indoor swimming pool, gym,
sauna, garden; 6-hole golf course,
driving range, tennis court, croquet,
clay-pigeon shooting **Credit cards**
AE, MC, V **Children** welcome
Disabled access possible (2 adapted
ground floor rooms) **Pets** accepted
Closed Jan **Proprietors** ICMI
Management

Isle of Eriska Hotel
Island mansion

A splendid hotel that has the twin
advantages of seclusion, since it is set
on its own remote island, and accessibility:
it is connected to the mainland by a short
road bridge. And for those who like to keep
themselves occupied during their stay, its
leisure centre, which includes a magnificent
17-metre heated swimming pool, and its
sporting opportunities, will appeal.

Built in 1884 in grey granite and warmer
red sandstone, in Scottish Baronial style,
the hotel is a reminder of a more expansive and confident era. If it reminds you in
feel, if not in appearance, of Balmoral, you
will not be surprised to learn that the
original wallpaper on the first-floor landing
is also found in the royal castle. In fact the
experience of staying here is very much
like being in an old-fashioned grand private
house, comfortable rather than stylish,
with a panelled great hall, and roaring log
fires and chintz fabrics much in evidence.
In the library-cum-bar you can browse
through the books with a malt whisky in
hand, while excellent six-course dinners
are served in the stately dining room. The
handsome bedrooms vary in size and out-
look. In 2016 the hotel changed hands
from the Buchanan-Smith family to ICMI
Management: we'd be interested to hear
reports on whether the same spirit abides.

Isle Ornsay, Sleat, Isle of Skye
IV43 8QR

Tel (01471) 833332
Fax (01471) 833275
e-mail hotel@eileaniarmain.co.uk

Nearby Clan Donald Centre; Aros
Heritage Centre; Dunvegan Castle.
Location on water's edge, on estate
between Broadford and Armadale in
the S of the island, 20 mins drive
from Skye Bridge or Mallaig ferry
point; ample car parking
Food breakfast, lunch, dinner
Price £££
Rooms 16;12 double, twin or triple,
4 suites; all with bath; all rooms have
phone, hairdryer
Facilities sitting room, 2 dining
rooms, boutique shop, Gaelic
Whisky, art gallery; anchorage for
yachts
Credit cards all major
Children welcome
Disabled no special access
Pets dogs welcome by prior arrange-
ment
Closed never
Proprietor Lady Noble

Eilean Iarmain
Seafront hotel

Hearing the soft lilt of the voices of the
staff is one of the pleasures of a stay
at this traditional Skye hotel, and a sure
sign that you are in the Hebrides. This is a
bi-lingual establishment, and the friendly
and welcoming staff are fluent in both
Gaelic and English.

The hotel is part of an estate belonging to
Lady Noble. Its three buildings are beautifully situated right on the water's edge, on the
small rocky bay of Isle Ornsay, looking
across the Sound of Sleat to the mainland
Knoydart Hills beyond. If you are lucky, you
may see otters on the shore.

The hotel's core is a white-painted
Victorian inn, which comprises the reception area, two appealing dining rooms and
six bedrooms. A further six bedrooms are
in a building opposite, while the latest
addition houses four split-level suites. All
the rooms are traditional in character,
hospitable and homely, with modern fittings and smart bathrooms. In each is a
complimentary miniature bottle of whisky
supplied from the distillery. The restaurant
specializes in local fish, shellfish and game,
and enjoys a local reputation.

Isle of Mull, Argyll

Ise of Mull, Argyll and Bute,
Scotland PA69 6ES

Tel 01681 705232
e-mail info@tiroran.com
website www.tiroran.com

Nearby Iona, Staffa, castles, mountains, beaches and wildlife.
Location countryside, by a loch with a private beach, large gardens
Food breakfast, lunch, dinner, afternoon tea, room service
Price ££££
Rooms 10; 5 double/twin, 5 double, all have shower, all have TV, hairdryer, tea/coffee facilities **Facilities** 2 drawing rooms, conservatory and dining room, gardens, beach
Credit cards MC, V
Children welcome
Disabled limited, 1 ground floor room with walk-in shower
Pets accepted, 4 rooms for pet owners
Closed rarely
Proprietors Laurence and Katie Mackay

Tiroran House
Country house hotel

An omission from earlier editions. This is about as good as a small country house hotel gets. It's secluded, but not remote, in large gardens beside a loch; you're face-to-face with terrific wildlife... but that is just a start.

One of our trusted reporters describes it as 'one of those gems' which the *Charming Small Hotel Guides* are all about, in fact it surpasses all our criteria.

He wrote of a recent visit: 'We were greeted on the doorstep by Laurence Mackay', who owns and runs the place with his wife Katie. 'The staff were a delight. The food was superb. The wine list is impressive and Laurence clearly knows a good deal about single malt whisky. The freedom from intrusive modern technology was a pleasure, although had I wanted to listen to some decent music for a quiet hour, there was discreet equipment to make it possible. The old world charm of the two very different sitting rooms, then a contrasting two-level dining room, as well as the seriously comfortable and tasteful bedrooms, makes this a seriously good hotel.'

There's also self-catering accommodation in separate buildings in the garden, with access to the hotel's facilities – perfect for families.

Killiecrankie, By Pitlochry,
Perthshire PH16 5LG

Tel (01796)473220
Fax (01796) 472451
e-mail enquiries@killiecrankieho-
tel.co.uk **website** www.kil-
liecrankiehotel.co.uk

Nearby Pitlochry; Pass of
Killiecrankie; Blair Atholl; Glamis.
Location in 4 acres, 3 miles (4.5 km)
N of Pitlochry, just off A9 on the
B8079; ample car parking
Food breakfast, lunch, dinner
Price ££
Rooms 10; 8 double and twin, 2 sin-
gle, 1 suite, 8 with bath, 2 with
shower; all rooms have phone, TV,
hairdryer
Facilities sitting room, 2 dining
rooms, bar, conservatory, garden
Credit cards MC, V
Children accepted
Disabled access possible
Pets accepted by prior arrangement
Closed 3 Jan to 14 Feb **Proprietor**
Henrietta Fergusson

Killiecrankie Hotel
Country house hotel

A sensible, reassuring sort of establishment in a delightful setting that somehow encapsulates the modest Scottish
country hotel. Built as a private home for
a local clergyman in 1840, it stands at the
foot of the Pass of Killiecrankie, formed by
the River Garry slicing through the surrounding granite hills, and it has its own
attractive grounds – a lovely place in which
to relax and watch out for wildlife, including red squirrels and roe deer.

The ten comfortable bedrooms are
individually decorated in country house
fabrics and fine custom-made furniture
and fittings. An unexpected touch: beds are
turned down each evening. The painted
panelling in the bar helps make it a cosy,
convivial place in which to gather for
drinks, and a bright conservatory section
is set for light lunches and supper. Guests
eat breakfast in a second conservatory,
overlooking the garden. In the main
restaurant, chef Mark Easton, prepares a
large and daily-changing 'modern British'
menu. Special diets are also catered for.

Tweed Mill Brae, Kingussie,
Inverness-shire PH21 1TC

Tel (01540) 661166
e-mail relax@thecross.co.uk
website www.thecross.co.uk

Nearby Highland Wildlife Park,
Aviemore, Cairngorm Mountain
Railway
Location in Kingussie just off the
A9, 10 miles south of Aviemore.
Large car park
Food breakfast, lunch, dinner, after-
noon tea (prior booking advised)
Price ££££
Rooms 8 double and twin, all with
bath; all rooms have phone, TV,
DVD, hairdryer, tea/coffee
Facilities 2 sitting rooms, restau-
rant; garden and garden terrace
Credit cards AE, DC, MC, V
Children welcome
Disabled no special facilities; restau-
rant is accesible, rooms are not
Pets accepted by arrangement
Closed Christmas, Jan (open for
Hogmanay) **Proprietors** Derek and
Celia Kitchingman

The Cross
Restaurant-with-rooms

Since the Kitchingmans took over twelve
years ago they have invested heavily in
the basics – including better heating and
refurbished rooms – and continue to relish
the ongoing challenge of upgrading this
charming restaurant-with-rooms. They've
rightly maintained standards in the kitchen,
with a young chef from north of the border serving 'contemporary Scottish cuisine'
that wins awards. A review in *The Scotsman*
has praised the huge amount of work that
goes in to reasonably priced dishes, for
example, the chicken liver parfait, which
'seemed to be created by a nerdy perfec-
tionist. It was silky and musky, with a sprin-
kle of sea salt on the top, and a dark, sticky-
sweet fig and apple jam, as well as two
rough oatcakes, on the side. Joy.' *Sic.*

Our own trusted reporter confirmed
that it's business as usual in this beguiling
19thC tweed mill, though we would welcome more reports on the nature of the
welcome and the atmosphere. Besides
good food, The Cross's charm is its secluded 4-acre setting, in a pretty valley above
Kingussie with the River Gynack alongside,
where you might see salmon swimming
and herons fishing. The lofty sitting room is
especially appealing.

Kylesku, Sutherland

Kylesku, Sutherland IV27 4HW

Tel 01971 502 231
e-mail info@kyleskuhotel.co.uk
website www.kyleskuhotel.co.uk

Nearby Loch Glencoul and Loch Glendhu, bird watching, wildlife spotting, fishing, walking, climbing, beaches
Location good parking. Access from A894, 35 miles N of Ullapool or 95 miles NW of Inverness.
Food breakfast, lunch, dinner
Price £-££
Rooms 8 double/twin rooms: 6 with bath/shower; 2 with private shower room. All rooms have tea/coffee, TV, hairdryer
Facilities wi-fi, residents' sitting room, bar, dining area and beer garden. **Credit cards** MC, V
Children welcome
Disabled no special access
Pets welcome
Closed Dec-Feb
Proprietors T Lister and S Virechauveix

Kylesku Hotel
Lochside hotel

'It's no beauty, but it is a charmer', writes a trusted reporter of this newcomer. A group of southerners, including Tanja Lister and Sonia Virechauveix, bought it in 2010 and set about renovation in stages. 'Above all else, it is warm and comfortable, which in north-west Scotland means it has plenty going for it.'

The public spaces of this 1680s coaching inn have responded well to renovation, with wonderful views from picture windows.

The food is not far behind other grander places nearby, such as The Albannach (see following page) – if not behind at all. The friendly enthusiasm with which it is prepared and presented adds to the charm. Bedrooms are fresh, plain and white-and-grey contemporary, with dots of understated colour here and there. The north end of the hotel is actually the village local and makes a cheery, cosy drinking place. 'An inexpensive, helpful small hotel that deserves to succeed'.

It's a handy stopping place on the road to Cape Wrath, the far north-western tip of mainland Britain, next to the old Kylesku ferry slip, and right by the Kylesku Bridge, in wonderful scenery. Fish for the dinner table are landed on the slip.

Baddidarroch, Lochinver,
Sutherland IV27 4LP

Tel 01571 844407
e-mail info@thealbannach.co.uk
website www.thealbannach.co.uk

Nearby Suilven and Canisp peaks,
Achmelvich beach, boat trips to
islands
Location Lochinver
Food breakfast, lunch, dinner
Price ££££
Rooms 5; 3 suites, 2 doubles
Facilities terraces, garden, slipway
Credit cards MC, V
Children over 12 accepted
Disabled 2 specially-adapted rooms
Pets not accepted
Closed never
Proprietors Colin Craig and Lesley
Crosfield

The Albannach
Country house hotel

'Up a small hill just outside the pretty port of Lochinver,' writes a trusted reporter, 'the building is not particularly attractive externally – but compared with the alternative places in Lochinver, where terms such as barracks and youth hostel come to mind – it is better than OK.'

Inside, the welcome is warm and the way they handle your booking during arrival is pleasantly personal. 'Our room was well heated, tastefully furnished and well equipped.' All the bedrooms are individually decorated and have views to the sea loch and mountains beyond.

The public parts have a Highland ambience, or as our reporter puts it, 'a slightly Gothic feel – my wife was a little anxious that on a dark staircase she might meet Norman Bates, or his mother.'

But the food is far from Gothic: as we went to press this was the most northerly Michelin-starred restaurant in Britain. Our reporter was given fat oysters as a pre-dinner appetiser, and the food thoroughly deserved its star.

Not inexpensive – without the Michelin star, it would be overpriced, but this is an interesting place in a terrific location, made better by the food. There's a self-proclaimed 'draconian' no smoking policy in the hotel, but the terrace is convenient for this purpose – umbrellas provided.

Higher Oakfield, Pitlochry,
Perthshire PH16 5HT

Tel (01796) 473473
Fax (01796) 474068
e-mail
bookings@knockendarroch.co.uk
website www.knockendarroch.co.uk

Nearby Blair Castle; Killiecrankie
Pass; Loch Tummel, Edradour
Distillery.
Location close to town centre, 26
miles (41 km) N of Perth on A9;
ample car parking
Food breakfast, dinner
Price £-££
Rooms 12 double and twin, all with
bath; all rooms have phone, TV,
hairdryer, radio
Facilities 2 sitting rooms, dining
room; garden
Credit cards AE, MC, V
Children accepted over 10
Disabled access limited
Pets not accepted
Closed mid-Nov to mid-Feb
Proprietor Struan and Louise
Lothian

Knockendarroch
Town mansion

Pitlochry is a particularly agreeable
Highland town, and Knockendarroch
House is the place to stay. Built in 1880 for
an Aberdeen advocate, it displays more
château-esque elegance than Scottish
Baronial pomp. It stands on a plateau
above the town, surrounded by mature
oaks (its Gaelic name means Hill of Oaks).

Furnished in careful good taste, the
house feels gracious and welcoming. There
are two interconnecting sitting rooms in
which to relax, with log fire, white cor-
nices and new carpets – all very soothing.
The dining room is light and spacious, with
many windows and some attractive furniture.

Most of the bedrooms have views; those
from the second floor are spectacular.
They are all well furnished and two have
small balconies.

Guests attending the famous Pitlochry
Festival Theatre (which began here at
Knockendarroch) are served an early dinner, and a courtesy bus is laid on to take
them to and from the town.

As we went to press we heard from
some well-travelled 30-year-olds who
stayed here recently and said the description above is spot on. They enjoyed the
grandeur, the comfort and the good food.

Port Appin, Argyll PA38 4DF

Tel (01631) 730236
Fax (01631) 730535
e-mail airds@airds-hotel.com **web-site** www.airds-hotel.com

Nearby Oban; Glencoe; 'Road to the Isles'; Ben Nevis.
Location between Ballachulish and Connel, 2 miles (3 km) off A828; ample car parking
Food breakfast, lunch, dinner; room service **Price** ££££ **Rooms** 8 double and twin, 3 suites, all with bath/shower; all rooms have Bulgari toiletries, bathrobes and slippers; phone, TV and DVD players, hairdryer; 2 self-catering cottages.
Facilities 2 sitting rooms, conservatory, dining room, whisky bar, garden and croquet lawn, shingle beach
Credit cards DC, MC, V **Children** accepted; none under 8 in dining room after 7.30pm
Disabled no special facilities **Pets** accepted, not in public areas
Closed last three weeks Jan
Proprietors Jenny and Shaun Mc Kivragan

Airds Hotel
Boutique luxury hotel

The owners of Airds have very sensibly taken every advantage of its superb location on the shores of Loch Linnhe: the dining room, the conservatory and many bedrooms face the loch. To capitalize further, they have also created, across the road, an attractive lawn and rose garden in which guests can sit and admire the view across the loch to the island of Lismore. The sunsets here are stunning.

Despite its fairly ordinary exterior, Airds Hotel is a smart and decorous establishment, impeccably run and maintained. The interior is elegant, with two sitting rooms prettily furnished with comfortable chairs, deep-pile carpets and open log fires. Each of the bedrooms are individually furnished and decorated with designer wallpapers and fabrics, and kitted out with fancy Bulgari toiletries Fresh flowers, books and paintings are in abundance throughout the hotel.

The food at their recently modernized restaurant is highly praised and often features such local delicacies as Lismore oysters, smoked salmon or venison. Each day the dinner menu and wine list is left in your room, so that you can consult it at leisure, give your orders by late afternoon, and relax before dinner with an aperitif, confident that there will be no unecessary delays.

Portree, Isle of Skye

Portree, Isle of Skye, IV51 9EU

Tel (01478) 612217
Fax (01478) 613517
e-mail info@viewfieldhouse.com
website www.viewfieldhouse.com

Nearby Trotternish peninsula.
Location on outskirts of town, 10 minutes walk S of centre; from A87 towards Broadford, turn right just after national garage on left; with ample car parking
Food breakfast, packed lunch, dinner
Price ££
Rooms 11 double and twin, 10 with bath; all rooms have phone, radio, hairdryer **Facilities** sitting room, dining room, TV room, washer and tumble drier for guests
Credit cards MC, V **Children** welcome **Disabled** one specially adapted room on ground floor **Pets** accepted, but not in public rooms
Closed mid-Oct to mid-Apr
Proprietors Iona Macdonald

Viewfield House
Country guesthouse

'It won't suit everyone,' writes our reporter about Viewfield House, 'but for those seeking an age gone by, the experience would be memorable.'

This is an imposing Victorian country mansion, which, as the name suggests, has some fine views from its elevated position. The need for costly repairs to the roof prompted Evelyn Macdonald, Hugh's grandmother, to open Viewfield House to guests. The delight of it is that the distinctive character of the house was preserved; and though you will not lack for comfort or service, a stay here is likely to be a novel experience. The house is full of colonial memorabilia: stuffed animals, and birds; *objets d'art*; and a magnificent collection of oil paintings and prints.

The rooms are original, right down to the wallpaper in one instance (though all but one now have *en suite* bathrooms in the former dressing-rooms); there is a classic Victorian parlour and a grand dining room with a huge oak table, which seats up to 16 people. Dinner can be taken each evening at 7.30, by prior arrangement. Breakfast features a wide selection of cooked items including Mallaig kippers, smoked haddock and porridge.

The day-to-day running of the hotel is currently being passed on to Hugh's daughter, Iona, and her partner Jasper.

Scarista, Isle of Harris HS3 3HX

Tel (01859) 550238
e-mail timandpatricia@scarista-house.com
website www.scaristahouse.com

Nearby beaches; golf; boat trips.
Location 15 miles (24 km) SW of Tarbert on A859, over-looking sea; in 2-acre garden, with ample private car parking
Food breakfast, packed/snack lunch, dinner
Price ££££
Rooms 6; 2 double, 1 twin, 3 suites in Glebe House, all with bath; all rooms have phone, hairdryer
Facilities library, 2 sitting rooms, dining room
Credit cards MC, V
Children welcome
Disabled no special facilities
Pets by arrangement
Closed Dec-Feb
Proprietors Tim and Patricia Martin

Scarista House
Island guesthouse

Harris has little in the way of hotels, but Scarista would stand out even among the country houses of the Cotswolds.

The converted Georgian manse stands alone on a windswept slope overlooking a wide stretch of tidal sands on the island's western shore. The decoration is elegant and quite formal, with many antiques, but the atmosphere is relaxed and, by the open peat fires, conversation replaces television. The bedrooms, all with private bathrooms, have selected teas and fresh coffee, as well as home-made biscuits. Three of the bedrooms are in the main house, with three refurbished suites available in The Glebe building, just behind the house.

Tim and Patricia Martin continue to maintain a high standard. They aim to be welcoming and efficient, but never intrusive, and to preserve that precious private home atmosphere.

One of Scarista's greatest attractions, particularly rewarding after a long walk over the sands, is the meals. The imaginatively prepared fresh local and garden produce and an impressive wine list ensure a memorable dinner in the candle-lit dining room.

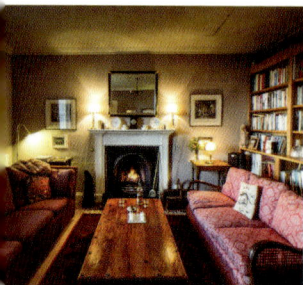

Sleat, Isle of Skye

Sleat, Isle of Skye IV43 8QY

Tel (01471) 833214
Fax (01471) 833277
e-mail reservations@kinloch-lodge.co.uk
website www.kinloch-lodge.co.uk

Nearby Clan Donald Centre.
Location in 60-acre grounds, 6 miles (9.5 km) S of Broadford, one mile (1.5 km) off A851; ample car parking
Food breakfast, lunch, dinner, afternoon tea
Price ££
Rooms 14 double, all with bath; all rooms have TV/DVD player, radio, hairdryer
Facilities 3 sitting rooms, bar, dining room, spa, wi-fi; fishing
Credit cards AE, MC, V
Children accepted **Disabled** access reasonable – one ground-floor bedroom **Pets** accepted by arrangement but not in public rooms
Closed Christmas
Proprietors Lord & Lady Macdonald

Kinloch Lodge
Country hotel

This white-painted stone house, in an isolated position with uninterupted sea views, at the southern extremity of the Isle of Skye, now known as the North House, was built as a farmhouse around 1700 and later became a shooting lodge. But it escaped the baronial treatment handed out to many such houses – 'thank goodness,' says Lady Macdonald, whose style is modern interior-designer rather than dark panelling and tartan. It has that easy-going private-house air. The guests' sitting rooms are comfortably done out in stylishly muted colours; there are open fires, honesty bar and family oil paintings grace the walls. The dining room is more formal, with sparkling crystal and silver on the tables.

Bedrooms used to be rather small, but have recently been reconfigured to give more space, and all now have en-suites, some with roll-top baths. The South House has accommodation for the Macdonalds and five more double rooms for guests. This building is quite remarkable as it looks, both inside and out, as old as its 18th century neighbour, and includes a magnificent stone spiral staircase, as wells as a wealth of books, portraits and *objets d'art*.

The food, under Marcello Tully, at Kinloch Lodge is renowned – Lady Macdonald has written cookery books and gives cookery demonstrations.

Sleat, Isle of Skye

Sleat, Isle of Skye IV44 8RE

Tel 01471 820200
e-mail info@skyehotel.co.uk
website www.skyehotel.co.uk

Nearby new Torabhaig Distillery, Knock Castle ruin, coast, mountains, wildlife, bird-watching, villages, ferry to mainland
Location just outside Ferrindonald on the A851, accessible by seaplane, ferry, train, bus and air, parking available.
Food breakfast, lunch, afternoon tea, dinner; full and half board available, lunch not included in price.
Price ££-£££
Rooms 9 double and twin, all have showers, some have baths, all have TV and hospitality tray
Facilities sitting room, restaurant, gardens, yacht trips
Credit cards MC, V
Children accepted over 5
Disabled no special facilities
Pets not accepted
Closed never
Proprietors Captain Ken Gunn and Anne Gracie

Toravaig House
Country house

Toravaig House is an unimposing, plain white building nestled in Skye's Sleat peninsula overlooking the Sound of Sleat. The smooth lines, silky fabrics and twinkling lights inside are a sharp contrast to what's out: craggy cliffs, an often boiling sea and the said-to-be-haunted ruin of Knock Castle.

Some of the rooms are considerably smaller than others, and not all face the sea, but each is named after a Hebridean island and individually designed. Huge, chequered headboards, spotty cushions and bold colours are found throughout, as are satellite TV and wi-fi: the decoration here is thoroughly and unexpectedly modern. That said, one room does feature a magnificent wooden sleigh-bed and the sitting room, warmed by an open log fire, is filled with comfortable, elegant seating.

One of the main draws of Toravaig is undoubtedly the food. Chef Miles Craven menus are strictly seasonal and ingredients are locally sourced – langoustines and lobsters from local waters and home-grown leaves and herbs. The restaurant itself – The Islay – benefits from great views over the gardens and mountains beyond.

Service is described as extremely warm and welcoming: owners Captain Ken Gunn and Anne Gracie 'make the place seem like home'.

Spean Bridge, Inverness-shire

Loch Lochy, by Spean Bridge, Inverness-shire PH34 4EA

Tel (01397) 712685
Fax (01397) 600052
e-mail info@corriegour-lodge-hotel.com **website** www.corriegour-lodge-hotel.com

Nearby Cawdor Castle; Urquhart Castle; Loch Ness; Glencoe.
Location on road to Skye, between Spean Bridge and Invergarry, in own grounds, 17 miles (27 km) N of Fort William on A82; ample car parking
Food breakfast, dinner
Price £££ **Rooms** 9; 7 double and twin, 2 single, all with bath/shower; all rooms have TV, hairdryer on request **Facilities** sitting room, bar, dining room; terrace, private beach, jetty, fishing, waterfall
Credit cards AE, DC, MC, V
Children welcome
Disabled access possible
Pets not accepted
Closed end of Nov until the week before the Easter holiday
Proprietors Ian and Christian Drew

Corriegour Lodge
Lochside hotel

A former Victorian hunting lodge commanding outstanding views over Loch Lochy and set in six acres of mature woodland and garden within the 'Great Glen'. With its own attractive private beach and jetty on the loch, as well as a fishing boat and the services of a private fishing school at its disposal, this is an obvious choice for keen anglers, as well walkers and climbers, pony trekkers and sailors.

When guests arrive they are always greeted by a member of the family, whether it be Christian, Ian or James; their friendliness and enthusiasm for the hotel they run is infectious. The decoration throughout the rest of the hotel is cosy and pleasant, with a log fire in the sitting room and magical views over the loch from the large picture windows in the restaurant. Many of the comfortable bedrooms have the same view.

Food is an important element here. The restaurant is Michelin Recommended, using local meat, fish and game. Expect bold flavours: for a main you could have Aberdeen Angus steak with anchovy butter and truffle *jus*, followed by an iced baileys parfait.

The staff are genuinely friendly and willing to help. Beacause of its location wi-fi is unavailable, but this are to be expected in old lodges and are more than made up for by the views and food.

Strontian, Argyll

Strontian, Argyll PH36 4HY

Tel (01967) 402257
Fax (01967) 402041
e-mail enquiries@kilcamblodge.com
website www.kilcamblodge.com

Nearby ferry to Isle of Mull and Skye; Castle Tioram; Glencoe.
Location Corran ferry to Ardgour from the A82 near Ballachulish, then follow A861 to Strontian; in 19 acres with ample car parking
Food breakfast, light lunch, dinner (formal dining in restaurant, informal dining in their Driftwood Brasserie)
Price £££
Rooms 11 double and suites, all with bath; all rooms have TV, hairdryer, phone **Facilities** 2 sitting rooms, bar, restaurant, brasserie, garden, private beach, fishing, mountain bikes
Credit cards MC, V
Children welcome
Disabled no special facilities
Closed first two weeks of Dec & Jan
Pets dogs accepted by arrangement, £12 per night
Proprietors David and Sally Fox

Kilcamb Lodge
Lochside hotel

There is a sense of adventure in travelling to a hotel by ferry, particularly when it then involves a ten-mile journey, first alongside a loch and then over a pass through a steep-sided glen. Drop down through the glen, pass through the small village of Strontian, and there, in a romantic setting on the shores of Loch Sunart, is Kilcamb Lodge.

Originally built in the early 18thC, with Victorian additions, Kilcamb is a beautifully restored country house with ten bedrooms, some with a loch view. Set amidst lawns and woodland, filled in spring with the colours of rhododendrons, azaleas and many wild flowers, it is a romantic and calming bolthole, the perfect choice for nature lovers: sea otters, seals, pine martens, red and roe deer and golden eagles can all be seen.

The ground floor public rooms are pleasantly furnished with light and attractive pastel fabrics. There is a wonderful Victorian wrought-iron staircase and a large stained glass window. All the bedrooms are individually decorated and have triple-lined curtains (it stays light very late in summer). Chef Gary Phillips prepares fresh Scottish food using locally-sourced fish, shellfish and meat from the Ardnamurchan Peninsula.

Tobermory, Isle of Mull, Argyll
PA75 6QE

Tel 01688 302321
e-mail
enquiries@glengormcastle.co.uk
website www.glengormcastle.co.uk

Nearby Tobermory, Calgary,
Dervaig.
Location on coast, easy to find with
satnav
Food breakfast, lunch can be pur-
chased in hotel's coffee shop
Price ££-££££
Rooms 5; 4 doubles, 1 double/twin,
all have bath/shower
Facilities dining room, library with
complimentary whisky, seating in
hall area, sitting room with pool
table and board games
Credit cards MC, V
Children welcome
Disabled no special facilities
Closed mid-Dec to beginning Feb
Pets accepted
Proprietors Marjorie and Tom
Nelson

Glengorm Castle
Country house guesthouse

At the northernmost tip of Mull,
Glengorm castle – really a grandiose
Victorian country house – boldly surveys
the Sound of Mull, Ardnamurchan
Peninsula and, vivid at sunset in the far distance, the Outer Hebrides. It stands on a
5,000-acre estate that is yours to roam.
"Everything," says Tom Nelson, "that Mull
is noted for, from white-tailed eagles to
whales, can be seen at Glengorm."

There are five guest bedrooms occupying the principal bedrooms of the house:
spacious (two are huge) and charming,
with characterful bathrooms and pretty
wallpapers. These rooms are a delight,
especially with the lack of televisions and
telephones.

This is a family affair, with Tom, Marjorie
and their three children living in one wing
of the castle. There's a lofty hall and sitting
room (well-worn sofas, board games, big
fire). You can also relax in the library,
where whisky is complimentary and the
fire can be lit if you wish.

Dinner isn't served at Glengorm, but
the Macdonald Arms Hotel in Tobermory
(four miles away) is well worth a trip. In
the morning, enjoy the excellent and
hearty breakfast in front of those stunning
views. We thought that the prices were
rather high, but the scenery, breakfast and
family-feel made them worthwhile.

Aboyne, Aberdeenshire

Struan Hall
Guesthouse

Looking at the solid mass of grey stone that is Struan Hall, we could hardly believe that its original site was five miles away. The house dates back to the 1800s, but in 1904 it was dismantled, moved stone-by-stone, and rebuilt here. Set in two acres of grounds, with lawns and an Indian-style pavilion, a rockery and carp pool, Struan Hall makes a restful, comfortable base. Judith is a marvellous host, welcoming guests with tea and cake, and a sherry in the evenings.

The decoration is comfortable and cosy, with lovely Scottish furnishings: tartan carpets harmonize with the pine staircase and creamy palettes. Upstairs, the Scottish theme continues. The bedrooms are named after castles and have pine bedheads carved with Scottish motifs.

Ballater Road, Aboyne,
Aberdeenshire AB34 5HY

Tel 01339 885599
e-mail judith@struanhall.co.uk
website www.struanhall.co.uk
Food breakfast
Price £
Closed first two weeks of Feb
Proprietors George and Judith Anderson

Colbost, Isle of Skye

Three Chimneys
Seaside restaurant-with-rooms

For 30 years chef Shirley Spear and her husband Eddie have run Three Chimneys as an award-winning seafood restaurant in an idyllic seaside location in the north-west corner of Skye. The six suites created in a new building called the House Over-By, are luxurious – if under-stated – rooms designed to blend with the seascape and the changing light. Each contemporary, spacious and high-ceilinged room has direct access to the beach; bathrooms are heavenly. Breakfast is served in a room overlooking the seashore and the islands in Loch Dunvegan.

As you would expect, the menu is a mainly fishy one, but Highland beef, lamb and game are also a feature, and the puddings are just as good. The kitchen is run by their new Head Chef, Scott Davies.

Colbost, Dunvegan, Isle of Skye
IV55 8ZT

Tel (01470) 511258 **Fax** (01470) 511358 **e-mail** eatandstay@three-chimneys.co.uk **website** www.three-chimneys.co.uk
Food breakfast, lunch, dinner
Closed 1st Dec – late Jan
Proprietors Shirley and Eddie Spear

Comrie, Perthshire

The Royal Hotel
Town hotel

From the moment you step inside The Royal Hotel, it feels right. Situated in the centre of this attractive little Highland town, and dating from 1765, it began life as a coaching inn, and earned its grand title after a visit by Queen Victoria, accompanied by her servant, John Brown.

The atmosphere is homely, yet at the same time elegant and stylish, with log fires in the public rooms as well as squashy sofas, antiques and oil paintings. The Lounge Bar is for informal dining, as well as the main restaurant.

Recent visitors enthused about the freshness of their rooms. All have been individually furnished with an eye for detail and design. It is managed by hands-on couple Jerry and Teresa Milsom.

Melville Square, Comrie, Perthshire PH6 2DN

Tel (01764) 679200
Fax (01764) 679219
e-mail reception@royalhotel.co.uk
website www.royalhotel.co.uk
Food breakfast, lunch, dinner; room service **Price** £££ **Closed** Christmas Day and Boxing Day **Managers** Jeremy and Teresa Milsom

Connel, Argyll

Ards House
Seaside hotel

This pretty Victorian villa has uninterrupted views westward over the Firth of Lorn to the Morvern Hills. Sunsets are truly spectacular.

The house itself tends to ramble, as additions have been made over the years to the original cottage. The most recent owners, Steve and Ilze Paterson, has retained the snug atmosphere, but no longer serves dinner. Breakfasts are especially generous. You could choose not only the usual fresh fruit salad, muesli and yoghurt but also kippers, smoked salmon and scrambled eggs, pancakes and bacon with maple syrup, haggis on toast (with whisky if you want).

Special terms are available for short breaks.

Connel, by Oban, Argyll PA37 1PT

Tel (01631) 710255
e-mail info@ardshouse.com
website www.ardshouse.com
Food breakfast
Price £
Closed Christmas and New Year
Proprietor Steve and Ilze Paterson

Muir of Ord, Ross-shire

Highfield, Muir of Ord, Ross-shire
1V6 7XN

Tel (01463)870090
Fax (01463)870090
e-mail info@thedowerhouse.co.uk
website www.thedowerhouse.co.uk
Food breakfast
Price £££ **Closed** up to a month,
off-season **Proprietors** Robyn and
Mena Aitchison

The Dower House
Farmhouse bed-and-breakfast

This former Dower House of a baronial home, which burnt down in the 1950s, was converted from thatched farmhouse to charming Georgian cottage ornée style in about 1800. It became a hotel in 1988, and is still run by the same owners. Something of an oasis in the rugged landscape between the rivers Beauly and Conon, it is set in beautifully-maintained gardens and grounds. The elegant red dining room makes a stunning setting for evening meals, and Robyn's self-taught cooking does not disappoint. The sitting room has comfortable chairs, flowery fabrics and an open fire. The three bedrooms vary in size and furnishings and are fairly simple. The largest is the most luxurious, with an enormous bed and spacious bathroom. A two-bedroom self-catering flat is also available).

Strachur, Argyll

Strachur, Argyll PA27 8BX

Tel (01369) 860279
Fax (01369) 860637
website www.creggans-inn.co.uk
Food breakfast, lunch, dinner
Price ££
 Closed closed over Christmas and
usually a couple weeks at the beginning of Jan
Proprietors The MacLellan family

Creggans Inn
Lochside hotel

Overlooking Loch Fyne, this former hunting lodge of the 3,000-acre Strachur Estate was first opened as an inn more than 40 years ago. The MacLellan family are still in charge, and have refurbished the place, starting with the sitting and dining rooms.

The food here is excellent: drawing heavily on local products such as scallops and langoustines from Loch Fyne, it is light, inventive and delicious. The wine list is unusually good.

A major natural advantage is the position of the inn. The views over Loch Fyne and across the Mull of Kintyre to the Western Isles are breathtaking. Many parts of the Strachur Estate, including the private flower garden, are open to guests.

Tarbert, Isle of Harris

Pier Road, Tarbert, Isle of Harris
HS3 3DG

Tel 01859 502364
Fax 01859 502578
email stay@hotel-hebrides.com
website www.hotel-hebrides.com
Food breakfast, lunch, dinner
Price £–£££
Closed Christmas Day **Proprietors**
Angus and Chirsty Macleod

Hotel Hebrides
Town hotel

A functional, modern hotel aimed at business travellers as well as tourists – and perhaps formulaic despite describing itself as a boutique hotel. Still, it's a useful address because it's 30 seconds from the ferry pier in Tarbert on the island of Harris where until now we've not found anywhere to recommend – in fact as we went to press there was nothing that reached this standard anywhere in the Outer Hebrides. Also, unusually, it has eight single rooms where you can stay for as little as £60 including breakfast. Some of the bedroom decorations are jarring, others plainer and more successful; the staff wear low-key uniforms, but it's owner-managed and its heart is in the right place.

Thurso, Caithness

Forss, Near Thurso, Caithness
KW14 7XY

Tel 01847 861201
email anne@forsshousehotel.co.uk
website www.forsshousehotel.co.uk
Food breakfast, lunch, dinner
Price ££–£££ **Closed** 23rd Dec – 5th
Jan **Proprietors** Ian and Sabine
Richards

Forss House Hotel
Country house

Sabine and Ian Richards bought this mellow country house, built 1810, in 2004. They have redecorated in a way that makes it look unchanged, though it is in fact new and fresh.

You'll find tartan carpeting, a malt whisky bar, a sunny conservatory for breakfast and a shallow Georgian staircase leading up to the light and spacious first-floor bedrooms. The food is highly rated and we thought it lived up to its reputation.

There's excellent salmon fishing at hand along the Forss, which flows in an arc around the hotel. With open, easy casting, it's well suited to beginners and children as well as the more experienced. In spring and summer the banks – thick with wild flowers – make pretty walking.

Urquhart, Morayshire

Meft Road, Urquhart by Elgin IV30 8NH

Tel 01343 843063
mobile 0774 8867825
e-mail info@oldchurch.eu
website www.oldchurch.eu
Food breakfast, dinner
Price £ Closed Nov-Apr
Proprietors Andreas Peter and Kyzysztof Plewicki

The Old Church of Urquhart **Village B&B**

Areader recommends this unusual, budget B&B – as we went to press two people can stay for as little as £66 including breakfast. Owners Andreas and Krzysztof have their own rooms in the converted church, and they are a presence, but you can feel private in the guest sitting room and dining room (dinner: £15). Bedroom decoration and furnishings are homespun and standardised. They also use the name 'B&B Parrandier'. Reports welcome.

Walls, Shetland Islands

Walls, Shetland Islands, ZE2 9PD

Tel (01595) 809307
e-mail info@burrastowhouse.co.uk
website www.burrastowhouse.co.uk
Food breakfast, light/packed lunch, dinner
Price ££
Closed Oct to Mar
Proprietor Pierre Dupont

Burrastow House
Seafront guesthouse

On the remote west side of Shetland, at the end of the single track road, on a rocky promontory overlooking Vaila Sound and the Island of Vaila, stands this calm, solid 18thC stone house. It has been run for the last thirteen years with enthusiasm by Pierre Dupont.

The four first-floor bedrooms in the main house are the ones to go for if you can. They are all large, one with a second bedroom which is perfect for children, and all have views. Some have splendid beds: a four-poster in one and a half-tester, draped in blue silk, in another. In the public rooms there are peat fires, books, an eclectic mix of furnishings and wonderful views from the windows. Pierre serves his natural, homely cooking in the cosy dining room.

Ireland area introduction

With a mild climate and a famously leisured way of life, Ireland (also described in tourist publications as the Emerald Isle) is a place of contrasts and changing light, of mountains, lakes and rivers, lush pastures, bog and wild moorland. There are 2,000 miles of coastline with small rocky coves, long sandy beaches and some of the highest cliffs in Europe. In the most remote parts of the country you can drive for miles without seeing anything but sheep. Among the most spectacular features are the golden beaches of Counties Wicklow and Wexford in the east, and the romantic lakes of County Sligo in the west. But if you want bright lights, music and good food, Ireland has any number of pubs that nightly celebrate the traditional Irish love of music and conversation. Northern Ireland, for a long time shunned by visitors because of the troubles, has been developing into a modestly popular destination.

Below are some useful back-up places to try if our main selections are fully booked:

Shores Country House
Bed-and-breakfast,
Castlegregory Tel 066 7139196 www.theshorescountryhouse.com
On Brandon Bay.

The Cliff Townhouse
Restaurant-with-rooms,
Dublin Tel 01 638 3939
www.clifftownhouse.ie
Airy, stylish restautant-with-rooms in central Dublin.

Rosturk Woods
Self-catering houses,
Mulranny Tel 087 6573840
www.rosturkwoods.ie
Secluded woodland houses near Clew Bay.

Magheralin, Co Armagh

58 Newforge Road, Magheralin,
Craigavon, Co Armagh BT 67 0QL

Tel (028) 9261 1255
e-mail
enquiries@newforgehouse.com
website www.newforgehouse.com

Nearby Belfast (25 km); Mountains
of Mourne (50 km).
Location clearly signposted, just off
A3, through Magheralin, 1st left
onto Newforge Road, with ample
private car parking
Food breakfast, dinner
Price £££
Rooms 6 doubles with bath/shower;
all rooms have phone, TV, DVD
player, hairdryer, wi-fi
Facilities drawing room, dining
room; large garden
Credit cards MC, V
Children under 1 and above 10
Disabled dining room accessible
Pets not accepted
Closed 3 weeks over Christmas
and New Year
Proprietors John and Louise
Mathers

Newforge House
Country guesthouse

For Northern Ireland, this is about as sophisticated as a guesthouse gets, in fact it's almost a small hotel. Instead of sharing the owner's home, you have the run of it, not least the graceful drawing room. John and Louise Mathers, the young owners, live in one outbuilding, while John's father has another. Six generations of Mathers (a linen family) have lived here; the latest bowed to the fact that it was too big and converted it to a guesthouse, restoring it in the process. The Georgian interior has been respected, but the walls have that clean, smooth modern finish and there's an optimistic, airy atmosphere – windows are tall. The dining room has separate tables, so no communal dining. Another bonus: John is a trained chef, with a professionally fitted kitchen and the food is good: three courses (£44) with two choices at each course, ingredients fresh each day. There's a license, and a wine list. Give a day's notice for dinner.

Even the smallest of the six bedrooms, named after family members, is roomy, and all are individually decorated in the best of taste. In fact, they're as smart as many we've seen in chic city hotels, and the spacious bathrooms gleam.

You're guaranteed a peaceful night here since the house stands well back from a quiet road just outside Newforge.

Bushmills, Co Antrim

The Bushmills Inn
Converted coaching inn

Chickens once lived on the first floor when this charming little inn was going through hard times. All that changed in 1987 when two partners spotted the potential of the building. The oldest part – now the restaurant – dates back to the 17th century. Almost the first thing to be seen, once inside, is a glowing fire, which is always lit. There's a warren of ground-floor rooms, with roaring fires and old flagstones; the Victorian-style bar has gas lighting, leather chairs and dark wood panelling. The older bedrooms have been converted into a cinema and conference room; newer ones in the Mill House extension – with river views – are larger, with wood panelling, rough white walls and their own sitting area.

9 Dunluce Road, Bushmills, Co Antrim BT57 8QG

Tel (028) 2073 3000
e-mail mail@bushmillsinn.com
website www.bushmillsinn.com
Food breakfast, lunch, dinner
Price ££
Closed never
Proprietors Alan Dunlop

Downpatrick, Co Down

Tyrella House
Country house bed-and-breakfast

Staying at Tyrella as David Corbett's guest is to experience in a genuine way the vanishing lifestyle of the Northern Irish landed gentry. It's a fine country house, dating from the 18th century, down a longish drive, not another building in sight. The nicely proportioned rooms contain the accumulated brown antique furniture and possessions of four generations of Corbetts. Don't expect immaculate paintwork or a trim drive; do expect a relaxed welcome, a large bedroom, a comfortable bed and the feeling of being in a home. The food gets some pleasant compliments in the visitors' book. The house still stands in some 300 acres of its own, now used for equestrian events (David is a horseman) and has its own private beach, which guests can use.

Tyrella House. Downpatrick Co Down

Tel (028) 4485 1422 **e-mail** tyrella.corbett@virgin.net **website** www.hidden-ireland.com/tyrella
Food breakfast; dinner on request, a day's notice needed. **Price** ££-£££
Closed never
Proprietor David Corbett

Aghadoe, Co Kerry

Aghadoe, Lakes of Killarney,
Co Kerry

Tel (064) 66 31711
Fax (064) 66 31811
e-mail charming@indigo.ie
website www.killeenhousehotel.com

Nearby Killarney, 4 miles (6 km);
Muckross House; Gap of Dunloe.
Location in countryside, 4 miles (6
km) from Killarney; car parking
Food breakfast, dinner
Prices €€-€€€
Rooms 23; 8 championship, 15 stan-
dard; 8 with king-size double and
single; 2 double, 5 twin, 2 single, 6
double and single; 22 with bath, 1
with shower; all rooms have phone,
TV, radio, hairdryer
Facilities bar, sitting room; garden,
terrace, tennis court, free wi-fi
Credit cards AE, DC, MC, V
Children welcome if well-behaved
Disabled not possible
Pets welcome
Closed 1 Nov to 1 Apr
Proprietors Michael and Geraldine
Rosney

Killeen House Hotel & Rozzers Restaurant

Country house hotel

We had to visit a hotel with 'charming' as its e-mail address. And there it was: a charming small hotel, a rectory built in 1838 and given a bright new white front and architectural twiddly bits painted in red by Michael and Geraldine Rosney, who took it over in 1992. Michael is a jolly, amusing – and kind – person who used to manage the Great Southern Hotel in Killarney. He has created a warm, cosy, entertaining and live-ly little place, where he spoils his golfing clients and indulges their every whim. He sees them off in the morning and waits for their return in the evening, like an anxious parent. Then he is to be found in The Pub, 'possibly the only place in the universe that accepts golf balls as legal tender', where he dispenses Guinness and sympathy. Nothing is too much trouble for him: he puts phone messages in envelopes and distributes them himself. All this activity provides loads of fun for everyone, especially Michael, and you don't have to be a golfer to benefit from his generous spirit. Comfortable, spacious bed-rooms are decorated in checks and plaids; there's a special one with a spa bath that he gives to regular guests as a 'thank you' for coming back again and again. Good show-ers; excellent food at Rozzers restaurant, one of the most popular in the Kerry area, with chef Paul O'Gorman at the helm.

Ardara, Co Donegal

Ardara, Co Donegal

Tel + 353 (0)86 17 65 431
website www.thegreengate.eu

Nearby Ardara (for tweed);
Glenveagh National Park.
Location 1 mile (1.6 km) from
Ardara, up a hill; with car parking
Food breakfast
Price €-€€
Rooms 3 adjoined thatched chalets,
sleeping 7 altogether (extra beds pos-
sible), plus 1 honeymoon suite with
sea and mountain views
Facilities garden, terrace
Credit cards not accepted
Children welcome, free for under
10s
Disabled access possible in 1 room
Pets dogs allowed
Closed Christmas
Proprietor Édouard Chatenoud
Manager Paula McMullen

The Green Gate
Cottage bed-and-breakfast

This little place, a tiny farmhouse with stone outbuildings, is bursting with charm. It was converted by a Frenchman who came to Donegal 15 years ago to write about "life, love and death". Paul Chatenoud left behind his musical book-shop and flat in Paris for a wilder exis-tence on the top of a hill overlooking the Atlantic, and created what must be the most beautiful small B&B in Ireland. So much love and care has gone into this enterprise, mostly done with his own hands, from thatching the cottage roof to whitewashing the guest rooms.

Suce Paul died the B&B has been man-aged by Paula McMullen, who has stayed true to his vision, extending the same care and attention to her guests: hot water bot-tles, a map in each room, a bath in which you can rest your head back and gaze out of the window at the sky and sea. The gar-den is filled with primroses, fuscia and small birds, with hundreds, if not thou-sands, of orange montbretia up the lane.

Breakfast is an informal affair, to be taken at any time in front of the peat fire of her cosy kitchen. The guests chat with each other while Paula prepares a break-fast of coffee/tea, granola with yoghurt and fresh fruit, a full Irish or pancakes – her famous speciality. Fruit and veg are often plucked straight from the garden.

Ballymacarbry, Co Waterford

Glenanore, Ballymacarbry, Co
Waterford

Tel (052) 6136134
Fax (052) 6136540
e-mail hanorascottage@eircom.net
website www.hanorascottage.com

Nearby Dungarvan, 18 miles (29
km); Clonmel, 15 miles (24 km);
Blackwater Valley.
Location in Nire Valley, 4 miles (6
km) out of Ballymacarbry; parking
available
Food breakfast, packed lunch, dinner
Price
Rooms 10; all double/twin; all with
Jacuzzi; all rooms with phone, TV,
hairdryer; tea/coffee making facilities
Facilities garden, terrace, spa tub
Credit cards MC, V **Children** not
accepted **Disabled** not possible **Pets**
not accepted **Closed** Christmas
week **Proprietors** Wall family

Hanora's Cottage
Riverside guesthouse

Changes have taken place since our last
edition at award-winning Hanora's
Cottage, built by a little bridge over the river
in the beautiful Nire Valley for late owner
Seamus Wall's great-grandmother. With the
village school and church next door, the picturesque group of buildings and their setting
made our inspector think of somewhere in
the Pyrenees. The guest-house is a favourite
with walkers, who come for the Comeragh
Mountains and nearby forests and lakes.
Mary Wall puts comfort high on her list and
pampers her guests. She has added five new
rooms, each with a spa tub, where guests
may rest aching limbs and emerge refreshed
for a candle-lit dinner in the new dining
room. Food is prepared by the Walls' talented Ballymaloe-trained son, Eoin, and his wife
Judith. In the new extension, brilliantly
designed to fit with the rest of the building, Mary has put in a drying and boot
room. Bedrooms are large, calm and
peaceful, with thick carpets, and most have
spa baths (superiors have double Jacuzzis).
There are books by the beds, some Tiffany
lamps, and quality bedlinen. The breakfast
room looks out on to the little stone
bridge and Seamus's renowned bread
recipes are still being used. Plenty of fruit
and freshly-squeezed juices, too. Ask for a
front room if you want to fall asleep to the
sound of the river.

Ballymote, Co Sligo

Ballymote, Co Sligo

Tel (087) 9976045
e-mail stay@templehouse.ie
website www.templehouse.ie

Nearby Sligo, 12 miles (19 km);
Yeats Country; Lissadell House;
Carrowkeel megalithic passage
tombs.
Location on 1,000-acre estate, 4
miles (6 km) from Ballymote; park-
ing available
Food breakfast, dinner
Price €
Rooms 6; 4 double, 1 twin, 1 family
room; 5 with bath, 6 with shower; all
rooms have hairdryer and free wi-fi
Facilities garden, woodland, farm,
lake fishing, boating
Credit cards MC, V
Children welcome, high tea in
kitchen for under-12s
Disabled access difficult **Pets** dogs
on leads (sheep); sleep in car **Closed**
15 Nov to 1 Apr **Proprietors**
Roderick and Helena Perceval

Temple House
Country house

Is this a dream? It begins as you enter the
gates of what is a gentle, gracious world
of its own. In parkland filled with fat sheep,
this is a whopper of a Georgian mansion,
the home of the Percevals since 1665.
Much of what you see was refurbished in
1864; electricity was not put in until 1962.
To be overcome by awe and wonder
would be easy were it not for the charm
and kindness of Roderick and Helena
Perceval together with their children and
four dogs. Temple House is very much a
home, and they want it to be enjoyed.

Bedrooms, with marble fireplaces and
much of their original Victorian furniture,
seem to be the size of football pitches –
one is called the 'half-acre'. All the bedrooms and bathrooms have been revamped
since 2005, when Roderick and Helena
took over from Roderick's parents, and
there is now wi-fi throughout the house.

As shadows fall, you could take a walk
across the farm land to the ruins of a 13thC
Knights Templar castle and a Tudor house
down by the lake. The family silver comes
out for dinner – an experience in itself; delicious dishes and freshly-baked bread. Guests
dine together at a vast mahogany table and
the atmosphere is that of a friendly house
party. Big breakfasts.

Ballyvaughan, Co Clare

Ballyvaughan, Co Clare, H91 CF60,

Tel +353 65 707 7005
e-mail stay@gregans.ie
website www.gregans.ie

Nearby Aran Islands, Cliffs of Moher, Aillwee Cave; Doolin and Kilfenora village
Location 5 km south of Ballyvaughan village on the N67
Food breakfast, light lunch, after-noon tea, dinner
Price €€€-€€€€
Rooms 21 (Classic, Superior, Junior Suite or Premier Suite); all come with reading, bathrobes, radios, tele-phone, hairdryer, Bamford toiletries, shower/bath, tea/coffee, wi-fi
Facilities reflexology and massage, restaurant, sitting rooms, gardens
Credit cards all major
Children welcome
Disabled fully accessible
Pets dogs allowed
Closed Dec, Jan and first half of Feb
Proprietors Simon Haden and Frederieke McMurry

Gregan's Castle
Country house hotel

This is not actually a castle. It's one of Ireland's Georgian houses, dating from 1750, and a relatively modest one at that, but exceptionally lovely all the same. The interior, both sweeping and intimate, has an elegant drawing room, charming corkscrew bar and a roaring fire. Simon, who was brought up here, trained in hos-pitality before returning, fortuitously with an interior designer wife. Frederieke has expertly wedded the house's traditional features and plentiful antiques with mod-ern colours, lighting and artworks.

The real cherry on the cake, however, is its magical location in the heart of Burren, a limestone county scattered with ancient burial tombs, stone forts and ruins. It's no wonder J.R.R Tolkein was inspired to write *Lord of the Rings* when he stayed here in the 1950s.

The modern menu, locally sourced and whipped up by talented chef David Hurley, more than lives up to the hotel's high stan-dards, as do the exceptional breakfasts.

English visitors currently only account 10 per cent of their guests. Our series edi-tor Fiona Duncan implores English readers to visit: privately owned, family-run and staffed by passionate locals, this breed of hotel is a rarity in England, and well worth making a trip for – not least for the great rambling country around Middle Earth.

Caragh Lake, Co Kerry

Caragh Lake, Killorglin, Co Kerry

Tel (066) 9769105
e-mail reservations@ardnasidhe.com
website www.ardnasidhe.com

Nearby Killorglin, 4 miles (7 km); Killarney, 21 miles (34 km); Dingle peninsula; Caragh Lake; golf; boating.
Location in lakeside gardens, 4.5 miles (7 km) from Killorglin; parking available
Food breakfast, dinner, afternoon tea **Price** €€€
Rooms 18 double, all with bath/shower; all rooms have phone, hairdryer; ironing board, wi-fi
Facilities gardens, terraces, boating, fishing, horse riding (at sister property), free entry to leisure centres and spas at sister hotels
Credit cards AE, DC, MC, V
Children not suitable
Disabled ground-floor room
Pets not accepted
Closed Oct to end of April
Proprietor Killarney Hotels

Ard na Sidhe Country House **Lakeside hotel**

When we visited Ard na Sidhe (Gaelic for Hill of the Fairies), there seemed to be no other guests about. The lovely wooded prize-winning gardens, with paths leading down to little grassy areas by the lake where there are benches to sit on and dream, were deserted. Most of the guests, we were told, were out playing golf. These golfing hotels are left like the Marie Celeste during the day, and lucky non-golfers may have the place to themselves.

This handsome Victorian stone house was built in 1913 by a Lady Gordon, and is so romantic that you can be as fanciful as you like. It certainly feels as if there are fairies about; indeed, behind the house is a fairy hill, with passages said to lead to a large cave. But these little creatures do not like to be seen.

All credit must be given to Killarney Hotels for keeping the house quite uncommercialized and unspoiled, and bringing in Roy Lancaster to advise them on the gardens. There are no facilities here, except natural ones. But guests are given complimentary use of the leisure centre and spa at the group's nearby sister hotels. Bedrooms (spacious) are in the main house and in the Garden House (very quiet and tranquil); all have impressive antiques Lady Gordon might well have chosen herself; excellent bathrooms.

Cashel Bay, Co Galway

Cashel Bay, Co Galway

Tel (095) 31111
Fax (095) 31117
e-mail info@zetland.com
website www.zetland.com

Nearby Connemara, Roundstone, Clifden, Westport, Aran Islands, fishing (some deep sea), shooting, golf, scuba diving, horse-riding, climbing.
Location in gardens overlooking Cashel Bay, on N340 to Roundstone from Galway; car parking
Food breakfast, dinner
Price ?
Rooms 22 rooms, all with television, shaving points, hairdryers and tea and coffee making.
Facilities gardens, bar, restaurant, open fires, lounge, Wi-Fi
Credit cards AE, MC, V
Children welcome
Disabled no special facilites (though there is 1 ground floor room)
Pets one room (with direct access to garden) is suitable for small dogs
Closed never **Proprietors** Colm Redmond

Zetland House Hotel
Country house hotel

Guests remark that they feel as if they are stepping back in time as they drive up to the Zetland House. It's an imposing, 19thC sporting lodge, which broods over a landscape of bogs, mountains, beaches, lakes and little else.

Inside, it's all soft, golden lighting, polished wood, open fires and plaid armchairs. The bedrooms are furnished chintzily but luxuriously, with carved wooden furniture and floral fabrics. Most have mesmerising views. Standard rooms are uniformly comfortable, but the deluxe rooms are truly charming: one has a king-size, four-poster bed, and all have sea views.

Downstairs, the restaurant's main feature is its stunning views over Cashel Bay and the surrounding area. Guests shouldn't just expect to feast their eyes, though – the Zetland has recently won several awards for catering and hospitality. The chef uses only locally-produced, fresh products and seasonal herbs and vegetables, and the wine list is interesting. The bar is cosy and wood-panelled, and offers a selection of Irish whiskys, as well as the black stuff. 'Life moves at a different pace, here' says one guest. 'People have time to stop and chat to you.'

Castlelyons, Co Cork

Castlelyons, Nr Fermoy, Co. Cork

Tel +353 25 36349
e-mail info@ballyvolanehouse.ie
website ballyvolanehouse.ie

Nearby Blarney Castle, Kinsale, St
Ballycotton, Cashel Rock, lots of
gardens, River Blackwater
Location set in 70 acres, 30 min
from Cork; 45 min from airport
Food breakfast, picnic lunch (on
request), dinner, afternoon tea
Price €€€-€€€€
Rooms 6; all with wi-fi, reading
material, bath, tea/coffee, cookies;
glamping on offer May-Sep
Facilities sitting room, dining room;
fly fishing, trout lakes, walled and
formal gardens, woodland
Credit cards all major
Children welcome
Disabled not suitable
Pets enquire before, small well-
behaved dogs sometimes allowed
Closed the week around Christmas
(re-opens 4/5th Jan)
Proprietors Justin and Jenny Green

Ballyvolane
Country house hotel

Like many Irish hotels, Ballyvolane
eludes classification. Somewhere
between a hotel, guesthouse and B&B, its
also a historic country house that's been in
the same family since 1953. Its interior is
both grand and homely, with smart wood-
en floors, shelves of books, paintings and
mirrors – and, loveliest of all, Italianate
painted panels on their doors depicting
flowers and birds. The mix of antique,
retro and contemporary has a boho-chic
feel, enhanced by quirky alternative offerings: 'Glamping' in bell tents with tea-light
chandeliers and a 'glamping pack' with all
the essentials.

The six stately bedrooms in the main
house are antique-laden, but with all the
modern comforts, paired with lovely old-
fashioned bathrooms. A charming sense of
informality pervades: there are no room
keys ("we lost them years ago," says Justin)
and dinner is served house party style on
a large communal table (with the option to
eat separately). Delicious suppers are
cooked by Tina, who's worked here several years, using vegetables plucked from
their magnificent walled garden. The team
are also keen foragers: expect the likes of
wild garlic, sorrel, pennywort and
damsons, alongside a menu of game and
salt-water fish.

383

Clifden, Co Galway

Ballyconneely Road, Clifden,
Co Galway

Tel (095) 21460
e-mail info@mallmore.com
website www.mallmore.com

Nearby Clifden; Connemara
National Park; Kylemore Abbey.
Location a mile out of Clifden town
centre; in own 35-acre grounds on
Ardbear peninsula; car parking
Food breakfast
Price €
Rooms 6; 3 double, 1 twin, 1 family
room with 1 double and 2 singles, 1
with 1 double and 1 single, all with
showers and spring water; all rooms
have wi-fi, most have hairdryers
Facilities gardens and woodland
Credit cards not accepted
Children welcome; 20% discount
Disabled possible
Pets not permitted in rooms
Closed 1 Nov to 1 Mar
Proprietors Alan and Kathleen
Hardman

Mallmore House
Country bed-and-breakfast

The Hardmans breed Connemara
ponies, for showing and dressage;
these hardy little natives are often kept
beside the drive to the family's lovingly
restored house with a cheery red front
door and late Georgian porch. The place is
stiff with historical interest: Baden Powell,
founder of the Boy Scouts, used to spend
his holidays here. Alan and Kathleen
Hardman came from The New Inn at
Tresco on the Isles of Scilly to work for
themselves and found the house in a
derelict state: only one room had been
used since the 1920s. From the back of the
house there is a lovely view through trees
over the bay to Clifden and out to the
Atlantic. You can walk down to the sea
through the orchard and past the old cottage. Rooms in this unusual and intriguing,
mainly single-storey house, with original
pitch pine floors, have a variety of views;
for water ask for Room 4. One room has
the original washbasin, and wallpaper with
a pattern of birds; another original wide
shutters, yellow paper, a Bonnard print and
spotless bathroom. Award-winning breakfasts are served in the dining room, which
also has its original shutters; tables have
pink cloths. On the menu: smoked salmon
pancakes; smoked mackerel; Irish bacon.
Very much a family affair; a daughter bakes
brown bread each evening.

Clifden, Co Galway

Beach Road, Clifden, Co Galway

Tel (095) 21369
e-mail res@thequayhouse.com
website www.thequayhouse.com

Nearby Connemara National Park;
Galway, 50 miles (80 km).
Location on quay, 3 minutes by car
from Clifden town centre; car park-
ing in road
Food breakfast
Price €€
Rooms 15; 5 superkings, 9 double (4
twin); all with bath or shower; all
rooms with phone, TV, radio,
hairdryer, balcony
Facilities sitting room; garden, ter-
race
Credit cards MC, V
Children welcome
Disabled ground-floor rooms
Pets not accepted
Closed end Oct to end Mar
Proprietors Paddy and Julia Foyle

The Quay House
Town house hotel

Paddy Foyle is a celebrated mover and shaker in this rapidly-getting-very-hip little seaside town, where he was born in room 12 of Foyle's Hotel. He is also the owner of the stylish Quay House, down on the harbour wall where the fishing boats tie up. A natural interior decorator, he has the boldness and panache of a set design-er: the house, built in 1820 for the har-bourmaster, is a stage for his fanciful ideas and outbursts of colour. You have the dis-tinct sense you are in a production of some kind – is it an opera? a film? – as you pass through the wondrous rooms. A favourite theme is Scandinavian: washed-out, dis-tressed paintwork; plenty of grey and Nordic blue; wooden panelling; striped fab-rics. One room is a riot of blue *toile de jouy*; there's a Napolean Room at the top of the house; another has a frieze of scallop sea shells. It's pretty; it's fun. But Paddy is a rest-less pacer, always moving on, so expect changes. He's already stuck a bay on to the old flat-fronted house, bought the place next door and turned it into studios.

On a recent visit we were once again enchanted by the originality of the place, and found Paddy as full of charm as ever. A must if you are in this part of Ireland, and well worth a detour.

Clones, Co Monaghan

Clones, Co Monaghan

Tel (047) 56007
e-mail mail@hiltonpark.ie
website www.hiltonpark.ie

Nearby Castle Coole and Florence
Court (National Trust); Armagh.
Location 3 miles (5 km) S of Clones,
near Clones Golf Club; in 500 acres
of parkland, woods, lakes and gar-
dens; car parking
Food breakfast, dinner
Price €€€
Rooms 6; 4 double, 2 twin; 5 with
bath; all rooms have hairdryer.
Facilities gardens; games room; bil-
liard room; grand piano; pike and
brown trout fishing; rods; boating on
lake; complimentary golf on 18-hole
course
Credit cards MC, V
Children welcome
Disabled not possible
Pets by arrangement
Closed end Oct to end Mar except
for group bookings
Proprietor Fred and Joanna
Madden

Hilton Park
Country house hotel

In the Hidden Ireland group of country
houses taking paying guests is Hilton
Park – home of the Madden family since
1734 and remodelled in the Italianate
manner in the 1870s. It is grand, beautiful,
and most evocative of the great days of
the Irish country house. Fred, having
trained in London, is now in charge of the
cooking. He prepares breakfast, which is
served in the old servants' hall below
stairs. He and his wife Joanna, who manages the front of house, are memorably
delightful hosts. Many family stories are to
be told about the guest bedrooms: one
was Johnny's when he was a child.

Little seems to have changed over the
years, though one of the rooms has been
renovated since our last visit. The wallpaper in the Blue Room, with a four-poster
bed and stunning view down to the lake,
was put up in 1830. On our visit, the lace
curtains had just come out of a box
opened for the first time since 1927. Next
door, a roll-top bath, marble washstand,
print of Landseer's Hunters at Grass, and
the scent of jasmine from plants in pots
arranged at the foot of the tall window, all
add to the grace and charm. Lucy's dinner
is by candle-light, with fresh produce from
her garden.

Dingle, Co Cork

Upper John Street, Dingle,
Co Kerry

Tel (066) 9151518
Fax (066) 9152461
e-mail info@pax-house.com
website www.pax-house.com

Nearby Killarney, 42 miles (68 km);
Mount Brandon; Tralee, 30 miles (48
km).
Location in countryside, half a mile
(0.8 km) out of Dingle town; sign-
posted on N86; car parking
Food breakfast
Price €€€
Rooms 13 all with choice of king
bed or 2 single beds; 10 seaview bed-
rooms; all have walk-in shower, some
also have separate bathtub
Facilities lounge, patio, terraces
Credit cards MC, V
Children accepted **Disabled** not
possible **Pets** if well-behaved
Closed 1st Dec to 1st Mar
Proprietor John O'Farrell

Pax House
Guesthouse

There is an abundance of wild fuchsia in
the hedgerows of the little lanes
around Pax House, high on a green hill
looking down over Dingle Bay. Before
breakfast, you can take an early walk down
to the shore, or, from the terrace, count
the cows coming out of the milking parlour of the farm below this rather odd
building that was once a retirement home.
John O'Farrell took over from the Brosnan-
Wrights in the summer of 2006, having
worked in the hospitality business for
more than 30 years, in such diverse places
as Switzerland, Thailand, America and
Spain. He has since repainted the house, all
bedrooms have fresh flowers, and a collection of original paintings, prints and sculp-
tures fill the house.

All rooms have walk-in showers, and
some have seaparate bathtubs; cold taps
produce water from the house's own spring
well. John serves a notably varied breakfast,
from a full Irish to pears in white wine,
honey and clove syrup, and kippers in a
lemon butter sauce. From the dining room
you can see the field on Sleahead that
starred in a film with Tom Cruise, and over
to the Ring of Kerry. The silence on the
green hill is blissful, but Dingle, a swinging little town, with its full share of traditional
music, pubs and restaurants, much frequented by celebs, is only a short walk away.

Drinagh, Co Wexford

Drinagh, Wexford, Co Wexford

Tel (053) 9158885
e-mail info@killianecastle.com
website www.killianecastle.com

Nearby Wexford; Rosslare Harbour
(Europort); Waterford Harbour;
Kilmore Quay.
Location on a dairy farm, 3 miles
(5km) from Wexford; 8 miles (13km)
from Rosslare Harbour; car parking
Food breakfast & dinner (booked in
advance)
Price €
Rooms 8; 4 double, 1 twin, 2 family;
8 with bath and shower; all rooms
with TV, hairdryer; iron in corridor;
tea/coffee making facilities under
stairs
Facilities garden, terrace; tennis
court; pitch & pitt course, golf driv-
ing range, farm walk
Credit cards MC, V
Children welcome
Disabled not suitable
Pets not in house
Closed 18 Dec to 12 Feb
Proprietors Jack, Kathleen & Paul
Mernagh

Killiane Castle
Farmhouse bed-and-breakfast

Those who have already found Killiane
Castle tend to have that special expression worn by people who have a secret
they want to keep to themselves. For this is
a remarkable place, and Kathleen Mernagh
is a most charming hostess. The Mernaghs'
early 17thC house was built inside the walls
of a largely intact 15thC Norman castle,
complete with tower (now listed). From
the back rooms, you see the ruins of a small
chapel in a field and the marshes running
down to the sea. Down a leafy lane, miles
from the main road, it seems centuries away
from everywhere else. Twice a day, you can
hear the hum of machines as the cows file
in and out of the milking parlour. Kathleen,
mother of five boys, loves what she does
and she does it extremely well. Long before
she married a farmer she worked in hotel
management. Their son Paul has recently
rejoined the hotel, preparing to take the
reigns over the coming years, having worked
in 5* hotels across the world.

Our reporter heard one guest say to
another at breakfast (Jack Mernagh serves
his wife's dishes): "It's just like a small hotel."
Some bedrooms overlook the weeping ash
at the front of the house; more interesting
ones overlook the courtyard and over the
castle walls to green countryside beyond.
All are spacious, well-equipped and comfortable.

70 Adelaide Road, Dublin 2

Tel (01) 475 5266
Fax (01) 478 2841
e-mail info@kilronanhouse.com
website www.kilronanhouse.com

Nearby Grafton Street; National
Gallery; Trinity College.
Location 5 minutes walk S of St
Stephen's Green; free off-street
parking
Food breakfast
Price €€
Rooms 15; 11 double (8 twin), 2 sin-
gle, 2 family; all with shower; all
with phone, TV, hairdryer; safe and
free internet in reception
Facilities sitting room
Credit cards AE, DC, MC, V
Children over 10
Disabled no special facilities
Pets not accepted
Closed 23-25th Dec
Proprietor Leon Kinsella
Manager Romi Gutu

Kilronan House
Town guesthouse

This veteran, reasonably-priced Georgian guest-house in a quiet, leafy, residential street near St Stephen's Green has been in business for more than 35 years and is perfectly situated for walking to some of the city's most famous landmarks and shops. A new owner has recently taken over and refurbished the place, bringing it up to date. Our reporter was impressed with the warm, yellow walls and parquet floor of the entrance hall and the welcoming reception area tucked under the stairs. Bedrooms are on four 'creaking' floors, and it is a long climb to the top. Some are on the small side. Colours tend to be yellow again, with elegant fabrics and pretty, white-painted wrought-iron bedheads, some pine furniture, heavy off-white curtains and the odd print on the walls. We were told of one room – below ground level – that was described as 'tiny', so it is clearly advisable to check in advance which rooms are available. The yellow sitting room has a big, gilt-edged mirror over the fireplace, antique furniture and a chandelier. The yellow extends to the breakfast room, with silver and white linens on the tables. The overall feel of the place is old-fashioned and relaxed. In late 2013 they refurbished the bedrooms and general areas – reports, please.

31 Leeson Close, Dublin 2

Tel (01) 676 5011
Fax (01) 676 2929
e-mail info@number31.ie
website www.number31.ie

Nearby St Stephen's Green;
National Gallery; Grafton Street,
Trinity College.
Location just off Lower Leeson
Street; 5 minutes walk from St
Stephen's Green; car parking
Food breakfast
Price €€€-€€€€
Rooms 20; 15 double (12 twin), 5
family; 17 with bath, 3 with shower;
all with phone, TV, hairdryer, wi-fi;
safe at reception **Facilities** sitting
room, breakfast room, conservatory;
garden
Credit cards all major
Children welcome
Disabled not suitable
Pets not accepted
Closed 24, 25 and 26th Dec
General Manager Ray Hingston

Number 31
Town guesthouse

This is a very special and visually pleasing place: a mews house designed in the mid-1960s by controversial Dublin architect, Sam Stephenson, and the Georgian house across the garden that was acquired giving much more space. Only a plate on the wall with '31' on it indicates this is somewhere you may stay. The Stephenson building is modern and open-plan, with painted white brickwork and much glass, wood and stone; kilims hang on the wall. There's a little sunken sitting area, with a black leather sofa custom-built around the fire. French windows and wooden decking lead to the garden and the back of the Georgian house. Generous and delicious breakfasts (home-made breads, jams, potato cakes, granola) are cooked by Delia and served in a white upstairs room on long tables with fresh flowers, sparkling silver, and white linen napkins.

Five stylish bedrooms are in the mews house (two have patios). Fifteen more are in the Georgian house, with moulded ceilings and painted in National Trust colours. A thorough refurbishment in 2007 introduced new bathrooms and beds and brought the place up to modern standards.

Dunkineely, Co Donegal

St John's Point, Dunkineely,
Co Donegal

Tel (07497) 37022
Fax (07497) 37330
e-mail info@castlemurray.com
website www.castlemurray.com

Nearby Donegal.
Location a mile (1.6 km) off the
main N56 from Donegal to
Killybegs, signposted in Dunkineely;
parking
Food breakfast (residents usually
cooked for on weekends but you
need to check ahead)
Price €€
Rooms 10 (9 with sea view); 7 double, 3 twin; all with shower and some
with bath; all with phone, TV,
hairdryer, tea/coffee making facilities, wi-fi **Facilities** bar; garden, terrace **Credit cards** MC, V
Children welcome
Disabled not possible
Pets small dogs in rooms
Closed Nov-Mar
Proprietors Marguerite Howley and
husband Peter Lawler

Castle Murray House
Boutique bed-and-breakfast

This charming little place is run by husband and wife Marguerite and Peter,
taking over from Marguerite's father. The
setting of Castle Murray House could be
called magical. In front of the house, bright
green fields with low, drystone walls run
down to the sea and a small ruined castle
on the point is illuminated as night falls.
Across the bay, the sun goes down over
the Slieve League, the highest sea cliffs in
Europe.

Since our last edition its status has
changed to a bed-and-breakfast, but food
is still an important part of the experience
– everything is homemade and locally
sourced. Peter smokes the mackerel himself (sourced from their family's fishing
buisness), while a polytunnel supplies him
with herbs and vegetables. He cooks delicious breakfasts each day, and weekend
meals for guests if given prior notice,

Up a pine staircase, bedrooms we felt were a
touch basic on our last visit have since
been redone, with modern bathrooms.
The Howleys have also turned their attention to the garden (situated at the front of
the property, 200 m from the sea) and
added a stone patio, where in fine weather
they host barbecues for guests.

Reports welcome.

Goleen, Co Cork

Gurtyowen, Toormore, Goleen,
Co Cork

Tel (028) 35324
Fax (028) 35324
e-mail fortviewhousegoleen@eir-com.net
website www.fortviewhouse.ie

Nearby Goleen; Mizen Head; Schull peninsula; Skibbereen; Bantry.
Location in countryside, 6 miles (10 km) from Goleen; car parking
Food breakfast
Price €
Rooms 5; 2 with 2 double, 2 with double and single, 1 with double and 2 single; 1 with bath, 4 with shower; all rooms with hairdryer
Facilities sitting room; garden, terrace **Credit cards** not accepted
Children over 6 welcome
Disabled not possible
Pets not accepted
Closed 1 Nov to 1 Mar
Proprietor Violet Connell

Fortview House
Farmhouse bed-and-breakfast

This place is a labour of love, and it radiates an appropriately warm glow. Richard Connell built the newer part of this house on the West Cork family dairy farm himself, out of stone, and roofed it in slate. The interior is the inspired work of his delightful wife, Violet. With her own ideas, and pictures from magazines, she has created something so fresh, welcoming and comfortable that it is hard to tear oneself away. You can tell what's in store by the two small bears in the retro pram in the hall and the boxy blue-and-red chairs in the sitting room. Violet's bedrooms are named after wild flowers: periwinkle; lavender; daffodil; fuchsia. In one, she has hung straw hats on the wall. She has made curtains out of striped mattress ticking and stencilled a bathroom with sea shells. In a family room with two single beds and pretty patchwork quilts, she props teddy bears up on the pillows as if they are waiting for new, young friends to come. The beamed dining room has a long table, terracotta tiles, wood-burning stove, and old pine furniture. Violet's breakfasts reflect the same attention and care: eggs from the Connell's own hens; freshly squeezed juices; hot potato cakes, salmon and crème fraîche. She has many admirers. Be sure to book early.

Goleen, Co Cork

Goleen, Co Cork

Tel (028) 35225
e-mail info@heronscove.com
website www.heronscove.com

Nearby Mizen Head; Cork, 75 miles
(120 km); Bantry, 25 miles (40 km);
Skibbereen, 24 miles (39 km).
Location on Goleen Harbour; car
parking
Food breakfast, dinner (a la carte
and set menu)
Price €
Rooms 4; 1 double, 2 twin, 2 double
with a single bed; 1 with bath, rest
with shower; all with TV, free wifi,
hairdryer, electric blanket, tea/coffee
tray
Facilities terrace
Credit cards AE, MC, V
Children by arrangement
Disabled not suitable
Pets not accepted
Closed Christmas and New Year
Proprietor Sue Hill

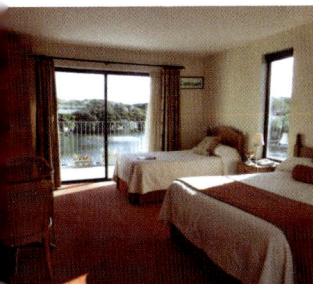

The Heron's Cove
Restaurant-with-rooms

Fish from trawlers on the West Cork coast are brought to the door of Sue Hill's white-painted, waterside restaurant, which offers 'fresh fish and wine on the harbour' and, most likely, a view of a heron. It is an idyllic spot, on this rugged stretch of the West Cork coastline. It is not surprising to hear from Sue that some of her guests do not want to do anything but simply sit and watch the tide come in and go out again. Three of the bedrooms in this modern house open on to balconies overlooking the little sheltered cove, and from the terrace of the restaurant on the ground floor – which is open from May to October – there are steps down to the shore. Guests are clearly those who relish the peace and quiet.

Along the upstairs landing runs a long shelf with a row of books. Bedrooms are well-equipped. There are posters of Aix-en-Provence on the walls and Sue has turned the staircase into a gallery for local artists. It's only a short walk to the village of Goleen and Sue sends all visitors off on the spectacular drive to Mizen Head, which is Ireland's most southwesterly point.

Gorey, Co Wexford

Gorey, Co. Wexford

Tel (053) 942 1124
Fax (053) 942 1572
e-mail info@marlfieldhouse.ie
website www.marlfieldhouse.ie

Nearby Waterford; Kilkenny;
Wexford; Rosslare; beaches.
Location in 35-acre gardens and
woodland, 1 mile (1.6 km) out of
Gorey on R742 Gorey-Courtown
road, or exit 23 off N11 from
Dublin/the south; with car-parking
Food breakfast, lunch, dinner
Price €€€€
Rooms 19 in main house; 17 double,
2 single, all with bath, phone, TV,
hairdryer. Duck Lodge house; sleeps
4 **Facilities** sitting room, bar, dining
room, sauna; garden, terraces, ten-
nis, croquet, 2 restaurants: The
Conservatory Fine Dining and The
Duck Restaurant **Credit cards** AE,
DC, MC, V **Children** welcome;
high tea for those under 8
Disabled access possible **Pets** dogs
welcome by prior arrangement
Closed 2nd Jan – beginning Feb
Proprietors Bowe family

Marlfield House
Country house hotel

A sign in the drive of this stunning
Regency house, once owned by the
Earls of Courtown and now a Relais and
Chateaux hotel since 1983 (one of the best
in Ireland), reads: 'Drive carefully, pheasants
crossing'. Not only is this a preserve of all
good things for people, but it is pretty comfortable for animals, too. There's a little dog
basket for a terrier beside the 18thC marble fireplace in the semi-circular architect-
designed hall. Mary Bowe's peacocks, ban-
tams, ducks and geese are cherished and
indulged almost as much as her guests. This
is a gorgeous, overblown place, a feast for
the eyes because of the Bowe family's passion for interior decoration. Her taste is
reflected in Waterford crystal chandeliers,
little French chairs, gilded taps and a domed
conservatory dining room. Garlanded with
awards – Hostess of the Year, Wine List of
the Year, Best Breakfast, One of the World's
Most Enchanting Hideaways, Best Boutique
Hotel – the hotel has a tradition of warm
hospitality and the Bowes' daughters,
Margaret and Laura, are now at the helm.
Bedrooms are sumptuous and charming.
Jewels in the crown are the State Rooms,
decorated with rich fabrics and fine antique
furniture: the French Room, with marble
bathroom, overlooks the lake; the Print
Room has views of the rose garden.
Outstanding food.

Inis Meáin, Co Galway

Inis Meáin, The Aran Islands, Co.
Galway

Tel +353 86 8266026
e-mail post @inismeain.com
website www.inismeain.com

Nearby coastal and cliff walks, bird
and wildlife watching, the island
pub, ferry to other islands and mainland. **Location** on Inis Meáin Island,
reachable by ferry, plane, private
boat or helicopter. **Food** breakfast
and packed lunch included, dinner in
restaurant **Price** €€€€ **Rooms** 5; 4
suites, 1 suite-apartment. Each has
seating area, mini-deli, wetroom
shower, books. Apartment has
lounge, dining area with wood-burning stove and guest rest-room.
Facilities restaurant, bicycles, fishing rod and binoculars provided
Credit cards MC, V **Children** welcome **Disabled** not suitable **Pets** no
specific facilities **Closed** Nov-Mar;
suite-apartment available for longer
stays during this time **Proprietor**
Ruairi and Marie-Therese de Blacam

Inis Meáin Restaurant and Suites **Island hotel**

I5 miles off the west coast of Ireland, Inis
Meáin is a landscape of terraced limestone, higgledy-piggledy fields and hundreds
of miles of dry-stone walls. Irish is the first
language of the islanders, and traditional
methods of farming, fishing, sport and
music are a large part of their lives.

This place sits by the coast on a rocky
outcrop. It's owned and run by Ruairi – a
native – and his wife, Marie-Therese.
Alongside winning a host of awards, they've
stuck to their aim of showcasing the best
of the island (quite literally: huge windows
offer amazing views). The restaurant, headed up by Ruairi, uses main ingredients
sourced mostly on Inis Meáin: lobster and
crab caught by local fishermen, wild food
from the surrounding countryside and
home-grown vegetables, fertilised with seaweed. It's great food: cooked simply, but by
all accounts superbly.

The bedrooms offer views of the coastline and island, and are uncluttered to let
the landscape do the talking. Walls are
painted in natural lime and furniture and
flooring is simple polished wood. The de
Blacams want the guests to 'appreciate the
peace and quiet' so bicycles, books and fishing rods are provided in place of TVs. This
is characteristically thoughtful: the couple
are praised by guests for their 'warm welcome and attention to the small things'.

395

Inistioge, Co Kilkenny

The Rower, Inistioge, Co Kilkenny

Tel (051) 423614 / (+353) 872523614 / US/Canada guests use free 1-844-363-4444
e-mail info@cullintrahouse.com
website www.cullintrahouse.com

Nearby Kilkenny, 19 miles (31 km); New Ross, 6 miles (10 km); Jerpoint Abbey; Waterford, ancient cairn nearby on farm.
Location in wooded countryside, 6 miles (10 km) from New Ross; car parking
Food breakfast, dinner
Prices €-€€ (usually minimum stay 2 nights)
Rooms 6; 5 double/twin, 1 family; 2 with bath, 4 with shower; hairdryer; all rooms equipped with hot water bottle **Facilities** courtyard; gardens, bridge for viewing countryside
Credit cards most credit cards
Children welcome
Disabled 1 ground-floor room but no special facilities (enquire before)
Pets welcome by arrangement
Closed never
Proprietor Patricia Cantlon

Cullintra House
Country house

Patricia Cantlon is known for her long, leisurely, candle-lit dinner parties at the 250-year-old ivy-clad farmhouse where she was born. Guests have reported moveable eating times. When our reporter called, Patricia had several important jobs to do before getting under way in the kitchen: station herself outside the front door with palette and brushes to finish off a painting; race off to the vet with one of her cats. The day begins when a guest knocks on her door to alert her that people are up and about and waiting for breakfast (could be noon). Her informality and originality have won friends and admirers all over the world. They leave messages in the visitors' book such as 'Great fun'; 'The house, the surroundings, the food, and most of all Patricia, were a magnificent find'.

She has, indeed, created a bewitching retreat. The low-ceilinged house abounds in artistic extras such as the imaginatively-designed rooms in the green-roofed barn, and the conservatory, where Patricia lights banks of candles for pre-dinner drinks. There are log fires, long walks (there are countless acres of woodland to explore), conversations with cats and foxes, swimming with Patricia in the river. She's a natural hostess, with persuasive powers to make her guests feel they have entered a place that is not quite of this world. It works.

Leenane, Co Galway

Leenane, Co Galway

Tel +353-954-2222
Fax +353-954-2296
e-mail info@delphilodge.ie
website www.delphilodge.ie

Nearby Westport; Kylemore Abbey; Clifden; golf.
Location by the lake in wooded grounds on private estate; with car parking
Food breakfast, lunch, dinner
Price €€€
Rooms 12; 8 double, 4 twin, all with bath; all rooms have phone; hairdryer on request **Facilities** drawing room, billiard room, library, dining room; garden, lake
Credit cards AE, MC, V
Children welcome
Disabled 2 ground-floor rooms
Pets not accepted
Closed mid-Dec to mid-Jan
Manager Michael Wade

Delphi Lodge
Fishing lodge

The 2nd Marquess of Sligo – who had been with Byron in Greece – thought this wild place as beautiful as Delphi, and built himself a fishing lodge here in the mid-1830s. When Peter Mantle, a former financial journalist, came across the house, it was semi-derelict. Falling under the same spell, he restored it with great care and vision, and Delphi is one of the finest and foremost sporting lodges in Ireland. Fishing is its main business, but everyone is made welcome here. He stepped back in 2011, and as we went to press the new manager was Michael Wade.

On our visit, wood smoke was rising from the chimney, a new delivery of Crozes Hermitage was stacked up in the hall and Mozart was playing in the snug library overlooking the lake. Among the guests were a couple of bankers in their waterproofs, a novelist, and some Americans. Salmon are weighed and measured in the Rod Room, creating frissons of excitement and stories for the communal dinner table; the ghillies come in during breakfast to discuss prospects for the day ahead. Bedrooms are unfussy but pretty, with pine furniture; larger ones have lake views. Book well ahead. Our most recent inspector was impressed: 'a unique and stunning location; the absolute country house experience.'

Lisdoonvarna, Co Clare

Lisdoonvarna, Co Clare

Tel (065) 7074025
Fax (065) 7074025
e-mail
ballinalackencastle@eircom.net
website www.ballinalackencastle.com

Nearby The Burren; Ballyvaughan;
Doolin Crafts Gallery.
Location in 100-acre grounds, 3
miles (5 km) S of Lisdoonvarna on
R477; car parking
Food breakfast, dinner
Price €€
Rooms 12; 2 suites, 10 doubles; 10
with bath, all with shower; all with
phone, TV, radio, hairdryer
Facilities sitting room, bar, restaurant,
wi-fi; garden
Credit cards MC, V
Children welcome
Disabled not suitable
Pets well-behaved dogs in room; not
in public areas
Closed end of Oct to end of Apr
Proprietors O'Callaghan family

Ballinalacken Castle Hotel **Country hotel**

This fascinating house, high on a green hillside with uninterrupted Atlantic views, was built as a 'villa' in the 1840s for John O'Brien, MP for Limerick. Not only does it have its own ruins of a 15thC O'Brien stronghold, but the entrance hall with cupola and green Connemara marble fireplace remains more or less unaltered. There is a newish, discreetish extension, but main house bedrooms have large, dark, old-fashioned pieces of antique furniture, huge wardrobes, and original shutters. From the bed in Room 4, you can see the Aran islands; and Room 7 has a view of the Cliffs of Moher. The lay-out is intriguing – mostly on one floor.

Chef Michael Foley uses fresh local ingredients to create dishes such as cannelloni of crab meat in a light salmon mousse, with shellfish jus, and Barbary duck with celeriac purree and Guinness and fresh honey sauce. The dining room has another cracker of a fireplace, turf fire, original wood floor, pink tablecloths. Nightcaps are served in the lounge bar, and you can steep yourself in the history of the place with locals and join in singalongs on weekend evenings, when live entertainment is laid on.

The O'Callaghans also offer self-catering accommodation in nearby Gentian Cottage.

Lisdoonvarna, Co Clare

Lisdoonvarna, Co Clare

Tel (065) 7074026
Fax (065) 7074555
e-mail info@sheedys.com
website www.sheedys.com

Nearby The Burren; Ballyvaughan;
Doolin Craft Gallery.
Location in centre of Lisdoonvarna,
on edge of the Burren; car parking
Food breakfast, dinner (restaurant
closed on Sundays, and intermittent
in April)
Price €
Rooms 11; 5 double, 6 twin; 9 with
bath, 2 with shower; all with phone,
TV, hairdryer; ironing board avail-
able
Facilities south-facing sun lounge,
seafood bar, sitting room, restaurant
Credit cards AE, MC, V
Children welcome
Disabled 1 ground floor room,
enquire beforehand
Pets not accepted
Closed end Sep to Mar (opens in
time for Easter)
Proprietors the Sheedy family

Sheedy's Restaurant & Hotel **Restaurant-with-rooms**

This small hotel was originally a farm-house where the Sheedy family began looking after visitors to this little spa town (it has sulphurous springs) in 1855. John Sheedy, ex-Ashford Castle head chef, has come home to cook; his delightful wife, Martina, looks after front of house and the wine list and adds her taste for contemporary design. John Sheedy's food is highly acclaimed and the restaurant has been given a completely new look to complement his celebrated 'Modern Irish' cooking. Walls are painted in a moody grey colour called 'Muddy River'. Martina, who used to work at Mount Juliet, has also transformed the hotel, bringing in help from the nearby Doolin Craft Gallery, renowned for sharp, simple design in wool, crystal, linen and tweed. The lobby heralds the exciting shape of things to come, with shiny wood floor, little curved reception desk, a bit of exposed natural stone, paintwork in gentian blue and terracotta red.

As we went to press a new conservatory was being built at the front of the house, for drinks before dinner. Bedrooms are being upgraded continuously. The aim is comfort, but with some modern design. A place to watch; reports, please.

Mallow, Co Cork

Mallow, Co Cork

Tel (022) 47156 **Fax** (022) 47459
e-mail info@longuevillehouse.ie
website www.longuevillehouse.ie

Nearby Blarney Castle & Parklands.
Location on 500 acres of wooded
estate, 3 miles (5km) W of Mallow
on Killarney road; ample free car
parking **Food** breakfast, daily lounge
menu, afternoon tea, Sunday lunch,
dinner - chef's seasonal menu plus
tasting menu with optional wine
pairings
Prices €€-€€€
Rooms 18; 12 double/twin with
bath; 6 suites; all with central heating, phone, hairdryer
Facilities drawing room, bar, 2 dining rooms; on-site fly fishing, brandy
distillery
Credit cards MC, V **Children** welcome **Disabled** easy access to public
rooms only on ground floor
Pets pet policy applies, please ask
Closed midweek Jan – Mar; Mon
and Tue all year
Proprietors William & Aisling
O'Callaghan

Longueville House
Country house hotel

One of the finest country house hotels
in Ireland: this elegant and imposing
pink listed Georgian house on a 500-acre
wooded estate has a three-storey block in
the centre built in the 1720s, later wings,
and a pretty Victorian conservatory. Inside,
it is full of ornate Italian plasterwork, elab-
orately framed ancestral oils and graceful
period furniture. The drawing room overlooks lawns and rows of oaks in the parkland; in the distance are the ruins of the
family's Dromineen Castle, demolished
under Cromwell, who dispossessed the
family. But, after 300 years, they are back.

Longueville House has everything,
including internationally recognised chef
and patron William O'Callaghan, who,
according to one leading food critic, cooks
'some of the finest food in Europe'.
Almost all of his ingredients come from
the estate farm and the walled kitchen garden. Some 25 acres of apple orchards provide apples for Longueville House's craft
apple cider, some of which William distils
into apple brandy in the Calvados style.

Bedrooms are comfortable and filled
with antiques. The ones at the front of the
house have the best views. The Presidents'
Restaurant is named after the portraits of
Irish past presidents that hang on the
walls. The wine list is superb, as is William's
seven-course Surprise Tasting Menu.

Mountrath, Co Laois

Mountrath, Co Laois

Tel (0502) 32120
e-mail info@roundwoodhouse.com
website www.roundwoodhouse.com

Nearby walking, horse-riding, fishing; Slieve Bloom mountains.
Location in countryside, 3 miles (5 km) N of Mountrath on Kinnitty road; with gardens and ample car parking
Food full breakfast, five-course dinner
Price €€€
Rooms 10; 8 double (3 twin), 2 family rooms; all with bath; all rooms have central heating
Facilities drawing room, study, dining room, hall, library
Credit cards AE, DC, MC, V
Children very welcome
Disabled not suitable
Pets accepted by arrangement
Closed 3 days at Christmas
Proprietors Hannah & Paddy Flynn

Roundwood House
Country house

A recent reporter reacted very well to the Flynns' operation. The house is 'not in perfect repair, but for the type of place they run, this didn't seem to matter': it's a 'wonderful place, and Hannah and Paddy really are charming and informal hosts'. The perfectly proportioned Palladian mansion is set in acres of lime, beech and chestnut woodland. The Kennans have wholeheartedly continued the work of the Irish Georgian Society, who rescued the house from near-ruin in the 1970s. All the Georgian trappings remain – bold paintwork, shutters instead of curtains, rugs instead of fitted carpets, and emphatically no TV. Despite this, the house is decidedly lived in, certainly not a museum.

For Paddy's plentiful meals, non-residents sit at separate tables; residents usually sit together (though not obligatory) – fine if you like to chat to strangers, not ideal for romantic twosomes. After-dinner conversation is also encouraged over coffee and drinks by the open fire in the drawing-room. You may well find the hosts joining in.

Four pleasant extra bedrooms in a converted stable block we thought were cosier and of a better standard than those in the main house. It's very child-friendly (the Flynns have two girls), with a lovely big playroom at the top of the house, full of toys.

Multyfarnham, Co Westmeath

Multyfarnham, Co Westmeath

Tel (044) 937 2191
Fax (044) 937 2338
e-mail stay@mornington.ie
website www.mornington.ie

Nearby Mullingar, Lough Crew, Tullynally Castle, Belvedere House, Newgrange, Lock's Distillery, Kibeggan.
Location in private grounds outside Multyfarnham
Food breakfast, dinner
Price €–€€
Rooms 4 double, with ensuite bathrooms and power showers **Facilities** drawing room, dining room, sitting room, walled gardens and 50 acres of grounds, wi-fi and broadband
Credit cards AE, DC, MC, V
Children by arrangement **Pets** not accepted **Closed** Nov 1st – Mar 31st. Open for groups on weekends in Nov **Proprietors** Warwick and Anne O'Hara

Mornington House
Country house

Mornington House stands a little apart from the tiny village of Multyfarnham, deep in the Westmeath countryside. Set back from the road by an acre or so of gardens, rolling up the drive to this place feels like taking a dip into the 1930s. It's not for those seeking glossy interior design and state-of-the-art equipment: it's proudly old-fashioned. Rooms have shelves of books and encyclopaedias rather than TVs; brass bedsteads and wooden dressing tables.

Guests eat together house party-style at a long, polished dining table after gathering in the drawing room for drinks. Candlesticks, chandeliers and family portraits adorn communal rooms (most with open fires and oriental rugs). There's an air of elegance, and the antiques are to be used rather than simply admired.

Cooking is done by owners Anne and Warwick, and is wonderfully hearty – their Guinness stew is a firm favourite with guests. Whenever possible, ingredients come straight from the walled garden and local suppliers. It's worth checking that you're staying on a night when dinner is served: the O'Haras take occasional breaks from cooking. According to reports, they're wonderful hosts: welcoming and full of stories about the building which has been in their family for hundreds of years.

Nenagh, Co Tipperary

Ardcrony, Nenagh, Co Tipperary

Tel (067) 38223
e-mail info@ashleypark.com **web-site** www.ashleypark.com

Nearby Lough Derg; Limerick, 27 miles (43 km); Shannon.
Location on private estate, with lake, 3.5 miles (6 km) out of Nenagh on Borrisokane road; car parking
Food breakfast, dinner
Price €€
Rooms 6; 3 double, 2 twin, 1 family; 3 with bath and shower, 3 with shower; TV and hairdryer on request **Facilities** garden; lake, boat, fishing rods, riding; public telephone
Credit cards not accepted
Children welcome
Disabled not possible
Pets accepted
Closed never
Proprietor Sean Mounsey

Ashley Park House
Country house bed-and-breakfast

A peacock was sitting, wailing, on the rail of the green veranda when we visited Ashley Park: one of the owner's beloved birds that are fed every morning in a ritual of the household. Mr Mounsey is insistent that nothing here should be like a hotel. He need have no fears on that front. This wildly atmospheric early 18thC house comes complete with ballroom, ruined chapel on an island on the lake, original stabling and farmyard in a more-or-less untouched state, and a scheduled Neolithic ring fort in the woods. The whole place is a nature reserve, too. Mozart is played at breakfast and Frank Sinatra at dinner.

We were unable to see any bedrooms, as they were occupied by a sleeping film crew, but, like all the other rooms in the house, they are huge, as are the bathrooms with their Victorian fittings. The former Irish President, Mary McAleese, has stayed in Room 2. Roses trail along the veranda that runs the length of the house and, to relax, you can sit and read in the octagonal Chinese Room. There are turf fires; Mr Mounsy's daughter, Magaret, bakes a delicious scone; fresh eggs can be ordered straight from the hen. Hotels just don't come like this.

Newmarket-on-Fergus, Co Clare

Newmarket-on-Fergus, Co Clare

Tel (061) 360500
Fax (061) 360700
e-mail info@carrygerryhouse.com
website www.carrygerryhouse.com

Nearby Shannon airport, 8 miles (13 km); Limerick, 20 miles (32 km); Ennis (32 km).
Location rural setting surrounded by green fields; car parking
Food breakfast, dinner
Price €€
Rooms 11; 6 superior double, 4 double, 1 twin, 1 family room, 10 with bath, 1 with shower; all rooms have phone, TV, hairdryer on request
Facilities restaurant, bar, courtyard
Credit cards AE, DC, MC, V
Children over 12
Disabled access possible
Pets accepted
Closed 24 to 27 Dec
Proprietors Niall and Gillian Ennis

Carrygerry Country House **County house hotel**

Being so conveniently close to Shannon airport – a ten-minute drive away – this could have settled for being a commercial hotel. But the kindness and warm hospitality of Niall Ennis and his wife, Gillian, have made this old manor house a place to remember for those staying for either their first or last night in Ireland.

Surrounded by green pasture, Carrygerry – built in the 18th century with a gable end and a remarkable courtyard entered through an archway – was a private house until as recently as the 1980s. Gillian is passionate about her house and she has filled it with antiques and pretty things. The two cosy sitting rooms, either side of the front door, are delightful places to pass away the time, with blazing fires, deep sofas, striped cushions, oriental carpets, and rich, dark colours. The house really seems to come alive in the evenings, when it positively glows in candle light. In the former coach house in the courtyard is a bar; some bedrooms are there, too.

At the end of a flight or a long drive, this is a comfortable, welcoming traveller's rest.

Rathnew, Co Wicklow

Newrath Bridge, Rathnew,
Co Wicklow, A67 TN30

Tel (0404) 40106
Fax (0404) 40338
e-mail reception@hunters.ie
website www.hunters.ie

Nearby Mount Usher Gardens,
Powerscourt Gardens; Russborough
House; Glendalough; golf.
Location in gardens on River Vartry,
in countryside half a mile from
Rathnew; car parking
Food breakfast, lunch, dinner
Price €€€
Rooms 16; 15 double/twin, 1 single,
15 with bath, 1 with shower; all
rooms with phone, TV, hairdryer;
hot water bottle
Facilities gardens, terrace
Credit cards MC, V
Children welcome
Disabled ground-floor room
Pets not accepted
Closed 24 to 26 Dec
Proprietors Gelletlie family

Hunter's Hotel
Coaching inn

The area around it is fast becoming part of Dublin commuterland, but not much changes here in this little island of constancy. In 1840, some Victorian travellers touring Ireland reported: 'We strongly recommend Mr Hunter's Inn at Newrath Bridge, which is, according to our experience, the most comfortable in the county.' The same applies today. This is a delightful, proudly old-fashioned place, built as a coaching inn for several big houses in the vicinity. You would not be surprised if you were to hear the sound of horses' hooves and carriage wheels clattering into the enormous stable yard, or trunks being carried into the beamed front hall, which still has the tiled floor laid in 1720. Nothing clashes, nothing jars, to spoil the old world charm that brings people from far and wide. Present owners, Richard and Tom Gelletlie (great-great-grandsons of the original Mr Hunter) get complete strangers talking in the small bar, with bare, wide wooden floorboards, beams, and a print of the 1900 Grand National winner, Ambush 11, on the wall. There is good, plain cooking; a lovely garden by the river; courtesy; glowing fires; charming bedrooms (ask for garden view); tea on the lawn; billowing wisteria.

Recess, Co Galway

Inagh Valley, Recess, Co Galway

Tel (095) 34706
Fax (095) 34708
e-mail inagh@iol.ie
website www.loughinaghlodgeho-
tel.ie

Nearby Recess; Oughterard;
Clifden; Galway.
Location in open country on shores
of Lough Inagh; car parking
Food breakfast, lunch, dinner
Price €€€
Rooms 13; 1 triple, 4 twin, 8 double;
all with bath and shower; all rooms
have phone, TV, radio, hairdryer,
trouser press; ironing board on
request, room service
Facilities garden, lake, fishing,
bicycles
Credit cards AE, DC, MC, V
Children welcome
Disabled suitable ground-floor
room **Pets** acccepted
Closed mid-Dec to mid-Mar
Proprietor Maire O'Connor

Lough Inagh Lodge Hotel **Country hotel**

This solid, well-proportioned Victorian shooting lodge, romantically placed on one of the most beautiful lakes in Connemara, was boarded up when Maire O'Connor and her late husband, John, came across it looking for somewhere suitable to run as a small hotel. Remarkably, some of the old sporting record books survive and may be read by guests. Little has been overlooked in the way of comfort. Each bedroom, named after an Irish writer, has a dressing room with trouser press (not that we rate these very highly as creature comforts, but they're useful for damp Connemara days). Views are of water and The Twelve Bens mountains. Maire has kept to rich dark Victorian colours and polished wood; her careful attention to detail and service is reflected throughout the comfortable, cosy house. She arranges the fresh flowers, which are sent from Clifden. Rooms downstairs have inviting log fires and warm lighting. The green dining room with yellow curtains and gleaming, dark wood floor is delightful. Seafood and traditional wild game dishes are specialities of the kitchen. Loughs Inagh and Derryclare are on the doorstep; for walkers, there are miles of tracks through the wild and rugged landscape. The hotel also has a stable of bicycles.

Riverstown, Co Sligo

Riverstown, Co Sligo

Tel (071) 9165108
e-mail ohara@coopershill.com
website www.coopershill.com

Nearby Sligo, 12 miles (20 km); Lough Arrow; Lough Gara.
Location 1 mile (1.5 km) W of Riverstown, off N4 Dublin-Sligo road; in large garden on 500-acre estate, with ample car parking
Food breakfast, light/packed lunch, dinner; restaurant licence
Price €€€
Rooms 8; 7 double, 1 twin, 7 with bath and shower, 1 with shower; all rooms have phone, tea/coffee
Facilities sitting room, dining room, snooker room, wi-fi; fishing, tennis, croquet **Credit cards** MC, V
Children welcome if well behaved
Disabled no access
Pets not allowed
Closed Nov to end Mar
Proprietor Simon O'Hara and Christina McCauley

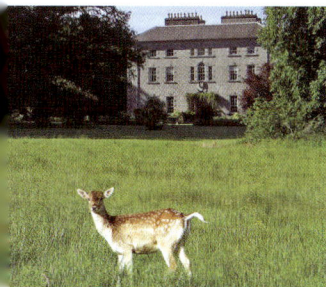

Coopershill
Country house hotel

Simon O'Hara runs this delightful country house with his wife and the chef, Christina. They took over from his parents eight years ago and have continued to subtly improve the style of the place without interfering with its essential appeal.

It is a fine house with splendidly large rooms (including the bedrooms, most of which have four-poster or canopy beds). It is furnished throughout with antiques; but remains emphatically a home, with no hotel-like formality.

The grounds are extensive enough not only to afford complete seclusion, but also to accommodate a river. Four-course dinners are available from a daily changing, seasonal menu. Much of the food is produced in the grounds, and the restaurant can make the unusual boast that the distance travelled from farm to plate for many of its ingredients is just 200 metres. The O'Haras rear fallow deer on the 500-acre estate, producing award-winning venison. The Restaurant Association of Ireland awarded them Best Hotel Restaurant in Sligo in 2016.

Slane, Co Meath

Rossnaree, Slane, Co Meath

Tel (041) 982 0975
e-mail rossnaree@gmail.com
website www.rossnaree.ie

Nearby Dublin (40 mins);
Newgrange, Knowth and Dowth
(Bru na Boinne)
Location the Boyne Valley; in own
grounds with ample car-parking
Food breakfast included; dinner (for
4 or more) to be booked in advance,
afternoon tea
Price €€
Rooms 4; 3 double, 1 twin; all with
own bath or shower
Facilities guided tours; Rossnaree
School of Art; fishing on the River
Boyne; summer cooking courses
Credit cards DC, MC, V
Children welcome
Disabled access difficult
Pets acccepted on request
Closed Nov – Feb
Proprietor Aisling Law

Rossnaree House
Country hotel

This 200-acre wooded estate is a true taste of Ireland. The north side of Rossnaree looks towards the Hill of Slane, where St. Patrick lit his paschal fire in defiance of the pagan King of Tara; the neighbouring glen is where the Battle of the Boyne took place. The house was purchased by the Law family in the early days of the Irish Free State (1925). It is now managed by Aisling Law, great granddaughter of Irish revolutionary Maud Gonne.

Aisling is a talented artist. Each of the four bedrooms has a unique and carefully considered theme: the 'bird' room with its subtle Oriental influences and murals with hand-painted birds and blossom trees; the 'tiger' room with its four-poster bed, draped with Congolese wall hangings; the period style 'William Morris' room, with original William Morris wallpaper; and the 'river' room, with magnificent views across the River Boyne and the Megalithic sites of Bru na Boinne.

Breakfast happens in the dining room during winter, beside a crackling open fire, on a pretty mahogany dining table laid with antique china and silverware. In summer, you can take a picnic basket to the River Boyne. They have a small farm with geese, guinea fowl, hens and roosters.

Tours of Rossnaree are also available for visitors who book in advance.

Ardmore, Co Waterford

Ardmore, Co Waterford

Tel 024 87800
e-mail info@thecliffhousehotel.ie
website www.thecliffhousehotel.ie
Food breakfast, lunch, dinner
Price €€€€
Closed 24th-26th Dec
Proprietors Barry and Gerri
O'Callaghan

Cliff House Hotel
Restaurant-with-rooms

Outside our usual territory, this modern steel, glass and slate building drops down a cliff to the sea in a series of levels. They're connected by a lift and a spiral staircase; all the rooms face the water. The decoration is somewhat bland, except for the shell mirrors and lamps in reception, the jazzy bar and the lime-green spa. The charm is in the special seaside setting, in the quality of the light that results, and in the charming local staff. A Relais & Chateau member. Food (Michelin star) by Dutchman Martijn Kajuiter.

Ballingarry, Co Limerick

Ballingarry, Co Limerick

Tel (069) 68508
Fax (069) 68511
e-mail mustard@indigo.ie
website www.mustardseed.ie
Food breakfast, lunch, dinner
Price €€€
Closed Feb
Proprietors Dan Mullane

The Mustard Seed at Echo Lodge **Country house**

The Mustard Seed was opened over thirty years ago by the acclaimed chef Dan Mullane, who moved his kitchen to this former convent. Since his retirement in 2016 the hotel has continued to flourish under John Edward Joyce (who previously worked as its manager for nearly 25 years). The painted yellow house is ageing gracefully, while John has put his own stamp on the interior with opulent draperies and designer wallpapers. 'Foodies' continue to flock to the blue-walled dining room for smooth and professional service under chef Angel Pirev. Breakfast could be Kenmare smoked salmon with potato farle and crème fraiche, while dinner might include sophisticated dishes such as turbot and scallop with parsnip, vanilla purèe and lime gel.

Ballylickey, Co Cork

Seaview House
Country hotel

Ronan O'Sullivan and his wife Suzanne are the third generation of O'Sullivans to take over Seaview House. This white Victorian house is a stone's throw from Ballylickey Bay, and well known for serving locally sourced ingredients, building on an international reputation.

The bedrooms are beautifully decorated in pastel colours and floral fabrics with stunning antique furniture – especially the bedheads and wardrobes. The rooms in the old part of the house are more irregular and individual.

There are two sitting-rooms – a cosy front room adjoining the bar and a large family room at the back. The menu changes daily, and the chefs are forever experimenting with new dishes – roast smoked pheasant on the day we visited.

Ballylickey, Bantry, Co Cork

Tel (027) 50073/50462
email info@seaviewhousehotel.com
website
www.seaviewhousehotel.com
Food breakfast, lunch (Sun only),
dinner **Prices** €€-€€€
Closed Nov-Easter
Proprietor Ronan O'Sullivan

Clifden, Co Galway

The Ardagh Hotel
Coast hotel and restaurant

The view from the restaurant over Ardbear Bay is fabulous: light and colours constantly change; sunsets are memorable. This small family hotel has an Alpine flavour that gives it charm. Monique Bauvet's the chef, housekeeper and gardener; her rooms are pristine and have recently been redecorated in a bright and contemporary style; she made the garden among the rocks. Her husband, Stéphane, can be found behind the front desk, or serving wine, and is always ready to help. Their hotel has a satisfying combination of friendliness and reliable, discreet efficiency. The four large suites on the top floor have sea views, for the rest you should check when booking. Tucked under the eaves, a sunny sitting room for residents has piles of magazines and a profusion of greenery.

Ballyconneely Road, Clifden,
Connemara, Co Galway

Tel (095) 21384
Fax (095) 21314
e-mail ardaghhotel@eircom.net
website www.ardaghhotel.com
Food breakfast, bar lunch, dinner
Price €€ **Closed** Nov to Easter or
April 1 **Proprietors** Monique and
Stéphane Bauvet

Cloyne, Co Cork

Cloyne, Middleton, Co Cork

Tel (021) 4652534
Fax (021) 4652534
e-mail info@barnabrowhouse.ie
website www.barnabrowhouse.ie
Food breakfast, lunch, dinner
Price €€€
Closed Christmas week
Proprietor Geraldine Kidd

Barnabrow House
Country house and restaurant

This could be called a 'cutting edge' country house. No faded chintzes or family portraits here. Semi-minimalist interiors, with bold, bright colours and vast expanses of gleaming wood floors look as if they have come out of glossy magazines. Behind the rejuvenated main house is a coach house with floors painted white and elsewhere much orange, pink and yellow; a rustic cottage; and restaurant with an outdoor timber terrace. Hens provide fresh eggs; organic produce for the table comes from the kitchen garden.

Barnabrow House's main business is now weddings, but B&B is still available Sunday to Wednesday, and all week in the quieter months. Barnabrow, under chef Stuart Bowes, is now also open for lunch on Sundays.

Innishannon, Co Cork

Innishannon, Co Cork

Tel (021) 4775121
e-mail info@innishannon-hotel.ie
website www.innishannon-hotel.ie
Food lunch, dinner
Price €€
Closed Feb
Proprietors Roche family

Innishannon House
Country hotel

This attractive, imposing 18thC house on the banks of the Bandon River was taken over by new proprietors the Roche family, whose son, Shane, is now General manager. While maintaining the rustic country house style, the new owners have been redecorating the place since they took over in 2005. No. 16 is a cosy attic room with an antique bedspread, No. 11 a fascinating circular room with small round windows, a huge curtained bed and a newly built bathroom with a stand-alone bath.

Jean-Marc is still in charge of the cooking – duck *confit*, fillet steak, smoked salmon – earning the place two rosettes. Innishannon is not the last word in seclusion or intimacy; there are facilities for conferences and wedding receptions of up to 200 guests.

We would welcome reports.

411

Kenmare, Co Kerry

Muxnaw Lodge
Bed-and-breakfast

Castletownbere Road, Kenmare,
Co Kerry

Tel (064) 41252
e-mail muxnawlodge@eircom.net
Food breakfast;
Price €
Closed Christmas Eve and Day
Proprietor Hannah Boland

Charming, gabled Muxnaw Lodge was built in 1801, one of the oldest houses in Kenmare, set on a hillside overlooking the suspension bridge – and equipped with an all-weather tennis court.

Hannah Boland has created an attractive period style for her lovely old house, with painted magnolia and blue walls, brass beds and lovingly-polished antique furniture. In the bedrooms, she hides the modern electric kettles away in wooden boxes so they don't spoil the general look. In a bathroom at the back of the house, you may sit in the corner bath and look at the sea. For breakfast, fresh eggs from the butcher are cooked on Mrs Boland's big red AGA in the kitchen. She is such a delightful hostess that guests may find themselves getting away rather later than planned.

Kilgraney, Co Carlow

Lorum Old Rectory
Country guesthouse

Kilgraney, Bagenalstown, Co Carlow

Tel (+353) 059 9775282
e-mail bobbie@lorum.com
website www.lorum.com
Food breakfast, dinner
Price €€
Closed Dec-Feb
Proprietors Bobbie Smith

There will come a moment in your stay at Lorum Old Rectory – perhaps during conversation at dinner, or in the afternoon as you glimpse owner Bobbie Smith collecting herbs from the garden – when everything clicks. That is when you will realize just how refreshed you are after such a short time and just how pleasant a place Lorum is. Much of this is down to Bobbie, whose warm manner gets people talking, and whose quirky but clever grip of flavours in the kitchen oils the wheels.

The rich Irish heritage helps too, whether in the form of a fine view of Mount Leinster from your bedroom; the inviting furniture in the communal areas; or perhaps a trip into nearby Kilkenny, a historic town with medieval roots

Kilkenny, Co Kilkenny

Butler House
Town house

This tall, grand Georgian house was once the dower house to Kilkenny Castle, family seat of the Earls of Ormonde. In the 1970s, the house was refurbished in contemporary style by Kilkenny Design, and the result is stunning.

The house has been refurbished again recently, with large spacious rooms, oak furniture and muted colours. The effect, with acres of white walls, is ordered, quiet and restful. Breakfast is now served in the Kilkenny Design Centre, a short stroll through the walled garden. Morning coffee, biscuits and cake are served on a pale oak table in the entrance hall. Superior bedrooms have bay windows and garden and castle views. Butler House is now run by the Kilkenny Civic Trust.

16 Patrick Street, Kilkenny,
Co Kilkenny

Tel (056) 7765707
Fax (056) 7765626
e-mail res@butler.ie
Food breakfast
Closed 24 to 29 Dec
Proprietors Kilkenny Civic Trust
Manager Gabrielle Hickey

Rathmullan, Co Donegal

Rathmullan House
Country hotel

Both outside and in, Rathmullan House is a feast for the eyes. Built as a grand Georgian holiday home, its plentiful original features include a striking row of bay windows along the façade, as well as ornate ceilings, doorways and marble fireplaces once inside. The Indian colonial-styled sitting room is particularly lovely, and even the later addition of a Regency-style wing brings a welcome contemporary element.

Aside from the lovely surroundings, our series editor Fiona Duncan likens the experience of staying here to that of finding a hot water bottle in a chilly bed: tensions immediately evaporate under Mark and Mary's hospitality, not to mention the healing hands of their in-house masseuse. The food's outstanding too, served in their characteristically elegant restaurant.

Kilgraney, Bagenalstown, Co Carlow

Tel (+353) 7491 58188
e-mail reception@rathmullan-house.com **website** www.rathmullanhouse.com
Food breakfast, lunch, afternoon snacks, pizzeria, formal dining **Price** €€€-€€€€ **Closed** Jan; from 9th Feb until Easter only open weekends
Proprietors Mark and Mary Wheeler

Shanagarry, Co Cork

Ballymaloe House
Country house hotel

We can't resist this rambling, creeper-clad house set in rolling green countryside. Readers have been 'immensely impressed' and found the staff 'well-drilled as an army, but jolly, with abundant charm'.

The Allens have been farming here for almost 70 years, started offering rooms in the 60s, adding more facilities and rooms over the years — those in extensions and converted out-buildings now outnumber those in the main house.

Despite quite sophisticated furnishings, the Allens have managed to preserve intact the warmth of a much-loved family home. Reporters have been impressed by the standard of food. Jason Fahey prepares the Classic French and Irish dishes. Just as much care is lavished on breakfast, and the famous children's high tea.

Shanagarry, Midleton, Co Cork

Tel (021) 4652531
e-mail res@ballymaloe.ie
website www.ballymaloe.ie.
Food breakfast, lunch, dinner
Closed Christmas
Proprietors the Allen family

Woodstown, Co Waterford

Gaultier Lodge
Beach B&B

Well above average B&B in a handsome, 18thC Georgian house with a five-star location beside the beach on Waterford Bay. Step straight out on to the broad sands. Busy, characterful hosts — Sheila (Irish) and her son Peter — who know their own minds. Smart, period-furnished bedrooms. Generous brunch. A guest reports confusion over bookings: get written confirmation, and pay any deposit required to be 100 per cent of the reservation.

Woodstown, Co. Waterford

Tel (0)51 382 549
Mobile (0)87 248 6283
e-mail gaultierlodge@yahoo.ie
website www.gaultierlodge.com
Food breakfast
Price €
Closed beginning of Nov-beginning of Mar
Proprietors Sheila and Bill

Index – Hotel names

In this index, hotels are arranged in order of the first distinctive part of their name; other parts of the name are also given, except that very common prefixes such as 'The' and 'La' are omitted. More descriptive words such as 'Hotel', 'B&B', 'St', 'Maison' and 'Auberge' are included.

Index – Hotel locations

In this index, hotels are arranged in order of the names of the cities, towns or villages they are in or near. Hotels located in a very small village may be indexed under a larger place nearby. An index by hotel name precedes this one.

Index – Hotel locations

Other Duncan Petersen titles

Buy your *Charming Small Hotel Guide* or other titles by post or e-mail directly from the publisher and you'll get a worthwhile discount. *

Titles:	Retail price	Discount price
Austria, Switzerland and the Alps	£14.99	£13.50
France	£14.99	£13.50
Germany	£14.99	£13.50
Italy	£16.99	£15.50
Spain	£14.99	£13.50

The *On Foot City Guides* are great companions for the *Charming Small Hotel Guides*. These books feature unique aerial-view maps, which show not only the city's street layout but the look of your surroundings too.

Titles:	Retail price	Discount price
London Walks	£10.99	£9.50
New York Walks	£10.99	£9.50
Paris Walks	£10.99	£9.50
Prague Walks	£10.99	£9.50
Rome Walks	£10.99	£9.50
Venice Walks	£10.99	£9.50
Florence Walks	£10.99	£9.50

We also publish an innovative series of country walking and cycling routes on cards in boxes, including *Walker's Britain in a Box,* the perfect companion to *Charming Small Hotels Britain & Ireland.* All these guides are stocked by Amazon. You can also e-mail us for more information on this series at duncan.petersen@zen.co.uk.

Please send orders to: Book Sales, Duncan Petersen Publishing Ltd, Studio 6, 82 Silverthorne Road, Battersea, London, SW8 3HE; or: duncan.petersen@zen.co.uk, giving: the title and number of copies; name and address; cheque made out to: Duncan Petersen Publishing Ltd, or card details. *Offer applies to this edition and UK only.

Exchange rates
As we went to press, $1 bought 0.81 euros and £1 bought 1.14 euros